Current Perspectives on Substance Use Disorders in South Asia

S. M. Yasir Arafat · Sujita Kumar Kar
Editors

Current Perspectives on Substance Use Disorders in South Asia

Public Mental Health Aspects

Springer

Editors
S. M. Yasir Arafat
Department of Psychiatry
Bangladesh Specialized Hospital
Dhaka, Bangladesh

Sujita Kumar Kar
Department of Psychiatry
King George's Medical University
Lucknow, Uttar Pradesh, India

ISBN 978-981-97-6618-5 ISBN 978-981-97-6619-2 (eBook)
https://doi.org/10.1007/978-981-97-6619-2

This Springer imprint is published by the registered company Springer Nature Singapore Pte Ltd.
The registered company address is: 152 Beach Road, #21-01/04 Gateway East, Singapore 189721, Singapore

(Late) Santosh Kumar Saha and
Mr. Amanullah Aman who shaped the
academic pathway of S. M. Yasir Arafat
(Late) Prof. Jitendra Kumar Trivedi and
Prof. Prabhat Sitholey, who shaped the
understanding of psychiatry and mentored
Sujita Kumar Kar

Preface

South Asia consists of eight countries with low- and middle-income (LMI) backgrounds. The people of this region share common cultures, beliefs, and behavioral patterns regarding physical and mental health. The region contains about 2 billion populations making up about a quarter of the global population. The prevalence of alcohol use disorder ranges from 0.4% to 2.4% and the prevalence of other substance use disorders ranges from 0.4% to 0.6% in 2019 in the region. However, the rate varies among the countries based on religion, availability, and purchase power of people as alcoholism is more prominent in India, Nepal, and Sri Lanka than in Afghanistan, Bangladesh, Maldives, and Pakistan. Substance abuse affects almost all spheres of life, i.e., personal, social, recreational, criminal, and family aspects; both physical and mental health; and economy of the society as well as the country. Advanced management and holistic prevention are the public health priorities. However, we found a little attention to the issues as a region as well as in countries like Afghanistan, Bangladesh, and Pakistan. We did not find any book focusing on the public mental health aspects of substance abuse in South Asia. We aimed to organize the public mental health and healthcare issues related to substance use disorder in a densely populated LMI setting. This book is the first of its kind of approach discussing public mental health aspects of substance use disorders in South Asian countries.

At the beginning, we highlighted the overview of substance abuse in South Asia, and subsequently we discussed the country-wise chapter for Afghanistan, Bangladesh, Bhutan, India, Nepal, Pakistan, and Sri Lanka. For an individual chapter, we highlighted geographical position and historical aspects of substance abuse, epidemiology and burden of substance abuse in a country, risk factors for substance abuse, prevalence of different substance abuse, help-seeking pattern for substance abuse, available services for managing substance abuse including treatment facility and rehabilitation programs (services structure), harm reduction strategy, resilience factors for treatment of drug abuse, physical and psychiatric co-morbidity of substance abuse, behavioral addictions, emerging addictions, law- and policy-related substance abuse, current status of research on substance abuse, and future direction for services development in a country. Then we discussed challenges and ways forward for substance use disorders in the South Asian countries followed by policy, legislation, and programs for substance abuse. We dedicated a chapter on public health aspects, preventions and interventions for substance abuse in the region. Subsequently, we included comorbidities of substance abuse and their management challenges, available evidence of substance abuse, and substance abuse in vulnerable groups (women and children).

This book highlights the public mental health needs and further ways out to deal with substance abuse in a densely populated LMI setting. It will be useful for researchers, academics, and professionals in the field of addiction medicine, mental health, public mental health, behavioral science, and social science. It may act as a catalyst of further research and development of culture-sensitive interventions for substance use disorders in South Asia.

Dhaka, Bangladesh S. M. Yasir Arafat
Lucknow, Uttar Pradesh, India Sujita Kumar Kar

Acknowledgement We acknowledge our colleague from Sri Lanka, Dr. Sayuri Perera for inviting us at the Colombo conference of 2023 where we planned the book.

Contents

About the Editors

Dr. S. M. Yasir Arafat is currently working as an Associate Consultant of Psychiatry at Bangladesh Specialized Hospital, Dhaka, Bangladesh. He is affiliated with Dnet as an honorary Research Fellow and Biomedical Research Foundation, Bangladesh as Senior Research Fellow. He was affiliated with the University of Bristol, UK as Visiting Senior Research Associate (August 2021–2023). He completed MD in Psychiatry from Bangabandhu Sheikh Mujib Medical University, Dhaka and MBBS from the Dhaka Medical College, Dhaka, Bangladesh. He also did an MPH in Health Economics and MBA in Marketing. Dr. Arafat has (co)authored more than 350 peer-reviewed articles and 50 book chapters, and (co)edited more than 10 books with Springer. He is the leading editor of the book series "South Asian Perspectives in Mental Health and Psychology" with Springer. He has been included in the global 2% researcher list in 2021, 2022, and 2023. He is acting as editorial member in more than 10 leading journals in mental health published by Elsevier, Frontiers, Wiley, Springer, and Taylor and Francis. His research focused on mental health, suicidal behavior, psychometrics, panic buying, and psycho-sexual disorders.

Dr. Sujita Kumar Kar is currently working as an Additional Professor of Psychiatry at King George's Medical University, Lucknow, Uttar Pradesh, India. He is the Editor-in-Chief of Indian Journal of Health, Sexuality and Culture. He is also the editorial board member and reviewer of various national and international journals. He had written 62 book chapters and more than 450 articles in various national and international journals and made 70 presentations at various national and international conferences. He has been included in the global 2% researcher list released by Stanford University in 2021, 2022, and 2023. His research interests include brain stimulation, neuropsychiatry, and suicide prevention.

List of Figures

List of Tables

Chapter 1
Overview of Substance Use Disorder in South Asia

Shinjini Choudhury, Tanmay Joshi, and Abhishek Ghosh

1.1 Introduction

The widespread misuse of substances poses a persistent global challenge, impacting public health, societal structures, and economies. The South Asian region, encompassing India, Pakistan, Bangladesh, Afghanistan, Sri Lanka, Nepal, Bhutan, and Maldives, exhibits vast linguistic, cultural, and socio-economic diversity. Historical, socio-economic, and cultural factors, along with a predominantly youthful population and rapid urbanization, shape the epidemiological landscape of substance use disorders (Arafat and Kar 2024). Neighboring Southeast Asian countries also influence substance use patterns through factors like accessibility, availability, and social norms.

A meta-analysis found alcohol use disorder as the most prevalent substance use disorder in South Asia, with a 13% prevalence, lower than the global rate of 32.5%, potentially due to cultural norms prohibiting alcohol use in Muslim-majority countries. Additionally, IV drug abuse prevalence was notable at 2.5%, higher than the global rate of 0.33% in 2015 (Naveed et al. 2020).

Besides traditional psychoactive substances such as alcohol, tobacco, cannabis, and opium, newer substances including synthetic drugs also contribute to the evolving patterns and prevalence of substance use disorders in South Asian countries.

The major stakeholders such as public health officials, policymakers, and healthcare professionals must acquire a better understanding of the epidemiology of

---

S. Choudhury
Department of Psychiatry, All India Institute of Medical Sciences, Patna, Bihar, India

T. Joshi
Department of Psychiatry, All India Institute of Medical Sciences, Bhopal, Madhya Pradesh, India

A. Ghosh (✉)
Department of Psychiatry, Drug Deaddiction and Treatment Centre, Postgraduate Institute of Medical Education and Research, Chandigarh, India
e-mail: ghosh.abhishek@pgimer.edu.in

S. M. Y. Arafat and S. K. Kar (eds.), *Current Perspectives on Substance Use Disorders in South Asia*, https://doi.org/10.1007/978-981-97-6619-2_1

substance use disorders (SUDs) to be able to design targeted interventions and evidence-based strategies for addressing this critical public health crisis.

In the following sections, we shall explore the salient features of substance use disorders in South Asian countries. The ensuing sections have been arranged according to the major drug classes, and available country-wise information for each has been incorporated.

1.2 Tobacco

The tobacco epidemic persists as a major global public health threat, causing over 8 million deaths annually. Out of the 1.3 billion tobacco users, 80% reside in low- and middle-income countries, including South Asian nations. Tobacco consumption patterns vary based on socio-demographic factors and cultural beliefs. Smokeless tobacco (SLT) use is increasing, especially in South Asia, posing significant health risks (Kendrick et al. 2021). Data from meta-analysis too reveals a similar picture with a higher prevalence of chewing tobacco compared to smoking (21% vs. 18.6%) in South Asian countries (Naveed et al. 2020). Despite some reductions, SLT-related diseases remain a concern, influenced by pricing, social factors, and industry strategies exploiting weak regulations.

Global smoking trend monitoring faces challenges due to variations in survey methodologies, hindering accurate comparisons (Reitsma et al., 2019). The Global Tobacco Surveillance System aims to enhance countries' tobacco control measures by monitoring key aspects of the WHO's Framework Convention on Tobacco Control and MPOWER technical package (Siddiqi et al., 2020).

1.2.1 Afghanistan

The 2015 Afghanistan Demographic and Health Survey, found smoking cigarettes was the most prevalent form of tobacco use for men (21.9%), while prevalence rates were lower for women (3.4%). Tobacco use was inversely associated with education, positively with certain occupations, and wealth influenced odds differently for men and women. Media exposure had limited influence on women but varied effects on men (UNODC 2018).

As for tobacco control measures, Afghanistan ratified the WHO Framework Convention on Tobacco Control (FCTC), leading to the implementation of smoke-free legislation and the MPOWER policies. The country enforces smoke-free public places and bans on tobacco advertising, though lacks a national anti-tobacco media campaign. Health warning labels lack pictorial representation, and taxes on tobacco products remain low, with no excise tax, violating WHO recommendations.

1.2.2 Bangladesh

Higher rates of production and consumption of tobacco, in diverse forms have been historically present in Bangladesh. Besides cigarettes, beedis, and hookahs, the use of smokeless tobacco with betel quid is also a popular form of tobacco use. Bangladesh was the first country to ratify the Framework Convention on Tobacco Control (FCTC) in 2003. The Smoking and Using Tobacco Products Control Act was first enacted in 2005 and subsequent amendments have been made since then. The International Tobacco Control Bangladesh Survey, conducted in 4 waves between 2009 and 2013 revealed that most exclusive cigarette users were unlikely to use any other forms of tobacco. Socio-economic and rural–urban disparities in tobacco use transitions were also noted. Rural smokers were more likely to transition to beedi or SLT use and to quit. Those belonging to a higher socio-economic status and who smoked tobacco exclusively as beedis were more likely to quit. Among those who exclusively used smokeless tobacco, males, younger individuals, higher educational qualifications and urban residence were the variables most associated with greater likelihood to quit (Chen et al. 2023).

1.2.3 Bhutan

Bhutan's pioneering ban on tobacco sales and public smoking in 2010 garnered global acclaim, but subsequent challenges like smuggling and a persistently high prevalence rate of around 24–25% indicated limited effectiveness. Amid the COVID-19 pandemic, the ban was lifted in 2021 due to smuggling concerns, marking a shift to regulated sales. Taxation changes followed, initially dropping to 0% but then reinstated to 100% under the Tax Act of 2022. These fluctuations raise worries about increased affordability and access to tobacco products, potentially driving up usage, particularly among youth.

1.2.4 India

India, with 267 million tobacco users, has high consumption rates, particularly in rural and lower socio-economic areas, and among men. Tobacco-related employment is prevalent but exploitative, especially for women. Tobacco contributes significantly to cancer, notably oral cancer, driven by smokeless tobacco products. India faces a substantial burden of smokeless tobacco-related diseases, with over 350,000 annual deaths. Ischemic heart disease, COPD, and stroke are the top causes of death attributable to tobacco, with significant economic burdens totaling USD 27.5 billion in 2018–2019, primarily from smoking-related costs.

Tobacco use has a higher prevalence among males (50–64) and females aged 65 years and above, particularly in rural areas and among lower socio-economic and education levels. Despite declining per capita cigarette consumption, tobacco remains the fourth highest risk factor, causing over 1.2 million deaths annually.

According to the second edition of the Global Adult Tobacco Survey conducted in India during 2016–2017 (GATS 2), there is a significant level of awareness among the adult population regarding the health hazards associated with smoking. However, beedis are often incorrectly perceived as healthier than conventional cigarettes due to the use of tendu leaf and areca nuts.

India ratified the FCTC in 2004 and implemented various tobacco control measures, yet execution remains incomplete. Despite bans on nicotine-containing food products in 2011 and efforts to increase awareness, a considerable number continue using such items. A prohibition of Heated Tobacco Products (HTPs) and e-cigarettes also exists. The total tax rate on cigarettes was 57.6% in 2022. Enforcement of smoking and advertising bans is moderate. The sale of HTPs and e-cigarettes is prohibited for all ages.

India ranks second globally in tobacco production, yielding 761,335 tons annually, primarily in three states, employing about 25 million workers. Since 2015, a Crop Diversification Scheme has reallocated 8.7% of the land designated for tobacco.

1.2.5 Nepal

In Nepal, both smokeless and smoking tobacco use are prevalent. Analysis of the Global Burden of Disease study indicates a decline in smoking tobacco from 1990 to 2015, particularly among females. Daily tobacco use decreased by 33% in men and 48% in women during this period. Regional variations show higher smokeless tobacco use in the plains and more smoking at higher altitudes. Misconceptions about the harmlessness of smokeless tobacco may contribute to its increasing use. The Nepal Demographic and Health Survey 2016 revealed a tobacco use prevalence of 52.3%, with smoking decreasing from 32.8% in 2006 to 27.3% in 2016. Smokeless tobacco use was 40.2%, surpassing rates in 2011 and India in 2015–2016. Policy measures like increasing tobacco taxation, currently at 15.5%, far below the WHO guideline of 70%, are crucial to further reduce tobacco use's high burden in Nepal.

1.2.6 Pakistan

In Pakistan, tobacco use poses a significant public health challenge, with over 20% of the population reported as tobacco users. The prevalence is higher among men (32%) than women (6%). Smokeless tobacco products are also widely consumed. Alarmingly, over a quarter of young individuals aged 13–15 are exposed to second-hand smoke within their homes. Approximately 19.1% of adults currently use tobacco in any form, with smoking being more prevalent (12.4%) than smokeless tobacco use (7.7%) and waterpipe smoking (3%). Among youth, 10.7% use some form of tobacco, while nearly 40% of young smokers initiate cigarette use before the age of 10.

Tobacco-related mortality in Pakistan is. Tobacco use accounts for 16.0% of male deaths and 4.9% of female deaths, contributing significantly to mortality from various diseases, including lung cancer, chronic obstructive pulmonary disease, heart disease, diabetes, and stroke (GBD 2019).

The economic burden of tobacco use is substantial, equivalent to 1.6% of Pakistan's GDP. This economic cost surpasses the revenue generated by the tobacco industry by fivefold. Moreover, tobacco expenditure by households impacts essential spending areas, particularly affecting poorer households who spend a significant portion of their budget (3.0%) on tobacco, more than they allocate to education (1.8%) (Nayab et al., 2021; WHO, 2019).

Pakistan became a party to the WHO FCTC in 2005 and has enacted key legislations, including ordinances mandating warning labels on cigarette packets and prohibiting smoking in enclosed spaces.

1.2.7 Sri Lanka

The Global Adult Tobacco Survey 2019–2020 in Sri Lanka found that 13.4% of adults used smokeless tobacco, while 9.1% smoked tobacco currently. Nearly half of smokers (47%) and around 31% of smokeless tobacco users were advised to quit by healthcare providers in the past year. Among 13–15-year-olds, 1.7% reported currently smoking tobacco, and 2.4% reported using smokeless tobacco. In 2010, WHO estimated that 24% of Sri Lanka's population aged 15 and above were tobacco users, with projections indicating a decrease to 21% by 2025. However, smoking rates remain high, especially among older men and women. Despite efforts to reduce tobacco use, Sri Lanka may not achieve the global target of a 30% reduction by 2025. Since ratifying the FCTC in 2003, Sri Lanka has implemented comprehensive tobacco control policies, including strict smoke-free laws and smoking cessation support through quit lines and healthcare facilities. Additionally, health warnings covering 80% of cigarette packages were mandated in 2015.

1.3 Alcohol

1.3.1 Afghanistan

With alcohol being regarded as taboo and the presence of total prohibition of alcohol use, data regarding its use are difficult to obtain. According to the latest Global Status Report on Alcohol and Health, the total alcohol per capita consumption by drinkers only in the year 2016 was 33.5 L. This disproportionately high figure suggests high consumption among those who drink alcohol. Meanwhile, total alcohol per capita consumption in the general population in 2016 was 0.2 L of pure alcohol, reflecting a low prevalence of alcohol use.

1.3.2 Bangladesh

In Bangladesh, alcoholic beverages, including beer, wine, spirits, and locally made varieties, are defined by an alcohol content of $\geq$0.5%. Bangladesh imposes strict prohibitions on alcohol use, yet it is widely available and locally produced, with government-approved companies and a privately licensed brewery producing various brands. Molasses from local sugar mills is used for spirit production, while rural areas also produce crude alcohol from rice, sugar cane, and molasses. Harmful alcohol use is a growing national concern. Law enforcement and healthcare providers report increasing alcohol misuse, particularly in urban areas.

1.3.3 Bhutan

Alcohol holds significant cultural acceptance in Bhutan, with alcohol being served at most religious ceremonies. Home-brewed rice-based liquor is found in the majority of households, and commercially produced varieties have been available since 1976. Alcohol Use Disorder (AUD) is prevalent, surpassing other substance use disorders. Bhutan's per capita alcohol consumption is higher (8.47 L) than the global average (6.2 L), with alcohol liver disease being a leading cause of death. Despite a decrease in alcoholic liver disease-related deaths, it remains the primary cause of mortality in Bhutan, with a prevalence of 37.5 cases per 10,000 population in 2018.

1.3.4 India

Global alcohol consumption trends have shifted, with declines in high-income nations and rises in low- and middle-income countries like India. In 2019, an estimated

340,000 deaths and 14.7 million disability-adjusted life years could be attributed to alcohol (Shield and Rehm 2021). This surge can be linked to heightened affordability driven by economic growth, as adult alcohol consumption nearly doubled from 2.3 to 5.5 L of pure alcohol per capita between 2000 and 2018. However, alcohol use remains male-dominated, with males having twice the prevalence of current drinking compared to females (Manthey et al. 2021).

The exacerbation of India's alcohol-related disease burden compared to high-income countries underscores the need for targeted prevention strategies within the constraints of limited healthcare resources. Understanding regional variations in alcohol use is paramount due to the diverse cultural, economic, and social factors across Indian states and union territories (UTs). These disparities stem from differences in alcohol policies, religious beliefs, educational levels, and economic status (Rehm et al. 2021).

The lack of a national-level policy for alcohol further contributes to these disparities. For example, while six states/UTs enforce complete alcohol prohibition, others have varying policies on legal drinking ages or have implemented temporary liquor bans in the past. Religious diversity also plays a crucial role in shaping alcohol acceptance and contributes to varying alcohol consumption patterns across regions.

Additionally, disparities in literacy rates and per capita income among states further shape alcohol use trends, with lower literacy and income levels potentially correlating with higher alcohol consumption rates.

1.3.5 Nepal

According to a study published in the Lancet under the Global Burden of Diseases Study in 2020, the prevalence of alcohol use above the "non-drinker equivalent (NDE)" has risen across all age groups in Nepal since 1990. The most significant increases occurred among males aged 15–39 and 40–64 (Kivimäki et al. 2022).

The Nepal Drug Users Survey of 2019 found that 64.8% of drug users had consumed alcohol at least once. Among alcohol users, 71.4% initiated use between ages 15 and 19, with females (73.9%) having a slightly higher initiation rate than males (71.3%). Regionally, Karnali Province had the highest proportion (97.7%) initiating alcohol use between ages 15 and 19.

1.3.6 Pakistan

As the World Health Organization shows in its 2018 Global Status of Alcohol and Health Report, total APC is very low, 0.3 L in Pakistan, with 96.5% being lifetime abstainers. The prevalence of alcohol use disorder is 0.4%, and alcohol dependence is 0.2%, one of the lowest in the world. However, among those who do drink alcohol, total alcohol per capita consumption is as high as 30 L in males and 11.5 L in females.

Due to religious beliefs and political restrictions, there is a dearth of treatment facilities for those affected. Despite strict prohibitions on alcohol, a study of male adolescent school students in Gilgit-Baltistan (mean age 16.9) reported surprisingly high lifetime alcohol use (44.9%) (Shahzad et al. 2020).

1.3.7 Sri Lanka

Sri Lanka experiences significant health challenges stemming from the rising misuse of alcohol. Between 2005 and 2018, per capita alcohol consumption surged from 2.6 to 4.1 L, indicating a worsening situation. (GSAH 2018) Approximately 28% of the population reported alcohol use within the past year, with urban areas showing higher prevalence rates. Average alcohol consumption was 14.6 L in 2016, with arrack being the dominant beverage. Unrecorded alcohol consumption, notably Kasippu, remains a significant concern. Heavy episodic drinking is widespread with a higher prevalence among males. Illicit alcohol, comprising 40% of total consumption, poses serious health risks due to its toxic nature.

1.4 Opioids

1.4.1 Afghanistan

The region comprising Afghanistan, Iran, and Pakistan, known as the "Golden Crescent," has historically been a hub for opium production and trafficking. In the late 1980s, Afghanistan emerged as a leading opium exporter, fueling political instability, violence, and corruption. Estimating drug use in Afghanistan is challenging due to ongoing conflict, dispersed population, and cultural factors (UNODC, 2020).

The Afghanistan National Urban Drug Use Study (ANUDUS) in 2009, found that 5.1% of the population reported recent drug use, with opioids being the most common, including opium, heroin, and pharmaceutical opioids (Cottler et al. 2014). The Islamic Republic of Afghanistan Ministry of Counter Narcotics—UNODC reported similar data in 2015, with opioids being the most frequently used drugs, with a prevalence of 4.9% among the general population and 8.5% in adults.

Opium poppy secures the livelihoods of many Afghans. In 2022, Afghanistan contributed to 80% of global opium production. However, the 2023 opium harvest might decrease significantly due to a national drug ban implemented in 2022, potentially impacting global heroin markets. Additionally, there's a shift towards methamphetamine production in Afghanistan, raising questions about its interconnection with the heroin market and its impact on the global drug trade (WDR 2023).

1.4.2 Bangladesh

Following the ban on cannabis sales in 1988 in Bangladesh, heroin use surged, along with the misuse of pharmaceutical opioids. However, stringent punishment measures for opioid use led to low treatment seeking for opioid use disorders. Treatment resources for substance use disorders are limited in Bangladesh, with harm reduction strategies falling short of meeting the population's needs. The 2022 Bangladesh Annual Drug Report reveals that treatment seeking for heroin-related opioid use disorders totaled 1438, while codeine use surged in 2022 after fluctuating admission rates. Injecting drug use, primarily involving buprenorphine, saw a gradual decline until 2021 but spiked by over 90% in 2022. These figures likely underestimate the true extent of opioid use and opioid use disorders in the country, highlighting the need for expanded treatment resources and harm reduction efforts.

1.4.3 India

Opioid usage is documented in 2.1% of the nation's populace, with heroin being the most prevalent at 1.14%, followed by pharmaceutical opioids at 0.96%, and opium at 0.52% (Ambekar et al. 2019). The prevalence of opioid use in India exceeds the global average by threefold. Compared to figures from 2004, overall opioid usage has risen, with heroin now surpassing opium in popularity. Opioid use disorder is most prevalent among heroin users (0.57%). State-wise variation is evident in the higher population prevalence rates in the northeastern states compared to greater numbers in the northeastern states. Between-state variability also exists in the types of opioids primarily misused. Additionally, a significant portion constitute the injecting drug use population, with far-reaching negative outcomes. India introduced harm reduction as a strategy for treatment for opioid use disorder in the early 2000s and there are ongoing efforts to increase its availability and accessibility. However, disparity between the legal provisions, national policies, and socio-political and geographical barriers all interfere with faster and more effective treatment delivery in this population.

According to the World Drug Report 2023, India is the largest opiate market in South Asia. Illicit opium cultivation primarily occurs in the northeastern and northwestern states. (UNODC 2023). Official reports suggest that more than half of the heroin found in India in 2017 entered the country from Pakistan and Afghanistan (53%) with the main trafficking route for heroin being across the India–Pakistan border, notably through the State of Punjab and the union territory of Jammu and Kashmir, from where the heroin is then trafficked to other states across the country.

1.4.4 Nepal

Opioids are the second most commonly used substance in Nepal, with various methods of consumption including smoking or inhaling heroin, injecting opioids like buprenorphine, or consuming high doses of tramadol in combination with other substances. Injectable drug users typically engage in a dangerous practice known as the "South Asian Cocktail," which involves combining opioids, benzodiazepines, and antihistamines, leading to numerous health, social, economic, and legal hazards.

Nepal has implemented opioid agonist therapy (OAT) programs, offering methadone and buprenorphine at both governmental hospitals and non-governmental organizations and following a "low threshold" approach, providing treatment to individuals with opioid use disorder.

1.4.5 Pakistan

In Pakistan, opium has been historically used and remains prevalent, despite the 1979 Hudood Ordinance banning its cultivation, sale, or use. The 1980s saw a rise in heroin use, primarily affecting males, with some regional pockets of higher female usage. Prescription drug misuse, including pethidine and morphine, has also persisted. Pakistan's location on a major drug trafficking route from Afghanistan exacerbates its drug-related challenges, with around 40% of Afghanistan's heroin and cannabis passing through Pakistan.

Since 1982, Pakistan has conducted national drug use surveys to monitor consumption trends. The 2012–2013 survey, led by UNODC and Pakistan's authorities, revealed 1.06 million regular opiate users aged 15–64 (1.0% of the population), with the highest prevalence in Balochistan (1.6%). Dependency was severe in Khyber Pakhtunkhwa and Balochistan, yet treatment access was limited due to financial constraints. Approximately 1.5% misused prescription opioids. Opium users were typically older, married, and rural, while heroin users were younger, unmarried, and often urban homeless. Many heroin users struggled with employment due to addiction-related issues. Polydrug use, particularly with cannabis and sedatives, was common among opioid users, who averaged 16 years of use. Reports of opioid overdose were increasing, emphasizing the need for updated substance use disorder data. A National Drug Use Survey Pakistan 2022–2024 is currently underway in Islamabad to track evolving drug use patterns nationwide.

1.4.6 Sri Lanka

In an earlier 2002 survey in Sri Lanka, using the snowballing technique across 18 cities, 6,664 heroin users were identified. Most were aged 21–40, literate, and unskilled laborers. Initiation through friends was common, with almost half married. Nearly one-third had used heroin for 6–10 years and most used more than one substance. A more recent survey in 2019, showed heroin as the second most commonly used illicit substance, with a prevalence of 0.61% of the total population above 14 years of age (NDDCB 2019).

1.5 Cannabis

According to the latest World Drug Report published in 2023, Cannabis remains the most prevalent illicit drug used across the globe. Cannabis is indigenous to this region and historical records of its use date back to around the third century BC. With regard to the cannabis legalization trends across the globe, none of the South Asian nations currently endorse this view. Newer synthetic cannabinoids have been reported in select cities, predominantly among the younger population.

1.5.1 Afghanistan

The UNODC Afghanistan Cannabis survey (2009) revealed Afghanistan's significant role as a global cannabis producer. Cannabis, primarily consumed as hashish, is the most prevalent illicit substance in the country. Approximately 60% of drug users had used cannabis. Male users showed more frequent use, with 70% reporting daily consumption. Cannabis use typically begins at 18–19 years. Most cannabis users had primary education, differing from other drug users who were often illiterate. Regional disparities showed higher cannabis use in Northern and Southern regions, corresponding to former and current production areas, respectively (UNODC 2009; UNODC, 2017).

1.5.2 Bangladesh

Cannabis has a significant historical presence in Bangladesh. Cannabis, marketed in various forms with different psychoactive properties, was socially accepted. There also exists a history of cannabis use for spiritual purposes across religions.

In the present date, cannabis remains the most widely used illicit drug in Bangladesh, similar to neighboring countries. According to the latest data, the number of cannabis dependent patients receiving treatment was 8459 in the year 2022. A large majority of illicit cannabis in Bangladesh seems to originate from the north-eastern and eastern states of India, with the districts of Comilla and Brahmanbaria in Bangladesh reportedly experiencing the highest trafficking rates (DNC 2022).

1.5.3 India

Cannabis grows naturally along the Himalayan foothills. Its use is intertwined with regional religious practices, dating back to ancient scriptures, and holds spiritual, and ceremonial significance in the Indian population. Its use among traditional medicine practitioners for various ailments continues in varying measures till this day.

Currently, cannabis ranks as the most prevalent illicit psychoactive substance used in the country, with approximately 2.8% prevalence of cannabis use in any form among people aged between 10 and 75 years. (Ambekar et al. 2019). Besides bhang, the consumption of cannabis in other forms such as resin is illegal according to the Narcotic Drugs and Psychotropic Substances (NDPS) Act of 1985. Although bhang is the most widely used form of Cannabis in India, the cannabis use disorder is higher in those using higher potency cannabis, mostly as ganja or charas. There also exists state-wise variation in the form of cannabis most widely used. Unlike the predominant national scenario, the states of West Bengal, Bihar, Sikkim, Mizoram, Nagaland, and Meghalaya report higher prevalence of illicit forms of cannabis use as compared to bhang. The latest nationwide drug use survey estimated the prevalence of cannabis use in harmful or dependent patterns to be 0.66%. There is significant state-wise variation, with higher prevalence rates in some states, such as Tripura and Punjab, while larger treatment requiring population in numbers in larger states such as Uttar Pradesh.

1.5.4 Nepal

Cannabis is a flora indigenous to Nepal. Its use as hemp and animal feed has been present for centuries. Traditional healers in this region have incorporated cannabis into their practices for medicinal purposes for many years. Up until the ban on the sale of cannabis in 1973 and the implementation of the Narcotics Control Act of 1976, Nepal was a favored destination among people from other countries seeking out cannabis. There are reports of wide availability of Cannabis across the country, with designated licensed dealers selling the cannabis resin or hashish in places such as Kathmandu.

According to the Nepal Drug Users Survey conducted in 2020, cannabis use is prevalent in 84.7% of the population using drugs, use cannabis. Early initiation of cannabis is another notable feature as suggested by the following findings.

1.5.5 Pakistan

Cannabis use is widely prevalent in Pakistan with about 3.6% of the population reporting cannabis use. The 2013 National Survey on Drug Use reported that more than 4 million people in Pakistan use cannabis regularly, most of whom started using cannabis and other drugs during their teenage years. The survey highlighted that the majority of cannabis users were men, with lower education levels compared to non-users. The typical cannabis user was a 33-year-old male with up to primary school education, engaged in full or part-time employment, and about half were married. Both male and female users exhibited high frequency and severity of cannabis use, with one-third reporting daily use and meeting criteria for drug use disorders. However, only 7% sought drug treatment. While few respondents considered cannabis the most harmful drug, 76% of regular opiate users reported cannabis as their first drug. Most problem drug users were introduced to cannabis by friends or family, often at weddings, with an average age of initiation at 21 years (UNODC 2013).

1.5.6 Sri Lanka

Cannabis is the most frequently used illicit drug in Sri Lanka. It is also the only drug that is grown illicitly, primarily in dry regions of the Eastern and Southern provinces. The prevalence of cannabis use is 1.9% among the population aged 14 years and above. A significant proportion of cannabis users also use other psychoactive substances, such as opioids, tobacco, or alcohol. Gender-wise differences in cannabis use patterns were noted with significantly higher prevalence among males (4%) versus females (0.2%) (NDDCB 2019).

1.6 Stimulants

According to the Global Cocaine Report, 2023, around 5% of overall global cocaine past-year users were from South Asia. Although cocaine consumption is notably minimal in this region, there is the greatest potential for a surge in cocaine users, primarily because of its large population. A country-wise overview of the primary findings from national and international level studies follows. Some countries for which adequate data was unavailable haven't been included (UNODC 2023).

1.6.1 Afghanistan

There has been a continued substantial increase in methamphetamine manufacture in Afghanistan, a trend that has been observed since 2012. The latest data show that increasing demands for synthetic drugs such as methamphetamine and their use in Afghanistan have been reported (UNODC, 2017; UNODC 2021).

1.6.2 Bangladesh

According to the World Drug Report 2023 data, Bangladesh is the leading methamphetamine market in South Asia. The South-East Asian region, primarily Myanmar continues to be the origin of the methamphetamine found in Bangladesh.

The proportion of patients admitted to treatment services for methamphetamine tablets in Bangladesh rose between 2014 and 2018, in tandem with an increase in seizures.

Yaba—a stimulant comprising methamphetamine and caffeine is one of the most common drugs misused in Bangladesh. Easy affordability and accessibility continue to be the main driving forces of a sustained high Yaba use, particularly among the younger population. Drug entry is primarily through the southeastern corner of the country, from Malaysia (DNC 2022).

1.6.3 India

Compared to the previously discussed drug classes, India has a much lower prevalence of stimulant use disorders. The estimated annual prevalence of cocaine use in India is about 0.11%, equivalent to approximately 1.1 million past-year users, with variations between genders. Arunachal Pradesh and Punjab, the union territories of Dadra and Nagar Haveli, Lakshadweep, and Maharashtra including Mumbai, report greater previous year prevalence of use. As for Amphetamine-Type Stimulants (ATS), an estimated 0.06% of the general population is dependent. Methamphetamine manufactured in Afghanistan is the most common source.

Moreover, Indian states along methamphetamine trafficking routes across Southeast Asia and South Asia such as Manipur (4.86%), Mizoram (0.31%), and Andaman and Nicobar Islands (0.78%) had a higher prevalence of past-year ATS use compared to the regional average. In terms of number of users, the western states rank higher (UNODC 2023).

1.6.4 Pakistan

While cocaine use is negligible in most areas of the country, its use was reported in Pakistan-administered Kashmir where approximately 2,300 people had used cocaine in the past year (Global Cocaine Report 2023).

Previously undetected in the country, trace levels of methamphetamine are now being reported with around 19,000 people estimated to have used this stimulant in the past year.

Regarding ATS, an emerging group of substances in Pakistan, Balochistan had the highest prevalence of methamphetamine use and Khyber Pakhtunkhwa had the highest prevalence of prescription amphetamine use (UNODC, 2013).

1.7 Other Drug Classes

Besides the above drug classes, some of the other psychoactive substances reportedly used include sedatives-hypnotics, hallucinogens, inhalants, cathinones, and areca nuts. Globally, 600 million people use Areca nut (AN). The countries of India, Bangladesh, Pakistan, and Sri Lanka report some of the highest consumption, besides Southeast Asian countries such as Myanmar and Thailand. AN is consumed in various forms, often wrapped in a betel leaf with additives. Despite established carcinogenic risks for oral and pharyngeal cancer, prevailing customs and beliefs contribute to its widespread use, along with its significant role in the export industry, particularly in lower socio-economic groups. Inhalants are another class of drugs with a higher prevalence in this part of the world, predominantly in younger age groups, including children and adolescents, particularly those belonging to lower socio-economic classes. Sedative-hypnotics, in particular benzodiazepines such as diazepam, and nitrazepam are also reported to be misused. Prevalence of sedative-hypnotics use in non-prescription patterns is estimated to be around 1.08% in India. A minority of them use sedatives-hypnotics in a dependent pattern, about 0.11% of the general population (Ambekar et al. 2019).

1.8 Maldives—A Snapshot

The Maldives has an import-oriented economy and a demographically young and mobile population. Drug legislation began in 1977, with an amendment in 2011 leading to the establishment of the National Drug Agency (NDA) aimed at encouraging treatment-seeking and combating illegal substance use.

A recent Situational Analysis conducted by the UNODC reveals a transition in substance use patterns in the last decade, with younger users and drug suppliers emerging alongside a growing elderly demographic. Trends include the rise of new psychotropic drugs, a shift in drug sources from South Asia to Europe, and changes in transportation methods. Challenges include limited access to treatment programs, local substance production, human trafficking among users, and health risks such as sharing needles due to syringe shortages (UNODC 2021, UNODC, 2012).

Despite the implementation of a complete ban on alcohol consumption, the latest Global Status Report on Alcohol and Health shows a disproportionately high value of the total alcohol per capita consumption, drinkers only, which was 33.7 L. Other than alcohol, the prevalence of cannabis and opioids has also shown an increasing trend.

The Health Protection Agency survey found a 23% tobacco use rate, with concerning rises among women and children. Early initiation poses health risks, including chronic diseases.

1.9 Changing Trends of Substance Use in South Asia

South Asia remains a major player in the global drug scenario. As the preceding sections show, the last decade has witnessed a transformation in multiple domains of substance use in this region. There is a growing trend toward the use of higher potency opioids as shown by the higher consumption of heroin and other opioids compared to natural opium as reflected by the latest data from almost all the countries. With easy availability and poor regulation of pharmaceutical products, this region also continues to be an important source of newer drugs, such as ATS with supply to the neighboring countries. With good access and transportation routes, South Asia lies on important drug trafficking routes, with consistently high seizure rates of different drugs primarily, opium and cannabis. Another worrying trend is the lack of consistent decline in alcohol consumption rates in this region, compared to the higher-income countries. Most of the population in South Asian countries experience the fallouts from social inequity, political unrest, and transitioning economies. With a predominantly young demographic in this region and easy access to the internet, drug experimentation and acquisition have become easier than ever. With regard to tobacco, the level of implementation of MPOWER strategies varies between the countries. Despite a declining trend of smoking prevalence in this region, the sheer magnitude in terms of numbers continues to heavily contribute to the global burden of disease associated with tobacco in this region. Rising levels of smokeless tobacco use heavily contributes to this. Emerging threats of other forms of newer nicotine and tobacco delivery systems continue to be reported intermittently.

1.10 Conclusion

This chapter provides an overview of substance use disorders (SUDs) in South Asia, laying the groundwork for deeper exploration in subsequent chapters. Despite this, a glimpse into current patterns reveals a complex interplay of factors shaping substance supply and demand. Limited standardized monitoring systems and national treatment registries hinder systematic data collection. Collaboration between local governments and global organizations can improve data collection through national surveys. Resource and capacity building are crucial for delivering effective preventive and treatment services. South Asia's predominantly young population, socio-economic disparities, and ongoing conflicts exacerbate the problem. Addressing SUDs requires a comprehensive strategy considering cultural, economic, and community-specific challenges. Continuous research and monitoring are essential to adapt preventive and therapeutic approaches to evolving social and economic changes. Stakeholders, including public health officials, policymakers, and healthcare professionals, must understand SUD epidemiology to design targeted interventions and evidence-based strategies.

References

Ambekar, A., Agrawal, A., Rao, R., Mishra, A. K., & Khandelwal, S. K. (2019). Magnitude of substance use in India. Ministry of Social Justice and Empowerment, Government of India

Arafat, S., & Kar, S. (2024). Epidemiology of psychiatric disorders and overview of access to mental health care in South Asia. In: Arafat, S.M.Y., Kar, S.K. *Access to mental health care in South Asia.* Springer Nature Singapore. https://doi.org/10.1007/978-981-99-9153-2_1

Chen, D. T.-H., Nargis, N., Fong, G. T., Huq, S. M., Quah, A. C. K., & Filippidis, F. T. (2023). A longitudinal study of transitions between smoking and smokeless tobacco use from the ITC Bangladesh Surveys: Implications for tobacco control in the Southeast Asia region. The Lancet Regional Health - Southeast Asia, 14. https://doi.org/10.1016/j.lansea.2023.100185

Cottler, L. B., Ajinkya, S., Goldberger, B. A., Ghani, M. A., Martin, D. M., Hu, H., & Gold, M. S. (2014). Prevalence of drug and alcohol use in urban Afghanistan: epidemiological data from the Afghanistan National Urban Drug Use Study (ANUDUS). The Lancet. Global health, 2(10), e592–e600. https://doi.org/10.1016/S2214-109X(14)70290-6

Department of Narcotics in Bangladesh (DNC) (2022). Annual Drug Report Bangladesh-2022. Ministry of Home Affairs Government of the People's Republic of Bangladesh.

Global Burden of Disease (GBD) 2019. Seattle, WA: Institute for Health Metrics and Evaluation (IHME), University of Washington; 2021. Available from: vizhub.healthdata.org/gbd-compare/

GSAH 2018: World Health Organization (2018). Global status report on alcohol and health 2018. World Health Organization. https://www.who.int/publications/i/item/9789241565639

Kendrick, P. J. et al (2021). Spatial, temporal, and demographic patterns in prevalence of chewing tobacco use in 204 countries and territories, 1990–2019: A systematic analysis from the Global Burden of Disease Study 2019. *The Lancet Public Health*, *6*(7), e482–e499. https://doi.org/10.1016/S2468-2667(21)00065-7

Kivimäki, M., et al. (2022). Alcohol and health. The Lancet, 400(10365), 1763-1764. https://doi.org/10.1016/S0140-6736(22)02183-1

Manthey, J., Kilian, C., Carr, S., Bartak, M., Bloomfield, K., Braddick, F., Gual, A., Neufeld, M., O'Donnell, A., Petruzelka, B., Rogalewicz, V., Rossow, I., Schulte, B., & Rehm, J. (2021). Use of alcohol, tobacco, cannabis, and other substances during the first wave of the SARS-CoV-2 pandemic in Europe: a survey on 36,000 European substance users. Substance abuse treatment, prevention, and policy, 16(1), 36. https://doi.org/10.1186/s13011-021-00373-y

Naveed, S. et al (2020). Prevalence of Common Mental Disorders in South Asia: A Systematic Review and Meta-Regression Analysis. *Frontiers in Psychiatry, 11.* https://www.frontiersin.org/articles/10.3389/fpsyt.2020.573150

National Dangerous Drugs Control Board, Presidential Task Force on Drug Prevention and Sri Lanka Police (2019). National Prevalence Survey on Drug Use—2019. National Dangerous Drugs Control Board.

Nayab D, Nasir M, Memon JA, et al. The Economic Cost of Tobacco-Induced Diseases in Pakistan. Pakistan Institute of Development Economics, Islamabad. 2021. Available at: https://tobacconomics.org/research/the-economic-cost-of-tobacco-induced-diseases-in-pakistan/

Reitsma MB, Kendrick PJ, Ababneh E, et al. ; GBD 2019 Tobacco Collaborators . Spatial, temporal, and demographic patterns in prevalence of smoking tobacco use and attributable disease burden in 204 countries and territories, 1990–2019: a systematic analysis from the Global Burden of

Disease Study 2019. Lancet. 2021;397(10292):2337–2360. https://doi.org/10.1016/S0140-6736(21)01169-7

Shahzad, S., Kliewer, W., Ali, M., & Begum, N. (2020). Different risk factors are associated with alcohol use versus problematic use in male Pakistani adolescents. *International Journal of Psychology: Journal international de psychologie*, *55*(4), 585–589. https://doi.org/10.1002/ijop.12617

Shield, K. D., & Rehm, J. (2021). Societal development and the alcohol-attributable burden of disease. Addiction (Abingdon, England), 116(9), 2326–2338. https://doi.org/10.1111/add.15441

Siddiqi, K., Husain, S., Vidyasagaran, A., Readshaw, A., Mishu, M. P., & Sheikh, A. (2020). Global burden of disease due to smokeless tobacco consumption in adults: An updated analysis of data from 127 countries. *BMC Medicine*, *18*(1), 222. https://doi.org/10.1186/s12916-020-01677-9

United Nations Office on Drugs and Crime (2012). National drug use survey Maldives 2011/2012.United Nations Office on Drugs and Crimes.

United Nations Office on Drugs and Crime (2013). Drug use in Pakistan 2013. (United Nations Publications).

United Nations Office on Drugs and Crime (2017). Afghanistan synthetic drugs situation assessment 2017. (United Nations Publications).

United Nations Office on Drugs and Crime (UNODC). (2018). Study on substance use and health among youth in Afghanistan. UNODC. Retrieved from https://www.unodc.org

United Nations Office on Drugs and Crime, UNICEF and Government of Afghanistan. (2020) Youth study on substance use and health. (United Nations Publications).

United Nations Office on Drugs and Crime (2023). World Drug Report 2023. (United Nations Publications).

United Nations Office on Drugs and Crime (2023). Global Report on Cocaine 2023- Local Dynamics, Global Challenges. (United Nations Publications).

World Drug Report 2009: United Nations Office on Drugs and Crime. (2009). World Drug Report 2009. United Nations. https://www.unodc.org/unodc/en/data-and-analysis/WDR-2009.html

World Health Organization (2019). WHO global report on trends in prevalence of tobacco use 2000–2025. World Health Organization. Available from: https://apps.who.int/iris/bitstream/handle/10665/330221/9789240000032-eng.pdf

World Drug Report 2021: United Nations Office on Drugs and Crime. (2021). World Drug Report 2021. United Nations. https://www.unodc.org/unodc/en/data-and-analysis/wdr2021.html

Chapter 2
Current Perspectives on Substance Use Disorders in Afghanistan

Omer Ahmed Shaikh, Sheikh Shoib, Fahimeh Saeed, and Sardar khan Nazari

2.1 Introduction

A major public health issue in Afghanistan, substance use disorders (SUDs) have an effect on people, families, and communities all over the nation. Drug use and other addictive behaviors have negative effects on mental health and well-being, which exacerbates already-existing vulnerabilities in the war-torn country. With a focus on how SUDs are currently affecting public mental health in Afghanistan, this chapter seeks to shed light on the situation.

Despite Afghanistan producing the bulk of the world's opium, little research has been done on the use of illicit drugs there. There are fewer reliable statistics on drug use in Afghanistan than in most other countries. Several challenges exist that include inadequate reporting processes and continuous security worries that may stand as a barrier to good quality research. Comprehensive data collection within the nation is

O. A. Shaikh
Faculty of Medicine, Ziauddin Medical University, Karachi, Pakistan

S. Shoib (✉)
Department of Health Services, Srinagar 190001, India
e-mail: Sheikhshoib22@gmail.com

Sharda University (SSh), Greater Noida, India

Psychosis Research Center, University of Social Welfare and Rehabilitation Sciences, Tehran, Iran

Healing Mind and Wellness Initiative Nawab Bazaar Srinagar, Srinagar, India

F. Saeed
Psychosis Research Center, University of Social Welfare and Rehabilitation Sciences, Tehran, Iran
e-mail: Fa.saeed@uswr.ac.ir

S. Nazari
Sakha Private Hospital, Kabul, Afghanistan
e-mail: dr.sardarkhan2019@gmail.com

S. M. Y. Arafat and S. K. Kar (eds.), *Current Perspectives on Substance Use Disorders in South Asia*, https://doi.org/10.1007/978-981-97-6619-2_2

particularly challenging due to a number of variables, including inadequate reporting techniques and continuous security concerns (Bewley-Taylor et al. 2023).

This report strives to give significant insights for policymakers, healthcare practitioners, researchers, and other stakeholders to handle this pressing issue effectively by assessing the prevalence, risk factors, treatment choices, preventative initiatives, and the existing policy framework.

2.2 Current Situations in Afghanistan

Opium, heroin, and methamphetamine cultivation and trafficking have historically been heavily concentrated in Afghanistan. A favorable environment for the production and distribution of drugs has been established by the country's geographical position as well as decades of war and unrest. As a result, drug abuse has become pervasive and has had negative effects on the public's health. Afghanistan has long been acknowledged as the main opium producer in the world, expected to account for 85% of all output by 2020 ("GLOBAL OVERVIEW: DRUG DEMAND, DRUG SUPPLY," 2021).. Opium poppy cultivation has gradually risen, with an average yearly expansion of 4,000 hectares, ever since routine monitoring started in 1994 (UNODOC-Afghanistan Opium Survey 2021). Additionally, according to early evidence, Afghanistan is developing a robust black market for methamphetamine following an increase in production in 2016. Data on drug seizures, for instance, showed that between the years 2014–2018 and 2019–2021, a rising proportion of methamphetamine confiscated in neighboring countries originated in Afghanistan. Substance use disorder poses a serious issue given Afghanistan's growing illicit drug economy, which might account for up to 14% of the country's GDP in 2021 (UNODOC-Afghanistan Brief 2021). Due to the accessibility of cheap illicit drugs, unchecked poverty, and decades of conflict, all of which cause significant population relocation, many Afghans are at risk for substance use and the subsequent health and societal consequences. Opium, heroin, and methamphetamine cultivation and trafficking have historically been heavily concentrated in Afghanistan. A favorable environment for the production and distribution of drugs has been established by the country's geographical position as well as decades of war and unrest. As a result, drug abuse has become pervasive and has had negative effects on the public's health. Afghanistan has the most opiate users in the world, with 12.6% of Afghan people using drugs on average in 2015. This is much higher than the world average of 5.2%. (Jake Tacchi—The Organization for World Peace 2020) Most likely, this number has gone up over the past 7 years. (Jake Tacchi—The Organization for World Peace 2020).

The limited literature that is currently available, though, indicates a possibly epidemic-scale problem with substance use. In 2005, Afghanistan conducted the country's first-ever population-based drug usage study, which revealed that 3.8% of people there admitted to using illicit drugs, with cannabis and opiates being the most popular substances (UNODOC—Afghanistan Drug Use Survey 2005). According to a follow-up survey conducted in 2009, drug use was prevalent among adults aged 15–64 at 8%, with frequent opium and heroin users increasing by 53% and 140%, respectively, since 2005 (UNODOC-Drug use in Afghanistan 2009).

According to a 2015 poll (Afghanistan National Drug Usage Poll), which employed biological indicators that had been independently verified (Colombo Plan-Afghanistan National Drug Use Survey 2015), the country-wide prevalence of drug use among those 15 and older was 12.8% in 2015. The global rate for adults of the same age that year was 5.3%; this rate was higher (UNODOC—Global Overview 2017). With an 8.5% prevalence rate, opioids surpassed cocaine as the most widely used illegal drug in Afghanistan, surpassing cocaine's 4.42% prevalence rate in North America, according to the 2015 Afghanistan National Drug Use Survey (Colombo Plan—Afghanistan National Drug Use Survey 2015; UNODOC—Global Overview 2017).

Opioids are the most harmful illegal drugs, dramatically increasing the morbidity and death associated with SUDs. Between 2016 and 2019, opioids alone were responsible for more than 70% of disability-adjusted life years (DALYs) attributed to SUDs (UNODOC—Global Overview 2021; Degenhardt and Charlson 2018). Opioids are the most frequently injected substances, with an overall frequency of 83% among drug users (Degenhardt et al. 2017). The most hazardous drug administration method is injection, which has a substantial impact on health. In comparison to non-injection drug users, PWID had a higher risk of being addicted to drugs (Novak and Kral 2011; Strang et al. 1998), having numerous overdoses (Darke 2003; Shrestha et al. 2021), and passing away for any reason (Onyeka et al. 2016). While oral ingestion and inhalation have traditionally been the common way of drug uptake in Afghanistan, recent data show that displacement within Afghanistan as well as migration backward and forward the neighboring countries, Iran and Pakistan, may have contributed to the rise of injecting among drug users (Griffin and Khoshnood 2010).

Due to the high ubiquity of illicit opioid use in a country with some of the lowest socioeconomic and public health indicators in the world (The World Bank Group in Afghanistan 2021; The Global Health Observatory—WHO 2021), as well as the punitive laws surrounding substance use that are frequently influenced by religion (Drug Situation and the practice of drug 2019; Todd et al. 2007), drug users in general, and PWID in particular, may experience devastating health and social outcomes. Malaria, the rapidly proliferating human immunodeficiency virus (HIV), and viral hepatitis among drug users are all endemic in Afghanistan. The prevalence of communicable diseases is very high there (Wallace et al. 2002; Mumtaz et al. 2014). Health metrics are further complicated by a severe lack of social and medical infrastructure brought on by years of conflict and poverty. This prompts us to discuss the dangers.

2.3 Risk Factors

Several interconnected risk factors have an impact on the development of SUD in Afghanistan. Socio-economic problems including poverty, unemployment, and a lack of educational opportunities have a significant impact on substance use. Drug use is more prevalent among those from low socioeconomic backgrounds than in other categories. The level of commitment to or interaction with important institutions in society among teenagers and young adults is one of the most prominent risk factors for substance use. As seen by criminal behavior in kids, almost all forms of drug use (as well as underage smoking and drinking) are highly connected with general disobedience from societal standards (Darker and Whiston 2015).

Children in Afghanistan who use opiates have less academic success; some have to drop out of school and work as a result of a family member's drug use (UNODC—World Drug Report 2014). The United Nations Office on Drugs and Crime (UNODC) discovered through a survey that drug usage had also contributed to domestic violence. Many workers have lost their employment, and other families have been compelled to borrow money because family members are drug users. As a result, drug use has caused financial issues for families. Drug usage has led to a rise in crime, early death, corruption, workplace challenges, and security issues. Drug-related operations are a significant source of corruption that threatens political systems or government institutions, particularly in provinces where marijuana is grown (UNAFEI 2023).

Money laundering has tarnished banks across the Gulf and internationally. Premature deaths are a significant issue, and one of Afghanistan's main consequences of opiate abuse is the loss of potential productivity due to incapacity (World Drug Report 2013). Due to a lack of infrastructure and insufficient support from the public and commercial sectors, only 3% of opioid users may be treated annually. Additionally, drug treatment is not prioritized on the agendas of the relevant ministries. Significant barriers include the lack of adequate protocols and standards for the treatment of drug users as well as a government budget that has not been set aside to address the issue. Drug use in households and family issues, peer pressure and influence, lack of sports and entertainment facilities, tension related to war, ineffective drug prevention programs and treatment facilities, easy access to drugs and insufficient law enforcement, unemployment and job insecurity, and migration are some of the factors that contribute in the usage of opiates in the citizens of Kabul.

Lack of awareness about drug hazards and addiction's harmful impacts, particularly among adolescents and the younger generation, is one of the key risk factors for drug addiction. Unfortunately, there aren't many consultation and awareness services available to educate the next generation about the risks of drugs in Kabul's schools, mosques, and even on the news. Although mosques and schools can play an important part, this doesn't now happen or happens on a very tiny basis (Haidary 2016).

Cultural influences, such as the normalization of drug use in some locations, have an impact on the issue as well. Additionally, free borders and lax law enforcement lead to easy access to drugs, which facilitates substance usage. The bulk of the young population is still illiterate as a result of the war. Peer pressure, drug use among peers, a lack of community involvement, poor family ties, and other socialization-related risk factors are all prevalent among Kabul residents.

The ongoing war in Afghanistan has made the problem much worse by increasing the prevalence of mental health comorbidities among those with SUDs. Inequalities frequently coexist with mental health illnesses and are exacerbated by them. The likelihood of having mental health issues is increased by factors like unemployment and poverty, and frequently, the most vulnerable populations also receive the least help in terms of advocacy and access to healthcare. Low- and middle-income nations are disproportionately affected by mental health issues. According to estimates, only 29% of psychosis patients worldwide receive mental health care; in high-income nations, that number is closer to 70%, while it is as low as 12% in low-income nations (World Mental Health Report 2022). There are still large treatment gaps despite the high prevalence of poor mental health, which are typically caused by a lack of human resources, stigma, prevention and promotion activities, and the integration of mental health into primary care settings (World Health Organization.Regional Office for South-East Asia (2022)). Afghanistan also lacks adequate money for mental health services; it is believed that just 4% of the nation's overall health budget is devoted to this field (Pedneault 2020). An effective strategy would involve increased investment by national and international stakeholders in human capital and the integration of mental health initiatives through leveraging existing public health efforts (Patel 2007).

The Afghan population at large is confronted with pervasive and enduring distress, which has had devastating consequences for the nation over an extended period. According to a poll conducted by the European Union in 2018, a significant majority of individuals from Afghanistan, specifically 85%, indicated that they had encountered or observed at least one distressing occurrence. On average, these individuals reported experiencing four such events (Human Rights Watch 2020). The experience of trauma is frequently internalized and downplayed, hence increasing the potential for the development of mental health issues. However, it is evident that mental health treatments in Afghanistan are below standard, and the medical profession has challenges due to limited resources and insufficient knowledge in this particular domain. Afghanistan's populace struggles to effectively communicate mental health problems and challenges due to the country's poor level of mental health literacy. Due to a lack of appropriate words to explain their experiences, Afghans have limited options when asking for help (Harsch et al. 2021). Research from 2021 states that 10% of people use some kind of mental health care (Pedneault 2020). Still, people who do use them may be abused, such as by being made to get medical care (Pedneault 2020) or by family members taking them to a place of worship where they may be held down and chained (Ashna 2019). Misunderstandings cause people to think that mental illness is a personal failure or weakness, and its signs are often seen as punishments from God (Ashna 2019). WHO study from 2022 says that there is still a stigma against mental health and that people with mental health problems are often seen as weak, lazy, and not smart (World Mental Health Report 2022). These effects may not only affect the person but also his or her family. People often think that one person's "bad" behavior can make a family member sick or even make them unable to work. People with mental illnesses are often told to pray for healing instead of taking psychiatric drugs or getting other kinds of help, or they are just forgotten by the rest of the community. Psychosomatic diseases are underdiagnosed in Afghanistan because somatic symptoms are sometimes given more weight than psychic symptoms. Patients who present with psychosomatic diseases often receive medication instead of psychological treatment, such as for stomach problems, due to misdiagnosis and overprescribing (Pedneault 2020). If Afghans don't access healthcare, they might turn to self-medication for mental health issues. Evidence connects substance use, a common form of self-medication, to depressive disorders (Jake Tacchi—The Organization for World Peace 2020). Because of a combination of things, like high levels of stress and instability, high levels of stigma, and very few resources, there are a lot of SUDs in Afghanistan, and the mental health system isn't ready to deal with them.

2.4 Psychological Burden of SUDs

In Afghanistan, there are differences in both the prevalence and causes of poor mental health. Different groups of people in society are treated differently and have different ways to get help. Women in Afghanistan are more likely than men to have sadness, anxiety, and post-traumatic stress disorder (PTSD). This is likely because they have to deal with more social and cultural pressures (Cardozo et al. 2004). A study done in 2019 found that more than 90% of Afghan women who killed themselves did so because of untreated mental illness. A poll done in 2021 found that 9.1% of women had ever thought about killing themselves. Even if there isn't a single reason why there are so many people with mental illnesses, abuse is one thing that can lead to a mental illness. A study by the United Nations Population Fund found that 62% of Afghan women have been abused in many ways, and 87% of them have been physically, sexually, or mentally hurt at least once in their lives. There is widespread violence against women and girls. (Safi—BBC News 2018) In addition to the stigma associated with mental illness, there is also a great deal of guilt associated with abuse, which prevents many women from speaking out.

Even though women are more likely to face more trauma, men should not be ignored when seeking mental care. Specifically, young men have challenges, and more often the stigma attached to asking for help is higher for men than it is for women, which makes them less willing to do so. If this lack of assistance for men is disregarded, it may indirectly affect women because of the prominent association between domestic violence and trauma (Gibbs et al. 2018).

Afghanistan has a large number of young people, and poverty and economic trouble affect young people more than any other age group ("The Need for Evidence-Based Narratives Around Afghanistan's Youth," 2014). Young people have lost decades of opportunities in terms of education, health, jobs, and being able to vote because of the war in Afghanistan. Armed non-state groups have taken advantage of young people's trustworthiness and lack of hope by coming up with effective ways to radicalize and recruit people that the government isn't ready to deal with. Whether from abroad or in Afghanistan, children who have been radicalized and trafficked typically experience serious psychological trauma as a result. However, when it comes to effective interventions for the recovery and reintegration of radicalized youth, these kids do not have access to enough structured psychological support services.

Rural individuals are more negatively impacted by regional disparities in the availability and quality of mental health care. In 2018, 87% of Afghans, according to a WHO poll, resided within two hours of a medical facility (WHO 2022). However, in recent times, violence and prejudice have grown in Afghanistan's rural Andrab, Panjshir, and some districts of Balkhab. Due to the lack of mental healthcare, this has an impact on how healthcare is offered. Remote populations reported needing to travel up to nine hours to access even basic medical care, including those in Badakhshan.

2.5 Impact on Public Mental Health

2.5.1 The Impact on Families

According to the 2014 UNODC study, substance use increases the risk of domestic violence; more than half of the family members surveyed admitted to having been struck by or retaliated against by a drug-using relative during a dispute over the latter's drug usage. Family members reported that 60% of drug-using relatives who had been employed before using drugs had later lost their jobs, underscoring the correlation between drug use, unemployment, and poverty. As a result of the drug use in the family, nearly 50% of the family members who were interviewed claimed they had to borrow money, and nearly 70% said that they had experienced financial troubles.

2.5.2 The Impact on Children

The same UNODC 2014 report enlightens the fact that youngsters who are exposed to drug use in the home struggle academically; more than one-third of the youngsters surveyed reported having to quit school because of a family member's drug usage. Key informants' information also revealed that some kids were made to work as a result of a family member's drug addiction. Additionally, 15% of the kids who were interviewed stated that drug use in their family had an impact on their behavior, and 7% reported that they had become ill as a result.

2.5.3 Impacts on Communities

Most communities perceive drug use as a concern. Over half of key informants claimed to know drug users who had passed away as a result of their addiction, and the majority of them considered that drug usage had a negative impact on their community. More than 80% of the government personnel surveyed thought that drug usage in their neighborhood had a detrimental effect on the operations of their organizations. One of the effects mentioned by those interviewed was the development of a toxic work environment and a higher inclination for corruption. Additionally, more than 20% of drug users who were interviewed said that law enforcement personnel had physically assaulted them.

2.6 Treatment and Rehabilitation

Accessing SUD treatment and rehabilitation options in Afghanistan is extremely difficult. Many people are deterred from seeking help by the stigma attached to addiction, and there aren't many specialized institutions available, especially in rural areas. Treatment-seeking behavior is also influenced by cultural variables. Despite these difficulties, some organizations are setting the bar for novel initiatives like harm reduction tactics and community-based rehabilitation programs. To effectively address SUDs in Afghanistan, there is a need for more extensive and accessible treatment alternatives. Evidence-based treatments, according to a study, for SUDs and adaptation to low-resource settings include the following:

The MCN's mandate includes reducing drug demand and developing policies. It manages the eight pillars of the National Drug Control Strategy from 2006 with a focus on drug abuse prevention and treatment. Among the policy texts created since 2005 are:

(a) The National Drug Treatment Guidelines, of which the latest version is currently under dispute.
(b) The National Guidelines for Drug Education.
(c) National Harm Reduction Strategy.

2.6.1 Treatment with Methadone Maintenance

The French NGO *Medecins du Monde's* nationwide pilot project in Kabul has not been without criticism. However, the outcome has been governmental confusion regarding the legitimacy of OST and limited permission confined to three monthly import licenses only. It is still unclear at what level the issue sits. This is a concern since locating methadone and negotiating imports takes time, and the requirement for signatories can cause supplies to run out before the next batch is delivered to

Kabul. Due to the lack of tolerance and relapse into using street drugs, this has in the past led to fatalities. To create a united and harmonious strategy, UNODC and WHO may find it helpful to have a national consensus conference based on knowledge and local experiences. Creating policy advice involves collaborating with all parties.

Other initiatives as part of the Afghan preventive programs included religious [mosque-based] outreach in 24 provinces in collaboration with the Colombo Plan, which offered job placement, training, and limited job referrals due to the work options. Peer support groups for the 12-step program, drug education during Friday prayers (average: 3000), attendance at mosques for religious and social instruction (500), and after-care programs centered on food are other sources of assistance.

The patients getting treated claimed there was a lot of equipment sharing in Kabul prior to the harm reduction, education, and needle and syringe exchange programs. Antiseptics and safer injection techniques are now used. They said that before these programs, they were similarly unaware of the dangers of hazardous injections (United Nations Office on Drugs and Crime 2013).

The most successful evidence-based medications for treating SUDs include those for OUD, AUD, and nicotine use disorders. Only those treatments have been shown to help people with and without other mental health problems at the same rate in treating nicotine use disorder (Anthenelli et al. 2016). The general ideas behind SUD maintenance therapies include the use of partial or full agonist therapies, in which the medication effectively replaces and stabilizes neural pathways that have become unstable due to long-term substance use, and antagonist therapies, in which the medication stops substances from getting to receptors in affected, SUD-reinforcing neural pathways. These include buprenorphine and methadone for OUD, nicotine replacement therapy and varenicline for AUD, and acamprosate, topiramate, and gabapentin for OUD.

Drugs like naltrexone and bupropion, which are used to treat OUD and AUD, and nicotine use disorder, are two instances of antagonist treatment. Some drugs, like the selective agonists buprenorphine and varenicline, work in ways that are different from both agonist and antagonist drugs that are used to stop people from using drugs again. Disulfiram, a nasty drug, is used to treat AUD. The acetaldehyde that is made when alcohol is broken down is then broken down by acetaldehyde dehydrogenase. Disulfiram blocks acetaldehyde dehydrogenase, which can cause acetaldehyde to build up in the body when alcohol is present. This buildup of acetaldehyde can cause adverse reactions like flushing and nausea, as well as possible heart problems, low blood pressure, and chest pain. In places with limited resources, it may be better to use drugs with few side effects and good tolerability, like buprenorphine, varenicline, and acamprosate, instead of those with more severe side effects that need lab monitoring, like methadone or disulfiram, or with less good tolerability, like naltrexone or clonazepam. A warning about somatic treatments that may be used but haven't been proven by science is also helpful.

The differences in sex-specific responses to pharmacotherapies are mainly unknown because women are underrepresented in many clinical investigations. However, there is growing data that suggests that different SUD medications may affect men and women differently. For instance, when compared to nicotine replacement therapy, meta-analytic research indicated that varenicline was more successful in treating nicotine dependence in women than in men (Smith et al. 2017). In the majority of trials, men and women saw the same clinical outcomes with buprenorphine/naloxone treatment for OUD.

SUD therapy is appropriate for pregnant or recently delivered women who also have SUDs. The placenta absorbs the bulk of addictive substances, many of which are teratogens or have the potential to be teratogens. Therefore, both the mother's health and the development of the fetus need to make an attempt to include pregnant SUD women in prenatal and substance use care (Jones et al. 2010). Methadone or buprenorphine, which are both agonists that have been shown to help pregnant women with OUD, is now the usual treatment for these patients. For women who are pregnant or just gave birth, behavioral therapies remain an essential intervention.

2.7 Prevention and Harm Reduction Strategies

The three drugs that kids and teenagers use the most commonly are alcohol, cigarettes, and cannabis. Adolescence is when substance usage typically begins. Early frequent substance use is linked to problems with physical and mental health as well as a higher risk of dependency or harmful use in later life, even if there is no clear causative relationship. Effective prevention, which starts early, is built on the best scientific evidence currently available. A number of industries, most notably the health sector, have a role to play, but the education sector may also have a big role to play in protecting children and teenagers from substance abuse while also creating an environment where getting help for problematic drug use is not stigmatized.

The relevance of providing preventative and treatment services is outlined by SDG Target 3.5, "Strengthen the prevention and treatment of substance abuse, including narcotic drug abuse and harmful use of alcohol." The second revised edition of the UNODC and WHO International Standards on Drug Use Prevention (UNODC 2020) gives an overview of the most recent studies on the policies and treatments that have been proven effective in preventing drug use as well as other related risky behaviors.

Effective interventions and policies have been adopted across a wide range of contexts (family, school, community, workplace, health sector, etc.) and risk levels (universal, selective, and advised). Early childhood education, prenatal and postpartum care, and treatments for expectant mothers are all beneficial interventions in infancy and the early years. Programs to improve the classroom environment, policies to keep children in school, parenting education initiatives (effective also in early adolescence), and policies to address mental health disorders (relevant also in adolescence) are all effective strategies for middle childhood (roughly 5–10 years of age).

Mentoring, substance use policies at schools, school-wide efforts to strengthen school ties, and preventive education with a social impact and competency focus are other effective strategies for reducing substance use in early adolescence. Additional effective strategies for usage in later adolescence and adulthood include brief intervention, tobacco and alcohol legislation, as well as multi-component programs in the workplace, in the community, and in entertainment venues. Media campaigns can also be quite beneficial without stigmatizing drug users. There is a dearth of research on the different factors that may influence the success of prophylactic measures for both men and women. The little data point to a variety of etiological factors for girls and women (UNODC 2016).

When it comes to substances that are produced and distributed legally, such as prescription drugs that cause dependence, commercial health issues may have an impact on the amount and type of drug use. The rapidly growing cannabis industry has become a distinct area of the private commercial sector in several countries, where it is legal to promote cannabis-related products and potentially unhealthy lifestyle choices. The impact of these extra variables on preventative tactics and policies might be positive or negative.

Health professionals are in a unique position to identify patients who abuse psychoactive substances and to intervene early before substance use disorders and other serious issues manifest. Strong evidence supports the value of screening and prompt interventions for hazardous and harmful alcohol intake in primary healthcare settings. Short interventions following screening can be effective when dealing with drugs other than alcohol-related psychoactive substances, according to a study. With the use of the WHO ASSIST package, health professionals can intervene at the early stages of substance use to prevent the formation of substance use disorders (WHO—MHGAP Intervention Guide 2019).

In order to effectively treat Afghans' mental health needs, a framework of family-focused and community-based care must be established and maintained. Due to Afghanistan's low resources, long-term provision of independent clinical mental health care is not viable. A framework where social, public health and clinical services are provided concurrently at the community level can help to fill the gaps in previous models of healthcare, particularly by improving care coordination, addressing the comorbidity of physical and psychological conditions, and lowering the need for referrals from outside sources. The most vulnerable members of society in Afghanistan, where the family is the most important social unit, would also benefit greatly from family-centered care. For instance, the mental health of a woman is significantly influenced by that of her husband; therefore, resolving the primary issues of the family head (often the husband or father) may have a positive effect on the health of the other family members. The primary caregiver's—often the mother's—health needs must be managed like how a kid is handled.

2.8 Policy and Legal Framework

The legal and legislative framework in Afghanistan regarding substance use disorders needs to be thoroughly reviewed and improved. A more public health-oriented attitude that places an emphasis on prevention, treatment, and rehabilitation needs to replace the existing punitive approach. To establish evidence-based programs that effectively manage SUDs while preserving cultural sensitivities, policymakers must collaborate with healthcare professionals, researchers, and organizations like the WHO.

Human rights abuses, poor health outcomes, early death, and economic losses on a global and national scale are all caused by mental health issues. The United Governments Human Rights Council passed a resolution on mental health and human rights, which acts as a catalyst for tackling this issue and affirms governments' commitment to doing so. The next phase should be an iterative process with a defined plan based on the needs of the local people and culture because different countries are expanding their mental health services at different speeds.

While policies are important, it's also important to make sure that they will benefit and have an impact on the local population. The policy's implementation should be carefully prepared and the revision procedure should be made public. A well-designed program to achieve strategic localization and implementation of evidence-based policy is PRIME (PRogramme for Improving Mental Health CareE) (Lund et al. 2012). The PRIME project intends to generate evidence on the application and scaling up of integrated packages of treatment for priority mental disorders in primary and maternal healthcare settings in Ethiopia, India, Nepal, South Africa, and Uganda. Breuer and associates (Breuer et al. 2016) talked about how the PRIME program developed integrated mental health treatment plans for particular regions using the theory of change (ToC).

The products of this procedure include a description of the applied ToC map, an outcomes route, significant interventions, crucial assumptions, and indicators, to name just a few. Despite claiming that the transformation process was beneficial, the authors said that the method prevented stakeholder buy-in and bottom-up development. This was a missed opportunity, and moving forward, initiatives should make an effort to gain support and buy-in from the community to improve programs. The community is a strength in many LMICs, as we have highlighted. Local regulations are important, but global leaders must also consider how global architecture and civil society may affect the laws governing mental health.

2.9 Research and Data Gaps

Research and statistics on SUDs in Afghanistan are seriously lacking. It takes top-notch epidemiological research to fully comprehend the scope and character of the issue. Research on efficient interventions, preventative measures, and the cultural adaptability of current methods is also crucial. Prioritize research to inform evidence-based policies and practices among funders and policymakers.

The best approach to reducing drug use is through treatment, which is also the most economical option for society. Despite this data, fewer than 20% of those in need of therapy actually receive it, and implementing improved treatment and facilitating better access face numerous obstacles.

Even the most knowledgeable and well-intentioned treatment clinician, researcher, or state substance abuse director finds it challenging to stay up to date with the science given the boom of knowledge occurring in the field of understanding the biology of the brain and the causes of addiction. New policy questions develop as a result of the new scientific knowledge, which in turn raises new treatment-related queries and new research directions. To deliver the advantages of treatment research to the consumer of drug treatment and society, it is crucial to improve the sharing of information and knowledge among the research, treatment, and policy fields.

The three main pillars of the drug abuse treatment community—therapy, research, and policy—do not communicate well with one another. These gaps are brought about (or made worse) by several crucial impediments to improved coordination and communication. Lack of advocacy initiatives and training opportunities (and requirements) in substance misuse treatment and research for all health-related professions are additional impediments. Additionally, many CBOs struggle with the difficulties of a fluctuating political and financial context while lacking organizational resources to apply new treatment discoveries. The following chapter describes a range of models to help in this endeavor. The committee decided that there are ways to get around the obstacles and close the gaps.

2.10 Recommendations

NGOs and the medical community may take several essential steps to better address Afghanistan's mental health problems.

2.10.1 *Advocacy for Change: Getting Community Feedback*

Promoting mental health from the ground up and increasing awareness of the problem should be a major focus. When the target community is encouraged to actively participate in problem-solving and in deciding how mental health care is delivered in a way that is acceptable to its members on a social and cultural level, advocacy is most effective.

2.10.2 *The Value of National Authorities Leading by Example*

It would be wise to make use of medical leadership's influence. It is impossible to de-stigmatize a population without also altering the beliefs and attitudes of the medical professionals who are assisting them. Afghan society is a highly decentralized collectivist one in which local leaders' perspectives are greatly respected.

2.10.3 Improving the Practicability of Health Professionals

Realistically, investment in people and services rather than physical infrastructure, training, and ongoing supervision of health workers is necessary to reach more Afghans in need. Because large hospitals or health centers are not always geographically or socially accessible, it is essential to increase the competency of rural health practitioners, those dealing with women, and those who have access to minority communities.

2.11 Conclusions

Public mental health in Afghanistan is severely hampered by the prevalence of substance use disorders. Adopting a multifaceted strategy that includes prevention, treatment, rehabilitation, and policy reforms is essential. To effectively address the difficulties of SUDs, a collaborative effort involving policymakers, healthcare professionals, researchers, and other stakeholders is essential.

References

Afghanistan Brief 2021—UNODC. https://www.unodc.org/documents/data-and-analysis/Afghanistan/Afghanistan_brief_Nov_2021.pdf [Internet]. Accessed on 27th October 2023.

Afghanistan Drug Use Survey 2005—UNODC. [Internet]. https://www.unodc.org/pdf/afg/2005AfghanistanDrugUseSurvey.pdf, Accessed on 27th October 2023.

Afghanistan National Drug Use Survey 2015—Colombo Plan. https://colombo-plan.org/wp-content/uploads/2020/03/Afghanistan-National-Drug-Use-Survey-2015-compressed.pdf, [Internet]. Accessed on 27th October 2023.

Afghanistan Opium Survey 2021—UNODC. https://www.unodc.org/documents/crop-monitoring/Afghanistan/Afghanistan_Opium_Survey_2021.pdf, [Internet]. Accessed on 27th October 2023.

Afghanistan: Little help for Conflict-Linked trauma. (2020, October 28). Human Rights Watch. [Internet]. Accessed on 27th October 2023. https://www.hrw.org/news/2019/10/07/afghanistan-little-help-conflict-linked-trauma.

Anthenelli, R. M., Benowitz, N. L., West, R., St Aubin, L., McRae, T., Lawrence, D., Ascher, J., Russ, C., Krishen, A., & Evins, A. E. (2016). Neuropsychiatric safety and efficacy of varenicline, bupropion, and nicotine patch in smokers with and without psychiatric disorders (EAGLES): a double-blind, randomized, placebo-controlled clinical trial. Lancet (London, England), 387(10037), 2507–2520. https://doi.org/10.1016/S0140-6736(16)30272-0.

Ashna, M. (2019). Stigma and Taboos: The absence of mental health awareness in Afghanistan. Khaama Press. https://www.khaama.com/stigma-and-taboos-the-absence-of-mental-health-awareness-in-afghanistan-87654/.

Breuer, E., De Silva, M. J., Shidaye, R., Petersen, I., Nakku, J., Jordans, M. J. D., Fekadu, A., & Lund, C. (2016). Planning and evaluating mental health services in low- and middle-income countries using theory of change. *British Journal of Psychiatry*, 208(s56), s55–s62. https://doi.org/10.1192/bjp.bp.114.153841.

Bewley-Taylor, D., Eventon, R., & Southwell, M. (2023). From bad to worse? drug use and treatment in Afghanistan. Global Drug Policy Observatory, Swansea University. http://www.swansea.ac.uk/media/Policy-Brief-19.pdf

Cardozo, B. L., Bilukha, O. O., Crawford, C. A., Shaikh, I., Wolfe, M. I., Gerber, M. L., & Anderson, M. (2004). Mental health, social functioning, and disability in postwar Afghanistan. JAMA, 292(5), 575–584. https://doi.org/10.1001/jama.292.5.575.

Country Update—The World Bank Group in Afghanistan. [Internet]. Accessed on 27th October 2023. https://documents1.worldbank.org/curated/en/451181617171930719/pdf/The-World-Bank-Group-in-Afghanistan-Country-Update.pdf.

Darke, S. (2003). Heroin Overdose: Research and Evidence-Based Intervention. *Journal of Urban Health-bulletin of the New York Academy of Medicine*, 80(2), 189–200. https://doi.org/10.1093/jurban/jtg022.

Darker, C., & Whiston, L. (2015). Drug Use and Abuse: Psychosocial Aspects. In International Encyclopedia of the Social & Behavioral Sciences (Second Edition). https://doi.org/10.1016/b978-0-08-097086-8.14090-5.

Degenhardt, L., Charlson, F. J. (2018). The global burden of disease attributable to alcohol and drug use in 195 countries and territories, 1990–2016: a systematic analysis for the Global Burden of Disease Study 2016. The Lancet Psychiatry, 5(12), 987–1012. https://doi.org/10.1016/s2215-0366(18)30337-7.

Degenhardt, L., Peacock, A., Colledge, S., Leung, J., Grebely, J., Vickerman, P., Stone, J., Cunningham, E. B., Trickey, A., Dumchev, K., Lynskey, M., Griffiths, P., Mattick, R. P., Hickman, M., & Larney, S. (2017). Global prevalence of injecting drug use and sociodemographic characteristics and prevalence of HIV, HBV, and HCV in people who inject drugs: a multistage systematic review. *The Lancet. Global health*, 5(12), e1192–e1207. https://doi.org/10.1016/S2214-109X(17)30375-3.

Drug Demand Reduction Projects in Afghanistan. (2013, July). United Nations Office on Drugs And Crime. [Internet]. Accessed on 27th October 2023. https://www.unodc.org/documents/evaluation/Independent_Project_Evaluations/2013/AFG_H09_H87_G68_Cluster_Evaluation_Final_Report_22JUL2013.pdf.

Drug Use in Afghanistan, 2009 Survey—UNODC. [Internet]. Accessed on 27th October 2023. https://www.unodc.org/documents/data-and-analysis/statistics/Drugs/Drug%20use/Drug_use_in_Afghanistan_2009_survey.pdf.

Gibbs, A., Corboz, J. & Jewkes, R. Factors associated with recent intimate partner violence experience amongst currently married women in Afghanistan and health impacts of IPV: a cross sectional study. *BMC Public Health* 18, 593 (2018). https://doi.org/10.1186/s12889-018-5507-5.

Global Overview of Drug Demand and Supply—UNODC. [Internet]. https://www.unodc.org/wdr2017/field/Booklet_2_HEALTH.pdf, Accessed on 27th October 2023.

Global Overview: Drug Demand, Drug Supply—UNODC. [Internet]. Accessed on 27th October 2023. https://www.unodc.org/res/wdr2021/field/WDR21_Booklet_2.pdf.

Griffin, N., & Khoshnood, K. (2010). Opium Trade, Insurgency, and HIV/AIDS in Afghanistan: Relationships and Regional Consequences. Asia Pacific Journal of Public Health, 22(3_suppl), 159S-167S. https://doi.org/10.1177/1010539510374524.

Guidelines on drug prevention and treatment for girls and women (n.d.). United Nations: Office on Drugs and Crime. https://www.unodc.org/documents/drug-prevention-and-treatment/unodc_2016_drug_prevention_and_treatment_for_girls_and_women_E.pdf, [Internet]. Accessed on 27th October 2023.

Haidary, A.S. (2016). Socioeconomic factors associated with opioid drug use among the youth in Kabul, Afghanistan.

Harsch, S., Jawid, A., Jawid, E., Saboga-Nunes, L., Sørensen, K., Sahrai, D., & Bittlingmayer, U. H. (2021). Health literacy and health behavior among women in Ghazni, Afghanistan. *Frontiers in Public Health*, 9. https://doi.org/10.3389/fpubh.2021.629334.

International Standards on Drug Use Prevention. (n.d.). United Nations : Office on Drugs and Crime. https://www.unodc.org/unodc/en/prevention/prevention-standards.html, [Internet]. Accessed on 27th October 2023.

Jake Tacchi (2020, November 5). Conflict Continues to Drive a 'Mental Health Crisis' In Afghanistan. The Organization for World Peace. https://theowp.org/reports/conflict-continues-to-drive-a-mental-health-crisis-in-afghanistan/.

Jones, H. E., Kaltenbach, K., Heil, S. H., Stine, S. M., Coyle, M. G., Arria, A. M., O'Grady, K. E., Selby, P., Martin, P. R., & Fischer, G. (2010). Neonatal abstinence syndrome after methadone or buprenorphine exposure. *The New England journal of medicine*, 363(24), 2320–2331. https://doi.org/10.1056/NEJMoa1005359.

Lund, C., Tomlinson, M., De Silva, M., Fekadu, A., Shidhaye, R., Jordans, M. J. D., Petersen, I., Bhana, A., Kigozi, F., Prince, M., Thornicroft, G., Hanlon, C., Kakuma, R., McDaid, D., Saxena, S., Chisholm, D., Raja, S., Kippen-Wood, S., Honikman, S., ... Patel, V. (2012). PRIME: a programme to reduce the treatment gap for mental disorders in five low- and Middle-Income countries. *PLOS Medicine*, 9(12), e1001359. https://doi.org/10.1371/journal.pmed.1001359.

Mental Health and Substance Use. (2019). MHGAP Intervention Guide—version 2.0. https://www.who.int/publications/i/item/9789241549790, Accessed on 27th October 2023. www.who.int.

Mumtaz, G. R., Riedner, G., & Abu-Raddad, L. J. (2014). The emerging face of the HIV epidemic in the Middle East and North Africa. *Current Opinion in Hiv and Aids*, 9(2), 183–191. https://doi.org/10.1097/coh.0000000000000038.

Novak, S. P., & Kral, A. H. (2011). Comparing Injection and Non-Injection routes of administration for heroin, methamphetamine, and cocaine users in the United States. Journal of Addictive Diseases, 30(3), 248–257. https://doi.org/10.1080/10550887.2011.581989.

Onyeka, I. N., Basnet, S., Beynon, C., Tiihonen, J., Föhr, J., & Kauhanen, J. (2016). Association between routes of drug administration and all-cause mortality among drug users. *Journal of Substance Use*, 21(6), 559–565. https://doi.org/10.3109/14659891.2015.1112847.

Patel, V. (2007). Mental health in low- and middle-income countries. *British Medical Bulletin*, 81–82(1), 81–96. https://doi.org/10.1093/bmb/ldm010.

Pedneault, J. (2020). Afghanistan's silent mental health crisis. Human Rights Watch. [Internet]. Accessed on 27th October 2023. https://www.hrw.org/news/2019/10/07/afghanistans-silent-mental-health-crisis.

Safi, B. S. (2018, June 30). Why female suicide in Afghanistan is so prevalent. BBC News. [Internet]. Accessed on 27th October 2023. https://www.bbc.com/news/world-asia-44370711.

Shrestha, S., Stopka, T. J., Hughto, J. M. W., Case, P., Palacios, W. R., Reilly, B., & Green, T. C. (2021). Prevalence and correlates of non-fatal overdose among people who use drugs: findings from rapid assessments in Massachusetts, 2017–2019. *Harm Reduction Journal*, 18(1). https://doi.org/10.1186/s12954-021-00538-9.

Smith, P. H., Weinberger, A. H., Zhang, J., Emme, E., Mazure, C. M., & McKee, S. A. (2017). Sex Differences in Smoking Cessation Pharmacotherapy Comparative Efficacy: A Network Meta-analysis. Nicotine & tobacco research : official journal of the Society for Research on Nicotine and Tobacco, 19(3), 273–281. https://doi.org/10.1093/ntr/ntw144.

Strang, J., Bearn, J., Farrell, M., Finch, E., Gossop, M., Griffiths, P., Marsden, J., & Wolff, K. (1998). Route of drug use and its implications for drug effect, risk of dependence and health consequences. *Drug and Alcohol Review*, 17(2), 197–211. https://doi.org/10.1080/09595239800187001.

Substance use and Co-Occurring mental disorders. March 2023 (n.d.). National Institute of Mental Health (NIMH). https://www.nimh.nih.gov/health/topics/substance-use-and-mental-health, [Internet]. Accessed on 27th October 2023.

The Drug Situation and the Practice Of Drug—ProQuest. (2019). [Internet]. https://www.proquest.com/indexingvolumeissuelinkhandler/1036373/Himalayan+and+Central+Asian+Studies/02019Y07Y01$23Jul-Dec+2019$3b++Vol.+23+$283$2f4$29/23/3$2f4, Accessed on 27th October 2023. and jsessionid=81D940B70742840961DE64B9AC09AFD3.i-0f330c6873c5dfe9a.

The Global Health Observatory—WHO. https://www.who.int/data/gho/data/countries/country-details/GHO/afghanistan?countryProfileId=5f0ca8ad-037c-4241-a792-b3f06bddd40e, [Internet]. Accessed on 27th October 2023.

The Need for Evidence-Based Narratives Around Afghanistan's Youth (2014). https://www.pressreleasepoint.com/need-evidence-based-narratives-around-afghanistan-s-youth, [Internet]. Accessed on 27th October 2023.

Todd, C.S., Nassiramanesh, B., Stanekzai, M.R. et al. Emerging HIV epidemics in muslim countries: Assessment of different cultural responses to harm reduction and implications for HIV control. Curr HIV/AIDS Rep 4, 151–157 (2007). https://doi.org/10.1007/s11904-007-0022-9.

UNAFEI (2023). https://www.unafei.or.jp/about/pdf/brochure_e_2023.pdf, [Internet]. Accessed on 27th October 2023.

United Nations Office on Drugs and Crime. (2017). World Drug Report 2017 (ISBN: 978-92-1-148291-1, eISBN: 978-92-1-060623-3, United Nations publication, Sales No. E.17.XI.6). https://www.unodc.org/wdr2017/field/Booklet_2_HEALTH.pdf

Wallace, M. R., Hale, B., Utz, G., Olson, P. E., Earhart, K. C., Thornton, S. A., & Hyams, K. C. (2002). Endemic infectious diseases of Afghanistan. *Clinical Infectious Diseases*, 34(Supplement_5), S171–S207. https://doi.org/10.1086/340704.

World Drug Report 2013—UNODC. https://www.unodc.org/unodc/secured/wdr/wdr2013/World_Drug_Report_2013.pdf, [Internet]. Accessed on 27th October 2023.

World Drug Report 2014—UNODC. https://www.unodc.org/documents/wdr2014/World_Drug_Report_2014_web.pdf, [Internet]. Accessed on 27th October 2023.

World Health Organization. Regional Office for South-East Asia. (2022). Addressing mental health through primary care and community engagement in the WHO South-East Asia Region. [Internet]. https://apps.who.int/iris/handle/10665/361248, Accessed on 27th October 2023.

World Health Organization: WHO. (2022). Afghanistan's health system is on the brink of collapse: urgent action is needed. www.who.int. https://www.who.int/news-room/feature-stories/detail/afghanistan-s-health-system-is-on-the-brink-of-collapse-urgent-action-is-needed, [Internet]. Accessed on 27th October 2023.

World mental health report 2022: Transforming mental health for all. https://www.who.int/publications/i/item/9789240049338, Accessed on 27th October 2023.

Chapter 3
Current Perspectives on Substance Use Disorder in Bangladesh

Mohammad Muntasir Maruf, Lisanul Hasan, Antara Chowdhury, and Mohammad Hayatun Nabi

3.1 Introduction

Substance abuse is a major public health concern in Bangladesh pervading the social, cultural, economic, and legal spheres of the country. History reveals that the British colonial rules familiarized the consumption and commercial operations of substances in the Indian subcontinent to earn revenue which was sustained even after the liberation of Bangladesh. Alongside, some substances were consumed as a traditional and ritualistic practice on various occasions in certain populations. Until the mid-80s, substance was not regarded as a problem. Various high-risk behaviors of the users called for a prohibition that time on particular substances. Cannabis was banned officially in 1988, which led heroin and later a codeine-based cough syrup to take over the market. From the early 2000s, methamphetamine started to gain popularity among abusers (Department of Narcotics Control 2022). Several geographic and socio-economic factors have likely contributed to the spread and upsurge of drug use, the effects of which are many-fold.

In the view of geographical location, Bangladesh is situated in the heart of the three notorious narcotics producing and trading route zone: the *Golden Crescent*, the *Golden Triangle*, and the *Golden Wedge*. The south-east part of Bangladesh is vulnerable to the *Golden Triangle*, an intimidating zone consisting of Myanmar, Thailand, Laos, and Vietnam. The West is exposed to the *Golden Crescent*, the

M. M. Maruf (✉) · A. Chowdhury
Department of Community and Social Psychiatry, National Institute of Mental Health, Dhaka, Bangladesh
e-mail: marufdmc@gmail.com

L. Hasan
Department of Psychiatry, Dhaka Medical College, Dhaka, Bangladesh

M. H. Nabi
Department of Public Health, School of Health and Life Sciences, North South University, Dhaka, Bangladesh

S. M. Y. Arafat and S. K. Kar (eds.), *Current Perspectives on Substance Use Disorders in South Asia*, https://doi.org/10.1007/978-981-97-6619-2_3

trafficking route of especially opium produced in Afghanistan, Pakistan, and Iran. The *Golden Wedge* is a relatively newer route linking the northern part of the country to some of the states of India, Nepal, and Bhutan. Due to the easy access to the Bay of Bengal and penetrable borders both with India and Myanmar, the country has become a lucrative transit point for drug smugglers who route their consignments to the markets of other zones of the world including Africa, Europe, and America. In the process, Bangladesh has become an emergent market for substances due to the elevated risk of easy availability of drugs although it does not produce or supply the majority of the illicit drugs (Department of Narcotics Control 2019; Kamal et al. 2018). The influx of Rohingya populations from Myanmar contributed to the drug trade. A part of Rohingya refugees, who infiltrated in Bangladesh in 2016–17, became involved in drug dealing because of their squalid living conditions in the camps and the connection with drug syndicate in Myanmar which has emerged as a major global producer of methamphetamines in the late 1990s (International Crisis Group 2023).

In the backdrop of the condition, the country needs to undertake measures to deal with the detrimental situation successfully. Effective management strategy needs to identify and analyze various aspects of addiction like its etiology, profiles of the abusers, gaps in the available services, etc. However, there is a dearth of evidence-based findings about substance abuse in Bangladesh. Hence, the aim of this chapter is to shed light on the current scenario of substance abuse in the country from the medical perspective with available data which can also depict the gaps in the field of research. In this chapter, we begin with the epidemiology of substance abuse in Bangladesh, followed by the co-morbidities, risk factors, available services, and legal aspects. We have also discussed the current challenges and recommendations for developing effective services.

3.2 Epidemiology of Substance Use Disorder in Bangladesh

3.2.1 Prevalence of Substance Abuse Among Various Populations

The Department of Narcotics Control (DNC) in Bangladesh reported an upward trend of substance use in the country over the last 20 years. In 2022–23, 19,844 patients received treatment in the government drug addiction treatment centers, including the Central Drug Addiction Treatment Center (CTC) in the capital city, whereas the number was 3793 in 2009–10, which indicates a five-fold increase in the number of patients receiving treatment in these centers (DNC 2023). On the grounds of lack of exact data, the number of substance abusers in Bangladesh is stipulated as more than 6 million (DNC 2017). The National Institute of Mental Health (NIMH), under the Ministry of Health and Family Welfare (MoHFW) in Bangladesh reported that 3.3% of the adult population of the country has a history of substance use (except tobacco and caffeine). The prevalence was found 1.5% and 0.2% among adolescents

(12–17 years) and children (7–11 years), respectively (MoHFW 2021a). Among high-school-going adolescents, lifetime use of alcohol and any other drug (except tobacco) was found to be 15.1% and 14.4%, respectively (Moonajilin et al. 2021). The rate of substance abuse was higher among male juvenile offenders (38.4%) (Maruf et al. 2015).

The latest Global Adult Tobacco Survey (GATS) by the Bangladesh Bureau of Statistics (BBS) reported that about one-third (35.3%) of the adults (>15 years) were current tobacco users in any form, while the rate of tobacco smoking was 18% (BBS 2019). NIMH survey reported the rate of tobacco users as 45.3% (MoHFW 2021a). More than one-fifth (21.2%) of high-school-going adolescents had a history of smoking (Moonajilin et al. 2021).

The studies estimating the prevalence of substance abuse have a major drawback of underreporting (Khalili et al. 2021). The same concern is valid for the research in Bangladesh that underestimates the actual burden of the problem. In addition, wide variations have been noticed in the findings on the most commonly abused substances and socio-demography of the substance abusers because of the differences in methodologies adopted for the studies.

3.2.2 Commonly Abused Substances

Tobacco has been mentioned as the most frequently used substance in the studies which considered it as a substance. Regarding the other substances, most of the users used multiple substances, the rates varying from 71.9% to 91.4% (DNC 2018; Maruf et al. 2016). Studies found cannabinoids, methamphetamine, and opioids as commonly used substances among the abusers taking treatment in CTC, various drug rehabilitation centers and in the community, cannabis being the most common in the community and CTC and methamphetamine (Yaba) being the most common in drug rehabilitation centers (DNC 2017, 2018, 2022; Hawlader et al. 2020). Community-based NIMH survey found cannabis (42.7%) as the most commonly used substance, followed by alcohol (27.5%) and methamphetamine (15.2%) (MoHFW 2021a).

3.2.3 Sociodemographic Factors

In most studies, >90% of the substance users are male (DNC 2017, 2018, 2022; MoHFW 2021a; Hawlader et al. 2020; Kamal et al. 2018; Maruf et al., 2016). However, a hospital-based study reported that 35% of the treatment-seeking substance users were female (Ahmed et al. 2020).

Commonly abused substances and other sociodemographic characteristics of substance users found in various studies are summarized in Table 3.1.

Table 3.1 Commonly abused substances (except tobacco and caffeine) and sociodemographic characteristics of substance abusers

Author and year	Study type	Study place	Mean age (in years)	Commonly abused substances	Majority of the substance abusers were–
DNC (2022)	Cross-sectional	CTC, Dhaka	21–25 (age range of most users)	Cannabis, Opioids	Illiterate unemployed
Ahmed et al. (2020)	Cross-sectional	Hospitals having mental health services	39.2	Alcohol, Cannabis, Amphetamine	Having institutional education (62.6%) Married (83.2%)
DNC (2018)	Mixed method	Community	30.4	Cannabis (68.2%), Yaba (48.2%), opioids (25%)	Studying degree or above (52.4%) Married (48.1%) Doing business (30.7%)
Kamal et al. (2018)	Narrative review	Both community and hospital	28.1	Heroin (67%) Yaba (44%) Cannabis (39%)	Of urban background (94%) Graduate (26.07%) Unemployed (33%) Unmarried (63%)
DNC (2017)	Mixed method	Drug rehabilitation centers	28.7	Methamphetamine (94.2%) Cannabis (87.8%) Phensedyl (52,5%)	Completed HSC or above (52.5%) Doing business (26.6%)

(continued)

Table 3.1 (continued)

Author and year	Study type	Study place	Mean age (in years)	Commonly abused substances	Majority of the substance abusers were–
Roy and Miah (2017)	Cross-sectional	A private psychiatric hospital in Sylhet	155	Opioid, Alcohol, Sedatives	Of urban background (71.6%) HSC passed (34.2%) Unmarried (51.6%)
Maruf et al. (2016)	Cross-sectional	A private drug de-addiction center, Dhaka	28.8	Opioids (79.0%) Cannabinoids (55.2%) Alcohol (41.0%)	Of urban background (92.4%) Unmarried (57.1%) Completed HSC or above (76.2%) Unemployed (31.4%)

3.2.4 *Age of Onset of Substance Use*

Substance abusers begin to use tobacco at an earlier age than other substances. A study by DNC reported that the average age of initiating cigarette/tobacco was 16.4 years, and for other drugs, it was 21 years. About half of the abusers started using tobacco products at the age of less than 15 years and other substances before the age of 20 years (DNC 2018). The mean age of starting daily smoking was found to be 19.3 years in the latest GATS in Bangladesh (BBS 2019). Among hospitalized substance abusers, 37.1% began smoking nicotine, and 22.9% started other substances before the age of 15 years (Maruf et al. 2016).

3.2.5 *Persons Who Inject Drugs (PWID)*

According to the mapping and size estimation study, the estimated number of PWID in Bangladesh ranges from 26,186 to 33,067 (MoHFW 2016a). A study among inpatient PWIDs reported their mean age as 32.5 ± 21.3 years, while 9.2% of the respondents were females. Buprenorphine was the choice for most (40%) participants. Half of the respondents (50.8%) smoked cannabis as the first drug. About one-third (30.8%) of the participants used injectable drugs for the first time during the age of 25–34 years, which is the highest among the age groups. About three-fourths (73.3%) of the respondents shared needles sometimes in life (Islam et al. 2015).

3.3 Risk Factors for Substance Use Disorder in Bangladesh

There are several risk factors for substance abuse in Bangladesh. Many of them are similar to other countries of the world. Although the amount of research done to find out risk factors specifically for Bangladesh is minimal, those have been crucial to identify these factors.

In most of the studies, common risk factors for substance abuse in Bangladesh include peer pressure, availability of drugs, curiosity, and mental health conditions. The risk or contributing factors for substance abuse in the country may be divided into three broad categories—family factors, socio-cultural factors, and personal factors (Table 3.2). According to a study, personal and psychological factors were responsible for substance abuse for one-fourth of the respondents while sociocultural factors were attributed for about two-thirds (Patoari 2021).

Bhuiyan et al. (2023), Moonajilin et al. (2021), Patoari (2021), MoHFW (2021a), DNC (2018), Kamal et al. (2018), Hasam and Mushahid (2017), Islam and Hossain (2017), Roy and Miah (2017), Islam et al. (2015), Zaman et al. (2015), Khan (2015), Maheira et al. (2013), Riya et al. (2013), Maruf et al. (2012), Roy et al. (2010).

3.4 Co-morbidities in Substance Use Disorder in Bangladesh

3.4.1 Psychiatric Co-morbidities in Persons with Substance Abuse

Co-morbidity of substance abuse and psychiatric conditions is a common phenomenon. Co-morbid psychiatric disorders were found in 11% of persons seeking treatment for substance abuse in the hospitals having services for mental health. Among the disorders, the most common was depressive disorder, followed by somatic symptoms disorders and anxiety disorders (Ahmed et al. 2020). Among the hospitalized substance abusers, the prevalence of psychiatric disorders was even higher, estimating more than one-fourth in opioid abusers and about one-third in methamphetamine abusers (Maruf et al. 2021, 2013). The rate of psychiatric disorders among male adolescents with substance abuse was found more than 75% both in a drug addiction center and in a juvenile correction center (Khan et al. 2021a, b; Maruf et al. 2015).

There is another chapter titled *Substance Use and Mental Health Conditions: Co-existence of Dual Problems in Bangladesh* that has been published in 2024 describing in detail various aspects of co-occurring substance abuse and psychiatric disorders. That chapter discusses psychiatric disorders both as a risk factor and a co-morbidity for substance abuse. Details of the issue can be explored in that chapter (Maruf et al. 2024). That chapter also mentioned that other than diagnosed disorders, psychiatric

Table 3.2 Risk factors for substance abuse in Bangladesh

Familial factors	Sociocultural factors	Personal factors
Neglectful parenting Lack of supervision of guardians Familial disharmony Conflict between parents Lack of family bonding Family history of mental illness, especially substance use The poor financial condition of the family contributing to the inability to bear educational expenses Death of a loved one	Easy availability of drugs Peer pressure Failure of law and order situation Deteriorating social values Lack of social support Lack of recreational facility Less empowerment of women The negative effect of media Prostitution	Excessive curiosity Getting pleasure Depression Frustration Sorrow Boredom Loneliness Personality disorder Psychoticism as a personality trait Relationship issues Failure in love Divorce Delinquency Truancy Poor school record Failure in examination Unemployment Lack of capacity to find a job Excessive use of social media or smartphone Inadequacy in sexual performances Desire to express oneself among others Inability to feel relaxed Seeking happiness Worrying about a personal problem Desire to become healthy or strong Late-night sleeping Relation with drug dealers Affluence of money

symptoms like cranky mood, depression, loss of interest in work, decreased concentration, anxiety, fear, fatigue, aggression, abnormal behavior, insomnia, sexual problems, and suicidal attempts were commonly found among the substance abusers. On the other hand, substance use, especially sedatives, alcohol, and cannabis, other than tobacco, is also prevalent commonly in patients with various psychiatric disorders (Maruf et al. 2024).

3.4.2 *Physical Co-morbidities in Persons with Substance Abuse*

Persons with substance use disorders also experience various physical health conditions. Co-morbid physical illnesses were found in 34.2% of hospitalized substance abusers in Sylhet and 42.2% of opioid abusers in Dhaka (Roy and Miah 2017; Maruf et al. 2013). Among substance abusers undergoing detoxification in CTC, 16.3% had sexually transmitted infections (Hossain et al. 2013). The majority (85.8%) of the PWID seeking treatment in a private center admitted that drug use was affecting their health (Islam et al. 2015). Another study among PWID found that about one-thirds of respondents suffered symptoms of sexually transmitted infections in the last 12 months, and one-third suffered abscesses in the last 3 months. Fever and cough were common current complaints for them, followed by chest pain, sudden weight loss, lesion in mouth, jaundice, tuberculosis, and chronic diarrhea (MoHFW 2017). HIV and Hepatitis C virus (HCV) are two of the major concerns among PWID. HIV prevalence among PWID is estimated to be 2.5%. Among the newly diagnosed HIV cases in 2019, 24% were from PWID. The prevalence of hepatitis B and hepatitis C among PWID is 7% and 31%, respectively. (Harm Reduction International 2023). Another study reported anti-HCV antibody in 4.4% of the persons attending an HIV testing center in Dhaka, the highest rate (37.8%) being in PWID (Rahman et al. 2018). Chronic liver diseases and hepatocellular carcinoma have been reported due to long-term abuse of alcohol (Dewan and Chowdhury 2015). More than two-thirds of substance abusers had dental caries. Gingivitis, xerostomia, and meth mouth were also common complaints among substance abusers (Hossain et al. 2018).

3.5 Healthcare Seeking Behavior of Substance Abusers

Despite the increasing trend of substance abuse and related health issues in the country, most of the abusers are reluctant to seek out professional help. According to a nationwide survey, two-thirds of the substance abusers did not avail professional healthcare services. Among the substance users who got in-patient treatment from a rehabilitation center, more than two-thirds (70.2%) were hospitalized against their will (DNC 2018). This rate of treatment gap was found even higher in a regional study, where 89% of the substance abusers remained distant from treatment coverage. Among the rest 11%, majority underwent short term treatment and had history of relapse (Sarker et al. 2023). Even in the tertiary care centers in the capital city, more than 90% of the substance abusers were hospitalized involuntarily (Soron et al. 2017). Study among relapsed substance abusers in 50 drug treatment centers in Bangladesh reported that 70% of them were taken there against their will. Though in most cases, they were taken by family members or relatives, some were taken by law enforcement agency, NGO, social workers, and recovery addicts (Masud et al. 2020). Involuntary admission was also reported in more than two-thirds of the opioid abusers and methamphetamine abusers (69.9% and 69.6%, respectively) (Maruf et al. 2013, 2021).

There is no structured referral pathway for SUD patients in Bangladesh (Arafat et al. 2024). People might choose to take help from traditional or religious healers in the first place instead of accessing the modern allopathic health care service for SUD treatments. A study on healthcare seeking behavior among the hospitalized injectable drug abusers reported that local registered physicians were the primary contact for about one-third (33.3%), followed by private centers (19.2%), government hospitals (10.8%), medicine shops (10.0%), and paramedics, alternative or traditional health care providers (8.3%) (Islam et al. 2015).

Though the challenges in seeking treatment for substance abuse in Bangladesh have not been systematically investigated yet, lack of public healthcare facilities, and skilled professionals, limited funding, high stigma as well as the inappropriate attitudes, approaches, and practices of the professionals are generally considered as the barriers to treatment-seeking for the mental health conditions (Hasan et al. 2021; Shultana 2022). In a study, majority of the injectable drug abusers reported that they did not know where to get the treatment. Many were reluctant about healthcare seeking because of the preconceived idea of high treatment costs, and ineffectiveness of the treatment (Islam et al. 2015). Therefore, unless substance abuse causes severe disturbances in important areas of life, persons remain distant from seeking treatment. Rather, they embrace various alternative approaches from traditional healers. Transient relief from those approaches in turn deters scientific treatment-seeking, if not causing physical and psychological detriments complicating the prognosis (Hossain et al. 2014).

3.6 Services for the Management of Substance Abuse

Many service providers with different levels of training and different credentials work in the sphere of SUD treatment. This treatment requires a range of services provided by different organizations starting from government bodies to NGOs and private organizations.

3.6.1 Primary Healthcare Settings

Primary healthcare centers under MoHFW include union sub-centers and upazila health complexes at the government level, municipality, and city corporation-run hospitals and clinics and also some local private clinics, NGO-run clinics, general physicians' private chambers, etc. Medical graduates, village doctors (*pollichikitsok*), nurses, medical assistants, etc. are the first-line providers of our healthcare system and by default first-line providers of SUD treatment. The quality of service provided by them is not satisfactory as they lack adequate training in the treatment of SUD.

Trained psychiatrists and clinical psychologists are mainly based in the cities and rarely work in a primary healthcare setting.

3.6.2 Secondary Healthcare Settings

Secondary healthcare comprises government-run district hospitals, NGO-run hospitals and private clinics, and also some private chambers. There are some privately owned rehab centers at the secondary level providing focused in-patient care to SUD patients. Three divisional-level drug addiction treatment centers in Chattogram, Rajshahi, and Khulna run by the DNC may fall under this category as well. The type of manpower is the same as the primary level with a little bit more access to specialist consultation. However, some of the physicians and nurses from primary and secondary health care got some sort of training on substance abuse as a part of the training on mental health issues thanks to the initiative of the Directorate General of Health Services (DGHS) of Bangladesh with the collaboration of World Health Organization (WHO), and NIMH.

3.6.3 Tertiary Healthcare Settings

Tertiary healthcare for SUD treatment includes CTC, NIMH, and Department of Psychiatry of Bangabandhu Sheikh Mujib Medical University (BSMMU) in Dhaka, the mental hospital in Pabna, the Department of Psychiatry of government and non-government medical colleges and several well-run private and NGO clinics, private chambers, etc. Psychiatrists, child and adolescent psychiatrists, clinical psychologists, counseling psychologists, child psychologists, social workers, addiction counselors with various titles, medical officers, and nurses provide care for SUD patients at this level. Besides, counseling services for addiction can also be availed in the Department of Clinical Psychology of University of Dhaka.

CTC in Dhaka was established in 1988 under the Ministry of Health. But later, the center was transferred to the President's Secretariat in 1990, and to DNC under the Ministry of Home Affairs in 1991. Mental hospital Pabna, established in 1957, about 210 km distant from the capital city, launched its addiction unit in 1988. The Department of Addiction Psychiatry at NIMH started its separate inpatient services in 2022.

3.6.4 Inpatient and Outpatient Services

DNC-run 4 centers have 199 in-patient beds altogether. Among those, 24 beds are allocated to adult females and 10 for children. Besides that, Pabna Mental Hospital allocates 30 beds for addiction patients and NIMH has 15 beds allocated to adult males with substance use disorder. The Department of Psychiatry of BSMMU and government medical colleges don't have any ward or bed dedicated to the treatment of patients of SUD. DNC-approved 365 private facilities have around 5000 inpatient beds for the treatment of addiction. Besides, there are some illegal and unauthorized facilities providing care for SUD patients.

Apart from inpatient services, most of the above-mentioned facilities provide outpatient treatment services (psychiatric consultation and various forms of counseling) for SUD patients. Psychiatrists and psychologists provide service in their private chambers as well.

3.6.5 Hospitalization and Cost of Service

Mental Health Act (2018) has enumerated details of different types of hospitalizations but in reality, the majority of the hospitalizations are done on an involuntary basis with permission from legal guardians. Rarely, patients come voluntarily or they are brought by law enforcement agencies.

While the government facilities don't charge much or at all for hospital stays, most of the private facilities are paid from out-of-pocket expenditures by the patient parties. Health insurance is not prevalent in the overall health system of Bangladesh and insurance practically doesn't cover treatments of addiction.

3.6.6 Assessment of Persons with Substance Abuse in Bangladesh

Most of the professionals and treatment centers assess the aspects of addiction by interviewing the person and the guardians. The translated Bangla version of the *Alcohol, Smoking and Substance Involvement Screening Test*, *Addiction Severity Index*, and *Brief Assessment of Recovery Capital-10* are used for screening, assessment of severity of addiction, and assessment of recovery capital respectively in some treatment centers including CTC. For confirmation of diagnosis, dope tests are available in CTC, NIMH, Pabna Mental Hospital, BSMMU, some medical colleges, and private diagnostic centers.

3.6.7 Treatment of Substance Abuse in Bangladesh

In the government treatment centers, the aim of inpatient treatment of persons with substance abuse is mainly detoxification. The patients remain admitted for around one month in CTC and NIMH. During hospitalization, they are treated by psychiatrists or doctors trained in psychiatry or substance abuse issues with medication to mitigate withdrawal symptoms. Counseling and other psychosocial treatments including family psychoeducation are provided mostly as outpatients. DNC-approved private drug addiction treatment centers allow for long-term inpatient treatment where they treat patients mainly with medication, individual counseling, family counseling, and life skills training (DNC 2018).

Self-help support groups are emerging yet inadequate in number in Bangladesh. In the capital city of Dhaka, 18 Narcotics Anonymous (NA) groups and one Alcoholics Anonymous (AA) group are active. Besides, there are two NA groups in Chittagong and one in Sylhet.

3.6.8 Utilization of Services

In the years 2020, 2021, and 2022, government addiction treatment centers have treated 149,552, 100,014, and 16,316 patients, respectively. Licensed private centers have treated 15,181, 9876, and 16,316 patients in those years, respectively. Apart from treatments, government drug addiction treatment centers have arranged regular counseling sessions (every Wednesday) for patients suffering from SUD and their families. Up until June 2023, 9487 people have availed these counseling services. Moreover, private facilities have counseled more than 150,000 people just in the year 2022–2023 (DNC 2023).

But most of the persons having substance issues remain outside the coverage of treatment services. NIMH survey reported that the treatment gap in adults with psychiatric disorders was 92% where persons with substance use disorders were highest in comparison to other disorders. Only 4.8% of substance abusers could reach professional services. More severe symptoms and a family history of psychiatric illness were the factors that increased the possibility of having the services (Huque et al. 2023). This is hard to explain by only poor knowledge and financial constraints, as a study among the literate and persons belonging to higher socioeconomic conditions found a treatment gap of 79% (Islam and Hossain 2017).

3.7 Harm Reduction Interventions in Bangladesh

In Bangladesh, harm reduction programs for PWID have been operating since 1998. Among the presently deployed harm reduction interventions, the distribution of sterile needles, syringes, and condoms free of cost, opioid-substitution therapy, peer education using Behaviour Change Communication (BCC) or Information, Education and Communication (IEC) approach, testing, and counseling for HIV, antiretroviral therapy for HIV positive persons, management of STI and referral for tuberculosis are of special mention (Khan et al. 2019a, b).

3.7.1 Opioid Substitution Therapy (OST)

OST was launched in Bangladesh, initially as a part of a regional project of United Nations Office on Drugs and Crime (UNODC) in 2010. After the success of the pilot project, the OST service was scaled up in Dhaka city in 2012, with financial support from the Global Fund and Government of Bangladesh (Khan et al. 2019a, b). Currently, methadone is available for opioid substitution to around 2600 patients in 13 centers in Dhaka, Cumilla, Gazipur, Narayanganj, and Rajshahi, run by several NGOs under the supervision of DNC. Buprenorphine is not provided currently. No OST is available for the prison population.

3.7.2 Needle and Syringe Program (NSP)

NSP is a vital part of the comprehensive harm reduction approach currently serving around 19,000 PWID (out of an estimated 33,067 PWID) across 22 districts through 45 harm reduction centers (Harm Reduction International 2023). The services are provided through outreach workers recruited primarily from the PWID community. Service coverage of NSP in Dhaka city is above 80% but either very poor or fully unavailable in other cities. Currently, each PWID gets around 300 needles or syringes per year (Khan et al. 2019a, b). During the COVID-19 pandemic, the secondary distribution of needles and syringes was carried out by peer educators.

3.7.3 National Harm Reduction Strategy

Bangladesh adopted the *National Harm Reduction Strategy for Drug Use and HIV 2017–2021* in 2016. The goal of this strategy is to prevent drug-related HIV by controlling the use of drugs and improving the quality of life of abusers. The National AIDS/STD Programme (NASP) of DGHS is responsible for updating and implementing the strategy and developing a partnership among the concerned ministries of Health and Family Welfare, Home Affairs, Education, Youth and Sports, Social Welfare and Women and Children Affairs to make HIV prevention and control measures effective (MoHFW 2016b).

3.8 Laws and Policies Related to Substance Abuse

There is no unified law that regulates the management of substance abuse in Bangladesh rather there are several laws dealing with several aspects of substance abuse. Narcotics Control Act (NCA), 2018 and Mental Health Act (MHA), 2018 are two prominent acts that play vital roles when it comes to substance abuse in this country. Furthermore, the constitution of Bangladesh also states its commitment to providing medical care to its citizens in case of sickness and disability. Clause 18 of the constitution urges the state to take necessary steps for the prohibition of alcohol use and the use of other narcotic drinks and herbs injurious to health.

NCA, 2018 replaced the NCA, 1990. Besides making provisions for the management of drug abuse, this act also intends to control, reduce supply and demand, and prevent abuse and smuggling of narcotic drugs. The act consists of 7 chapters and 70 clauses divided into these chapters. The first and seventh chapters discuss the definition and treatment of addictions under this act (NCA 2018). Alcohol Control Rules, 2022, and Rules for the establishment and maintenance of drug addiction treatment centers, drug addiction rehabilitation centers and drug addiction counseling centers in the non-government sector, 2021 have been introduced to implement the NCA, 2018 effectively.

The act empowers DNC to take an active role in the management of substance abusers by establishing and monitoring government and private treatment and rehabilitation centers for them. DNC is also supposed to conduct research and surveys for the collection of information related to substances and take steps to control the production, use, and supply of those substances.

Moreover, substance use disorder, being a non-communicable disease under mental disorder, falls within the territory of MHA, 2018 as well. MHA (2018) came to replace the infamous Lunacy Act, 1912. It distinguished mental illness and mental disorder as two separate but related entities (MHA 2018). This act allows the government to establish and operate psychiatric hospitals and separate psychiatric units in medical colleges and district hospitals where substance abusers can access healthcare services (Karim and Shaikh 2021).

Different government bodies and different laws have created ethical and professional dilemmas in the field of addiction management in Bangladesh. Moreover, considering individuals with substance use disorder as criminals from a legal perspective hinders their access to proper healthcare. Though persons with substance abuse problems who are not involved in any other substance-related crime may have the offer of getting rehabilitation from the relevant authorities, in reality, this provision has not been practiced appropriately (Rahman 2019).

In addition to these two acts, there is an act especially addressing the most common substance of abuse in the country—the "Smoking and Tobacco Usage (Control) Act, 2005" which imposed a ban on smoking at public places and advertisements of tobacco products. In addition to that, Bangladesh is a signatory of the "Framework Convention on Tobacco Control (FCTC)" passed by WHO on its 56th Convention, on 16 June 2003 and ratified on 10 May 2004.

Before these acts, Bangladesh had several other acts to cover the domain of substance use, some of which were inherited from the British and Pakistan period before its liberation in 1971 such as the Opium Act, 1857, Opium Act, 1878, Excise Act, 1909, Dangerous Drugs Act, 1930 and Opium Smoking Act, 1932, etc. However, nowadays, these acts are not valid in reality.

3.9 Non-government Organizations (NGO) Working in the Field of Substance Abuse

Besides the government initiatives, there are a number of organizations that contribute a significant role in the field of addiction management. In Bangladesh, there are 79 NGOs working on various aspects of substance abuse. Notable organizations include the Bangladesh Rehabilitation and Assistance Center for Addicts (BARACA), Ashokti Punorbashon Nibash (APON), and Dhaka Ahsania Mission (DAM). These organizations mainly focus on drug prevention, education, training, treatment, counseling, research, and rehabilitation. Their activities also involve providing training to networking members, developing relevant materials, organizing meetings and discussion sessions, lobbying with policymakers, and raising awareness about the harmful effects of drugs.

BARACA, started in the year 1988 as the central undertaking of Caritas Bangladesh, has four drop-in centers and two nocturnal accommodations for persons with substance abuse. APON, established in 1994, is the sole Addiction Rehabilitation Residence that operates a school within its premises, specifically designed for the children who are undergoing treatment, many of whom are street children. DAM, commencing its activities in 1990, has established centers for the treatment and rehabilitation of male individuals grappling with drug addiction in Gazipur and Jashore, and for female individuals in Dhaka. Some NGOs are involved in harm reduction programs. OST centers are run by ICDDR,B, Save the Children, CARE and Ashokta Punorbashon Songstha. Numerous licensed and unlicensed drug rehabilitation facilities can be found throughout Bangladesh's districts that treat patients with substance use disorders as well as host small-scale awareness campaigns.

The other chapter *Substance Use and Mental Health Conditions: Co-existence of Dual Problems in Bangladesh* discusses more about the NGOs working in the field of substance abuse. Interested readers are referred to that chapter for the details (Maruf et al. 2024).

3.10 Current Status of Research on Substance Abuse

Good-quality researches on substance abuse are limited in the country, despite having national-level surveys in addition to some single center-based studies. DNC is a source of information regarding substance use scenarios in the country as it publishes annual drug report regularly. Available researches mostly concentrate on determining the frequency and pattern of substance use and its comorbidity among various populations. Some studies investigated the reason or risk factors and effects of addiction. Aspects of management and service delivery are neglected as research topics.

Clinic or rehabilitation center-based researches have limitations including small sample size, convenient sampling, inappropriate use of diagnostic instruments, and other issues that limit the generalizability of their findings. There is some indistinctness also in the nationwide surveys. A community-based study claimed to use *The Alcohol, Smoking and Substance Involvement Screening Test (ASSIST)* to ascertain the frequency of substance use in Bangladesh which allowed to gather information regarding lifetime substance use, as well as substance use and related issues during the previous three months (MoHFW 2021b). But it was unclear from the study whether the reported *screen-positive cases* applied to lifetime usage or use within the last three months. Again, despite 25.2% screen-positive instances, the prevalence of substance use among respondents, regardless of age categories, was determined to be 2.9%. Furthermore, the study reported the prevalence of substance use, not *disorders,* despite the study procedures claiming that psychiatrists verified the diagnosis of *substance use disorders* based on DSM-5 criteria. There was no mention of the risk score or risk category that ASSIST assigns (MoHFW 2021b).

The frequency and pattern of comorbid psychiatric illnesses in substance use disorders were investigated in another study carried out in 13 selected hospitals which used Mini International Neuropsychiatric Interview (MINI) for screening and psychiatrists initially confirmed the psychiatric diagnoses based on DSM-5 before obtaining socioeconomic, clinical, and substance-related information (Ahmed et al. 2020). Standard MINI diagnoses 17 major mental disorders; however, in the study, 20 categories of psychiatric disorders were reported to be co-morbid in addition to the "others" category. In some cases, both a single category of disorders and a disorder included in that particular category were considered separately to calculate the total frequency. For example, while the frequency of *schizophrenia spectrum and other psychotic disorders* was estimated overall, the frequency of *delusional disorder* was added separately in the total frequency calculation. In the same way, the frequency of *anxiety disorders* in general, and *panic disorder* and *specific/social phobia* were shown separately and added to estimate the total frequency.

3.11 Challenges for Service Development

It poses several challenges such as a lack of treatment facilities, funding, and skilled professionals (e.g. psychiatrists, psychologists, addiction counselors, peer counselors, medical doctors or general physicians, mental health nurses, medical assistants, etc.), lack of proper government supervision, involvement of law and order agencies, lack of public awareness and education, social stigma attached to people suffering from SUDs and generalized hopelessness among the common public about the chance of people getting better with scientific treatment, so the need for investment in this sector.

3.11.1 Lack of Treatment Facilities and Additional Services

There is only one bed available for every 13,142 persons with SUD in government healthcare facilities. This statement indicates the dire need for the development of newer facilities and adding more beds in existing facilities. As there are only 365 DNC-approved private drug addiction treatment and rehabilitation centers with 4996 inpatient beds for SUD patients (DNC 2023) and there is no reliable list of all private facilities providing outpatient services, more authentic and trust-worthy private facilities (both inpatient and outpatient) need to be built besides government facilities. Additional services for the management of substance abuse including treatment for comorbid psychiatric disorders, housing, employment, etc. are not well-organized or integrated in the country. While residential treatment or hospital admission is an important aspect of many SUD patients' recovery journey, at the same time substantial amount of outpatient and additional services is also required to meet the various needs of the substance abusers of Bangladesh.

3.11.2 Lack of Manpower and Funding

With around 270 psychiatrists and 565 psychologists for the mental health needs of the total population, Bangladesh seriously lacks skilled manpower in this sector (World Health Organization 2020). CTC planned to develop trained manpower in this field based on the "Universal Treatment Curriculum" of the International Centre for Credentialing and Education of Addiction Professionals and around 2300 persons got basic level training. But most could not proceed to next of the four levels of training as after 10 years of the effort of CTC, only 54 completed the examination after basic training. As creating skilled manpower requires time and funding, it is a major obstacle to be overcome. Finance is a major challenge as the government allocates less than 0.5% of the total health budget for mental health (Arafat et al. 2024). On the other hand, the DNC allocates a major part of its budget to the control of drug trafficking and other legal sides of addiction, while funding for treatment gets relatively less attention.

3.11.3 Lack of Supervision

There is a serious lack of government supervision of both approved and unapproved SUD treatment facilities that leave scope for unscientific, inhumane, and substandard treatment programs. There is no unified government body that ensures accreditation and quality control of substance use professionals. Different people with different levels of training or often no training come to this field and provide care with various titles. This mismanagement is a huge barrier that needs to be addressed for the development of quality service delivery platforms.

3.11.4 Lack of Quality Research and Quality Data

The actual burden of substance-related disorders in Bangladesh is yet to be estimated. The quality of data in the few researches regarding substance abuse conducted in community and rehabilitation centers is dubious due to the study design and methods. Reports regarding legal issues related to substance, seizure of drugs, treatment facilities, and the number of service consumers are published yearly by DNC but from the perspective of treatment of substance use disorder, those data contribute a little. There is a gap in quality data regarding various aspects of substance-related disorders including co-occurring physical and mental disorders, the efficacy of current management approach, treatment gap, substance literacy, cultural contexts, etc. in addition to actual prevalence of substance abuse.

3.11.5 Stigma and Lack of Awareness

Public perception of SUD patients is still highly stigmatized. Persons with substance use disorders perceive social stigma, suffer bullying, feel isolated, and lack support (Hawlader et al. 2020). Lack of awareness about the issue and poor overall mental health literacy in Bangladesh might be contributing to the stigma (Arafat et al. 2018). A significant number of the general public including healthcare providers view addiction as a personal failing of the affected person. This creates a punitive environment that is not congenial to recovery in the long run. NIMH survey reveals statistically significant (37.8–94.4%) negative attitudes among common people to mental health service that covers SUD treatment services as well (MoHFW 2021b). Law and order agencies involved in this predicament might complicate the overall scenario sometimes while enforcing laws.

3.11.6 Human Rights Concerns

SUD treatment services might require admitting patients involuntarily. MHA, 2018 mentions about the procedure and duration of involuntary admission of persons with mental health conditions though this issue has not been clearly addressed in NCA, 2018 (MHA 2018; NCA 2018). For inpatient admission, this is often the case and this has substantial abuse potential if not monitored carefully and regularly by proper legal authorities. Moreover, MHA, 2018 does not contain a comprehensive list of patient's rights except for their rights to health, dignity, property, education, etc. It also does not mandate the proper training of healthcare providers about patients' human rights (Karim and Shaikh 2021).

3.12 Future Directions for Service Development

Given the growing need for SUD treatment services, it is inevitable that novel services will be developed with time. The use of new technologies like artificial intelligence (AI) and telemedicine, community-based care and harm reductions in addition to developing more addiction treatment centers, skilled manpower, proper funding, awareness and literacy about substance abuse, and quality research are going to be the major directions where these service delivery platforms are heading towards.

3.12.1 Increasing Manpower, Infrastructure, Funds, and Research

To develop skilled manpower, short-term and long-term plans need to be made. More scope for post-graduation in psychiatry and clinical psychology and graduation for other relevant professionals and job opportunities for them should be created. For short term, basic training for all the personnel working in the field of substance abuse based on culture-sensitive and locally contextualized training modules should be conducted by concerned authorities. More healthcare facilities dedicated to the management of substance-related disorders incorporating integrated services should be established in both government and private sectors, and licensing processes for such facilities should be easier and hassle-free. For developing infrastructures, manpower, and other services for substance abuse, the government should emphasize more budget allocation. More funding from NGOs and international agencies should also be encouraged. Besides, quality data are important for estimating the actual burden and planning a proper service. Hence, the emphasis should be on good quality research by trustworthy and capable researchers dedicated to the field.

3.12.2 Community-Based Care

As SUD is such a prevalent condition that needs to be addressed in an urgent but delicate manner, providing care by trained para-professionals and giving community-based care by bringing people of the same community going through difficulties for SUD under one roof can be a smart and effective solution. SUD treatment requires a persistent commitment to recovery and abstinence on the patient's part. However, as the saying goes, relapse is a part of recovery in this healing journey and evidence suggests that being part of a community where people can share their difficulties and draw strengths from each other can be therapeutic, a community-based care model incorporating therapeutic groups under proper supervision is crucial. At the same time, such a model can reduce the burden on the existing services.

3.12.3 Harm Reductions

The harm reduction principle is widely used in the management of SUDs globally. It focuses on the disease model of addiction rather than the moral model. Several harm reduction approaches are already used in Bangladesh by different organizations working with SUD patients such as ICDDR,B and Save The Children in conjunction with CTC. Considering its proven efficacy in reducing overall mortality and morbidity of addiction, several existing harm reduction approaches such as NSP, free distribution of condoms, educating about STIs, running screening programs and providing Antiretroviral therapy for HIV-positive patients, TB treatment, OST, etc. should be strengthened and extended. This will reduce the burden on the overall health care system and at the same time save lives at a minimum cost. There will be significant challenges in implementing these strategies. For example, OST requires controlled substances such as methadone to be distributed by non-government bodies. Distributing sterile needles for injection or distributing condoms for preventing STIs can be viewed negatively by many conservative members of society. But, if new platforms can design any service delivery model that is not only based on harm reduction principle but also sensitive to the culture and religion of the country, they can create a great impact on the overall SUD treatment scenario of Bangladesh.

3.12.4 Multi-sectoral Collaboration for Integrated Services

Effective management of substance abuse problems in society requires multi-sectoral and multi-professional collaboration. Government agencies, ministries of Health and Family Welfare, Home Affairs, Law, Justice and Parliamentary Affairs, Education, Social Welfare, Youth and Sports, Labour and Employment, and Finance, among others are major stakeholders in substance-related issues. Therefore, effective coordination among these ministries, related departments, and concerned non-government and voluntary organizations is imperative for effective and integrated service delivery. A case management approach for substance abusers can be beneficial for the coordination among various support systems involved.

3.12.5 Developing Awareness and Literacy

To decrease stigma as well as demand for substances, increasing awareness and literacy involving extensive educational programs are necessary targeting the community leaders, teachers, and journalists alongside the youth. According to Section (E) of NCA, 2018, the anti-drug campaign to create public awareness against harmful effects of substances is one of the major activities of the DNC (NCA 2018). Distribution of posters, leaflets, stickers, and festoons containing anti-drug information and slogans can be an effective way to draw public attention to the fact that drug abuse is a preventable and controllable public health issue. Anti-drug documentaries, films, dramas, talk shows, etc. can have an impact. Social media can be a vital platform for awareness-building especially among the youth.

3.12.6 Addressing Human Rights Concerns with Proper Supervision and Legal Reforms

Irrespective of the amount of existing services and the planned new services, no service will be complete and effective if supervision under proper authority is not ensured. Any system is subject to mismanagement leaving scope for human rights abuse if not monitored from time to time. So, rigorous and regular supervision is paramount for effective services safeguarding human rights. Legal reforms and amendment of the existing laws are necessary for addressing human rights issues. Creating patients' rights advocacy groups and incorporating them in this system is worth considering for the betterment of overall service delivery.

3.12.7 Use of New Technologies

Smartphone and web-based technology dedicated to SUD patients can play a pivotal role in reducing the treatment gap while it also posing risk to patient privacy and confidentiality. Trained clinicians can give people living in rural areas and resource-poor areas access to high-quality care via digital technologies such as mobile app, SMS alert, crisis hotline, AI-based chatbot service, web-based platform for tele-access to NA/AA group meetings facilitating screening, early diagnosis, treatment of SUD and storage of data at central servers Bangladesh government's pledge to build a *Digital Bangladesh* can be rightly utilized to develop such services. A plethora of such services are already in the market that the ICT Divisions of the government incentivize. ICT-based services for psychiatric issues and addictive behaviors were effective in various countries (Guo et al. 2023; Fonseca and Osma 2021). However, the efficacy of such service delivery in terms of affordability, patient autonomy, data privacy, and user experience in Bangladesh is yet to be objectively determined.

3.13 Conclusion

In Bangladesh, substance abuse is a neglected entity from the viewpoint of healthcare. Persons with substance abuse are stigmatized and approached more from a legal point of view with a mostly punitive attitude rather than from a medical point of view. Though there is an alarming up-surging trend of substance abuse in the country due to its geographical location and easy availability of illicit substances, the services dedicated to the management are insufficient. Although there are government initiatives and laws to deal with the situation, lack of trained manpower, health care facilities and other logistics in this arena prevails. Lack of awareness, high stigma, poorly coordinated and complicated system of treatment services, ambiguous and discrepant legal system, etc. are other significant challenges in proper management. Substance abuse needs to be managed delicately, based on scientific evidence. For that, more meticulous research, change of public perception, and embracing modern treatment techniques are also very important alongside rigorous efforts from law and order agencies. Finally, digital technologies can help to bridge the treatment gap and provide affordable and sustainable treatment options for people in need.

References

Ahmed, H. U., Alam, M. T., Sarkar, M., Alam, M. F., Hossain, M. D., Bhowmik, A. D., Khan, N. M., Uddin, M. M. J., Royle, R. K. S., Khan, M. Z. R., Sarkar, A. A., Hossain, R., Islam, M. R., Podder, B. R. R., Kalam, M., Acharjee, P., & Hossain, M. J. (2020). Psychiatric comorbidity among the patients with substance use disorders in Bangladesh. *Archives of NIMH, 3*(1), 7–12.

Arafat, S. M. Y., Giasuddin, N. A., Mazumder, A. H. (2024). Access to mental health care in Bangladesh—current status, potential challenges, and ways out. In: S. M. Y. Arafat, S. K. Kar (Eds.) *Access to mental health care in South Asia.* Springer Nature Singapore. https://doi.org/10.1007/978-981-99-9153-2_3.

Arafat, S. M. Y., Ahmed, S., Uddin, M. (2018). Depression literacy status in Bangladesh: a cross-sectional comparative observation. *Journal of Behaioural Health,* 7(2), 91–97.

Bangladesh Bureau of Statistics. (2019). *Global adult tobacco survey Bangladesh report 2017.* (project report). Dhaka: Ministry of Planning, Bangladesh. https://ntcc.gov.bd/ntcc/uploads/editor/files/GATS%20Report%20Final-2017_20%20MB.PDF (accessed on 1 Nov, 2023).

Bhuiyan, S. M. A. U., Islam, M. A., Kamal, A. H. M. K. M., Jahan, M. A. (2023). Factors associated with relapse amongst substance abusers. *International journal of research in medical sciences, 11*(5), 1444–1449. https://doi.org/10.18203/2320-6012.ijrms20231021.

Department of Narcotics Control. (2017). *Baseline study on drug addiction in Bangladesh.* (Project report). Dhaka: Ministry of Home, Bangladesh. https://dnc.gov.bd/site/files/f20344f2-c63b-4761-9535-ff4f49b97cf8 (accessed on 10 Nov, 2023).

Department of Narcotics Control. (2018). *Cause and victim of drug addiction and way forward for establishment of adequate treatment and rehabilitation facilities at private sector in Bangladesh.* (Project report). Dhaka: Ministry of Home, Bangladesh. https://dnc.gov.bd/site/files/f20344f2-c63b-4761-9535-ff4f49b97cf8 (accessed on 10 Nov, 2023).

Department of Narcotics Control. (2019). *Identifying and mapping the routes of drug trafficking in Bangladesh: Pitfalls and way forward.* (Project report). Dhaka: Ministry of Home, Bangladesh. https://dnc.gov.bd/sites/default/files/files/dnc.portal.gov.bd/files/1e26d081_8f8a_4721_a1f1_5

98d55a9f455/2021-08-18-08-50-7958b2da82e5935bd45b770e0d386fea.pdf (accessed on 10 Dec, 2023).
Department of Narcotics Control. (2022). *Annual drug report Bangladesh 2022*. Dhaka: Ministry of Home, Bangladesh. https://dnc.gov.bd/site/view/annual_reports/- (accessed on 19 Nov, 2023).
Department of Narcotics Control. (2023). *Annual report 2022–23*. Dhaka: Ministry of Home, Bangladesh. https://dnc.gov.bd/site/view/annual_reports/- (accessed on 9 Nov, 2023).
Dewan, G & Chowdhury, F. R. (2015). Alcohol use and alcohol use disorders in Bangladesh. *Asia pacific journal of medical toxicology, 4*, 83–90. https://doi.org/10.22038/apjmt.2015.5091.
Fonseca, A., & Osma, J. (2021). Using information and communication technologies (ICT) for mental health prevention and treatment. *International journal of environmental research and public health, 18*(2), 461. https://doi.org/10.3390/ijerph18020461
Guo, H., Yang, H., Yuan, G., Zhu, Z., Zhang, K., Zhang, X., Lu, X., Zhang, J., Du, J., Shi, H., Jin, G., Hao, J., Sun, Y., Su, P., Zhang, Z. (2023). Effectiveness of information and communication technology (ICT) for addictive behaviors: An umbrella review of systematic reviews and meta-analysis of randomized controlled trials. *Computers in human behavior, 147*, 107843. https://doi.org/10.1016/j.chb.2023.107843.
Harm reduction international. (2023). https://hri.global/publications/harm-reduction-information-note-bangladesh/ (accessed on 21 Dec, 2023).
Hasam, M. A., & Mushahid, M. (2017). Drug addiction in urban life of Bangladesh: A sociological study for exploring the causes. *Asia pacific journal of multidisciplinary research, 5*(2), 1–11.
Hasan, M. T., Anwar, T., Christopher, E., Hossain, S., Hossain, M. M., Koly, K. N., Saif-Ur-Rahman, K. M., Ahmed, H. U., Arman, N., & Hossain, S. W. (2021). The current state of mental healthcare in Bangladesh: part 1 – an updated country profile. BJPsych international, 18(4), 78–82. https://doi.org/10.1192/bji.2021.41
Hossain, K. J., Karim, M. R., Karim, A., & Kamal, M. (2013). Sex-habit and sexually transmitted infection (STIs) among the drug abusers undergoing detoxification. *Journal of medicine, 14(1)*, 5–10. https://doi.org/10.3329/jom.v14i1.14529.
Hossain, K. M. S., Kakoli, A. S., Mesbah, S. B., & Mian, A. H. (2018). Prevalence of oral and dental diseases and oral hygiene practices among illicit drug abusers. *Journal of alcoholism and drug dependence, 6*(1), 1–6. https://doi.org/10.4172/2329-6488.1000301.
Hossain, M. D., Ahmed, H. U., Chowdhury, W. A., Niessen, L. W., & Alam, D. S. (2014). Mental disorders in Bangladesh: a systematic review. *BMC psychiatry, 14*, 216. https://doi.org/10.1186/s12888-014-0216-9.
Huque, R., Azad, A. K., Ahmed, H. U., Amin, M. R. (2023). Mental health care seeking behavior in Bangladesh: Evidence from the National Mental Health Survey 2019. (preprint). https://doi.org/10.21203/rs.3.rs-2736863/v1.
International Crisis Group. (2023). Crisis mounts for Rohingya refugees in Bangladesh. (Project Report). https://www.crisisgroup.org/asia/south-asia/bangladesh/355-crisis-mounts-rohingya-refugees-bangladesh. (accessed on 20 Dec, 2023).
Islam, A., & Hossain, M. F. (2017). Drug abuse and its impact on Bangladesh. *International journal of sociology and anthropology, 9*(11), 143–156. https://doi.org/10.5897/IJSA2016.0736.
Islam, S. M. S, Biswas, T., Bhuiyan, F. A., Islam, M. S., Rahman, M. M., & Nessa, H. (2015). Injecting drug users and their health seeking behavior: a cross-sectional study in Dhaka, Bangladesh. *Journal of addiction, 2015*, 756579. https://doi.org/10.1155/2015/756579.
Kamal, M., Huq, N., Mali, B., Akter, H., & Arafat, S. M. Y. (2018). Epidemiology of substance abuse in Bangladesh: A narrative review. *Journal of mental disorders and treatment, 4*, 165. https://doi.org/10.4172/2471-271X.1000165.
Karim, M. E., & Shaikh, S. (2021). Newly enacted mental health law in Bangladesh. *BJPsych international, 18*(4), 85–87. https://doi.org/10.1192/bji.2021.1.
Khalili, P., Nadimi, A. E., Baradaran, H. R., Janani, L., Rahimi-Movaghar, A., Rajabi, Z., Rahmani, A., Hojati, Z., Khalagi, K., & Motevalian, S. A. (2021). Validity of self-reported substance use: research setting versus primary health care setting. *Substance abuse treatment, prevention, and policy, 16*(1), 66. https://doi.org/10.1186/s13011-021-00398-3.

Khan, T. H. (2015). Debunking the drug abuse-crime interplay a study on the youths of selected urban areas of Munshiganj district, Bangladesh. *Society & change, 9*(3), 44–63.

Khan, S. I., Khan, M. N. M., Hasan, A. M. R., Irfan, S. D., Horng, L. M., Chowdhury, E. I., & Azim, T. (2019a). Understanding the reasons for using methamphetamine by sexual minority people in Dhaka, Bangladesh. *The international journal on drug policy, 73*, 64–71. https://doi.org/10.1016/j.drugpo.2019.07.009.

Khan, S. I., Reza, M. M., Crowe, S. M., Rahman, M., Hellard, M,, Sarker, M. S., Chowdhury, E. I., Rana, A. K. M. M., Sacks-Davis, R., Banu, S., Ross, A. G.(2019b). People who inject drugs in Bangladesh—The untold burden! *International journal of infectious diseases, 83*, 109–115, https://doi.org/10.1016/j.ijid.2019.03.009

Khan, N. M, Mullick, M. S. I., & Hussain, S. (2021a). Psychiatric comorbidity among adolescents with substance use disorder. *American journal of psychiatry and neuroscience, 9*(3), 98–106. https://doi.org/10.11648/j.ajpn.20210903.14.

Khan, S. I., Khan, M. N. M., Irfan, S. D., Rumayan Hasan, A. M., Ross, A. G., Horng, L. M., Lachowsky, N., Knudson, G., & Azim, T. (2021b). The effects of methamphetamine use on the sexual lives of gender and sexually diverse people in Dhaka, Bangladesh: A qualitative study. *Archives of sexual behavior, 50*(2), 479–493. https://doi.org/10.1007/s10508-020-01674-2.

Maehira, Y., Chowdhury, E. I., Reza, M., Drahozal, R., Gayen, T. K., Masud, I., Afrin, S., Takamura, N., & Azim, T. (2013). Factors associated with relapse into drug use among male and female attendees of a three-month drug detoxification-rehabilitation programme in Dhaka, Bangladesh: a prospective cohort study. *Harm reduction journal, 10*, 14. https://doi.org/10.1186/1477-7517-10-14.

Maruf, M. M., Alam, M. T., Khan, N. M., Khan, M. Z. R., Begum, K., Mamun, A. A., & Chowdhury, M. W. A. (2012). Substance abuse among male patients with major depressive disorder. *Bangladesh journal of psychiatry, 26*(1), 54–63.

Maruf, M. M., Chowdhury, A., & Islam, M. R. (2024). Substance use and mental health conditions: Co-existence of dual problems in Bangladesh. In SMY Arafat (Ed.), *Mental health in Bangladesh: From bench to community*. Springer Nature Singapore. https://doi.org/10.1007/978-981-97-0610-5_7.

Maruf, M. M., Jahan, N., Bhowmik, A. D., Syed, S. E., Alam, M. T., Rahman, F., Sarker, M., & Khan, M. Z. R. (2013). Opioid use: Sociodemography and some related factors. *Bangladesh journal of psychiatry, 27*(1), 20–27.

Maruf, M. M., Jahan, N., Khan, M. Z. R., Haq, A. I., Akhter, J., Rishad, M. M., & Kamal, M. (2021). Co-Morbidities and family history among methamphetamine users. *Bangladesh medical journal, 50*(2), 15–20. https://doi.org/10.3329/bmj.v50i2.61173.

Maruf, M. M., Khan, M. Z. R., & Jahan, N. (2016). Pattern of substance use: Study in a de-addiction clinic. *Oman medical journal, 31*(5), 327–331. https://doi.org/10.5001/omj.2016.66.

Maruf, M. M., Rahman, F., Khan, M. Z. R., & Jahan, N. (2015). Psychiatric morbidity and substance abuse among male juvenile offenders in Bangladesh. *Life: International journal of health and life-sciences, 1*(1), 161–171. https://doi.org/10.20319/lijshls.2015.s11.161171.

Masud, I., Nabi, M. H., Humaira, T., Hussain, A., Naz, F., Zaman, S., Hawlader, M. D. H. (2020). Treatment seeking pattern of relapse cases of substance use disorder in Bangladesh. *Indian journal of public health research and development, 11*(3), 770–774.

Mental Health Act. (2018). Bangladesh. https://legislativediv.gov.bd/site/page/3c13bbde-76b4-41fc-89cab738dd04a0bb (accessed on 12 Dec, 2023).

Ministry of Health and Family Welfare (2016a). Mapping study and size estimation of the key population in Bangladesh for HIV/AIDS Programs 2015–2016. (Project report). Dhaka: Ministry of Health and Family Welfare, Bangladesh. https://asp.portal.gov.bd/sites/default/files/files/asp.portal.gov.bd/page/4129b6d9_3565_48d5_8f89_ef37abb51732/2020-08-10-22-44-b3e531318d037988784a2aebe3458cfb.pdf (accessed on 23 Nov, 2023).

Ministry of Health and Family Welfare. (2016b). *National harm reduction strategy for drug use and HIV 2017–2021*. (Project report). Dhaka: Ministry of Health and Family Welfare, Bangladesh.

https://asp.portal.gov.bd/sites/default/files/files/asp.portal.gov.bd/page/2d04f70c_c5e5_4d3d_9a13_e8cc7e5af9c9/2021-01-05-16-25-0968e6a4a8a5106d2188a4b98544f10f.docx (accessed on 24 Nov, 2023).

Ministry of Health and Family Welfare. (2017). *End line survey (behaviour) on continuation of the prioritized HIV prevention services among key population in Bangladesh funded by the Global Fund*. (Project report). Dhaka: Ministry of Health and Family Welfare, Bangladesh. https://asp.portal.gov.bd/sites/default/files/files/asp.portal.gov.bd/page/4129b6d9_3565_48d5_8f89_ef37abb51732/2020-04-28-14-55-957a925c30c246e938a35336c26e29ca.pdf (accessed on 20 Nov, 2023).

Ministry of Health and Family Welfare. (2021a). *Prevalence and associated factors of substance use in Bangladesh*. (Project report). Dhaka: Ministry of Health and Family Welfare, Bangladesh. https://nimh.gov.bd/english/wp-content/uploads/2021/11/Substance-Use-Full.pdf (accessed on 29 Nov, 2023).

Ministry of Health and Family Welfare. (2021b). National Mental Health Survey 2019. (project report). Dhaka: Ministry of Health and Family Welfare, Bangladesh. http://nimh.gov.bd/wp-content/uploads/2021/11/Mental-Health-Survey-Report.pdf (accessed on 29 Nov, 2023).

Moonajilin, M. S., Kamal, M. K. I., Mamun, F. A., Safiq, M. B., Hosen, I., Manzar, M. D., & Mamun, M. A. (2021). Substance use behavior and its lifestyle-related risk factors in Bangladeshi high school-going adolescents: An exploratory study. *PloS one, 16*(7), e0254926. https://doi.org/10.1371/journal.pone.0254926.

Narcotics Control Act. (2018). Bangladesh. https://legislativediv.gov.bd/site/page/3c13bbde-76b4-41fc-89cab738dd04a0bb (accessed on 12 Dec, 2023).

Patoari, M. M. H. (2021). Socio-cultural, psychological and family aspects of drug addiction of adolescents and its impact: An analysis from Bangladesh perspective. *Journal of advanced research in social sciences and humanities, 6*(1), 1–14. https://doi.org/10.26500/JARSSH-06-2021-0101.

Rahman, K. F. (2019). *Is punitive action enough to prevent abuse of drug?*. The daily star. https://www.thedailystar.net/law-our-rights/law-analysis/news/punitive-action-enough-prevent-abuse-drug-1697473 (accessed on 10 Nov, 2023).

Rahman, M., Hossain, M. E., Afrad, M. H., Hasan, R., Rahman, M., Sarker, M. S., & Azim, T. (2018). Hepatitis C virus infections among clients attending an HIV testing and counseling center in Dhaka, Bangladesh. *Journal of medical virology, 90*(2), 383–387. https://doi.org/10.1002/jmv.24955.

Riya, S., Rahman, M., Sadeque, M. Z., Kabir, A., & Umar, B. U. (2013). Pattern of drug abuse among patients in some selected addiction rehabilitation centers in Dhaka City. *Faridpur medical college journal, 8*(2), 63–66. https://doi.org/10.3329/fmcj.v8i2.20371.

Roy, J., Morshed, N. M., Qusar, M. M. A. S., Nahar, J. S., Miah, M. A. S., Shah, M. A., Shams, S. F., Shahid, S. F. B., Ikbal, M. M., & Khanom, M. M. (2010). Personality traits of substance users in Bangladesh. *BSMMU journal, 3*(2), 76–81. https://doi.org/10.3329/bsmmuj.v3i2.7056.

Roy, S., & Miah, M. Z. (2017). Socio-demographic and clinical profile of substance abusers attending a regional psychiatric hospital in Sylhet, Bangladesh. *Journal of addiction research and therapy, 8*(5), 342. https://doi.org/10.4172/2155-6105.1000342.

Sarker, A. K., Raju, F. R., Sultana, M. P., Milon, M. M. M., & Akter, S. (2023). Exploration of drug addiction prevalence among young generation of Pabna district, Bangladesh. *Journal of drug delivery and therapeutics, 13*(3), 78–84. https://doi.org/10.22270/jddt.v13i3.5764.

Shultana. F. (2022). Exploring barriers in seeking mental health services. M.phil thesis. (unpublished).

Soron, T. R., Siddike, P. M. A., Ahmed, H. U., & Chowdhury, C. A. (2017). Social and family determinants of substance abuse among the patients of two hospitals in Bangladesh. *Journal of addiction research and therapy, 8*, 340. https://doi.org/10.4172/2155-6105.1000340.

World Health Organization. (2020). Bangladesh WHO special initiative for mental health situational assessment. WHO. https://www.who.int/docs/default-source/mental-health/special-initiative/

who-special-initiative-country-report---bangladesh---2020.pdf?sfvrsn=c2122a0e_2 (accessed on 3 Dec, 2023).

Zaman, B., Ahmed, S. M., Hossain, M. M., & Kamal, M. M. (2015). Psychosocial illness among the drug abusers undergoing detoxification in Dhaka, Bangladesh. *South East Asia journal of public health, 4*(2), 36–41. https://doi.org/10.3329/seajph.v4i2.23693.

Chapter 4
Current Perspectives on Substance Use Disorder in Bhutan

Damber Kumar Nirola

4.1 Introduction

Bhutan is a small landlocked nation situated in the Eastern Himalayas between China to the north and India to the south. The Kingdom of Bhutan is also known locally as "Druk Yul" or "Land of the Thunder Dragon". The total land area is 38,394 square kilometres and has a population of around 727,145. Bhutan's political system is a constitutional monarchy, with the King, also known as Druk Gyalpo, serving as the head of state and the Prime Minister leading the government. The major state religion is Vajrayana Buddhism, with the Je Khenpo as its religious head. Thimphu, the capital and largest city, is home to approximately one-seventh of the population.

Bhutan has undergone significant changes and development, particularly in the latter half of the twentieth century. The country's development philosophy is rooted in the concept of Gross National Happiness (GNH), which seeks to balance material and spiritual well-being for all living beings. The four pillars of GNH are sustainable and equitable economic growth and development, preservation and sustainable use of the environment, preservation and promotion of cultural heritage, and good governance.

Aligned with the Sustainable Development Goals (SDGs), GNH guides Bhutan's development strategy. The country has made significant strides in human development and graduated from the Least Developed Countries (LDCs) category in 2023. However, Bhutan faces challenges such as economic diversification, income inequality, environmental conservation, and climate change adaptation. In recent years, substance use among adolescents has emerged as a major challenge. Alcohol, the most used and abused substance in Bhutan, is associated with high rates of mortality, morbidity, suicide, and violence.

D. K. Nirola (✉)
Jigme Dorji Wangchuck National Referral Hospital, Thimphu, Bhutan
e-mail: dknirola@jdwnrh.gov.bt

S. M. Y. Arafat and S. K. Kar (eds.), *Current Perspectives on Substance Use Disorders in South Asia*, https://doi.org/10.1007/978-981-97-6619-2_4

4.2 Patterns of Drug Use

Bhutan shares a 699 km long border with India in the south, and due to its porous nature, these substances are easily accessible. This poses enormous challenges to law enforcement agencies as smugglers can easily enter and exit at several points along the border.

While "hard drugs" such as heroin, amphetamine, and methamphetamine are not prevalent, a typical pattern of drug use in Bhutan has been observed. Teenagers often begin experimenting with volatile substances (paint thinner, glue, petrol, etc.) before progressing to cannabis (marijuana). Marijuana grows wild in Bhutan, and people harvest, process and sell it on the black market.

More harmful substances include pharmaceutical products containing opioids such as Spasmo-Proxyvon (SP), cough mixtures containing codeine (Corex), and Nitrazepam (N10), a benzodiazepine. Recently, cases of brown sugar (crude heroin) addiction have emerged in the border town of Phuentsholing. While these opioid containing substances are available in India by prescription, they are banned in Bhutan.

Numerous studies have been conducted on the impact of alcohol consumption, yet data on other substances remain scarce. The per capita consumption of pure alcohol among adults (over 15 years of age) significantly exceeds global consumption (8.47 L compared to 6.2 L). Consequently, alcoholic liver disease (ALD) is the primary cause of mortality among the male population in Bhutan (International, Movendi 2016, January).

According to the most recent reports from the National Statistics Bureau of Bhutan (2021), there were 141 deaths due to ALD. This figure represents a decrease of approximately 25 deaths from 2020. However, ALD has been the leading cause of mortality in the country for the past decade. The number of ALD cases has been rising annually, reaching a peak of 2,771 cases in 2021. In 2019, the prevalence of heavy episodic drinkers in the population was 17.5%, and ALD continues to rank among the top ten causes of mortality in Bhutan (Tshering Pelden 2022).

The "Alcohol Use and Abuse in Bhutan" report published by the National Statistics Bureau in 2019 (Tshering Pelden 2022) revealed that the prevalence of current alcohol use among the population aged 15 years and above was 38.6%, with a higher proportion of males (50.3%) than females (26.4%). The prevalence of heavy episodic drinking among current drinkers was 17.5%, with a higher proportion of males (23.8%) than females (9.4%). The prevalence of alcohol use disorder among current drinkers was 11.5%, with a higher proportion of males (15.4%) than females (6.3%) (Dorji 2012).

Similarly, the prevalence of current tobacco use among the population aged 15 years and above was 24.6%, with a higher proportion of males (37.1%) than females (11.9%) (Aneja and Gopal 2023). The prevalence of current cannabis use among the population aged 15–64 years was 2.1%, with a higher proportion of males (3.2%) than females (0.8%). According to Royal Bhutan and other sources, the prevalence of current use of other illicit drugs, such as opioids, stimulants, and inhalants, among the population aged 15–64 years was 0.8%, with a higher proportion of males (1.1%) than females (0.4%) (Dechen Tshomo 2017). The 2018 annual health report noted 1,472 cases of mental and behavioural disorders due to alcohol and other substances treated in various health facilities, including the National Referral Hospital in Thimphu (Ministry of Health, Bhutan 2018).

4.3 Policies and Laws

The government of Bhutan has implemented several measures to address the Substance Use Disorder (SUD) problem, including the enactment of policies and laws, the establishment of the Bhutan Narcotic Control Authority, the provision of treatment and rehabilitation services, and the promotion of awareness and education. However, further efforts are required to prevent and reduce the harmful use of substances and to enhance the well-being of the Bhutanese people.

4.3.1 Alcohol Policy

The National Policy and Strategic Framework to Reduce Harmful Use of Alcohol 2015–2020 was approved by the 90th session of the Lhengye Zhungtshog on December 2, 2015. According to this, the permissible age for alcohol consumption is set at 18 years. Sales of alcohol are restricted to those under the age of 18 years. Further, sales of alcohol in bars are prohibited before 1 pm and after 10 pm. All foreigners are allowed to carry a maximum of 1 L of alcoholic spirits on them. Some religious sites and monasteries have restrictions on carrying alcohol within the premises.

4.3.2 The Narcotic Drugs Psychotropic Substances and Substance Abuse (NDPSSA) Act

This act was initially introduced in 2005, revised in 2015, and amended in 2018. Amendments: The NDPSSA Act underwent a significant amendment in 2015 after an incident in 2013 where a Bhutanese woman was caught smuggling Ketamine at Suvarnabhumi International Airport in Bangkok, Thailand.

The Act includes provisions for education, early intervention, treatment, and rehabilitation.

a. Control and Regulation: The Act controls and regulates operations related to narcotic drugs and psychotropic substances.

b. Forfeiture of Property: The Act provides for the forfeiture of property derived from, or used in, illicit traffic in narcotic drugs and psychotropic substances.
c. Implementation of International Conventions: The Act implements the provisions of the International Conventions on Narcotic Drugs and Psychotropic Substances.

4.4 Professional Services

To consolidate all mental health-related services, the Pema Secretariat was established on January 22, 2022, by the Royal Command of Her Majesty Gyaltseun Jetsun Pema, the Queen of Bhutan. This initiative, the first of its kind in Bhutan, became operational on June 16, 2021, with the primary objective of addressing the mental health and well-being of the Bhutanese population.

The Pema Secretariat has initiated the establishment of a 100-bed treatment and rehabilitation centre, which is expected to be operational shortly. Additionally, the Pema Centre, a 60-bed hospital catering to clients with mental disorders and substance and alcohol use disorders, is under construction.

The mandate of the Pema Secretariat encompasses the following:

1. Support the development and implementation of policies and programs that promote mental health and mitigate the harm caused by alcohol and other substance use, self-harm, and violence.
2. Foster multi-sectoral partnerships and collaborations among various stakeholders, including government agencies, civil society organizations, the private sector, media, and international organizations, to address the mental health challenges and needs of the population.
3. Engage and empower communities and individuals to take ownership and responsibility for their own mental health and well-being, and to support others in need.
4. Establish and strengthen a proactive and reliable service delivery network that provides accessible, affordable, and quality mental health care and support services for all.

The Pema Secretariat comprises three core divisions: Self-harm Prevention, Violence Prevention and Response, and Substance Use Prevention and Care. While each division has a specific focus and function, they collectively work towards achieving the common vision and mission of the Secretariat.

Several professional and semi-professional counsellors have been trained through the Colombo Plan's Drug Advisory Program in the field of Universal Treatment Course for Addiction Professionals. Bhutan's first batch of National Trainers were trained between 2012 and 2015, and three of them have since become Global Trainers. The Universal Prevention Course for School Principals was initiated in May 2015, with certification completed in 2018.

Through the initiatives of the erstwhile Bhutan Narcotic Control Authority (BNCA), national trainers have continued the Universal Treatment Course (UTC) training, educating numerous health workers (primarily doctors and nurses), school counsellors, and peer counsellors. Many of these individuals have successfully passed the international certification test and are now International Certified Addiction Professionals I (ICAP I), serving as frontline workers in the field of addiction.

The Bhutan Narcotic Control Authority has since been merged with other regulatory bodies under the Bhutan Food and Drug Authority, forming the Controlled Substances and Medical Devices Division. This division functions primarily as a regulatory authority, with limited involvement in service provision to clients.

With assistance from experts at the All India Institute of Medical Sciences, New Delhi, several batches of medical doctors have been trained in drug and alcohol de-addiction. These trained medical professionals carry out detoxification of clients with substance and alcohol use disorders before initiating rehabilitation. The Mental Health Program from the Ministry of Health has developed the Standard Treatment and Counselling Guidelines for Alcohol and Drug Dependence as a reference for this purpose.

The Khesar Gyalpo University of Medical Sciences initiated a bachelor's program in clinical counselling at the Faculty of Nursing and Public Health in 2015, with the first batch graduating in 2019. The curriculum includes the treatment of SUD.

While clients with alcohol or substance use disorders can avail treatment at various health centres, the majority seek treatment at the Jigme Dorji Wangchuck National Referral Hospital (JDWNRH).

4.4.1 Rehabilitation Centres

4.4.1.1 Bhutan Institute of Wellbeing

This institute is a pioneering initiative of Her Majesty Gyalyum Tseyring Pem Wangchuck, the President of the Bhutan Youth Development Fund. Situated approximately 25 kms from Thimphu, the capital city, it offers a diverse range of facilities and services for young individuals dependent on drugs and other practitioners. The institute promotes programs for the prevention and treatment of substance use disorders through the modelling and promotion of a holistic education process. It also provides training and support to organizations involved in substance use treatment that aspire to develop conditions inspired by Gross National Happiness (GNH).

The institute comprises two primary centres: i. **Centre for Treatment and Rehabilitation of Substance Use Disorders**: This centre provides quality treatment and rehabilitation services to all young individuals dependent on drugs and alcohol, particularly those from disadvantaged backgrounds. It offers a three-month, holistic GNH-inspired treatment and rehabilitation program, known as the "Happiness Model". ii. **Centre for Skills Development and Re-integration**: This centre focuses on upskilling recovering substance users and reintegrating them into society as productive citizens.

Since its inception in 2004, the institute has rehabilitated over 2500 young individuals with substance use disorders (SUDs).

4.4.1.2 Centre for Mind and Wellness

The Chithuen Phendey Association of Bhutan, a Civil Society Organization and the brainchild of the first psychiatrist of Bhutan, has established this rehabilitation centre near Thimphu city. It primarily focuses on relapse prevention and advocacy.

4.4.1.3 Happiness Centre, Phuentsholing

This small setup, initiated by an individual and supported by a CSO called Nazhoen Lamten, functions primarily as an aftercare service for individuals with SUD in recovery.

4.4.2 Compulsory Treatment Centre

This centre caters to individuals with SUD and legal conflicts. Clients are mostly referred to the centre after a rigorous assessment process by a treatment assessment panel comprising mental health professionals, Royal Bhutan Police, and legal officers. Initially established by the BNCA, it is now managed by the Pema Secretariat. Counselling is provided to those identified as peddlers and traffickers with SUD in prison settings, currently available only in Thimphu.

4.4.3 Supply Reduction

In Bhutan, the supply reduction strategies for drugs are primarily managed by the Royal Bhutan Police (RBP) and the Bhutan Narcotics Control Agency (BNCA). The RBP has established a special task force, various drug units, and police stations across the country to crack down on drug traffickers and related issues. They conduct surveillance and patrolling and monitor towns, cities, check posts, and borders. Their primary focus is on tracking down individuals trafficking drugs through the borders. Due to enhanced vigilance, numerous clients are sent for treatment, and peddlers and traffickers are apprehended.

4.5 Constraints and Limitations

Data related to substance use is limited. No comprehensive nationwide survey has been conducted to determine the prevalence of substance use. There is a lack of qualified professionals to provide effective treatment in remote areas, and all the rehabilitation centres are based in or around Thimphu.

4.6 Conclusion

In conclusion, Bhutan's approach to addressing substance use is influenced by its unique development philosophy and the challenges posed by its porous border with India. The high prevalence of substance use, particularly alcohol, is a significant concern for public health and societal well-being. This chapter highlights the commendable efforts of the government in mitigating the harmful impact of substance use through policies, laws, and the establishment of the Pema Secretariat. Professional services, training programs, and rehabilitation centres play crucial roles in addressing substance use disorders by providing a comprehensive framework for prevention, intervention, and recovery. The collaboration among different stakeholders, both national and international, demonstrates a concerted effort to tackle the complex aspects of substance use. However, the chapter acknowledges persistent challenges, such as limited data availability, a shortage of qualified professionals in remote areas, and the concentration of rehabilitation services in specific regions. It emphasizes the importance of adopting a more extensive and nuanced approach to address the diverse patterns of substance use. This includes community engagement, increased awareness, and capacity building. As Bhutan continues its journey towards holistic well-being, the chapter advocates for sustained efforts, research initiatives, and the strengthening of infrastructure to comprehensively address the changing landscape of substance use in the country.

References

Dechen Tshomo. (2017, July 4). *Kuenselonline*. Retrieved from Kunesel online web site: https://kuenselonline.com/bhutan-tops-tobacco-and-marijuana-users-in-south-east-asia/

Dorji, L. (2012). *Alcohol Use and Abuse in Bhutan*. Thimphu: National Statistics Bureau.

International, Movendi. (2016, January 15). *Bhutan: Alcohol Policy Adopted*. Retrieved from Movendi International. https://movendi.ngo/news/2016/01/15/bhutan-alcohol-policy-adopted/

Kashish Aneja and Sanjana Gopal. (2023, February 1). *Blog, Tobacco Control*. Retrieved from Blog Tobacco Control web site: https://blogs.bmj.com/tc/2023/02/01/bhutan-reverses-sales-ban-on-tobacco/

Ministry of Health, Bhutan. (2018). *Annual Health Report*. Thimphu: Minstry of Health, Royal Government of Bhutan.

Tshering Pelden. (2022, March 24). *Business Bhutan*. Retrieved from Business Bhutan Web site: https://businessbhutan.bt/ald-continues-to-be-major-cause-of-death-in-the-country/

Chapter 5
Current Perspectives on Substance Use Disorders in India—Public Mental Health Aspects

Ragul Ganesh and Siddharth Sarkar

5.1 Introduction

Substance use disorders have gained significant attention within India's public health policy framework. Effectively addressing the issue of substance use disorders necessitates a comprehensive understanding of the current perspectives on substance use disorders in India. India is an extensive and diverse nation with numerous geographical and environmental factors influencing the patterns of substance use in the country (Ambekar et al. 2019; Murthy et al. 2010). Different states of India have different cultures, languages, and traditions; they encounter distinct challenges when addressing substance abuse depending on the use of specific substances within their respective populations.

India has a long history of using cannabis, opium, and alcohol for medicinal, religious, and recreational purposes (Kethineni et al. 1995; Sharma 1996). In ancient India, Amanita muscaria played a significant role in religious practices, being one of the ingredients in the sacred beverage known as Soma, as mentioned in the Rigveda. During British colonial rule, the production and sale of substances like opium and alcohol were regulated (Sharma et al. 2010). This had a significant impact on the availability and consumption patterns of these substances. After gaining independence in 1947, India implemented various policies to regulate and control substance abuse. These policies have evolved over the years and have included measures like prohibition in some states and the regulation of alcohol sales. India is situated between the

R. Ganesh
Department of Psychiatry, Jawaharlal Institute of Postgraduate Medical Education and Research (JIPMER), Puducherry 605006, India

S. Sarkar (✉)
National Drug Dependence Treatment Centre, All India Institute of Medical Sciences, New Delhi 110029, India
e-mail: sidsarkar22@gmail.com

S. M. Y. Arafat and S. K. Kar (eds.), *Current Perspectives on Substance Use Disorders in South Asia*, https://doi.org/10.1007/978-981-97-6619-2_5

world's two largest regions of illegal opium production, known as the Golden Crescent and the Golden Triangle (Patil and Pandey 2022). Historically, this geographical placement has been considered a potential vulnerability to the use of opium and heroin, as it has made India a destination for and a conduit through which opiates from these regions flow (Dorabjee and Samson 1998). India is also one of the largest legal producers of opium. In recent decades, there has been a rise in the use of synthetic drugs, prescription medications, and inhalants, consequently resulting in individuals presenting to healthcare services with disorders related to these substances.

The present chapter puts forth perspectives on substance use disorders in India. The perspective provided is a clinically oriented one, and we appreciate that perspectives can be from different viewpoints as well, for example, regulatory, sociological, economic, and others. We present the salient aspects of epidemiology and burden, help-seeking patterns, comorbidity, emerging substances, legal and policy-related aspects, stakeholder perspectives, and gradual recognition of complementary and alternate treatment for substance use disorders. We subsequently reflect upon what can be done further about the substance use disorder situation in India. We reckon that the chapter is not a comprehensive and complete review of literature, and there is adequate useful literature on substance use disorders in India (Balhara et al. 2022; Basu et al. 2016; Murthy et al. 2010; Sarkar et al. 2022; Sarkar and Ghosh 2019). However, we have aimed to highlight the major facets of substance use disorders in the country, especially from a clinical angle.

5.2 Epidemiology and Burden of Substance Use Disorders in India

Several epidemiological surveys have explored the landscape of substance use in India. In 2004, a collaboration between the United Nations Office on Drugs and Crime (UNODC) and the Ministry of Social Justice and Empowerment resulted in the release of the inaugural National Survey on the Extent, Pattern, and Trends of Drug Abuse in India (Ray 2004). The "National Mental Health Survey of India (NMHS)" in 2015–2016 also contributed valuable epidemiological insights into substance use. The NMHS revealed that tobacco use disorder affected roughly 20.9% of the population, alcohol use disorder was prevalent in approximately 4.7%, and other substance use disorders were identified in 0.6%. The 2019 report titled "Magnitude of Substance Use in India," published by the Ministry of Social Justice and Empowerment, indicated that approximately 14.6% of the population had reported alcohol use, and about 2.8% had used some form of cannabis product within the past year. Approximately 2.1% of the country's population had used opioids, which encompassed opium, heroin, and a range of pharmaceutical opioids. The consumption of alcohol is significantly more prevalent among men (27.3%) than women (1.6%). The prevalence of current alcohol use among men in the previous survey conducted by Ray et al. in 2004 was 21%. This suggests a potential increase in alcohol use among men over the last decade (Parmar et al. 2023a).

Among individuals who use alcohol, country liquor, often called '*desi sharab*,' constitutes about 30% of consumption, while spirits or Indian Made Foreign Liquor account for around 30% of consumption. The use of the legal form of cannabis, known as bhang, was reported at 2%, while the use of illegal cannabis products like *ganja* and *charas* accounted for 1.2% of consumption. Among opioids, heroin is the most frequently used, with a prevalence of 1.14%. Pharmaceutical opioids follow this at 0.96% and opium at 0.52%. The prevalence of other drug categories, such as Cocaine (0.10%), Amphetamine Type Stimulants (0.18%), and Hallucinogens (0.12%), is lower, indicating utilization by a relatively small proportion of the country's population. Inhalants had an overall prevalence of 0.7%. However, the current use among children and adolescents (1.17%) exceeds that of adults (0.58%).

Additionally, national surveys like the "National Non-Communicable Disease Monitoring Survey (NNCDMS)" in 2017–2018, the "National Family Health Survey (NFHS)," and the "Longitudinal Ageing Study in India (LASI)" in 2020–2021 have delved into the prevalence and patterns of substance use across the country. The NNCDMS revealed that the prevalence of current alcohol use was reported at 15.9%.

According to the Global Adult Tobacco Survey India (2016–17), nearly 267 million adults in India, constituting 29% of the adult population (15 years and above), are tobacco users. The predominant form of tobacco use is smokeless, with commonly used products including khaini, gutkha, betel quid with tobacco, and *zarda*. Smoking forms of tobacco include bidi, cigarette, and hookah. In recent years, there has been a noticeable decrease in tobacco use in India. Specifically, among men, the prevalence of tobacco use has decreased from 45% during NFHS-4 in 2015–2016 to 39% in NFHS-5 in 2019–2021. Similarly, among women, there has been a reduction from 7 to 4% during the same period, as indicated by the surveys. These trends are further supported by data from separate GATS surveys, where a notable 7% decrease in current tobacco users was observed from GATS-1 in 2009–2010 to GATS-2 in 2016–2017.

The prevalence of substance use in India exhibits significant heterogeneity, indicating substantial variation across different regions. According to the Magnitude of Substance Use in India survey report (Ambekar et al. 2019), Chhattisgarh (35.6%) and Tripura (34.7%) demonstrate a notable prevalence of alcohol use, followed by Punjab (28.5%), Arunachal Pradesh (28%), and Goa (28%). Sikkim (7.3%), Nagaland (4.7%), and Odisha (4.5%) surpass the national average in cannabis use. The states with the highest percentage of the population affected by opioid use include Mizoram, Nagaland, Arunachal Pradesh, and Sikkim in the northeast, along with Punjab, Haryana, and Delhi.

Thus, the prevalence of different substances of use has been fairly high in India. Due to the high population in India, the actual number of those using substances and suffering from substance use disorders is quite high (for example, the estimated number of individuals with alcohol use disorders in India is more than the total population of countries like Australia, Sri Lanka, or Romania).

5.2.1 *Emerging Addictions*

Amphetamine-type stimulants (ATS) have a global presence, with approximately 0.7% of the world's population aged 15–64 reported to have used amphetamines, and 0.4% have used ecstasy in the past year (ATS 2023). ATS usage is associated with a wide range of adverse effects, including physical and psychological health issues, as well as an elevated risk of engaging in high-risk behaviors. India is one of the frequently mentioned countries in the context of illicit shipments of ephedrine and pseudoephedrine, the precursors used in producing ATS. ATS is used by 0.2% of the country's population aged 10 to 75 years, with 0.02% suffering from amphetamine dependence. Another qualitative study, conducted across five Indian states with a limited sample of 100 ATS users, revealed that ecstasy and methamphetamine pills were the most commonly used ATS (2023).

Several reports have highlighted instances of seizures related to new psychoactive substances (NPS), including substances like mephedrone, in various regions of India. India, often mentioned alongside China in UNODC reports, is recognized as a significant source of NPS. Given its prominence in global pharmaceutical exports, the country has also witnessed seizures of drug precursors, such as N-acetyl anthranilic acid and N-phenethyl-4-piperidone. These findings underscore the need for vigilance and regulatory measures to address the challenges posed by the trafficking and misuse of such substances and their precursors in India.

Apart from these, forays are being made into the assessment of newer psychoactive substances in India (Chadda et al. 2023). Understanding the profile of newer psychoactive substances can help in preparing for the future challenges of substance use disorders in India.

5.3 Help-Seeking Pattern for Substance Use Disorders

Substance use disorder treatment services are available through three distinct sectors in India: government facilities, which are overseen by the Ministry of Health and Family Welfare, non-governmental organizations (NGOs) operating under the Ministry of Social Justice and Empowerment, and the private sector. Government facilities for substance use disorder treatment encompass medical colleges and district or civil hospitals. The Drug De-Addiction Program, administered by the Ministry of Health and Family Welfare, is designed to offer accessible, affordable, and evidence-based care for individuals grappling with substance use disorder. The National Drug Dependence Treatment Centre (NDDTC), AIIMS, New Delhi, serves as the nodal center for capacity building among healthcare professionals in the identification and management of substance use disorders, collaborating with various healthcare institutions in this endeavor. The National Action Plan for Drug Demand

Reduction (NAPDDR), overseen by the Ministry of Social Justice and Empowerment, is crucial in supporting addiction treatment efforts. It provides financial assistance to support the operation of Addiction Treatment Facilities within government hospitals. Additionally, NAPDDR extends its assistance to non-governmental organizations (NGOs) for the maintenance and upkeep of Integrated Rehabilitation Centres for Addicts (IRCAs).

The study examining the utilization of treatment and the preferences for treatment settings among individuals with substance use disorders revealed that there are distinct patterns based on the type of substance (Dhawan et al. 2016). Specifically, the demand for treatment related to illicit drugs such as heroin, opiates, and cannabis was more pronounced in the Government sector. In contrast, injection drug use showed a higher prevalence among those seeking treatment in Non-Governmental Organization (NGO) settings. Notably, the private sector saw a higher proportion of individuals seeking treatment for alcohol-related issues.

According to the survey on the magnitude of substance use in India, it was found that merely 25% of individuals dependent on alcohol who tried quitting the substance received any form of treatment (Ambekar et al. 2019). Similar patterns were observed regarding treatment-seeking behavior among those who tried quitting illicit drugs. According to NMHS 2015–16, the treatment gap for substance use disorders was notably greater compared to psychiatric disorders, with an 86.3% gap observed for alcohol use disorder and an even higher 91.8% gap for tobacco use disorder (Murthy 2017). The findings suggest a significant disparity between the prevalence of substance use issues and the corresponding rates of individuals receiving appropriate treatment in India.

Multicentric studies have provided substantial evidence regarding the effectiveness of buprenorphine and methadone in managing individuals with opioid dependence. This robust body of research has been pivotal in establishing opioid substitution therapy as a trustworthy and accepted treatment strategy in India for addressing opioid dependence (Ambekar et al. 2018). In the context of relapse prevention for alcohol use disorder in India, disulfiram has been the most frequently studied pharmacological agent (Bharadwaj et al. 2018). Recent research in India has also centered on exploring the efficacy of acamprosate and naltrexone as anti-craving agents. In addition, other medications like baclofen and topiramate have been noted in studies over the past few years.

In September 2022, India introduced the fifth edition of the National List of Essential Medicines (NLEM). This updated list plays a crucial role in managing public health by ensuring access to medications essential for addressing important health disorders in the country. The recent additions to the NLEM include notable medications such as buprenorphine sublingual tablets, buprenorphine plus naloxone sublingual tablets, and nicotine gum (Parmar et al. 2023c). These additions underscore the recognition of these medications as essential tools in addressing substance use disorders within the country.

5.3.1 Complementary and Alternative Treatment

Complementary and alternative treatment for substance use disorders has received due focus, especially with the popularization of yoga in recent times. Yoga has been shown to have clear documented evidence for some of the substance use disorders (Kuppili et al. 2018; Sarkar and Varshney 2017). Studies are available on the use of yoga for alcohol use disorders, opioid use disorders, tobacco use disorders, and others. Rarely yoga has been used as a stand-alone treatment with a medication comparator. Rather studies have taken an approach of using yoga as an add-on treatment and found benefits on non-substance parameters (like quality of life), and sometimes substance use parameters. This suggests that there is a need to critically evaluate how, when, and where would yoga be useful for individuals with substance use disorders.

Apart from yoga, Ayurveda and Homeoopathy are the alternate systems of medicine that have shown benefits for patients with substance use disorders (Rathi and Rathi 2020; Singh et al. 2023). Ayurvedic approaches have endorsed meditation, a nutritious diet, inculcation of morals, environmental (and peer) changes, reduction by small quantities to reduce withdrawal symptoms, and utilization of medications like "*Bruhan Rasayana*". From a homeopathic perspective, medications that have been used in treatment have included Arsenic album, Nux vomica, Pulsatilla, Lycopodium, Sulfur, Ipecac, Staphysagria, Belladonna, Chamomilla, Phosphorus, Rhustox, and Lachesis. There is some evidence of the efficacy of acupuncture in the treatment of substance use disorders, but this modality has been rarely used in India.

5.4 Physical and Psychiatric Comorbidity of Substance Use Disorder

A significant correlation exists between drug use disorders and psychiatric comorbidities, with shared risk factors contributing to mental health conditions and drug use disorders. Additionally, individuals dealing with drug use disorders often face adverse health repercussions from their drug use, including non-fatal overdoses, the risk of contracting infectious diseases such as HIV and hepatitis C, and an increased likelihood of premature death.

Reports suggest prevalence of HIV is highest among people who inject drugs (PWID). The 17th HIV Sentinel Surveillance under the National AIDS and STD Control Program (NACP), along with biomarkers for Hepatitis B and Hepatitis C, was implemented in 2021 across eight population groups, including injecting drug users.

The latest report on the HIV epidemic in India highlights a concerning trend: the adult prevalence of HIV is particularly significant among PWID, with an estimated 200,000 individuals engaging in this behavior. Within this demographic, the HIV prevalence is estimated to be 6.23%. This underscores the heightened vulnerability and substantial impact of the virus within the injecting drug user community in India.

A recent systematic review found that the HIV prevalence varies significantly, with rates ranging from 9.9% to 52.9% among PWID across different parts of the nation (Pachuau et al. 2022).

India contributes significantly to the global burden of HCV, with a higher HCV seroprevalence among its general population (from 0.4% to 1.0%) compared to several Southeast Asian countries. One of the regional studies conducted in India revealed that 28% of patients enrolled in opioid substitution therapy tested positive for the Hepatitis C virus. The study also highlighted an increasing prevalence of HCV seropositivity in correlation with the number of years of injection drug use (Kumar et al. 2023).

In a comprehensive multicentric study conducted in India, researchers examined 13,014 cases of chronic liver disease (Mukherjee et al. 2017). The participants had a median age of 43 years, and 73% of them were male. The results of the study revealed that cirrhosis was predominantly associated with alcoholism, making up 34.3% of the 4,413 cases analyzed.

The presence of psychiatric disorders alongside substance use disorders is frequently linked to less favorable treatment outcomes, a more severe trajectory of illness, and increased utilization of services. The most prevalent psychiatric disorder among patients with alcohol use disorders (AUD) is mood disorders, ranging from 26 to 71%, with depressive disorders emerging as a commonly associated comorbidity (Singh and Balhara 2016). Anxiety spectrum disorders are present in 10% to 45.8% of patients with AUD, encompassing conditions such as agoraphobia and panic disorders. Additionally, psychosexual disorders are commonly reported in individuals with alcohol dependence.

Most of the Indian studies indicate that prevalent psychiatric comorbidities associated with cannabis use include cannabis-induced psychosis, schizophrenia, mania with psychosis, and unspecified psychosis (Sarkar et al. 2003). The individuals using cannabis exhibited predominantly positive symptoms and, notably, experienced a faster rate of remission of these symptoms upon receiving treatment (Aich et al. 2004). Research studies have reported cognitive disturbances, including poor attention span and memory deficits, in individuals using bhang (Singh and Balhara 2017).

Thus, research has explored the prevalence and connotations of comorbidities in individuals with substance use disorders in India. The substance use disorder treatment services need to be geared toward handling these comorbidities.

5.5 Law and Policy Related to Substance Abuse

5.5.1 *Laws Related to Substance Availability*

There are several laws governing substance use in India. Parmar et al. have reviewed the drug-related laws and policies and synthesized their salient features (Parmar et al. 2023b). The Narcotic Drugs and Psychotropic Substances Act of 1985 is a comprehensive law in this regard that proscribed the sale, purchase, cultivation, production, and consumption of narcotic drugs and psychotropic substances in the country. The Act came into force as India was a signatory to the Single Convention on Narcotic Drugs of 1961, and the Convention on Psychotropic Substances of 1971. The law has a largely punitive approach. The Act has a provision of immunity from prosecution for 'addicts' who volunteer to get medical de-addiction treatment (Section 64A). However, this provision has rarely been utilized. There is a scope for greater diversion to the treatment of individuals who have been suffering from substance use disorders. The application of the law may serve a deterrent value when used for expedited sentencing of drug peddlers, rather than being used as an instrument of intimidation for convenience.

The Cigarettes and Other Tobacco Products Act of 2003 aimed to prevent smoking in public places, restrict advertisement (including surrogate advertising), limit the sale of tobacco products to minors and near educational institutions, and introduce warnings on packaging consistently. While smokeless tobacco use has been common, spitting in public places has been made illegal. Under the Goods and Services Tax which has made the taxation uniform across the country, tobacco products have been put in the highest tax brackets. Consequent to these interventions or otherwise, the prevalence of tobacco use in India has been declining (Chhabra et al. 2021). This also potentially translates to reduced tobacco use disorders in the country. Alcohol in India is a state subject, and hence, there are a variety of laws regulating alcohol supply and availability across the country. While a few states prohibit the availability of alcohol, other states have different ages at which individuals can legally procure and consume alcohol. The prevalence of alcohol use varies across the Indian states. It has been remarked that while alcohol contributes significantly to the revenues of the states, the health consequences are immense.

5.5.2 *Laws Related to Treatment*

The Mental Health Care Act (MHCA) of 2017 considers substance use disorders under the ambit of mental illness. Hence, for the treatment of substance use disorder, the provisions of MHCA apply, including outpatient treatment, inpatient treatment (including supported admissions or non-voluntary treatment), and rehabilitation. The law has been aspirational and has found challenges in implementation at the ground level in India, given the variety of healthcare contexts across the country, and the diversity of legal awareness and complexity of requisite compliances. Individuals with substance use disorders also come under the purview of the Rights of Persons with Disability (RwPD) Act of 2016 as substance use disorders fall under the rubric of 'mental illness' covered under the Act. This law also envisages a rights-based approach and suitable accommodations, though the extent of its application for individuals with substance use disorders remains to be examined.

However, there exists a high treatment gap for substance use disorders. This has resulted in the mushrooming of unregulated 'de-addiction'/'rehabilitation' centers across the country catering to societal demand and familial helplessness. There have been reported instances of human rights violations, which have necessitated legal interventions to clamp down on such centers in specific states. Nonetheless, from a utilitarian perspective, the existence of such centers reflects the purpose served to 'save' the family and society from difficult behaviors exhibited by some individuals with substance use disorders.

5.5.3 Policy Related Aspects

The policy at the governmental level has also seen substantial changes and evolution with time. The National Mental Health Program (NMHP) was launched in 1982, and its operational component of District Mental Health Program had a limited focus on substance use disorders. To address substance use disorders across the country, two central government approaches namely the Central Sector Scheme for Prevention of Alcoholism and Substance (Drug) Abuse by the Ministry of Social Justice and Empowerment (MoSJE) in 1985 and the Drug De-Addiction Program of India by the Ministry of Health and Family Welfare (MoHFW) in 1988 were launched. The expansion has occurred in the capacity of treatment through training of treatment providers and centers that provide specialized care for individuals with substance use disorders. Inpatient services at larger dedicated centers have been supplemented with the opening of Addiction Treatment Facilities and Drug Treatment Clinics. The Government of India also brought out the National Policy on Narcotic Drugs and Psychotropic Substances in 2012 to provide explicit directions and coordinate actions of different government departments dealing with substances covered under the NDPS Act of 1985. While the policy largely attends to supply reduction measures, treatment of individuals with substance use disorders has been also given due importance to the provision for expansion of services. The MoSJE launched the National Action Plan for Drug Demand Reduction (NAPDDR) in 2018 to provide a comprehensive approach to address substance use, under which the Nasha Mukt Bharat Abhiyaan has been launched to provide outreach and raise awareness at the grass root level.

5.5.4 Stakeholders Perspective

There are different stakeholders in the treatment process for substance use disorders. The treatment is provided in the broad socio-economic and cultural context of legislation, healthcare system, societal approach, stigma (many consider substance use disorder as purely a moral failing), economic disparity, the profile of substances being used, and being considered harmful. In this, the stakeholders in the treatment process include patients, their family members, representatives of the community, healthcare professionals, legislators, and healthcare administrators. Being oblivious to the concerns of the various stakeholders may result in a disconnect between the services and the service users. Though there have been some organized voices from the different stakeholders, bringing them on a common platform so that they can interact with each other may result in a more effective, responsive, and locally customized approach to substance use disorders.

From a schematic perspective, the stakeholders in the substance use disorder perspective have been shown in Fig. 5.1. The necessity of the stakeholder perspective emerges from the fact that many of the programs, policies, and help approaches are designed from the 'expert' perspective, wherein the responsible officer or expert, vested with legislative, administrative, and financial authority, makes decisions. The stakeholder perspective can bring in complementary views of the service users, facilitators, and providers to make the help provision customized to the needs of the population. Gradually, there is some move toward including different stakeholders' views in decision-making.

Support groups like Alcoholics Anonymous and Narcotics Anonymous have found strong footing in various parts of India. They offer an avenue of self-help

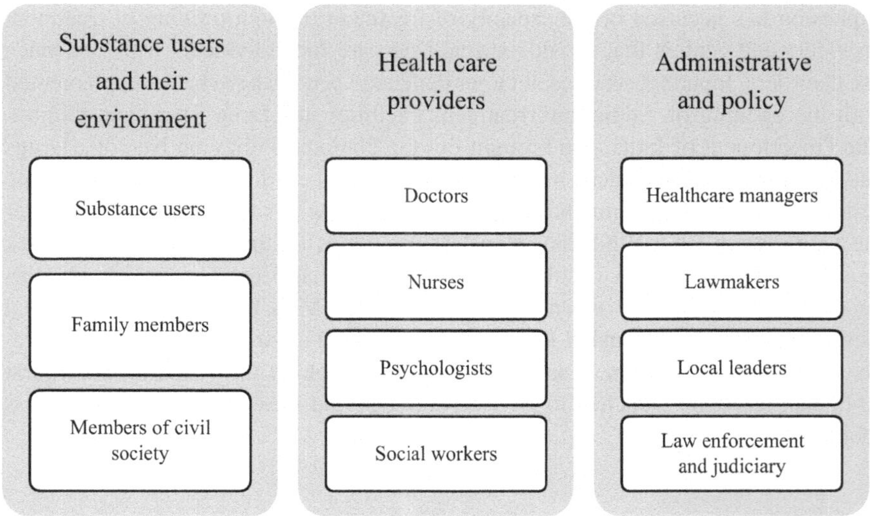

Fig. 5.1 Stakeholders in the substance use disorders help processes. *Source* Authors

and directions to individuals with substance use disorders from recovered 'addicts' about what could be done to abstain from substances and make positive changes. The subtle religious tonality of these groups, however, sometimes limits their acceptance in selected parts of the country. Another support-based approach that has been found to help some individuals with substance use disorders include 'Jamaat' (travel with a congregation for deeper religious understanding) among Muslims and seeking help from religious figures among Hindus.

Family members are quite often affected due to substance use and often are important support systems in treatment for individuals with substance use disorders (Sarkar et al. 2016). Several adverse consequences of substance use include domestic violence, burden, financial distress, psychological distress (which may even lead to psychiatric disorders), and courtesy stigma. Nonetheless, families not only provide coercion, impetus, and reasons for change and treatment engagement but also ensure the continuation of treatment and monitoring. Hence, their views are important in better treatment outcomes. Greater recognition of family interventions (formal and informal during clinical encounters) would probably utilize the strengths of the families in India in the therapeutic processes (Chadda and Deb 2013; Sarkar and Kaloiya 2019). We also need to be cognizant of changing family dynamics in the recent decades in India with the fragmentation of the family, smaller families, value shifts about occupational pursuits, greater recognition of the necessity of equality and gender sensitivity, legislative and judicial progress, and overall changes in societal outlook.

5.6 Public Mental Health Initiatives in India for Preventing Substance Abuse

Several public mental health efforts have been made in India to prevent substance abuse. Substance abuse prevention encompasses a range of measures varying from educational approaches in the community, integrating substance use-related counseling in general medical services, appropriate treatment of mental health conditions, harm-reduction measures, and enhancing resilience among students and young individuals. The efforts can be either government-driven, or may be propelled through the non-governmental organization sector, or may be initiated through the private sector (sometimes through their corporate social responsibility schemes). Some of these initiatives are enumerated as follows:

- Nasha Mukt Baharat Abhiyaan of the Government of India—This scheme envisages providing education pertaining to substance use and related problems. The three-pronged strategy involves curbing supply by the Narcotics Control Bureau; outreach, awareness, and demand reduction by Ministry of Social Justice and Empowerment; and provision of treatment facilities.

- A school program "I decide—I will not take drugs" was launched under the auspices of the United Nations Office of Drugs and Crime and the Ministry of Social Justice and Empowerment, Government of India (Pattojoshi and Tikka 2020). It reached about 400,000 students across 250 schools in several states of India.
- Another initiative known as Mobilizing Youth for Tobacco-Related Initiatives (MYTRI) was launched focusing on tobacco prevention. More than 14,000 students across 32 schools were reached in Delhi and Chennai as a part of this work.
- Among the states, the Punjab Substance Abuse Prevention Plan (PSAP) has a holistic approach to substance use prevention. It ranges from prevention to supply, demand, and harm-reduction measures. The program envisages collaboration between the government and the NGO sector.
- Several NGOs have been working in the field of prevention of substance use disorders. Some of the examples are available at (*List of NGOs for Drug Abuse Rehabilitation | Women & Child Development | Government of Assam, India* 2023). Some of these NGOs have health as their overall ambit of function.
- As a measure of capacity building, the National Drug Dependence Treatment Centre was involved in training of the General Duty of Medical Officers from various states of India. This was with the intent of increasing the number of medical officers who could provide treatment at early stages of substance use disorders or counsel patients for substance use cessation prior to the development of substance use disorder.
- NGOs working in the field of substance use disorders have developed educational curriculum material for addressing life skills for preventing drug use (Reid and Kalyani 2022). Similar life skills-based modules have also been developed from the government sector for use among school students (Uthaman et al. 2020).

5.7 Current Challenges in the Prevention of Substance Use Disorders in India

There are several challenges in the prevention of substance abuse in India. The major challenges with regard to prevention efforts are summarized in Box 5.1. The first and foremost is the lack of coordination among the stakeholders. India being a big and diverse country has probably too many stakeholders who can be accommodated on the table. This means that at some point in time, some of the voices are left out. Furthermore, hierarchies (implicit or explicit) and abeyance to authority or interest-based resistance may both result in coordination and direction of policy/efforts being affected, potentially resulting in a disarrayed profile of vehement efforts. The prevention efforts should preferably be aligned with each other, and different 'actors' tend to work according to their own mandates. However, some mandates (for example, providing opioid substitution) may not be aligned with another (rehabilitation aiming at a 'cure' of substance use disorder). Additionally, policies planned with best interests in mind do not have an objective measure of determining success (or failures) or of engaging meaningfully with the potential recipient of the efforts. This makes clear assessments of impact difficult, resulting in personal perceptions, peer appraisals, and projection as benchmarks of effect. The sustainability of the efforts is another consideration, as the political, societal, group, and individual commitment toward preventive efforts may wax and wane with time. The prevention strategies focus on one or two major means (for example, school information campaigns) and other prevention measures involving certain vulnerable populations. A common constraint of relying on one prevention mode versus another is the lack of culturally valid evidence. Local conditions, healthcare system characteristics, social outlook, and acceptable norms may have an influence on the efficacy, acceptability, and scalability of psychosocial interventions. Thus, there is a want for locally relevant proven interventions and strategies. And finally, human resource constraints are there, which can be partially circumvented by training teachers, nurses, and different cadres of doctors for prevention efforts.

Box 5.1: Major challenges in the prevention of substance abuse in India

Lack of coordination across stakeholders.
Alignment of prevention efforts.
Policy impact appraisal systems are yet to be in place.
Sustainability of prevention efforts.
Continuum of prevention strategies.
Lack of culturally valid evidence.
Human resource constraints.

5.8 Further Ways Forward in Substance Use Disorders in India

While there have been several notable strides in the recognition, advocacy, and treatment of substance use disorders in the country, there is much more to be done. Box 5.2 presents some of the options and directions that can be considered. The first aspect is the recognition of substance use disorders in the community and vulnerable populations. Substance use is often hidden and misreported (especially when there is a fear of legal consequences to disclosure of illicit substance use). Methods like respondent-driven sampling can help to reach out to this hidden population, but their application should also be cognizant of their challenges. Nonetheless, forays have to be made to understand the extent of substance use, especially gendered minorities, migrant populations, school and college populations, and commercial sex workers. Furthermore, female populations have been often under-represented in the assessed population, and they should also be systematically studied for the presence of substance use disorders.

Box 5.2: Ways ahead for recognition and treatment of substance use disorders in India

Recognition of substance use disorders

- Assessing vulnerable populations
- Assessing hidden 'users'
- Early warning systems for newer substances of use.

Treatment provision

- Mainstreaming of services
- Availability of a range of services
- Cultural adaptation of service.

Cross-talk and liaison

- Other treatment providers
- Law enforcement
- Community awareness and involvement.

Research

- Consistent use of validated methods
- Cross-cultural research
- International consortia.

Training

- Continued training of treatment providers
- Training of newer professionals
- Accreditation and quality control.

Treatment provisions for individuals with substance use disorders must be strengthened. Not only resource allocation is important, but the mainstreaming of services can help (by providing services in the context of general health care). Reduction of stigma among substance users and leveraging already existing healthcare services can be done by training currently posted healthcare staff in psychiatric, medical, surgical, and emergency services. Additionally, a range of treatment options should be made available. This may range from pharmacotherapy, psychotherapy, rehabilitation, neuromodulation, self-help, and other approaches. The National List of Essential Medicines should be revised keeping in view the necessity of substance use disorder treatment. We need to recognize the cultural context of the care process. Often, the patients and family members are seeking 'medicines' as a 'cure' for the 'disease' of substance use disorder. It can be a fair bit of a challenge to convince them about the utility of various approaches including counseling to 'control' the problem of substance use disorder. Psychotherapies also need to adapt to cultural demands, though we also should be able to cater to those who are ready and willing to engage with structured psychotherapy and its prerequisites.

There is a need for greater cross-talk of the medical providers with other treatment providers who cater to individuals with substance use disorders. Specialized addiction treatment services should be able to have an open dialogue with other specialists such as gastroenterologists, cardiologists, neurologists, and emergency medicine physicians who also cater to individuals with substance use disorders. Law enforcement and policymakers need to be sensitized about the addictive processes and the treatment of substance use disorders, and potential provisions can be made tweaking of laws (and enforcement of existing laws) to facilitate the treatment of those who require treatment. Community awareness and involvement can also help to use community resources to help people in recovery and strengthen avenues of community wellbeing.

The research and training landscape also needs some attention. Consistent use of validated methods of research and adoption of good research practices may help to enhance confidence in the research coming from the country. Cross-cultural research may be strengthened, to see whether the patterns, attributes, predictors, service delivery, and outcomes are similar across settings in the country or different. Participation in international consortia can help to contextualize the findings, and efforts have been made in that direction too (Bhad et al. 2023; Narasimha et al. 2022). Similarly, training can be enhanced for practitioners of various fields who deal with individuals with substance use disorders. Efforts have been made to develop a superspecialty in addiction psychiatry in India (De Jong et al. 2021). The expansion and entrenchment of this specialty should be cognizant of ground realities and would provide a focus for future concerted work in the field of substance use disorders in India. Furthermore, quality control of accreditation of a range of treatment providers (using suitable benchmarks and assessment criteria) would help to keep the field accountable, with known standards of care, and in high esteem among the medical fraternity.

5.9 Conclusion

India has recognized and made commendable efforts to tackle the problem of substance use disorders, with active involvement of mental health services. While efforts may have been made in India, it's imperative to acknowledge that addressing substance use disorders is a complex undertaking that requires sustained commitment from multiple sectors. Medical fraternity and healthcare services are one aspect of providing help to individuals suffering from substance use disorders. A comprehensive, evidence-based, and collaborative approach involving diverse stakeholders—such as the government, healthcare system, community organizations, and individuals—is vital to creating a significant and lasting impact on this public health challenge.

References

Aich, T. K., Sinha, V. K., Khess, C. R. J., & Singh, S. (2004). Demographic and Clinical Correlates of Substance Abuse Comorbidity in Schizophrenia. Indian Journal of Psychiatry, 46(2), 135–139.

Ambekar, A., Agrawal, A., Rao, R., Mishra, A. K., Khandelwal, S. K., Chadda, R. K., & on Behalf of the Group of Investigators for the National Survey on Extent and Pattern of Substance use in India. (2019). Magnitude of Substance Use in India. New Delhi: Ministry of Social Justice and Empowerment, Government of India.

Ambekar, A., Rao, R., Agrawal, A., & Kathiresan, P. (2018). Research on opioid substitution therapy in India: A brief, narrative review. Indian Journal of Psychiatry, 60(3), 265–270. https://doi.org/10.4103/psychiatry.IndianJPsychiatry_385_18.

ATS. (2023). https://www.unodc.org/wdr2013/en/ats.html.

Balhara, Y. P. S., Ghosh, A., Sarkar, S., Mahadevan, J., Pal, A., Narasimha, V. L., Kattula, D., Prasad, S., Parmar, A., & Kathiresan, P. (2022). Clinical care of patients with dual disorders in India: Diverse models of care delivery. Advances in Dual Diagnosis, 15(4), 227–243. https://doi.org/10.1108/ADD-09-2022-0025.

Basu, D., Ghosh, A., & Sarkar, S. (2016). Addictions in India. In Neuropathology of Drug Addictions and Substance Misuse (pp. 1025–1035). Academic Press.

Bhad, R., Achab, S., Rafei, P., Kathiresan, P., Ardabili, H. M., Butner, J. L., Orsolini, L., Melby, K., Farokhnia, M., & Narasimha, V. L. (2023). The scope and needs related to training, research, and mentorship among early-career addiction medicine professionals: An online global survey followed by expert group discussions. Global Mental Health, 10, e44. https://doi.org/10.1017/gmh.2023.35.

Bharadwaj, B., Selvakumar, N., & Kuppili, P. P. (2018). Pharmacotherapy for relapse prevention of alcohol use disorder in the Indian setting: A systematic review. Industrial Psychiatry Journal, 27(2), 163–171. https://doi.org/10.4103/ipj.ipj_79_17.

Chadda, R. K., & Deb, K. S. (2013). Indian family systems, collectivistic society and psychotherapy. Indian Journal of Psychiatry, 55(Suppl 2), S299. https://doi.org/10.4103/0019-5545.105555.

Chadda, R., Jain, R., Lal, R., Rao, R., Quraishi, R., Garg, P., Bala, N., Singh, R., Padhy, S., Basu, A., & Krishnan, V. (2023). Detection of New Psychoactive Substances among Substance Abuse Treatment Seekers in India—Multi Centric Study. Department of Revenue, Ministry of Finance, Government of India.

Chhabra, A., Hussain, S., & Rashid, S. (2021). Recent trends of tobacco use in India. Journal of Public Health, 29(1), 27–36. https://doi.org/10.1007/s10389-019-01091-3.

De Jong, C. A. J., Crockford, D., Welle-Strand, G., Iskandar, S., Sarkar, S., Haber, P. S., & Miller, M. (2021). Pathways to the Specialty Recognition of Addiction Medicine. In N. el-Guebaly, G. Carrà, M. Galanter, & A. M. Baldacchino (Eds.), Textbook of Addiction Treatment (pp. 837–852). Springer International Publishing. https://doi.org/10.1007/978-3-030-36391-8_58.

Dhawan, A., Chopra, A., & Ray, R. (2016). Preferences for Treatment Setting by Substance Users in India. Indian Journal of Psychological Medicine, 38(1), 42–45. https://doi.org/10.4103/0253-7176.175105.

Dorabjee JD, Samson LJ (1998) Self and community based opioid substitution among opioid dependent populations in the Indian sub-continent. Int J Drug Policy 9:411–416. https://doi.org/10.1016/S0955-3959(98)00057-7.

Kethineni S, Guyon L, Fennick RM (1995) Drug use in India: Historical traditions and current problems. Int J Comp Appl Crim Justice 19:211–221. https://doi.org/10.1080/01924036.1995.9678548.

Kumar, A., Mahajan, H., Chaturvedi, S., Kumar, A., Kumar, S., Sahoo, G. C., Das, V. N. R., & Pandey, K. (2023). Hepatitis C virus seroprevalence among patients enrolled at the opioid substitution therapy center in Bihar: A cross-sectional study. PLOS ONE, 18(6), e0287333. https://doi.org/10.1371/journal.pone.0287333.

Kuppili, P. P., Parmar, A., Gupta, A., & Balhara, Y. P. S. (2018). Role of Yoga in Management of Substance-use Disorders: A Narrative Review. Journal of Neurosciences in Rural Practice, 09(01), 117–122. https://doi.org/10.4103/jnrp.jnrp_243_17.

Mukherjee, P. S., Vishnubhatla, S., Amarapurkar, D. N., Das, K., Sood, A., Chawla, Y. K., Eapen, C. E., Boddu, P., Thomas, V., Varshney, S., Hidangmayum, D. S., Bhaumik, P., Thakur, B., Acharya, S. K., & Chowdhury, A. (2017). Etiology and mode of presentation of chronic liver diseases in India: A multi centric study. PLoS ONE, 12(10), e0187033. https://doi.org/10.1371/journal.pone.0187033.

Murthy, P., Manjunatha, N., Subodh, B. N., Chand, P. K., & Benegal, V. (2010). Substance use and addiction research in India. Indian Journal of Psychiatry, 52(Suppl1), S189–S199. https://doi.org/10.4103/0019-5545.69232.

Murthy, R. S. (2017). National Mental Health Survey of India 2015–2016. Indian Journal of Psychiatry, 59(1), 21–26. https://doi.org/10.4103/psychiatry.IndianJPsychiatry_102_17.

Narasimha, V. L., Butner, J. L., Hanafi, E., Farokhnia, M., Bhad, R., Chalabianloo, F., Kouimtsidis, C., Baldacchino, A., & Arunogiri, S. (2022). Harm reduction and abstinence-based models for treatment of substance use disorders during the COVID-19 pandemic: A global perspective. BJPsych International, 19(3), 66–69. https://doi.org/10.1192/bji.2022.1.

Pachuau, L. N., Tannous, C., Dhami, M. V., & Agho, K. E. (2022). HIV among people who inject drugs in India: A systematic review. BMC Public Health, 22(1), 1529. https://doi.org/10.1186/s12889-022-13922-2.

Parmar, A., Bhatia, G., Sharma, P., & Pal, A. (2023a). Understanding the epidemiology of substance use in India: A review of nationwide surveys. Indian Journal of Psychiatry, 65(5), 498–505. https://doi.org/10.4103/indianjpsychiatry.indianjpsychiatry_791_22.

Parmar, A., Narasimha, V. L., & Nath, S. (2023b). National Drug Laws, Policies, and Programs in India: A Narrative Review. Indian Journal of Psychological Medicine, 025371762311705. https://doi.org/10.1177/02537176231170534.

Parmar, A., Pal, A., & Sharma, P. (2023c). National List of Essential Medicines 2022 of India: Perspectives from Psychiatrists. Indian Journal of Psychological Medicine, 45(4), 411–414. https://doi.org/10.1177/02537176231155328.

Patil K, Pandey A (2022) Drug Trafficking: A Growing Problem for India. Asian J Forensic Sci 1:34–41. https://doi.org/10.55141/AJFS.2022.000112.

Pattojoshi A, Tikka SK (2020) School-based substance use disorder prevention in India: A brief appraisal. Indian J Psychiatry 62:427–430. https://doi.org/10.4103/psychiatry.IndianJPsychiatry_43_19.

Rathi, R. B., & Rathi, B. J. (2020). Ayurveda perspectives toward prevention and management of nicotine and alcohol dependence: A review. Journal of Indian System of Medicine, 8(1), 14–20. https://doi.org/10.4103/JISM.JISM_68_19.

Ray, R. (2004). The Extent, Pattern and Trends of Drug Abuse in India: National Survey. Ministry of Social Justice and Empowerment, Government of India & United Nations Office on Drugs and Crime, Regional Office for South Asia.

Reid G, Kalyani V (2022) NAVCHETNA: A New Consciousness on Life Skills and Drug Education for School Children: Teacher Trainer Resource Modules. Society for Promotion of Youth and Masses and Ministry of Social Justice and Empowerment, New Delhi.

Sarkar, J., Murthy, P., & Singh, S. P. (2003). Psychiatric Morbidity of Cannabis Abuse. Indian Journal of Psychiatry, 45(3), 182–188.

Sarkar, S., & Ghosh, A. (2019). The magnitude and vicissitudes of substance use disorders in India. Indian Journal of Social Psychiatry, 35(2), 99–101. https://doi.org/10.4103/ijsp.ijsp_50_19.

Sarkar, S., & Varshney, M. (2017). Yoga and substance use disorders: A narrative review. Asian Journal of Psychiatry, 25, 191–196. https://doi.org/10.1016/j.ajp.2016.10.021.

Sarkar, S., Kaloiya, G. S., (2019). Family-based interventions for substance use disorders must look at the local needs and service delivery. Journal of Mental Health and Human Behaviour, 24(1), 1-3. https://doi.org/10.4103/jmhhb.jmhhb_53_19.

Sarkar, S., Patra, B. N., Kattimani, S., & others. (2016). Substance use disorder and the family: An Indian perspective. Medical Journal of Dr. DY Patil University, 9(1), 7–14. https://doi.org/10.4103/0975-2870.172413.

Sarkar, S., Tom, A., Das, S., Bharadwaj, B., & Ghosh, A. (2022). Systematic review: Rates and determinants of relapse to alcohol: A systematic review of Indian studies. Journal of Mental Health and Human Behaviour, 27(1), 8–18. https://doi.org/10.4103/jmhhb.jmhhb_191_20.

Sharma HK (1996) Sociocultural Perspective of Substance Use in India. Subst Use Misuse 31:1689–1714. https://doi.org/10.3109/10826089609063997.

Sharma HK, Tripathi BM, Pelto PJ (2010) The evolution of alcohol use in India. AIDS Behav 14 Suppl 1:S8-17. https://doi.org/10.1007/s10461-010-9727-7.

Singh, S., & Balhara, Y. P. S. (2016). A Review of Indian Research on Co-occurring Psychiatric Disorders and Alcohol use Disorders. Indian Journal of Psychological Medicine, 38(1), 10. https://doi.org/10.4103/0253-7176.175089.

Singh, S., & Balhara, Y. P. S. (2017). A review of Indian research on co-occurring cannabis use disorders & psychiatric disorders. The Indian Journal of Medical Research, 146(2), 186–195. https://doi.org/10.4103/ijmr.IJMR_791_15.

Singh, U., Singh, S., & Ram, H. (2023). Homoeopathic Perspective in the Management of Substance Use Disorders: A Systematic Review. Journal of Complementary and Alternative Medical Research, 22(4), 33–47. https://doi.org/10.9734/jocamr/2023/v22i4465.

Uthaman SP, Pillai RR, George S, et al (2020) Life Skills Education for Prevention of Substance Use Among Adolescents. Institute of Mental Health and Neurosciences, Kozhikode; National Institute of Social Defence, New Delhi; Postgraduate Institute of Medical Education and Research, Chandigarh, Kozhikode, Kerala, India.

Chapter 6
Current Perspectives on Substance Use Disorders in Nepal

Pawan Sharma, Sagun Ballav Pant, and Kedar Marahatta

6.1 Introduction

Nestled amidst the world's tallest mountains, Nepal is a landlocked nation. Large plains of the Indian subcontinent border it to the south, east, and west, while China's high Tibetan plateau borders it to the north. With a population of almost 30 million, the nation has a total land area of 147,181 square kilometers. Nepal is a transit hub for drug trafficking due to its physical location and proximity to the "Golden Triangle" and "Golden Crescent" (Thapliyal 1999). Drugs like cannabis and alcohol have been used in Nepal for centuries and have cultural significance. Cannabis especially has been used in religious celebrations as a means of honoring deities and for spiritual practices (Shakya et al. 2021). Also, opium is used to treat many ailments especially in hilly regions in the form of tincture and powder. The use of these psychoactive substances as part of the cultural norms did not create major social problems during that period.

In Nepal, the mid-1960s and early 1970s witnessed the emergence of the problem of psychoactive substance use. Due to the easy and affordable access to strong cannabis products, even in the local pubs and restaurants on the streets of Kathmandu, the capital city of Nepal, in the mid-1960s, the city was considered a significant destination for many "*hippies*." Initially, only a small number of elderly Nepalese people, as well as saints and hermits, smoked "*ganja*" and "*hashish*," but the hippies quickly replaced them with opiates, primarily heroin. Because of their way of life and

P. Sharma (✉)
Department of Psychiatry, School of Medicine, Patan Academy of Health Sciences, Lalitpur, Nepal
e-mail: pawan60@gmail.com

S. B. Pant
Department of Psychiatry, Institute of Medicine, Tribhuvan University, Kathmandu, Nepal

K. Marahatta
WHO Country Office for Nepal, Kathmandu, Nepal

S. M. Y. Arafat and S. K. Kar (eds.), *Current Perspectives on Substance Use Disorders in South Asia*, https://doi.org/10.1007/978-981-97-6619-2_6

mindset, a large number of young people in Nepal started abusing drugs (Shrestha 1992). The first case of heroin dependence that was treated in Nepal was in December 1976 when a patient was referred from a medical ward for psychiatric consultation (Kunwar 1981). The rehabilitation center for Nepali drug abusers was started by the NGO sector in 1976 (Upadhyaya 2015). Though the reports of heroin use started appearing by the 1960s, the number of heroin users considerably increased by the 1980s. There was a shift in the pattern of drug use from heroin chasing to injectable opioid preparations such as buprenorphine in the following decade (Ambekar et al. 2013). This change is primarily driven by the low cost of injectables, their easy availability, and the rising cost of heroin. Most drugs found on the streets come from unrestricted pharmacies and medical supply stores that users get from their friends, as well as neighboring countries (Chatterjee et al. 1996). The use of the "South-Asian cocktail," which is injecting benzodiazepines, antihistamines, and opioids simultaneously, is one big cause for concern. The risks to this group's medical, social, economic, legal, and health outcomes have increased as a result of this injection modality (Ojha et al. 2014). As drug users have switched from smoking or ingesting drugs to injecting them, more issues have emerged especially the burden of HIV/AIDS and viral hepatitis. Substance abuse has thus developed into a complicated problem in Nepal.

6.2 Epidemiology and Burden of Substance Abuse in Nepal

Nepal Drug Users Survey 2020 (NDUS 2020) conducted by the Ministry of Home Affairs (MOHA) using the indirect technique of multiplier/benchmark method and interview of 2000 samples of current drug users estimated that the number of current drug users was 1,30,424 in Nepal. Among them 93.3% were male and 6.7% were female. 76.2% of drug users were below the age of 30 years. The 2019 survey also showed the highest use was of cannabis (82.7%), tranquilizers (73.1%), Opiates (46.8%), inhalants, hallucinogens, and stimulants. The trend was similar to the 2013 survey on hard drugs. Among the total drug users, 69.1% of drug users were People Who Injected Drug (PWID) and 70.9% used poly-drugs (Nepal Drug Users Survey 2020).

As per the National Mental Health Survey 2020 conducted among 9200 adults above 18 years using translated and adapted Nepalese version of the Mini International Neuropsychiatric Interview (MINI), it was seen that the prevalence of Alcohol Use Disorder (past 12 months) was 4.2% and other Substance Use Disorder (past 12 months) was 0.2% excluding nicotine use (Dhimal et al. 2022). The WHO STEP-wise approach to NCD risk factor surveillance (STEPS) survey of Nepal conducted among 5593 adults of 15–69 years showed 28.9% (48.3% male and 11.6% females) were current users of tobacco, in any form. 17.1% of adults smoked tobacco and 18.3% used smokeless tobacco. However, there has been a decreasing trend in tobacco use as compared to the survey of 2013 where the prevalence was 37.1% (Mandal 2022). Also, the 2019 STEPS survey showed 23.9% of adults (38.6% of men, 10.8%

of women) were current alcohol users (consumed alcohol in the past 12 months). Almost 1 in 8 men (11.7%) drank daily or almost daily (Dhimal et al. 2019).

In the western region of Nepal, a cross-sectional survey conducted in schools with 460 students aged 15 to 19 revealed that 27.4% of teenagers enrolled in school had used at least one kind of psychoactive substance. Products containing tobacco (59.3%) were the most commonly used psychoactive substances, followed by cannabis (55.6%), marijuana (35.8%), hashish (23.5%), alcohol (22.2%), heroin (18.5%), nitrazepam pills (14.8%), sulfa (13.6%), and opium (13.6%), respectively (Bhandari et al. 2021a, b). Also, another study in Eastern Nepal among 291 drug abusers using the friendship snowball sampling method showed that 14% of users were below the age of 20 years and for the majority (58%) the gateway drug was marijuana (Niraula et al. 2015).

A case–control study among 150 matched pairs of drug users and controls in Eastern Nepal showed that less than 10 years of education, feelings of domination, short temper, undeniability nature, and depression were strong correlates of drug abuse (Niraula et al. 2009). A qualitative study among youths with substance use problems identified the problems in families like parental separation, detachment from family members, and poor parental supervision as contributing factors. Also, cultural acceptance of substances, easy availability of psychoactive substances in local markets, peer pressures, academic stress, and influence of media and celebrities as other factors contributed to substance use (Bhandari et al. 2021a, b). A school-based cross-sectional study among 460 students from 15 to 19 years of age identified being male and having peers or family members that used psychoactive substances as associated factors for the psychoactive substance use (Bhandari et al. 2021a, b).

6.3 Help Seeking Pattern for Substance Use Disorder in Nepal

In a descriptive study among 51 cases of alcohol dependent, 96% used some home remedies, 23.5% visited traditional healers, and 12% local drug stores. The reasons cited by them for treatment delay were not considering alcohol as a problem (68.6%), having no idea about treatment (17.6%), poverty (10%), and conservative attitude (10%) (Shakya et al. 2011). In a community sample of 1,983 adults in a district of central Nepal, 5% were screened positive for alcohol use disorder and only 1.3% sought treatment. The major barriers for help seeking were: not being able to afford the financial cost; being unsure where to go to get mental health care; concern that they might be seen as 'crazy'; concern that it might harm my chances when applying for jobs; and concern that they might be seen as weak for having alcohol-related health problems (Luitel et al. 2017). The repeat survey of the same cohort showed an increase in help seeking but the change was not statistically significant in terms of treatment coverage and barrier to mental health care (Luitel et al. 2019). A community-based study of 3482 adults showed among the screened positive for alcohol use disorder,

38% spoke to another person about their alcohol as problem and 80% had internalized stigma (Rathod et al. 2018).

6.4 Behavioral Addictions in Nepal

The prevalence of problem Internet use among Nepalese students was 12.9% as per a multinational cross-sectional study using Generalized Problematic Internet Use Scale-2 and the major correlate was psychological distress (Balhara et al. 2019). The range of prevalence of Internet addiction has been 4.7% to 39% as per different studies using different scales and cut-offs. The Internet addiction was associated with relationship with parents, parental control over the Internet use, perceived loneliness, male gender, lesser duration of weekly physical or sports activity, lower life satisfaction, psychological distress, poor sleep quality, etc. (Bhandari et al. 2017; Sharma et al. 2023, 2020; Acharya et al. 2023; Karki et al. 2021). Internet gaming disorder was seen among 2.9% of students from secondary and higher secondary levels as per a web-based cross-sectional survey among 417 students and was associated with aggression scores (Joshi et al. 2022). Another study showed the prevalence of gaming disorder to be 8.5% among medical students during COVID-19 lock down period (Shrestha et al. 2020a, b). The studies regarding other behavioral addictions are lacking.

6.5 Emerging Addictions in Nepal

The patterns of psychoactive substance use have witnessed some changes over the last few years. The slow but steady penetration of amphetamine-like stimulants is apparent among people who use drugs especially in major cities. Also, Nepal being an economy heavily dependent on tourism has experienced some surge in the use of hallucinogens like "magic mushrooms" and other party drugs. Most importantly, a novel pattern of poly-substance uses in the form of "formula" is gaining popularity among youths. A typical "formula" is a combination of multidose of pharmaceutical opioid (tramadol, tapentadole), anti-cough medication (dextromeorphan and phenylephrine), anti-spasmodic (dicyclomine), and Gabapentinoid (Pregabalin and gabapentin) (NDUS 2020). These patterns of psychoactive substance use are a new challenge for service providers (Sharma 2021).

6.6 Available Services

6.6.1 *Specialized Long-Term or Residential Treatment (Treatment and Rehabilitation Centers)*

This is one of the main approaches used for the management of substance use disorder in Nepal. The management of psychoactive substance use at long-term residential centers (rehabilitation centers) falls under the responsibility of MOHA, which is not consistent with the global paradigm of substance use disorder being regarded as a chronic health condition. About 300 treatment and rehabilitation centers are operational in Nepal. Across most treatment and rehabilitation centers, people who use drugs live in a communal environment with others who have similar conditions and commit to abstaining from psychoactive substances. Staying in a residential setting helps in the management of stressful environments and triggers, promoting abstinence and recovery. The most common modality of residential treatment in practice is the "therapeutic community" model (Gyawali et al. 2016). The program includes reducing the risk of relapse, developing coping skills, providing treatment for co-occurring disorders, improving personal and social functioning, building effective relationships, building a healthy family environment, reintegrating into the community, acquiring new social skills, acquiring healthier lifestyle habits, and advancing education and vocational skills (Pathak and Saxena 2019). However, there is a lack of a standardized treatment approach and most treatment and rehabilitation centers provide services based on personal experiences that lack scientific rigor and are sometimes inhumane as well. To address this, The Ministry of Home Affairs' "Directive on the Operation of Treatment and Rehabilitation Centers for people who use drugs, 2018" offers important guidelines regarding the licensing requirements for treatment and rehabilitation facilities, including requirements for infrastructure, staffing, responsibilities, monitoring, supervision, and compensation as well as the standardization of treatment fees (Pant et al. 2023).

6.6.2 *In-Patient Services in Psychiatry Unit (Teaching Hospitals and Some Government Hospitals)*

Specialized short-term inpatient treatment services for substance use disorder are provided through psychiatry units of general hospitals, private hospitals, and some government hospitals. These treatments focus more on detoxification and medically assisted withdrawal lasting for up to 4 weeks coupled with psychological interventions like motivational enhancement therapy, cognitive behavior therapy, and other individual and group interventions. One of the drawbacks of this form of service in Nepal is the lack of continuity of treatment in the community and the absence of engagement of service users and people with lived experiences in the management plan. The academic institutions run post-graduate programs where addiction medicine is a major component. Institute of Medicine has started a one-year post-graduate clinical fellowship program in addiction psychiatry from 2024 which is a major milestone.

6.6.3 Non-specialized Settings

Health professionals, medical officers, general practitioners, and nurses trained in the mental health treatment curriculum based on mhGAP have some level of proficiency in the management of alcohol and substance use disorder (Luitel et al. 2023). Health professionals trained in this curriculum can provide out-patient-based detoxification services (for alcohol use) and basic counseling in line with brief intervention for substance use disorder. Furthermore, one of the main objectives of non-specialized settings is screening and referral (Wang et al. 2007).

6.6.4 Specialized Out-Patient Treatment

In Nepal, Opioid agonist treatment services are provided through specialized out-patient treatment, which are directly observed treatment services for people with opioid use disorder. Such services are provided through government hospitals and nongovernmental organizations. These sites dispense methadone and buprenorphine on a daily basis for people with opioid use disorder (especially people who inject drugs) and additionally psychosocial support which is provided by a social support unit that includes people with lived experience, survivors, and champions.

6.6.5 Community-Based Approaches

Survivor-led fellowships, both Narcotics anonymous and Alcohol anonymous, provide some form of network-based services mostly limited to major cities in the country (Neupane and Bramness 2014). However, the availability of fellowship services is limited and restricted to a few cities across Nepal.

6.6.6 Harm Reduction Strategy in Nepal

Nepal was the first country in South Asia to establish a "Harm Reduction" program for people who use drugs. The Methadone Maintenance Treatment Program (MMTP) started in Nepal in 1994 at the Mental Hospital Lagankhel in Kathmandu valley (Shrestha et al. 2020a, b). Nepal is considered as one of the first countries in South Asia to start Methadone Maintenance Therapy (MMT) as Opioid agonist treatment (OAT) program (Ambekar et al. 2013). The Methadone Maintenance Treatment Program was stopped in 2002. There were about five years of gap in OAT services in Nepal. In November 2007, the Department of Psychiatry, Tribhuvan University Teaching Hospital, started the Methadone Maintenance Treatment Program in Kathmandu as an "Emergency Response for IDUs" under the financial and technical support of UNODC, GIZ, and in collaboration with the Ministry of Home Affairs of the Government of Nepal. Currently, the Needle Syringe Program (NSP) and Opioid agonist treatment (OAT) are the key interventions for people who inject drugs in Nepal which are funded by the Global Fund to fight AIDS, Tuberculosis, and malaria ("Opioid Substitution Therapy in Nepal" 2016) (Rao et al. 2013). The program is operated based on the programmatic guideline endorsed by the Ministry of Home Affairs (2013) and clinical guidelines drafted by the National Center for AIDS and STI Control (NCASC). Under the leadership of (NCASC), currently, the coverage of harm reduction services spans across 28 districts in Nepal. There are in total 14 OAT sites spread across major metropolitan cities, which provide services to a total of 1200 clients daily (NCASC 2020). People who use drugs in Nepal continue to lack access to sustainable, comprehensive health and psychosocial care and support systems. Despite being reintroduced almost 18 years back, OAT services have insufficient coverage, are concentrated only in urban areas, are unevenly distributed as well as there are other structural barriers including inflexible take-home dispensing and clinic timing. Additionally, OAT services have also not been able to effectively collaborate with other harm reduction services like needle and syringe programs and rehabilitation services.

6.7 Physical and Psychiatric Co-morbidity with Substance Abuse

Studies in Nepal about mental health co-morbidity among people who use drugs are very few. In one study done among 180 service users who were managed across seven residential treatment facilities for alcohol and drug use disorders in the Kathmandu valley of Nepal, more than half (51.1%) had experienced serious psychological distress in the previous month (Gyawali et al. 2016). A recent study done among OAT service users in Nepal found every fourth OAT service user experienced serious psychological distress in the last four weeks. Additionally, lifetime suicidality and lifetime depression were diagnosed in 26% and 24.2%, respectively, while current suicidality and depression were noticeably lower. The other substantial diagnoses were alcohol use disorder, PTSD, generalized anxiety disorder, lifetime psychotic disorder, and antisocial personality disorder. This study also reported that almost one in two OAT service users had co-morbid medical conditions grouped together which included tuberculosis, diabetes mellitus, hypertension, HIV, viral hepatitis, and thrombosis (Pant et al. 2022). According to the National Integrated Biological Behavioral Surveillance among people who inject drugs, the prevalence of HIV and hepatitis C among males was 2.8% and 13.3% while it was slightly less for females (HIV/AIDS Data Hub for the Asia Pacific 2022). Similarly, the cross-sectional studies have identified the co-morbidity of cannabis use disorder and alcohol with anxiety, depression, and psychosis (Sedain 2013; Shakya et al. 2021).

6.8 Law and Policy Related to Substance Abuse in Nepal

The legal foundation for drug control matters in Nepal is the Narcotic Drugs Control Act, 1976. Cannabis, medicinal cannabis, opium, processed opium, plants and leaves of coca, any substance prepared with mixing opium, coca extract, including mixtures or salts, any natural or synthetic narcotic drug, psychotropic substance and their salts, and other substances as may be specified by the Nepal Gazette notification are all considered narcotic drugs according to Section 3(a). Anyone who cultivates, produces, prepares, buys, sells, distributes, exports or imports, stores, or consumes any kind of narcotic drug faces a fine and a maximum sentence of life in prison (Nepal Law Commission 1976). While the non-physician-prescribed consumption of narcotics drugs is a criminal offense, the Act makes provision for the prevention and treatment of drug users. The Department of Narcotics Control and Disaster Management, under the MOHA, has overarching responsibility for narcotics issues in Nepal. In 2018, the Ministry of Home Affairs endorsed the "Directive on the Operation of Treatment and Rehabilitation Centers for the users of Narcotic Drugs" (Ministry of Home Affairs 2018). There have been other guiding documents prepared over a period of time but the common theme has been the identification of substance use disorder as a legal issue and failing to address substance use disorder as a health issue needing treatment. The extent of this criminalization of a complex medical condition, i.e., substance use disorder can be understood from the fact that one in two drug users have a history of being arrested by police and 21% of the total prison population in Nepal are actually drug offenders (Human Rights and Drug Policies in Nepal 2021). The MOHA recently endorsed a five-year action plan, the "Narcotic Drug Prevention and Control National Master Plan" which aims for policy reforms including formulation of a standardized treatment protocol for treatment and rehabilitation center, awareness and education programs that are delivered through various settings including schools, institutional partnership, expansion of other treatment services including harm reduction interventions, and research in emergent issues like the legalization of cannabis (Ministry of Home Affairs 2023). WHO in collaboration with both ministries (MOHP and MOHA) is partnering in developing a standardized treatment package for alcohol and substance use in Nepal which will be published soon.

6.9 Current Status of Research on Substance Abuse in Nepal

The research base in Nepal regarding substance use disorder has mainly focused on epidemiology. The nation-wide surveys regarding substance use have been conducted at regular intervals. The need for research for standalone substance uses and as co-morbid conditions to other diseases and disorders has been realized. Most of the research have been done by the medical colleges in the treatment seeking population and are mostly cross-sectional in nature. The NGOs are involved in the research mainly in the community setups. However, there is still a dearth of research regarding the intervention.

6.10 Future Direction for Services Development

Though there have been steps taken in different domains of management of substance use disorder still more needs to be done. There are a wide range of challenges in Nepal like huge treatment gap, poor help seeking, minimal funding for research in substance use disorder, inadequate and inequitable manpower, poor referral system, high stigma, lack of collaboration, and failure to recognize the medical and biological model of substance use disorder. There have been major concerns regarding the human right violation of human rights by people using psychoactive substances as per a nation-wide consultation with representatives of communities and civil society and focus group discussions with women and youth-led organizations. The major points focused were the prevalence of psychoactive substance use especially injectable and the prevalence of HIV among them, criminalization, lack of access to treatment, abuses in private treatment centers, poor uptake of harm reduction, and disproportionate impact on women who use substances (Human Rights and Drug Policies in Nepal 2021). We have provided a few recommendations for future directions for the proper management of substance use disorder in Nepal.

6.10.1 Providing Range of Services

There is a need for providing a range of services that are available, acceptable, and affordable starting from acute treatment, recovery, and rehabilitation. This could be done in a continuum from general hospital setting to a residential harm or day-care services. The plans of recovery and rehabilitation should be individualized, needs-based, and participatory based on informed decisions made by the individual about their own treatment plan. There should be proper monitoring and supervision of the service providers. The treatment should also acknowledge the special needs of vulnerable populations like school children, sexual minorities, co-morbid mental health issues, women, etc.

6.10.2 Capacity Building

For this, there is a need to increase the capacity of the mental health care workforce as well as infrastructures for Substance use care ranging from addiction specialists among psychiatrists, psychologists, occupational therapists, social workers, peer educators, outreach workers, and nursing and other health professionals. A universal training curriculum can be used for the provision of training targeting different levels of service providers.

6.10.3 Building the Evidence Base

Nepal needs its own culturally appropriate guidelines for policy and practice reforms. For this, extensive research is required to establish what works and what doesn't in the Nepalese population. Though plenty of international evidence for the prevention and treatment of substance use disorders is available there is a need to adopt and/or develop local innovations for both identification and management.

6.10.4 Decriminalization of Substance Use

Decriminalization of drug use and possession is an important and effective approach that shifts resources from punishment to public health. This would in turn reduce the negative impacts of drug use (Bratberg et al. 2023). This can reduce fear of arrest, stigma, and discrimination and encourage more people with substance use issues to seek treatment. Considering the global atmosphere and evidence, decriminalizing cannabis use can be a starting point.

6.10.5 Administrative Responsibilities

There is an urgent need for taking up leadership role by the Ministry of Health and Population for the formulation of treatment guidelines, guidelines for treatment centers, and implementation of all programs and services related to substance use disorder including harm reduction. The MOHA has been taking up overarching responsibility for narcotics issues in Nepal which needs a shift of responsibility.

6.10.6 Multisectoral Collaboration

There is a need to develop coordination and partnership among different stakeholders including representatives from relevant ministries, law enforcement authorities, academics, people with lived experience including champions, relevant NGOs, current service users, and self-help groups.

6.10.7 Integration with the Education Sector

There should be school-based programs to increase awareness about substance use. There should also be integration of these awareness materials in the curriculum which would help to shape the understanding of youths.

6.11 Conclusion

Substance use in Nepal is a major public health concern. There have been epidemiological studies which have highlighted the problem statement. There is the availability of different setups ranging from general hospitals to rehabilitation centers for the treatment of substance use. There is a major lack of adherence to monitoring guidelines by the rehabilitation centers. There is a need to take responsibility by the Ministry of Health and population regarding the issues related to the treatment and services for people with drug use, and research initiatives in order to develop culturally contextualized interventions and treatment protocols.

References

Acharya, S., Adhikari, L., Khadka, S., Paudel, S., & Kaphle, M. (2023). Internet Addiction and Its Associated Factors among Undergraduate Students in Kathmandu, Nepal. *Journal of Addiction, 2023*, e8782527. https://doi.org/10.1155/2023/8782527

Ambekar, A., Rao, R., Pun, A., Kumar, S., & Kishore, K. (2013). The trajectory of methadone maintenance treatment in Nepal. *International Journal of Drug Policy, 24*(6), e57–e60. https://doi.org/10.1016/j.drugpo.2013.06.001

Bhandari, P. M., Neupane, D., Rijal, S., Thapa, K., Mishra, S. R., & Poudyal, A. K. (2017). Sleep quality, internet addiction and depressive symptoms among undergraduate students in Nepal. *BMC Psychiatry, 17*(1), 106. https://doi.org/10.1186/s12888-017-1275-5

Bhandari, T. R., Khatiwada, B., Rajbhandari, B., Bestman, A., Mistry, S. K., Rayamajhee, B., Rawal, L. B., & Yadav, U. N. (2021a). A qualitative study to understand drivers of psychoactive substance use among Nepalese youth. *PLOS ONE, 16*(11), e0259021. https://doi.org/10.1371/journal.pone.0259021

Bhandari, T. R., Paudel, G., Bestman, A., Thapa, T. B., Gwayali, C. P., Ghimire, B., Sharma, S., & Yadav, U. N. (2021b). *Use of Psychoactive Substance and its Associated Factors among*

School Adolescents in Rupandehi District of Nepal. http://elibrary.nhrc.gov.np:8080/handle/20.500.14356/1140

Bratberg, J. P., Simmons, A., Arya, V., Bhatia, A., & Vakharia, S. P. (2023). Support, don't punish: Drug decriminalization is harm reduction. *Journal of the American Pharmacists Association: JAPhA, 63*(1), 224–229. https://doi.org/10.1016/j.japh.2022.12.017

Chatterjee, A., Uprety, L., Chapagain, M., & Kafle, K. (1996). Drug abuse in Nepal: A rapid assessment study. *Bulletin on Narcotics, 48*(1–2), 11–33.

Dhimal, M., Bista, B., Bhattarai, S., Dixit, L. P., & Hyder, M. (n.d.). *Noncommunicable Disease Risk Factors: STEPS Survey Nepal 2019 [Internet]. Kathmandu, Nepal: Nepal Health Research Council; 2020.*

Dhimal, M., Dahal, S., Adhikari, K., Koirala, P., Bista, B., Luitel, N., Pant, S., Marahatta, K., Shakya, S., Sharma, P., Ghimire, S., Gyanwali, P., Ojha, S. P., & Jha, A. K. (2022). A Nationwide Prevalence of Common Mental Disorders and Suicidality in Nepal: Evidence from National Mental Health Survey, 2019–2020. *Journal of Nepal Health Research Council, 19*(4), 740–747. https://doi.org/10.33314/jnhrc.v19i04.4017

Gyawali, B., Choulagai, B. P., Paneru, D. P., Ahmad, M., Leppin, A., & Kallestrup, P. (2016). Prevalence and correlates of psychological distress symptoms among patients with substance use disorders in drug rehabilitation centers in urban Nepal: A cross-sectional study. *BMC Psychiatry, 16*(1), 314. https://doi.org/10.1186/s12888-016-1003-6

HIV/AIDS Data Hub for the Asia Pacific. (2022). *HIV/AIDS Data Hub for the Asia Pacific*. Retrieved from https://www.aidsdatahub.org

Human rights and drug policies in Nepal. (2021). IDPC. Retrieved from https://idpc.net/publications/2021/12/human-rights-and-drug-policies-in-nepal

Joshi, A., Sharma, K., Sigdel, D., Thapa, T., & Mehta, R. (2022). *Internet Gaming Disorder and Aggression among Students on School Closure during COVID-19 Pandemic*. http://elibrary.nhrc.gov.np:8080/handle/20.500.14356/1003

Karki, K., Singh, D. R., Maharjan, D., C, S. K., Shrestha, S., & Thapa, D. K. (2021). Internet addiction and sleep quality among adolescents in a peri-urban setting in Nepal: A cross-sectional school-based survey. *PLOS ONE, 16*(2), e0246940. https://doi.org/10.1371/journal.pone.0246940

Kunwar, D. R. B. (1981). Treatment techniques of drug dependents in Nepal. *The First National Seminar and Workshop on Drug Abuse And Addiction*, 20–22.

Luitel, N. P., Garman, E. C., Jordans, M. J. D., & Lund, C. (2019). Change in treatment coverage and barriers to mental health care among adults with depression and alcohol use disorder: A repeat cross sectional community survey in Nepal. *BMC Public Health, 19*(1), 1350. https://doi.org/10.1186/s12889-019-7663-7

Luitel, N. P., Jordans, M. J. D., Kohrt, B. A., Rathod, S. D., & Komproe, I. H. (2017). Treatment gap and barriers for mental health care: A cross-sectional community survey in Nepal. *PLoS ONE, 12*(8), e0183223. https://doi.org/10.1371/journal.pone.0183223

Luitel, N. P., Pudasaini, K., Pokhrel, P., Lamichhane, B., Gautam, K., Adhikari, S., Makhmud, A., Salisbury, T. T., Votruba, N., Green, E., Chowdhary, N., Jordans, M. J. D., Kohrt, B. A., Dua, T., Thornicroft, G., & Carswell, K. (2023). Development and functioning of the mobile app-based mh-GAP intervention guide in detection and treatment of people with mental health conditions in primary healthcare settings in Nepal. *Cambridge Prisms: Global Mental Health, 10*, e90. https://doi.org/10.1017/gmh.2023.69

Mandal, A. K. (2022). Trend of tobacco use: Reviewing the STEPS surveys conducted in Nepal. *Journal of Health Promotion, 10*(1), 89–100.

Ministry of Home Affairs. (2018). Directive on the Operation of Treatment and Rehabilitation Center for the users of Narcotic Drugs. Retrieved from https://www.drugportal.gov.np/assets/uploads/publications/5c6eea2eec41f1550686500.pdf

Nepal Law Commission. (1976). Narcotic Drugs (Control) Act, 2033 (1976). Retrieved from https://lawcommission.gov.np/en/?cat=407

Ministry of Home Affairs. (2023). *National Master Plan on Prevention and Control of Narcotic Drugs*. Retrieved from https://moha.gov.np/en/page/national-master-plan-on-prevention-and-control-of-narcotic-drugs-2

NCASC (2020). Retrieved from https://www.ncasc.gov.np/WAD2020/Factsheet-2020-S.pdf

Nepal Drug Users Survey: 2076. (2020). Government of Nepal, Ministry of Home Affairs.

Neupane, S. P., & Bramness, J. G. (2014). Who seeks treatment for alcohol problems? Demography and alcohol-use characteristics of patients in taboo and non-taboo drinking groups attending professional alcohol services in Nepal. *Asian Journal of Psychiatry, 12*, 82–87. https://doi.org/10.1016/j.ajp.2014.06.017

Niraula, S. R., Chhetri, D. B., & Connell, F. A. (2015). *Drug abuse pattern and risk taking behaviors among drug abusers in Dharan, Nepal.*

Niraula, S. R., Chhetry, D. B., Singh, G. K., Nagesh, S., & Shyangwa, P. M. (2009). Risk Factors for Drug Abuse Among Nepalese Samples Selected from a Town of Eastern Nepal. *International Journal of Mental Health and Addiction, 7*(3), 430–440. https://doi.org/10.1007/s11469-009-9217-1

Ojha, S. P., Sigdel, S., Meyer-Thompson, H.-G., Oechsler, H., & Verthein, U. (2014). 'South Asian cocktail'—The concurrent use of opioids, benzodiazepines and antihistamines among injecting drug users in Nepal and associations with HIV risk behaviour. *Harm Reduction Journal, 11*(1), 17. https://doi.org/10.1186/1477-7517-11-17

Opioid substitution therapy in Nepal. (2016, July 9). *Healthy Developments*. https://health.bmz.de/studies/opioid-substitution-therapy-in-nepal/

Pal Singh Balhara, Y., Doric, A., Stevanovic, D., Knez, R., Singh, S., Roy Chowdhury, M. R., Kafali, H. Y., Sharma, P., Vally, Z., Vi Vu, T., Arya, S., Mahendru, A., Ransing, R., Erzin, G., & Le Thi Cam Hong Le, H. (2019). Correlates of Problematic Internet Use among college and university students in eight countries: An international cross-sectional study. *Asian Journal of Psychiatry, 45*, 113–120. https://doi.org/10.1016/j.ajp.2019.09.004

Pant, S. B., Gurung, B., & Howard, J. (2023). Recovery and Rehabilitation from Alcohol, Substance Use and Related Disorders in Nepal: Call for Paradigm Shift. *Journal of Psychosocial Rehabilitation and Mental Health, 10*(2), 131–134. https://doi.org/10.1007/s40737-023-00337-4

Pant, S. B., Thapa, S. B., Howard, J., Ojha, S. P., & Lien, L. (2022). Mental disorders and suicidality among Opioid Agonist Treatment service users in Nepal: A cross sectional study. *SSM - Mental Health, 2*, 100165. https://doi.org/10.1016/j.ssmmh.2022.100165

Pathak, D. C., & Saxena, S. (2019). Role of Rehabilitation Center to Reduce Drug Abuse in Reference to Birendranagar Valley. *Nepal Journal of Multidisciplinary Research, 2*(4), 1–8.

Rao, R., Agrawal, A., Kishore, K., & Ambekar, A. (2013). Delivery models of opioid agonist maintenance treatment in South Asia: A good beginning. *Bulletin of the World Health Organization, 91*(2), 150–153. https://doi.org/10.2471/BLT.12.111815

Rathod, S. D., Luitel, N. P., & Jordans, M. J. D. (2018). Prevalence and correlates of alcohol use in a central Nepal district: Secondary analysis of a population-based cross-sectional study. *Global Mental Health, 5*, e37. https://doi.org/10.1017/gmh.2018.28

Sedain, C. P. (2013). Study of psychiatric comorbidity of alcohol use disorder. *Journal of Nepal Health Research Council, 11*(23), 66–69.

Shakya, D. R., Shyangwa, P. M., & Sen, B. P. (2011). Help seeking behavior in patients with alcohol dependence in a tertiary care hospital in eastern Nepal. *Journal of Psychiatrists' Association of Nepal, 1*(1), Article 1. https://doi.org/10.3126/jpan.v1i1.9922

Shakya, D. R., Upadhaya, S. R., & Thapa, M. (2021). Cannabis Use and Abuse in Nepal: A Review of Studies. *JNMA: Journal of the Nepal Medical Association, 59*(241), 954–961. https://doi.org/10.31729/jnma.6931

Sharma, P. (2021). Pregabalin Abuse: An Area of Concern in Nepal. *Journal of Psychiatrists' Association of Nepal, 10*(2), 1–2.

Sharma, P., Shakya, R., Singh, S., & Balhara, Y. P. S. (2020). An online survey of problematic internet use and its correlates among undergraduate medical students of Nepal. *Neurology, Psychiatry and Brain Research, 37*, 95–99. https://doi.org/10.1016/j.npbr.2020.07.001

Sharma, P., Singh, S., Bhandari, A. R., Poudel, B., & Bhattarai, G. D. (2023). Mental health problems, perceived stress, and internet addiction among undergraduate college students of Kathmandu, Nepal. *Journal of Psychiatrists' Association of Nepal, 12*(1), 21–25.

Shrestha, D. M., Aich, T. K., Gautam, K., & Bajracharya, D. (2020a). Opioid Dependence And Methadone Maintenance Treatment (MMT) Programme In Nepal In Three Different Decades: An Exploratory/Comparative Study. *Journal of Psychiatrists' Association of Nepal, 9*(2), 3–11.

Shrestha, M. V., Shrestha, N., Sharma, S. C., & Joshi, S. K. (2020b). Gaming Disorder among Medical College Students during COVID-19 Pandemic Lockdown. *Kathmandu University Medical Journal (KUMJ), 18*(70), 48–52.

Shrestha, N. M. (1992). Alcohol and drug abuse in Nepal. *British Journal of Addiction, 87*(9), 1241–1248. https://doi.org/10.1111/j.1360-0443.1992.tb02733.x

Thapliyal, S. (1999). Potential for Cooperation in South Asia: The Need for a Sub-Regional Approach. *South Asian Survey, 6*(1), 51–61. https://doi.org/10.1177/097152319900600107

Upadhyaya, K. D. (2015). Mental health & community mental health in Nepal: Major milestones in the development of modern mental health care. *Journal of Psychiatrists' Association of Nepal, 4*(1), 60–67.

Wang, P. S., Aguilar-Gaxiola, S., Alonso, J., Angermeyer, M. C., Borges, G., Bromet, E. J., Bruffaerts, R., de Girlolamo, G., de Graaf, R., Gureje, O., Haro, J. M., Karam, E. G., Kessler, R. C., Kovess, V., Lane, M. C., Lee, S., Levinson, D., Ono, Y., Petukhova, M., … Wells, J. E. (2007). Worldwide Use of Mental Health Services for Anxiety, Mood, and Substance Disorders: Results from 17 Countries in the WHO World Mental Health (WMH) Surveys. *Lancet, 370*(9590), 841–850. https://doi.org/10.1016/S0140-6736(07)61414-7

Chapter 7
Current Perspectives on Substance Use Disorder in Pakistan

Muhammad Tahir Khalily, Abdul Wahab Yousafzai, and Fatima Khurram

7.1 Introduction

Illicit drug use and abuse have deep roots in Pakistani society, engrained for reasons individual and societal such as pleasure-seeking, cultural practices, and social events. Substance abuse in Pakistani society presents a complex challenge with far-reaching consequences. Pakistan's geographical position as a bridge between South Asia, Central Asia, and the Middle East contributes to the transit and availability of various substances. Historical aspects reveal a complex relationship between substance use and cultural practices, with substances like opium and cannabis (charas) having traditional, albeit controlled, roles in certain rituals and medicinal use. Historically, Cannabis has been blatantly abused. Pakistan has enacted various laws and regulations to combat substance abuse, primarily governed by the Anti-Narcotics Force (ANF) and the Control of Narcotic Substances Act, 1997 (Khalily 2001). The legal framework classifies narcotics into different schedules, outlining the severity of penalties corresponding to the type and quantity of substances involved. Despite these measures, the enforcement of anti-drug laws faces challenges such as limited resources, corruption, and the geographical terrain that facilitates illicit drug trafficking. Cannabis, opium, and heroin are among the most commonly abused substances in Pakistan. The cultivation of opium poppy remains a significant issue,

M. T. Khalily (✉)
Professor of Clinical Neuropsychology and Dean Faculty of Social Sciences and Humanities, Shifa Tameer-E-Millat University, Islamabad, Pakistan
e-mail: khalily64@gmail.com

Department of Neurosciences, School of Medical Sciences, Universiti Sains Malaysia, Kuta Baro, Malaysia

A. W. Yousafzai
Professor of Psychiatry, Shifa Tameer-E-Millat University, Islamabad, Pakistan

F. Khurram
Department of Clinical Psychology, Shifa Tameer-E-Millat University, Islamabad, Pakistan

S. M. Y. Arafat and S. K. Kar (eds.), *Current Perspectives on Substance Use Disorders in South Asia*, https://doi.org/10.1007/978-981-97-6619-2_7

especially in the border regions. The ANF conducts operations to eradicate these crops, but the influence of drug cartels and insurgent groups in these areas and neighboring Afghanistan poses substantial hurdles.

Furthermore, there is a growing concern about the rise of synthetic drugs, including methamphetamines, within the country. The legal framework is adapting to address emerging challenges, but the pace of policy change is often surpassed by the dynamic nature of the illicit drug trade. Substance abuse imposes a significant burden on Pakistan's healthcare system and society at large. The prevalence of substance abuse, including opioids, cannabis, and synthetic drugs, has escalated, leading to adverse health, social, and economic consequences. Factors such as poverty, unemployment, trauma, sociopolitical instability, injustice, and youth disenfranchisement exacerbate this issue. Treatment and rehabilitation for substance abusers are also addressed in the legal framework, emphasizing a balanced approach that includes punishment for offenders and rehabilitation for those seeking recovery. However, the availability and accessibility of rehabilitation facilities remain limited, hindering the effectiveness of these measures. Although the government in Pakistan has implemented a legal framework to tackle substance abuse, the multifaceted nature of the problem requires ongoing adaptation and improvement. Enhancing law enforcement capabilities, expanding rehabilitation services, and addressing socioeconomic factors contributing to drug abuse are essential components in the comprehensive approach needed to mitigate the impact of substance abuse on Pakistani society. It is worth mentioning that help-seeking behaviors for substance abuse in Pakistan are influenced by cultural stigmas and limited awareness. Access to services remains a challenge due to inadequate infrastructure and a shortage of trained professionals. Government initiatives and non-governmental organizations (NGOs) play a crucial role in providing treatment facilities and rehabilitation programs, albeit with limitations in reach and capacity.

The pervasive use of Cannabis is deeply embedded in certain societal traditions in Pakistan and neighboring Afghanistan and is often used to bring about euphoric states for users in these practices. However, many such users remain entirely oblivious to the link between Cannabis and potential mood swings, particularly manic states as well as potential long-term effects. Recent years have seen global attention on the association between cannabis use and psychiatric disorders, notably bipolar disorder, with studies indicating heightened risks as substance abuse frequency increases. Notably, using illicit drugs during psychiatric disorder treatments correlates with poorer clinical outcomes, underscoring the mental health aspect of this issue (Khalily et al. 2015). Apart from Cannabis, alcohol misuse in Pakistani society remains a concealed yet pressing concern. Despite strict regulations, the United Nations Office on Drug and Crime (UNODC) 2013 survey failed to capture the severity of the alcohol problem, often overlooked in Pakistan despite its significant physical, psychological, and social repercussions. Fatal binge drinking and cases of "poison drinking" frequently reported in the media underscore the lack of acknowledgment of alcohol misuse as a public health issue (Khalily 2011a, b, c).

Furthermore, new drugs like "ecstasy" and "ice" are surfacing as additional threats, particularly to young individuals. Youth, known universally as a time of vulnerability of personality, are under a deluge of synthetic drugs flooding schools, universities, and social settings. The ease of access to dangerously addictive substances to a psychologically vulnerable population has far-reaching consequences. This encroachment, akin to termites on wood, erodes the societal fabric. Pakistan's history marked by natural and manmade calamities further exacerbates vulnerability to irrational drug use. It's imperative to explore deeper into understanding illicit drug use and frame comprehensive policies that resonate with indigenous concerns rather than merely responding to external pressures. In the youth, the prohibitive surface societal stance to the phenomena of drug use coupled with the ease of access to substances promotes dangerous and secretive use which is often discovered due to calamitous consequences to health or functioning.

7.2 Substance Abuse in Pakistan

Substance abuse is a pervasive issue, impacting various strata of society and entwined with medical, psychological, and social needs within certain Pakistani sub-cultures. However, the traditional dynamics changed in the early eighties with the advent of heroin in the international market, influencing the drug use patterns in Pakistan. Beyond health consequences, drug addiction's ripple effects extend to psychological and social realms, significantly pronounced with highly addictive drugs like heroin and cocaine. In Pakistani society, multiple factors contribute (Khalily 2001) to the initiation, perpetuation, and cessation of drug abuse. Family dynamics, peer pressure, social acceptance, rebellion against norms, thrill-seeking behaviors, and self-concept significantly influence an individual's vulnerability to drug addiction. Disturbed family environments, conflicts, and parental neglect often push individuals toward drug abuse. Peer groups, especially in disrupted family settings, play a pivotal role in encouraging drug use. Psychological tensions within familial relationships or hostile attitudes toward authority figures might drive individuals toward substance misuse. Drug addiction often correlates with a weakened ego, incapacity to confront life's realities, and an escape from inherent human inadequacies. Social attitudes favoring intoxication and use reinforce drug-seeking behaviors, with persons misusing substances exhibiting more favorable stances toward drug use as compared to non-users. Family relationships and self-concept also greatly impact addiction tendencies. Poor interpersonal relationships, coupled with a negative self-concept, contribute significantly to drug abuse patterns. The personal values of persons abusing substances often reflect less concern for others, a negative perception of human nature, and a disregard for social norms. Additionally, they tend to exhibit higher risk-taking tendencies, low motivation levels, rebelliousness against conventional values, a strong inclination toward pleasure-seeking, and a higher susceptibility to peer influence. These characteristics differentiate persons addicted to substance misuse from non-users and contribute significantly to their vulnerability to drug addiction (Khalily, 2009). Media portrayal of substance use in a glamorous light and pervasive messages endorsing and promoting substance use and associated behaviors and lifestyles contribute to the acceptance of substance use in vulnerable individuals particularly adolescents and young adults.

Data collected from individuals dependent on substances validates the prevalence of certain drugs, particularly cannabis, acting as a gateway to more dangerous substances like heroin. The ease of availability and onset age of drug use, primarily during adolescence, underlines a critical period for intervention such as positive parental attention and redirecting of energies to healthy experiences and expression. Cannabis stands as the most frequently used drug globally, presenting a significant issue among young adults. In countries like Pakistan, its use is a traditional practice for mood elevation, often without awareness of its connection to manic symptoms, declined cognitive performance, or long-term effects like a motivational syndrome. The prevalence of cannabis use has surged, particularly in young adults in Western nations, according to a 2013 UNODC survey. In Pakistan, around four million people (3.6% of the adult population) use cannabis, predominantly among younger individuals and men, spanning various socio-economic backgrounds. Despite being illegal in Pakistan, cannabis is imported from Afghanistan, primarily in the form of hashish "charas" and "bhang," a cannabis leaf-based drink.

Motivations for cannabis use in Pakistan include peer influence, coping with stress, and seeking euphoric effects. Notably, cannabis consumption has been associated with excitement, grandiosity, and psychosis, aligning with international findings on its euphoria-inducing and social interaction-enhancing effects. Increasing evidence suggests a correlation between cannabis use and the development of psychosis, a poorer prognosis for existing vulnerabilities to psychosis, and a possible link to inducing manic or depressive episodes. However, disentangling the mood-altering effects of cannabis from non-substance-induced mood disorders remains challenging. A study on university students in Pakistan investigated the association between recreational cannabis use and the emergence of hypomania or manic symptoms (Khalily et al. 2015). Recreational cannabis users displayed elevated psychological well-being and notably increased elated mood, despite having no previous history of psychopathology. The cannabis-using group also exhibited higher levels of impulsivity, which aligns with prior research on impulsivity linked to substance misuse. This association between cannabis use and symptoms of elation and impulsivity highlights a need for increased awareness among clinicians (Khalily et al. 2015).

7.3 Epidemiology of Substance Use Disorder in Pakistan

The epidemiology of substance use in Pakistan presents a complex and multifaceted picture, influenced by various socio-cultural, economic, and geographical factors. Understanding the prevalence, patterns, and trends of substance use is crucial in formulating effective interventions and public health strategies. Substance use in Pakistan encompasses a range of substances, including opioids, cannabis, alcohol, and emerging synthetic drugs. In 2013, UNODC in collaboration with the Ministry of Narcotics Control and other stakeholders conducted a national survey which revealed that 9% of the adult male population and 2.9% of the adult female population, equivalent to 6.7 million people, had used a substance of abuse other than alcohol and tobacco in the past year. Moreover, 4.25 million individuals were reported to be drug-dependent. Another National Drug Use Survey, by the same stakeholders, is currently underway since 2022 and is due to be completed in 2024.

The prevalence rates vary across different regions and demographics. While accurate nationwide data remains a challenge due to underreporting, limited research, and varying methodologies, several studies shed light on the extent of the issue. Opioid use, particularly heroin and opium, remains a significant concern in Pakistan. The 2013 UNODC report showed annual prevalence in Pakistan of cannabis use is 3.6%, opioids 2.4%, tranquilizers 1.4%, amphetamine 0.08%, solvents 0.03%, and cocaine 0.01%. The country serves as a transit route for opium originating from neighboring Afghanistan, contributing to the availability of these substances. Heroin addiction, in particular, is prevalent among marginalized communities, with high rates reported in urban areas and along trafficking routes. Cannabis, commonly known as "bhang" or "Charas," holds cultural and recreational significance in certain regions. Its use spans across different socio-economic strata, with higher prevalence in rural areas. The first countrywide survey by the Narcotics Control Board of Pakistan in 1986 highlighted cannabis as the most abused drug (Khalily 2001). Despite efforts, the subsequent UNODC survey in 2013 revealed an increase in cannabis use, with approximately four million users aged 15 to 64 out of a total of 7 million illicit drug users (Khalily et al. 2015). This escalating trend across 35 years emphasizes the gravity of the situation. In Pakistani society, the problem of substance abuse intersects with the epidemic of HIV/AIDS and psychiatric comorbidity presenting a complex web of public health challenges. Substance abuse, including the misuse of opioids, heroin, and other psychoactive substances, contributes significantly to the spread of HIV/AIDS since intravenous drug use, often associated with unsafe needle-sharing practices, serves as a major route for the transmission of HIV. Alarmingly, a UNODC (2008) report noted a 100% increase in injecting drug use between 2000 and 2006. The societal stigma surrounding both substance abuse and HIV/AIDS exacerbates the problem, hindering preventive measures and access to healthcare services. People who inject drugs face discrimination and are socially marginalized, making it difficult to implement harm-reduction strategies and comprehensive HIV prevention programs (Khalily 2010) exacerbating both problems. Moreover, the co-occurrence of psychiatric disorders compounds the public health impact since individuals with psychiatric disorders may be more vulnerable to substance abuse, creating a dual burden on their overall health. Mental illnesses can therefore act as both a cause and a consequence of substance abuse, further complicating the management of these intertwined public health concerns. Despite its illegal status, cannabis consumption continues, albeit with varying degrees of social acceptance. Alcohol consumption is subject to legal restrictions in Pakistan due to religious and cultural norms. However, despite the prohibition, its use persists in certain communities and among non-Muslim populations. Home-brewed alcohol, locally known as "*desi Sharab*," contributes to this pattern, often resulting in health risks due to unregulated production methods. The emergence of synthetic drugs, including methamphetamine and ecstasy, poses a growing concern. Their availability, especially in urban centers, presents new challenges in substance abuse management. Moreover, misuse of prescription medications, such as benzodiazepines and opioids, adds complexity to the substance use landscape. A proportion of those misusing substances in Pakistan are adolescents and youth in educational institutes (Chuadry 2022) who are functional enough to escape traditional data recording; such cases typically come to light only in life-threatening or extreme circumstances, and the true numbers for the youth are not reliably known. Therefore, there are certain challenges in epidemiological data collection, including the stigma associated with substance use, limited resources for research, and fragmented data collection systems, which hinder a comprehensive understanding of the true prevalence and patterns. As a result, prevalence rates might be underestimated, leading to gaps in policy and intervention strategies. Certain populations are more vulnerable to substance abuse, including marginalized groups, individuals with low socio-economic status, and those affected by conflict or displacement. Risk factors such as trauma, unemployment, lack of education, lack of awareness of the harms of substance misuse, social disenfranchisement, and easy access to substances contribute to the initiation and continuation of substance use. Gender disparities exist in substance use patterns, with men exhibiting higher prevalence rates compared to women. However, there is a growing concern about the increasing substance use among women, necessitating gender-specific interventions and research. In the UNODC report of 2013, men displayed a high prevalence of common substances of abuse, such as heroin and cannabis, while misuse of prescription opioids and sedatives was more common in women.

The epidemiology of substance use in Pakistan reflects a complex interplay of socio-cultural, economic, and geographical factors. Understanding the prevalence, patterns, and determinants of substance use is crucial in developing targeted interventions, strengthening healthcare systems, and formulating evidence-based policies to address this public health challenge. Improved data collection methodologies, enhanced research efforts, and a holistic approach encompassing prevention, treatment, and harm-reduction strategies are vital in tackling substance abuse effectively in Pakistan.

7.4 Substance Abuse in an Islamic Perspective

Islamic theological reflections provide a starting point for professionals aiming to support Muslims struggling with substance dependence. Recognizing the belief system and theological stance of individuals dealing with addictive disorders can be advantageous in offering effective care. It's important to clarify that, one, in this discourse, "drug use" refers specifically to recreational consumption, excluding its medical application. Two, essential preconditions, predisposition, and availability are posited as necessary yet insufficient explanations for drug use. Various interdisciplinary theories, spanning biology, sociology, and psychology, attempt to elucidate the roots of substance abuse. Notably, the controversial "disease model" attributes addiction to biological inheritance, alleviating social stigma and emphasizing support over condemnation. Contrarily, the "moral model" places responsibility solely on the individual, criticized for its judgmental stance while stressing the user's liability for rehabilitation. These models, however, lack consideration for experiential aspects, spirituality, and religiosity inherent in human nature, factors with great weight in Pakistan, and similar countries, on account of a majority Muslim population. Research emphasizes the protective role of spirituality and religion, in reducing substance abuse and aiding in recovery among Muslims. The rediscovery of faith often catalysis abstinence for those recovering from substance abuse within Islamic communities.

Exploring theological models across different faiths, including Christianity, reveals varied perspectives on addiction, such as addiction as a sin or incarnational theology. Islamic perspectives, however, remain relatively scarce in literature. Notably, Malik Badri presents an approach attributing drug addiction to the West's liberal attitude toward sex, critiquing non-judgmental therapy and advocating for Islamic-rooted programs. The exploration of addiction models within an Islamic framework offers a deep insight into the theological, cultural, and practical considerations surrounding substance abuse. Examining the perspective on intoxicant use in Islamic scripture, particularly alcohol (khamr) use prevailing in the time of initiation of the Prophethood of the Prophet Muhammad, PBUH, provides foundational principles. Prohibition of alcohol occurred gradually, after spiritual firmness in Islam was established, reflecting Islam's deep comprehension of human nature and addiction. The Qur'an's treatment of intoxicants is primarily on alcohol, referred to as "khamr." The Qur'an categorically prohibits alcohol, labeling it the "Handiwork of Satan" (al-Ma'ida 5:90). This prohibition underwent three phases before becoming absolute, indicating Islam's nuanced approach toward intoxication. Initially, alcohol was indulged in and enjoyed by early Arab Muslims. When questioned about its moral standing, the Qur'an outlined that while there might be some benefit, the harm outweighs it (al-Baqara 2:219). The gradual prohibitions addressed the cognitive impairment during prayer and the social disturbances caused by alcohol-induced conflicts, culminating in its complete ban. The scripture of Islam, the Qur'an, therefore teaches risk–benefit analysis and addresses the natural human self-preservative tendencies and cognitive faculty which seek to limit harm to the self.

Although the Qur'an primarily addresses alcohol and its intoxicating effects, the term "khamr" is often interpreted to encompass all intoxicants despite the historical context focusing on alcoholic beverages prevalent during pre-Islamic times. While recreational drugs use like cannabis, khat, or opium are not explicitly mentioned in the Qur'an, historical texts, indicate their medicinal use in early Muslim medicine. Cannabis, for instance, was introduced into the Arab world from India and was used medicinally for its digestive aid and cognitive clarity benefits. Texts emphasize the therapeutic value rather than recreational consumption during the formative period of Muslim society. However, by the eleventh century, evidence surfaces of the addictive potential of cannabis. Scholars like Al-Biruni noted the spread of drug habits, marking a shift from medical to recreational use, illustrated in the cases of addiction among influential figures. This societal shift prompted legal scholars to engage with drugs from a legal perspective, drawing comparisons with alcohol to provide rulings on narcotics. Scholars of Islamic jurisprudence dealt with the absence of explicit Quranic prohibitions against drugs through different means. Some, like al-Qarafi, associated the effects of hashish to alcohol, advocating for its prohibition. Others, however, struggled with establishing clear legal rulings due to the absence of direct religious guidance, leading to varied interpretations and legal stances. The approach toward intoxicants in Muslim societies is multifaceted, incorporating both preventative measures and punitive actions. Legal scholars categorized drug use within the spectrum of sins and crimes, prescribing punishments ranging from corporal penalties to considerations in divorce proceedings under the influence of intoxicants. The discourse around drugs within Muslim society became contentious where supporters of the use of substances like hashish leveraged religious legal axioms to argue against their prohibition. Hashish, used by some as part of misunderstood Sufi practices and meditation, became intertwined with mystical experiences and spiritual connections further complicating this debate.

Islamic teachings and approach to addiction align with its understanding of human nature, emphasizing the interplay between the self (nafs) including al-Amara and al-Lawama and its vital connection with the soul (ruh). The Qur'an portrays humans as a paradoxical amalgamation of the sacred and profane, the ruh and the nafs, highlighting the perpetual struggle between the pursuit of spiritual purity and the pull of temptations of the flesh. In Islamic teachings, the concept of Ruh (soul) and Nafs delineates the celestial essence and the temporal desires contained within individuals. The struggle lies in the Nafs assuming control over the body when the Divine light of the Ruh is disrupted, allowing bodily urges to dominate. The Lower self ("Nafs Ammarah") is susceptible to these urges, providing access to Satan. This understanding forms the basis for a "spiritual ailment model," wherein substance dependence signifies succumbing to satanic impulses or impulses from the nafs-al-Ammara, the lower-self, severing the self from the soul and leading to a psychologically "dead" state. This model emphasizes the disruption of relationships with Allah, family, and society due to intoxicants, urging believers to refrain from substance abuse. In addressing addiction, Islamic teachings intersect with therapeutic approaches like Millati Islami, a fellowship in the USA that adapts the 12-step model of Alcoholics Anonymous (AA) for Muslims. This adaptation modifies certain steps to align with Islamic beliefs and provides a framework for personal redemption, acknowledging guilt and seeking psychic healing.

This comprehensive exploration of intoxicants in Islamic scripture and society illustrates Muslims' evolving stance on substances, ranging from alcohol to drugs, and the intersection of religious principles with the complexities of addiction and rehabilitation.

The relationship between spirituality (Tazkia), religion, and intoxication has long been debated. Spirituality is often seen as a personal connection with The Divine, while religion is viewed as an organized system of beliefs and practices. This separation has led to spiritual experiences being detached from established religious doctrines, allowing individuals to become "spiritual masters" with their own doctrines. However, there's an increasing need to bridge the gap between spirituality and religion, particularly in addressing the emotional suffering caused by this disconnect. Re-integrating spirituality into religion can expand the understanding of academics to encompass broad aspects of humanity, collective and individual, grounded in religious teachings. It is important to note that this separation of spirituality and religion is a disconnect not present in Islamic teachings but is present in the modern scholarly lens examining Islam because of the historical relationship between Western European academia and the Church. In the context of Islam, spirituality involves belief in and obedience to Allah, facilitating a direct connection through personal experiences guided by Islamic principles revealed to Prophet Muhammad (PBUH). In the past, spirituality and religion were sidelined in scientific discourse due to political and ideological reasons, leading to the dismissal of spiritual experiences as illusory. However, there has been a recent paradigm shift in Western culture, moving toward a naturalistic view that acknowledges personal experiences and emotions beyond the realm of physical science. This shift has paved the way for spirituality and religious practices to be studied in mental health care, forming the basis of transpersonal psychology. The focus of this discourse is a "Bio-psycho-social-spiritual model" aimed at addressing psychological ailments, particularly those related to the "Nafs" (self or psyche) in Islamic teachings. This approach does not refer to issues related to the "Ruh" (Soul), but rather encompasses a range of collaborative religious practices aimed at improving one's self from a "lower" level of existence, nafs-al-ammara state, to a higher state, Insan-e-Kamil, of a perfected human being. This spiritual path to perfection reframes psychological issues such as substance misuse as obstacles to overcome on the path of becoming better human beings and as such is a perspective focusing on the mental health of individuals rather than the mental illnesses. This approach contrasts the Islamic model sharply with the "disease model" which takes away agency from individuals by framing the debate biologically—the Islamic model empowers the individual and provides them with the means required, in the form of practices and theological cognitive framework, to take action to improve and better their state.

Therefore, understanding and addressing these psychological ailments require awareness of historical perspective, acknowledging the intertwining of religion, medicine, and spirituality, which were inseparable in the past, particularly when it comes to Islam (Khalily 2018). Scientific advancements have led to the recognition of religion as a crucial social institution, offering alternative or adjunct approaches to medicine and psychotherapy (Khalily and Hallahan 2012). Integrating alternative interventions rooted in religious teachings into mental health care has shown promise, but it requires mental health practitioners to be aware and open to diverse practices, ensuring they don't dismiss potentially effective interventions due to cultural differences or unexamined biases. Challenges persist in adopting spiritual approaches within mental health recovery, particularly in a system dominated by pharmaceutical and therapeutic interventions. The integration of spiritual perspectives requires both practitioners and clients to understand mental health including substance abuse issues within a broader, religious context, necessitating a therapeutic insight aligned with spiritual perspectives. To effectively incorporate spiritual aspects into mental health care, practitioners must consider cultural diversity, religious competency, and the understanding of the "Nafs" in conformity with Islamic teachings. Historically, Islamic teachings, addressing psychological ailments related to the "Nafs" (self or psyche). involve a holistic approach that integrates religious practices. Practitioners seeking to incorporate spiritual approaches into mental health care should therefore collaborate with religious scholars to grasp religious practices and prayers as well as enhance their understanding of the perspectives of their clients. Establishing a referral pathway and maintaining liaison with religious scholars can thus help to align religion and mental health care including treatment of those suffering from addiction more closely, enhancing the effectiveness of interventions grounded in religious and spiritual traditions. Specific ailments and maladies of the "Nafs," such as irascibility, resentful envy, rancor, avarice, stinginess, arrogance, conceit, delusion, and ostentation, are identified in Islamic literature. Understanding and addressing these maladies require practitioners to explore the depths of spiritual (Tazkia) teachings and guide individuals toward spiritual wellness (Khalily 2018).

The convergence of spirituality, religion, and mental health care necessitates a re-evaluation of traditional therapeutic approaches to accommodate spiritual perspectives. By acknowledging and integrating spiritual wisdom into mental health care and the treatment of addiction, practitioners can offer more holistic and culturally sensitive interventions to address the complexities of the human psyche and well-being (Ali 2014). To achieve this, a therapeutic insight aligned with spiritual perspectives, cultural diversity awareness, and religious competency is required.

To recap, the intertwining of spirituality, religion, and mental health care within the context of Islamic teachings requires a nuanced, integrated approach (Khalily 2011a, b, c). Bridging these domains offers the potential for more comprehensive, culturally sensitive mental health interventions that acknowledge the spiritual dimensions of human existence.

An Indigenous Solution to Cannabis Misuse

The Indigenously Adapted Community Reinforcement Approach (IA-CRA) was tested in a randomized controlled trial involving 120 individuals with cannabis misuse. Results showed that IA-CRA significantly promoted abstinence compared to the control group, while also reducing depressive and anxiety symptoms and improving quality of life. These effects were sustained even at the 36-week follow-up. The dearth of data on cannabis use trends in Pakistan calls for effective management strategies. Cognitive behavior therapy (CBT) interventions have shown mixed results, indicating the potential efficacy of behavioral modifications, particularly in countries with lower literacy rates and educational attainment. IA-CRA, based on a comprehensive behavioral treatment model, demonstrated significant reductions in cannabis use and improvements in psychological symptoms. The study's high completion rate further reinforced the intervention's validity (Khalily et al. 2023). Despite the promising outcomes, limitations included the study's focus on a relatively young population with short-term cannabis misuse, potentially limiting generalizability. Future studies should explore broader demographics and longer-term interventions; however, IA-CRA proves effective in managing cannabis misuse, providing benefits for psychological well-being. Its sustained effects underscore its potential for promoting lasting recovery, urging further research to validate these findings in diverse populations. During the indigenous adaptation of CRA, cultural and religious perspectives were kept in mind and relevant to the cultural and societal needs. The majority of the people in Pakistan identify themselves with the religion of Islam; therefore, understanding the Islamic perspective on substance addiction unveils intricate insights into the soul and the relationship with God for those afflicted. Later in this chapter, we attempt to address questions about addiction within an Islamic framework. We explore three theological models that shed light on this complex issue.

7.5 Treatment Facilities for Substance Use Disorder in Pakistan

Treatment facilities for substance use in Pakistan have undergone significant evolution and expansion in recent years. The country faces a considerable challenge in combating substance abuse, with a range of substances, including heroin, cannabis, and prescription drugs, contributing to a complex public health issue. Various governments and NGOs have initiated programs and facilities aimed at treatment and rehabilitation. Pakistan's approach to substance use treatment encompasses a multifaceted strategy, blending medical interventions, counseling, and community-based support mostly following the Minnesota Model for the treatment of addiction. Governmental bodies like the Ministry of Narcotics Control and provincial health departments oversee policies and regulations related to substance abuse treatment. Additionally, NGOs and private sector organizations play a pivotal role in implementing programs due to their reach and community engagement. The treatment landscape comprises different levels of care. At the primary level, numerous detoxification centers grounded in the Minnesota Model or no robust treatment policy provide initial assessments, counseling, and outpatient treatment services. These centers, often run by NGOs or the private sector, claim to offer a range of interventions, including individual and group counseling, cognitive-behavioral therapy, and motivational enhancement therapy.

However, the availability and accessibility of these facilities vary significantly across regions. Urban areas tend to have more resources and better-equipped treatment centers compared to rural areas, where access to such facilities might be limited due to logistical constraints and insufficient funding. For individuals requiring more intensive care, there are residential rehabilitation centers spread throughout the country. These centers offer a structured environment for individuals to detoxify, receive intensive therapy, and learn coping skills essential for recovery. While some of these centers are run by the government, many are operated by NGOs and religious organizations; nevertheless, there is no monitoring policy to assess the efficacy and effectiveness of these treatment facilities. One of the challenges in Pakistan's treatment facilities is the stigma associated with substance abuse and no uniform and robust treatment policy. Many individuals and families hesitate to seek help due to societal judgments and frequent incidences of relapses. Efforts are ongoing to raise awareness and reduce stigma through public education campaigns, community outreach programs, introduction of evidence-based treatment approaches such as CRA, and advocacy efforts led by both governmental and non-governmental entities. Moreover, there is a growing recognition of the need for a holistic approach that addresses not just the addiction itself but also the environmental factors and underlying mental health issues. Integrated treatment facilities catering to co-occurring disorders—substance abuse and mental health problems—are emerging to address this gap in the existing services. However, despite these efforts, there are still gaps and challenges in Pakistan's substance use treatment landscape. Limited funding, lack of robust and uniform treatment policy, inadequate infrastructure, and a shortage of trained professionals remain significant hurdles. Additionally, there's a need for better coordination between various stakeholders to ensure a more comprehensive and effective approach to treatment. The emergence of new challenges, such as the rise in synthetic drugs and changing patterns of substance abuse among youth, requires ongoing adaptation and innovation in treatment strategies. In recent years, Pakistan has also seen the integration of technology in providing support and treatment for substance abuse. Helplines, online counseling services, and mobile applications have been introduced to reach a wider audience and provide immediate assistance to individuals in need. Collaborations between governmental bodies, NGOs, healthcare professionals, and community leaders are crucial for enhancing the efficacy and accessibility of treatment facilities across the country. The development of standardized protocols, continuous training programs for healthcare providers, and increased public–private partnerships can significantly contribute to improving the quality of care and expanding the reach of these facilities. A holistic approach that integrates medical, psychological, religious/spiritual, and social interventions is essential for addressing the complex nature of substance use disorders in Pakistan.

Program, policy, and legislation related to substance use in Pakistan. Pakistan has enacted various laws and regulations to combat substance abuse, primarily governed by the ANF Act and the Control of Narcotic Substances (CNS) Act, 1997 (Khalily 2001). The legal framework classifies narcotics into different schedules, outlining the severity of penalties corresponding to the type and quantity of substances involved. Chapter VI of the CNS deals with the treatment and rehabilitation of those addicted to substance use. Articles 52 and 53 stipulate the responsibility of the Provincial Governments to register, treat, and rehabilitate those with substance addiction. Moreover, the cost of first-time compulsory detoxification is to be borne by the Federal government as per Article 52 of this Act (UNDCP 2002).

Moreover, the government of Pakistan in alliance with UNDCP prepared a comprehensive plan for Master Plan Drug Abuse Control which was approved by the Prime Minister's cabinet in 1999. In the Anti-Narcotics Force Act, the Anti-Narcotics Force (ANF) has been given primary responsibility for indicting individuals for the production, smuggling, and distribution of illicit psychotropic substances.

The enforcement of anti-drug laws faces challenges such as limited resources, corruption, and the geographical terrain that facilitates illicit drug trafficking. The cultivation of opium poppy remains a significant issue, especially in the border regions. The ANF conducts operations to eradicate these crops, but the influence of drug cartels and insurgent groups in these areas and neighboring Afghanistan poses substantial hurdles. Pakistan's approach to substance use treatment encompasses a multifaceted strategy, blending medical interventions, counseling, and community-based support mostly following the Minnesota Model for the treatment of addiction. Governmental bodies like the Ministry of Narcotics Control and provincial health departments oversee policies and regulations related to substance abuse treatment. Additionally, NGOs and private sector organizations play a pivotal role in implementing programs due to their reach and community engagement. Treatment and rehabilitation for substance abusers are also addressed in the legal framework, emphasizing a balanced approach that includes punishment for offenders and rehabilitation for those seeking recovery.

The legal framework is adapting to address the emerging challenge of the rising synthetic drugs of abuse, including methamphetamines, within the country, but the pace of policy change is often surpassed by the dynamic nature of the illicit drug trade. The Drug Abuse Prevention Resource Center (DAPRC) maintained by ANF works on demand reduction as a strategy to meet these modern challenges.

Enhancing law enforcement capabilities, expanding rehabilitation services, and addressing socio-economic factors contributing to drug abuse are essential components in the comprehensive approach needed to mitigate the impact of substance abuse on Pakistani society.

7.5.1 *Neurofeedback for Substance Use*

Keeping in mind the cultural sensitivity and confidentiality in a less expressive cultural environment, and strong beliefs in procedural intervention for self-exploration, Neurofeedback therapy an innovative approach is gaining recognition globally for its potential in treating various psychological and neurological disorders, including addiction. In the context of Pakistani society, where drug addiction poses a significant societal challenge, exploring alternative therapeutic interventions has become crucial. This chapter also explores the concept of neurofeedback therapy and its potential application in addressing drug addiction within the specific cultural and social landscape of Pakistan. Neurofeedback is a non-invasive therapeutic technique that considers real-time monitoring of brain changes through electroencephalography (EEG). The individual receives visual or auditory feedback based on their brainwave patterns, enabling them to self-regulate and optimize neural functioning. In the realm of addiction treatment, neurofeedback has shown promise in helping individuals regain control over their brain processes, particularly those associated with addictive behaviors (Khalily and Hallahan 2012). This technique has potential for application in Pakistan due to traditional cultural values and the prevalent stigma against discussion of topics perceived to be shameful, addiction being one of them.

Pakistani society grapples with a growing drug addiction problem, affecting individuals from diverse backgrounds. Factors such as socio-economic disparities, political instability, and limited access to quality healthcare contribute to the challenges of addressing addiction effectively. Neurofeedback therapy presents an opportunity to complement traditional approaches by offering a personalized and neurologically focused intervention. One notable aspect of Pakistani culture is the importance of community and family ties. Integrating neurofeedback therapy into the existing rehabilitation frameworks can capitalize on these communal values. By involving families in the therapy process, ensuring confidentiality, and family pride, there is potential for a more holistic and supportive approach to addiction treatment. Educating communities about the benefits and mechanisms of neurofeedback can contribute to reducing the stigma associated with addiction and seeking unconventional treatments (Khalily 2010). However, challenges in implementing neurofeedback therapy in Pakistan exist, including limited awareness among healthcare professionals, cost, and the general public. Addressing these challenges necessitates collaborative efforts between mental health professionals, policymakers, and community leaders to raise awareness, promote research, and integrate neurofeedback into existing addiction treatment programs in public sector facilities. Furthermore, cultural sensitivity is paramount in the implementation of neurofeedback therapy in Pakistan. Understanding the cultural distinctions and adapting the therapy to align with local and religious values is essential for its acceptance and effectiveness. Integrating traditional healing practices alongside neurofeedback can create a more comprehensive and culturally responsive approach to addiction treatment. The financial aspect of implementing neurofeedback therapy may be a concern in a country with economic challenges. However, investing in innovative and evidence-based treatments can lead to long-term societal benefits, including reduced healthcare costs associated with addiction-related issues. Nevertheless, neurofeedback therapy holds promise as a valuable tool in the treatment of drug addiction in Pakistani society. Its integration into existing rehabilitation frameworks can offer a personalized and culturally sensitive approach, addressing both the behavioral and societal aspects of addiction. Collaborative efforts from healthcare professionals, policymakers, and community leaders are crucial to overcome challenges in establishing neurofeedback therapy as a viable and effective intervention in the battle against drug addiction in Pakistan.

7.6 Prevention of Substance Abuse in Pakistan

Numerous risk factors contribute to substance abuse, including socio-economic disparities, peer pressure, availability of drugs, trauma, and mental health conditions. The prevalence varies across different regions and demographics, with urban areas often showing higher rates due to increased accessibility and exposure. The lack of awareness and education on these issues in Pakistani society hampers effective prevention and treatment efforts. Public health campaigns need to address cultural and social factors that contribute to the persistence of substance abuse and HIV/AIDS. Additionally, the healthcare system must integrate mental health services with substance abuse and HIV/AIDS programs to provide holistic care (Khalily 2011a, b, c). Efforts should also focus on reducing stigma and promoting inclusivity, encouraging individuals to seek help without fear of judgment (Shah et al. 2019). Community-based initiatives, alongside governmental policies, play a crucial role in creating an environment that supports individuals dealing with substance abuse, HIV/AIDS, and psychiatric disorders, ultimately contributing to a healthier society. Implementing harm-reduction strategies is crucial to mitigate the adverse effects of substance abuse. Initiatives like needle exchange programs, opioid substitution therapy, and education campaigns aim to minimize health risks associated with drug use.

In the context of primary prevention in Pakistani society, addressing substance abuse from an Islamic and cultural perspective involves a multifaceted approach that integrates religious teachings, social awareness, and community support. The preventive strategy within the Islamic and cultural framework emphasizes both individual responsibility and collective efforts to create a society that is resilient against the menace of substance abuse. Islamic teachings provide a moral and ethical foundation that discourages the consumption of intoxicants. The Quran and Sunnah of the Prophet Muhammad peace be upon him explicitly prohibit the consumption of alcohol and any substance that alters one's state of mind. This forms the basis for individual accountability, as adherents are expected to avoid substances that may impair their judgment and lead them astray from the righteous path outlined in Islamic teachings.

Education plays a pivotal role in the preventive strategy. Mosques, contemporary and Islamic schools, and community centers can serve as platforms for disseminating information about the dangers of substance abuse and the importance of adhering to Islamic principles. Religious leaders, as influential figures in Pakistani society, can play a pivotal role in raising awareness and guiding individuals away from engaging in activities that may lead to substance abuse. Family is considered the cornerstone of Muslim society, and strengthening family bonds is integral to preventing substance abuse. Parents, as the primary educators of their children, play a crucial role in instilling Islamic principles and cultural values. Open communication within families can create a supportive environment where individuals feel comfortable discussing their concerns and seeking guidance, thereby reducing the likelihood of turning to substances for solace. Community involvement is another key aspect of the preventive strategy. Establishing support networks within neighborhoods and communities can provide a safety net for individuals at risk of substance abuse. Mosques and community organizations can organize events and programs that promote healthy alternatives to substance use, fostering a sense of belonging and purpose of existence. In addition to religious teachings, emphasizing the detrimental impact of substance abuse on physical health, mental well-being, and social relationships aligns with Islamic principles of preserving life and promoting overall welfare. Collaborations between religious scholars, healthcare professionals, and educators can facilitate the integration of comprehensive awareness programs that address the holistic aspects of substance abuse. Government initiatives also play a crucial role in the preventive strategy. Policies and regulations aligned with Islamic principles can be implemented to control the availability and distribution of substances. Public health campaigns, supported by religious leaders and community influencers, can reinforce the message of abstaining from substance abuse as a societal responsibility (Khalily 2010).

7.7 Conclusions

Substance abuse in Pakistan is a growing concern, affecting about millions of people. High availability of drugs, poverty, and societal pressures contribute to its prevalence. Prevention efforts focus on education, community programs, and stricter law enforcement. Treatment involves counseling, support groups, and rehabilitation centers. Challenges persist due to stigma, limited resources, and inadequate mental health infrastructure, necessitating coordinated efforts between the government, NGOs, and the community to address this complex issue effectively (Abdullah et al, 2018). In sum, preventive strategy for substance abuse from the Islamic perspective within Pakistani society relies on a combination of religious teachings, education, family support, community involvement, and government initiatives. By fostering a culture that values individual responsibility and collective well-being, Pakistan can work toward creating a society resilient against the challenges posed by substance abuse.

References

Abdullah, M., Khalily, M.T., Ahmad, I. & Hallahan, B. (2018). Psychological autopsy review on mental health crises and suicide among youth in Pakistan. *Asia Pacific Psychiatry, 10*(4), e12338. https://doi.org/10.1111/appy.12338

Ali, M (2014), Perspectives on Drug Addiction in Islamic History and Theology. Religions 2014, 5, 912–928. https://doi.org/10.3390/rel5030912

Chuadry, M. A. et al. (2022). Prevalence of drug use among university students in Pakistan. *Annals of Medical and Health Sciences Research* 12:1–10.

Khalily, M. T. (2001). A comparison between the psychosocial characteristics of drug addicts and non-addicts. *Pakistan Journal of Psychological Research* 16, (3-4):113–128.

Khalily, M. T. (2009). Personality Characteristics of Addicts and Non-addicts Determined through Rorschach Findings. *Pakistan Journal of Psychology* 40 (1): 3–15.

Khalily, M. T. (2010). Developing a coordinated response to drug abuse in Pakistan. *Journal of Interprofessional care 24*(2): 168–172. https://doi.org/10.3109/13561820903163587

Khalily M. T. (2011a). Alcohol-related neuropsychological deficits an invisible disability. Irish Psychiatrist; 12 (2): 62–64.

Khalily, M. T (2011b). Mental health problems in Pakistani society as a consequence of violence and trauma; a case for better integration of care. *International Journal of Integrated Care.* 11: 1–7. https://doi.org/10.5334/ijic.662

Khalily, M. T., (2011c). Developing an integrated approach to the mental health issues in Pakistan. *Journal of Interprofessional care.* 20: 1–2. https://doi.org/10.3109/13561820.2011.573598

Khalily, M. T. (2018). Taking Faith seriously in therapeutic psychology. Iqbal International Institute of Research & Dialogue, Islamabad Pakistan.

Khalily, M. T. & Hallahan, B. (2012). The occurrence of neurological symptoms in currently abstinent misusers of alcohol. *Irish Journal Medical Science* 181; 473–477. https://doi.org/10.1007/s11845-011-0801-6

Khalily MT, Schwannauer M, Hallahan B (2015). Cannabis Associated Elation of Manic Symptoms in a University Cohort (Non-Clinical). J Addict Behav Ther Rehabil 4:3. https://doi.org/10.4172/2324-9005.1000144

Khalily, M.T., Hussain, B., Hallahan, B. et al. Indigenously Adapted Community Reinforcement Approach (IA-CRA) for Cannabis Users: a Randomized Controlled Trial. Int J Ment Health Addiction (2023). https://doi.org/10.1007/s11469-023-01189-6

Shah, I., Khalily, M. T., Ahmad, I., & Hallahan, B. (2019). Impact of Conventional Beliefs and Social Stigma on Attitude Towards Access to Mental Health Services in Pakistan. *Community mental health journal*, 55(3), 527–533. https://doi.org/10.1007/s10597-018-0310-4

UNDCP Global Assessment Programme on Drug Abuse & Narcotics Control Division, Anti-Narcotics Force, Government of Pakistan (2002), Drug Abuse in Pakistan—Results from the year 2000 National Assessment. https://www.unodc.org/pdf/gap_drug-abuse_pakistan_2000.pdf

UNODC. (2008). Illicit Drug Trends in Pakistan. https://www.unodc.org/documents/regional/central-asia/Illicit%20Drug%20Trends%20Report_Pakistan_rev1.pdf

Chapter 8
Current Perspectives on Substance Use Disorders in Sri Lanka: Public Mental Health Aspects

Anuprabha Wickramasinghe and Nuwan Darshana Wickramasinghe

8.1 Introduction

Sri Lanka is an island surrounded by the Indian Ocean, situated close to the southern peak of the Indian subcontinent, separated from it by a 54.8 km wide strip of water called Palk Strait. The island has a land area of 65,610 square kilometres (435 km in length and 225 km in width). Due to its unique location and shape, Sri Lanka is known as "the pearl of the Indian Ocean" (Sehgal 2024).

The country has a total population of 22 million, and 65% of people are in the working-age group. The labour force participation rate among working-age people is 50%. There is an obvious discrepancy between the employment rate between males and females, while 70% of working-age males are employed, only 30% of working-age females are employed. In keeping with the other South-East Asian cultures, Sri Lanka has a patriarchal society where males are considered the head of the household.

Life expectancy at birth in 2019 was 73 years in males and 79 years in females (WHO). In 2019, the mean monthly household income was 76,414 LKR, median monthly household income was 53,333 LKR, and mean monthly household expenditure was 63,130 LKR, of which food expenditure was 22 830 LKR. Average expenditure on liquor, narcotics, drugs, and tobacco per household is 960 LKR (Department of census and statistics, Sri Lanka). One Indian rupee is worth 3.9 Sri Lankan rupees in 2023.

Alcohol, tobacco, cannabis, and opium are the most commonly abused substances in Sri Lanka. While most of the alcohol for local consumption is produced by local companies in Sri Lanka, Ceylon Tobacco Company (CTC), a member of British

A. Wickramasinghe (✉)
Faculty of Medicine, Department of Psychiatry, University of Colombo, Colombo, Sri Lanka
e-mail: anuprabha@psych.cmb.ac.lk

N. D. Wickramasinghe
Faculty of Medicine and Allied Sciences, Department of Community Medicine, Rajarata University of Sri Lanka, Anuradhapura, Sri Lanka

S. M. Y. Arafat and S. K. Kar (eds.), *Current Perspectives on Substance Use Disorders in South Asia*, https://doi.org/10.1007/978-981-97-6619-2_8

American Tobacco, is the only legal manufacturer of cigarettes in Sri Lanka. Alcohol and tobacco sales are legal and under regulations, while trafficking, selling, or using drugs including cannabis are illegal in Sri Lanka.

8.2 Epidemiology of Substance Abuse in Sri Lanka

Three-year average of alcohol (pure) per capita consumption in the population of Sri Lanka above 15 years of age between the years 2015–2017 was 4.3 L per annum (males:females, 7.7:1.2 L) after adjusting for tourist consumption (Alcohol, Sri Lanka Country Profile, WHO 2018). Out of this 2.7 L were recorded alcohol and 1.6 L were unrecorded. Total alcohol (pure) per capita consumption is representative of the same figure for the South-East Asian region which was 4.5 L for the specified period (Alcohol, Sri Lanka Country Profile, WHO 2018).

Focussing on drinkers only who are above 15 years of age, per capita consumption of alcohol in Litres of pure alcohol was 18.9 L for males, 6.7 L for females, and 14.9 L for both sexes (Alcohol, Sri Lanka Country Profile, WHO 2018) for the above period. Among males, 32.6% were lifetime abstainers, while among females 62.4% were lifetime abstainers (for both sexes 48.3% were lifetime abstainers) (Alcohol, Sri Lanka Country Profile, WHO 2018).

Eighty-five per cent (85%) of the pure alcohol per capita consumption above 15 years of age was consumed as spirits, 13% as beer, <1% as wine, while about 2% belonged to other types (Alcohol, Sri Lanka Country Profile, WHO 2018). Among the male drinkers between 15 and 19 years of age, 47.8% showed heavy episodic drinking (Alcohol, Sri Lanka Country Profile, WHO 2018).

Age-standardised prevalence of tobacco use (smoked and smokeless) among the population above 15 years of age is 22% in the most recent WHO World Health statistics ("World Health Statistics" 2023). Age-standardised estimated prevalence of any tobacco smoking above 15 years of age male: female is 18% and 0.2% (both sexes 9.1%) (WHO Report on the Global Tobacco Epidemic, 2023: Protect People from Tobacco Smoke 2023). A large proportion of smoked tobacco is consumed as cigarettes although "Beedi", a cheaper alternative containing a lesser amount of tobacco, is popular among low-income groups (Sri Lanka, Overview of Tobacco Use, Tobacco Control, Legislation and Taxation 2017).

Betel quid chewing was widely practised in the past, mainly among older age groups in rural settings. A nationwide survey in 1995 showed 33.8% between 35 and 44 year age group, and 47.7% of the 65–74 years chewed betel quid (Abayaratna and Krishnarasa 1997). Traditionally about one-third or half of them include tobacco in their quid, more commonly by males. On average a person will use about 5 betel quid a day. A recent study conducted among 15–24-year-old persons in urban slum areas showed 44.9% chewed tobacco either in the form of betel quid or as a commercially prepared mix of tobacco and areca nut, out of whom 90.8% were males (Dhanapriyanka et al. 2022a, b). Smokeless tobacco use seems to be getting popular among deprived urban young communities in Sri Lanka. Manufactured tobacco products are cheap and are easily available which may be attractive to the young age group. About 8.6% of the youth are currently using smokeless tobacco in Sri Lanka (Somatunga et al. 2012).

Cannabis is the most commonly abused illicit drug with a prevalence of 1.9% of the total population above 14 years in Sri Lanka (Welagedara 2020). There are about 180,000 regular cannabis users in Sri Lanka (National Prevalence Survey on Drugs Use 2019, NDDCB Presidential Task Force on Drug Prevention, Sri Lanka Police 2019). Cannabis is cultivated illegally on a large scale (estimated 500 hectares in 2006) in the eastern and southern provinces of Sri Lanka ("United Nations Country Profile: Sri Lanka" 2006).

Heroin use above 14 year-old male population is 1.2%, and the female population is 0.018% (0.6% for both sexes). There are an estimated number of about 71,000 regular heroin users in Sri Lanka (National Prevalence Survey on Drugs Use 2019, NDDCB Presidential Task Force on Drug Prevention, Sri Lanka Police 2019).

Other drugs of abuse include ecstasy, stimulants, cocaine, methamphetamine, and other newer substances which are used by about 0.76% of the population above 14 years of age in Sri Lanka (National Prevalence Survey on Drugs Use 2019, NDDCB Presidential Task Force on Drug Prevention, Sri Lanka Police 2019). The pattern of drug use is shifting towards these substances. Rave/dance/Facebook/beach or warehouse parties mainly targeting younger crowds have been seen in recent years where various combinations and strengths of newer drugs are used (Raveendran and Hulathduwa 2021).

Abuse of pharmaceutical tablets was seen in 0.16% of the total population above 14 years old (National Prevalence Survey on Drugs Use 2019, NDDCB Presidential Task Force on Drug Prevention, Sri Lanka Police 2019).

Out of the drug users, only a small minority (1.6–4.3%) is injecting drugs. Among people who inject drugs, heroin (91%) was the most commonly injected, and dependence was largely on opioids. About 83% inject daily and at least 85% have shared their injecting equipment at least once (NSACP and NDDCB 2018).

The highest prevalence of illicit drug use was in the Western province and the Colombo district (National Prevalence Survey on Drugs Use 2019, NDDCB Presidential Task Force on Drug Prevention, Sri Lanka Police 2019). Eastern province, Central province, North Western province, and Sabaragamuwa province show a higher prevalence of substance use in Sri Lanka. Substance use is significantly higher in males (National Prevalence Survey on Drugs Use 2019, NDDCB Presidential Task Force on Drug Prevention, Sri Lanka Police 2019).

Several vulnerable groups of people are worth mentioning. About two-thirds of upcountry tea estate workers above 18 years of age are known to use alcohol. Toddy, an alcoholic drink made from fermented coconut palm sap, has become popular in this region due to its low cost. Supplies are known to arrive by early hours, and workers drink on loaned money or by pawning ornaments, ID cards, and passbooks (Abeysundara 2016). Toddy sold is believed to be not genuine and made using urea, ammonia, yeast and painkiller tablets (Abeysundara 2016).

Other vulnerable groups such as military personnel, students, gypsy communities, deprived urban communities, commercial sex workers, and certain occupational groups such as unskilled labourers and entertainment industry workers may be at a higher risk of using substances and facing complications.

8.3 Public Health Impact of Substance Abuse

Substance abuse poses a profound and multifaceted impact on public health, affecting individuals, families, communities, and societies at large. Similar to the global context, the consequences of substance abuse extend across physical, mental, social, and economic dimensions in Sri Lanka.

8.3.1 Health Consequences

Physical Health

In relation to the physical health consequences of alcohol abuse, among the multitude of medical conditions attributed to alcohol, liver diseases are the most common globally as well as in Sri Lanka.

Over the last three decades, Sri Lanka has witnessed a significant increase in liver cirrhosis cases. For liver cirrhosis, the number of alcohol-attributable deaths (AAD) in Sri Lanka in 2016 was 2880 for both sexes. It is noteworthy to observe the difference in the age-standardised death rates (ASDR) of liver cirrhosis in males and females, which were 57.4 and 9.7 per 100,000 population, respectively. The alcohol-attributable fractions (AAF) were 56.7% and 28.2% in males and females, respectively. For cancers, the number of AADs in Sri Lanka in 2016 was 646. More importantly, the AAF in males and females were 5.2% and 0.9%, respectively (WHO Alcohol Sri Lanka 2019 country profile). It is also important to note that Sri Lanka holds a concerning rank of 1.40 in alcohol-related deaths.

About tobacco smoking, there are several physical health outcomes identified which are attributable to smoking tobacco use, including ischaemic heart disease, chronic obstructive pulmonary disease, and cancers of the respiratory tract, viz., tracheal, bronchus, and lung cancer. When considering the all-cause and all-age smoking-attributable deaths, the per cent of deaths attributable to smoking is 8.2%, while the smoking-attributable death rate is 50.7 per 100,000. It is noteworthy that as in many South Asian countries, there is a substantial difference between males and females. The percentage of deaths attributable to smoking in Sri Lankan males is 13.6%, while the corresponding value for females is 1.6%. In a similar vein, the smoking-attributable death rate per 100,000 in males is 95.6 as opposed to 8.6 in females (Reitsma et al. 2021).

As per the national statistics, Injecting Drug Users (IDUs) are predominantly concentrated in Colombo and coastal areas, rather than being widely dispersed throughout the entire island. Needle sharing among IDUs contributes to the spread of infectious diseases, such as HIV/AIDS and Hepatitis. Furthermore, risky sexual behaviours contribute to the spread of sexually transmitted infections. As per the findings of a survey conducted in 2017, 16% participated in sexual activities with casual partners, 14% were involved in sexual encounters with commercial sex partners, and 26% engaged in anal intercourse. Notably, the majority of individuals involved in sexual activities with casual partners practised unprotected sex (Fernando et al. 2017).

Mental Health

The statistics related to alcohol dependence suggest that the prevalence of alcohol dependence in 2016 for both sexes was 2.6%, which is relatively lower than the corresponding prevalence in the WHO South-East Asian region. However, the prevalence in males and females was 4.9% and 0.6%, respectively (WHO Alcohol Sri Lanka 2019 country profile).

In addition, a prospective case series in the Sri Lankan context reported that the co-ingestion of alcohol is independently linked to poorer hospital outcomes in individuals who have self-poisoned with the organophosphate insecticide profenofos (Dhanarisi et al. 2018).

Drug dependence is one of the most important health consequences of substance abuse worldwide. In the year 2022, a total of 1,996 reported drug users received treatment services. Among the reported drug users, 41% were treated at the Kandakadu Treatment and Rehabilitation Centre under the Bureau of Commissioner General of Rehabilitation, while 37% sought assistance from the treatment and rehabilitation centre affiliated with the National Dangerous Drugs Control Board (NDDCB). An additional 18% sought support from non-governmental organisations (NGOs), and 3.4% were treated at the prison drug treatment rehabilitation programme.

8.3.2 Social Consequences

In Sri Lanka, harmful alcohol consumption leads to a multitude of negative social ramifications including poverty (Baklien and Samarasinghe 2005), domestic violence (Subramaniam and Sivayogan 2001) and unintentional injuries in children (Punyadasa and Samarakkody 2016).

With regard to the negative social implications related to alcohol use, most of the evidence is based on qualitative studies conducted in different settings in the country. Domestic violence and gender-based violence were unfortunately normalised in various settings, often viewed as an inevitable outcome of alcohol consumption. The abuse of women within their homes by their "drunken" husbands was acknowledged, yet, tragically accepted either as destiny or attributed solely to the influence of alcohol. Moreover, the unfortunate consequences of paternal alcohol abuse, leading to the deprivation of children's needs, were perceived as a regrettable misfortune for the affected children (Baklien and Samarasinghe 2005).

A recent scoping review on alcohol use, self-harm, and suicide brings attention to the significant impact on Sri Lankan women, who are frequently noted to be affected by the alcohol use of someone else (commonly their husband or father). This, in turn, has been identified as a contributing factor to incidents of self-harm or suicide among these women. The review highlights that interpersonal conflict arising from alcohol use is a prevalent theme, often intertwined with struggles over socio-economic issues (Sørensen et al. 2023a, b).

Local evidence highlights that substance abuse also leads to social disintegration, with families and communities suffering from the breakdown of relationships and social structures. Children of substance-abusing parents face neglect and abuse, perpetuating a cycle of dysfunction. Substance use is also linked to unemployment, decreased productivity, and economic strain on individuals and families, contributing to poverty and creating additional burdens on social welfare systems (South Asia Regional Profile—Sri Lanka).

8.3.3 Public Safety Concerns

One of the main public safety concerns related to alcohol use in Sri Lanka is road traffic accidents. For road traffic injuries, the number of AADs in Sri Lanka in 2016 was 646. More importantly, the AAF in males and females were 5.2% and 0.9%, respectively (WHO Alcohol Sri Lanka 2019 country profile).

In Sri Lanka, 152,979 individuals were arrested for drug-related offences in 2022, which highlights a 36% increase in comparison to the previous year. More alarmingly, the prevalence of drug-related arrests in 2022 was 751 persons per 100,000 population. Furthermore, the total number of imprisonments reported for drug-related offences was 30,331 of which 63% were narcotic drug offences. In addition, it was noted that in 2022, there were a total of 21,953 drug-related road traffic accidents in Sri Lanka and there were 2515 deaths. Even though there has been a slight reduction in the total number of accidents since 2019, there were no drastic reductions in the numbers in comparison to the previous year (Handbook of Drug Abuse Information in Sri Lanka 2023).

8.3.4 Economic Burden

About household-level economic burden, the Annual Trend Survey on Alcohol consumption in Sri Lanka reports that the median monthly expenditure among current alcohol consumers was approximately LKR 4000.00 (Annual Trend Survey on Alcohol consumption in Sri Lanka 2021).

Similarly, the Annual Trend Survey on Tobacco consumption in Sri Lanka reports that the median monthly expenditure among current alcohol consumers was approximately LKR 6720.00 (Annual Trend Survey on Tobacco consumption in Sri Lanka 2021).

In 2015, the comprehensive economic impact of alcohol in Sri Lanka amounted to USD 885.85 million. Direct costs constituted USD 388.35 million (44%), while indirect costs reached USD 497.49 million (56%). The most substantial cost category was the loss of productivity due to premature mortality, totaling USD 388.86 million, representing 44% of the total cost. The in-patient care cost amounted to USD 293.75 million, constituting one-third of the overall expenditure (Ranaweera et al. 2018).

8.3.5 Disability-Adjusted Life Years (DALYs)

Smoking tobacco use accounted for 7,313,000 (245,000–396,000) disability-adjusted life-years in Sri Lanka. The per cent of DALYs attributable to smoking is 5.5%, and smoking-attributable.

DALY rate is 1430 per 100,000. Expectedly, the corresponding values for males are substantially higher representing 288,000 DALYs for males and 24,600 DALYs for females. Similarly, the per cent of DALYs attributable to smoking in males and females is 9.3% and 0.9%, respectively (Reitsma et al. 2021).

8.4 Treatment Settings and Infrastructure to Deal with Substance Use Disorders in Sri Lanka

8.4.1 Universal Health Cover to All Sri Lankan Citizens

Universal health care is provided free to all citizens of Sri Lanka by the well-established government health service under the Ministry of Health, which looks after 95% of in-patient care and 50% of the out-patient care (Rajapaksa et al. 2021). The role of the private sector is growing but is accessible only to a fraction of the population who are more affluent.

Services for substance users are mainly provided under the mental health directorate, although acute detoxification and treatment of physical health complications will fall under acute medical in-patient care services.

Psychiatry in-patient care is available in 23 of the 26 districts. Altogether there are 61 in-patient units, 3 child in-patient units, and 2 forensic in-patient units. There are 7 tertiary care hospitals in Sri Lanka, each with psychiatry in-patient units and out-patient clinics. Mental health clinics in hospitals are run by consultant psychiatrists and outreach mental health clinics are run by medical officers of mental health, under the supervision of a consultant psychiatrist. Community mental health teams are not in place in Sri Lanka, but community psychiatric nurses and psychiatric social workers attached to hospital psychiatry units carry out domiciliary visits when needed.

8.4.2 Acute Management and Liaison Work

Patients with substance abuse and dependence are often detected when they present to the hospital with trauma or medical complications at which point acute detoxification may take place depending on the needs of the patient. Patients with complicated withdrawals are usually treated in the acute medical setup. Following this, patients are referred to liaison psychiatry services available through hospital-based psychiatrists for client engagement, follow-up, therapy, and for the initiation of relapse prevention interventions.

8.4.3 Mental Health In-patient Service

Some of these clients with mental and behavioural presentations will be transferred to psychiatry in-patient services at this point where their psychological needs will be addressed. Facilities are available for patients to complete detoxification regimes in the psychiatry wards if not already completed. A minority of these patients who are voluntarily accepting in-patient rehabilitation treatment will be referred to rehabilitation centres, a process facilitated by the psychiatry social workers. Others may be discharged with a plan to follow up in the general adult out-patient clinic or in dedicated substance clinics when available.

The characteristic feature of the referrals coming through the liaison psychiatry service is that they are often unplanned admissions and patients have not had prior therapy, motivational work, or the opportunity to make a conscious decision to stop substances. Therefore, a high relapse rate is observed in these patients who are opportunistically seen by the described services.

8.4.4 Patients Presenting Through the Criminal Justice System

Substance-abusing offenders are brought to hospital-based services after arrests for different reasons such as judicial medical officer (JMO) reports, treatment of withdrawal features, or treatment for psychological disturbances. Depending on the individual's needs they will be able to access psychiatry services offered as in-patients or out-patients, but they are later followed by the prison hospitals. At least 10 of the prisons have designated substance treatment centres, and most of the prisons have prison hospitals and prison medical officers. Two well-established forensic psychiatry services are available in Colombo and Kandy districts. In other districts, hospital psychiatrists conduct prison mental health clinics and supervise substance services offered in prison hospitals.

Offenders with drug abuse who do not require prison sentences are placed in one of the two drug rehabilitation centres for offenders for up to a year of treatment and rehabilitation from drug use. At other times they are also placed in the National Dangerous Drug Control Board (NDDCB) rehabilitation centres along with voluntary patients.

8.4.5 *Patients Who Voluntarily Seek Treatment*

A substantial proportion of substance users seek help via psychiatry out-patient clinics, primary care services, or private general practitioners. Patients who actively seek treatment will have access to admissions for detoxification in acute psychiatry wards, rehabilitation placements, community detoxification, or other out-patient treatment options including relapse prevention treatment. These patients are at an advantage as detoxification and rehabilitation often happen as components of a long-term treatment plan, and they are already complying with community follow-up.

8.4.6 *Out-patient and Community Follow-Up*

Only a few centres have dedicated substance use clinics as addiction psychiatry as a subspeciality has not been rolled out in the country yet. Follow-up for substance use disorders often happens via general psychiatry clinics with a working-age focus, but also catering for child, old age, and forensic patients.

The multidisciplinary team available for patients with substance use disorder in a non-specialised psychiatry clinic includes the consultant psychiatrist, psychiatry medical officers and trainees, clinic nurses, psychiatry social workers, occupational therapists, health care assistants, and community psychiatry nurses who offer assessment, diagnosis, treatment, and signposting for rehabilitation services.

Psychological interventions in this setup are offered by any of the above-mentioned staff categories as clinical psychologists are not recruited routinely in the public health service. Some of the fortunate university psychiatry units have the service of psychologists. Specialised psychological interventions for addiction such as group therapies are available depending on the interest of the staff in the absence of a dedicated service. Such therapies were some of the first services to be interrupted during the COVID-19 pandemic.

8.4.7 Routine Investigations

Clinical history examination tools such as CAGE and AUDIT are used to detect and quantify the amount of alcohol use which heavily depends on patient's readiness to divulge information to the doctor. Indirect biomarkers that look at the effect of alcohol on organ systems and body chemistry such as Gamma-glutamyl Transferase (GGT), Alanine Transaminase (ALT), and Mean Corpuscular Volume (MCV) are commonly combined with the above which will corroborate the clinical findings.

Public or government hospitals do not routinely check blood alcohol concentration or breathalyses in acutely intoxicated patients. Needless to say that Sri Lanka has not got access to newer direct alcohol biomarkers like phosphatidylethanol (PEth test) which has a 2–4 week window of detection and correlates with the amount of alcohol consumed in the previous weeks. Urinary drug screening using dipstick tests has recently been introduced in hospitals. Facilities to check blood levels of psychoactive substances are available in the main cities in specialised laboratories.

8.4.8 Standard Pharmacological Treatment

The standard treatment choice for alcohol detoxification is chlordiazepoxide which is available in the hospitals. Most of the substitute medications such as lorazepam and diazepam are available in the public sector except for oxazepam. Generic thiamine IV, IM, and oral preparations are widely available and used during the detoxification.

Disulfiram is intermittently available in the public sector hospitals. Naltrexone and acamprosate are not available in the public sector and many patients cannot afford to buy these in the private pharmacies where these drugs are available.

None of the smoking cessation medications are available in the public sector hospitals and even private sector pharmacies do not have medication consistently.

A methadone programme is not available for heroin-addicted patients, except for methadone in the tablet form on a named patient basis which is rarely used due to the fear of misuse and diversion. A methadone programme is deemed to be unsuitable in the current state due to the risk of diversion, difficulty in regularisation, and lack of conclusive evidence for success. Heroin withdrawals are currently managed symptomatically with medications such as painkillers, antiemetics, and sedatives.

8.4.9 Rehabilitation Centres

In 2022, there were 7 government alcohol de-addiction rehabilitation centres (in Gampaha, Kandy, Jaffna, Batticaloa, Kurunegala, Badulla, and Kilinochchi) where clients are admitted voluntarily for treatment programmes.

Drug rehabilitation centres are mainly run by the National Dangerous Drug Control Board (NDDCB) and are situated in Thalangama, Nittambuwa, Unawatuna, and Kandy. Before voluntary admission to rehabilitation centres, the counsellors will assess and engage the patient in several therapy sessions in preparation for admission. During the rehabilitation placement, individual, group, and family therapies are offered. The programme also involves health education, spiritual development, skills development, vocational training, and aftercare programmes. After two month in-patient rehabilitation period is over, the client is required to enter a relapse prevention programme, where parents and guardians are involved. These centres also admit non-voluntary patients through courts.

Kandakadu drug treatment and rehabilitation centre was established by the Ministry of rehabilitation and prison reforms as a centre for drug-addicted persons who are referred through the courts. People are treated with counselling, sports, religious and aesthetic activities, and educational and vocational training. Senapura rehabilitation centre located in Polonnaruwa district also serves as a drug rehabilitation centre for offenders. Drug rehabilitation centres have attracted criticism from human rights organisations for the military-like approach of the programme (Satkunanathan 2021).

There are privately run rehabilitation centres which are supervised by the NDDCB. Religious organisations have various setups that may not be registered as rehabilitation centres but accept patients for boarded interventions for breaking substance habits. Such facilities and treatment programmes are often unregulated and unsupervised by the authorities.

8.4.10 Community Organisations with a Key Role

There are several other services that can be approached by the people using substances or their families directly for information, psychological therapies, and rehabilitation.

National Dangerous Drug Control Board (NDDCB)

National Dangerous Drug Control Board (NDDCB) was established following the National Dangerous Drug Control Board Act No 11 of 1984 by the Sri Lankan parliament as the principle national institute charged with the formulation and review of a national policy relating to the prevention and control of the abuse of dangerous drugs, and the treatment and rehabilitation of the drug users, and as the institution that has the power to advise and make recommendations to the minister on such policy (National Dangerous Drug Control Board (NDDCB), Sri Lanka). Currently, NDDCB is governed by the Ministry of public security.

NDDCB offers a dedicated telephone line "1927" for the drug users or their families for information, telephone counselling, and referral to outreach officers. NDDCB has outreach officers in all 25 districts in Sri Lanka who are attached to divisional secretariat offices. They offer individual therapies and group therapies by themselves or jointly with local health staff, mainly for drug users and also for alcohol users.

NDDCB monitors and assists designated drug treatment centres in prisons and private treatment centres. NDDCB also provides rehabilitation and treatment for patients who come through court orders and community rehabilitation orders. Another objective is the reduction of personal and social disruptions associated with the drug use and the improvement of the quality of life of the client and his or her family. NDDCB does not have a needle exchange programme for IV drug users but they use other services like the National STD/AIDS control programme for sexually transmitted infection screening and harm reduction work.

NDDCB operates the National Narcotics Laboratory (NNL) which provides laboratory and scientific services for drug control and prevention services in Sri Lanka. They carry out drug analysis for investigations, provide drug detection test kits for consultancy services, and are involved in capacity building on the identification of emerging drugs, and countermeasures against Internet and social media drug sales and postal or courier drug trafficking.

NDDCB also carries out training programmes for skills development in prevention and promotes evidence-based practices in schools, universities, workplaces, and prisons. NDDCB issues certificates of being drug free, conducts workplace drug testing, carries out capacity building work for medical and counsellors, and conducts research (*National Dangerous Drug Control Board (NDDCB), Sri Lanka*).

National Authority on Tobacco and Alcohol (NATA)

In response to the globalisation of the tobacco epidemic, countries developed the framework convention of tobacco control of the WHO (WHO-FCTC), and as a result, The National Authority on Tobacco and Alcohol (NATA) was established by the National Authority on Tobacco and Alcohol Act, No. 27 of 2006. NATA is the pioneer government institution that will enact the legal aspects of tobacco and alcohol prevention in Sri Lanka with a mission to mobilise all social sectors to liberate society from harm caused by tobacco and alcohol (National Authority on Tobacco and Alcohol (NATA) 2024).

NATA advises the government on the implementation of the National policy on tobacco and alcohol; encourages health promotion through media and community projects; recommends measures to minimise the harm from consumption of tobacco and alcohol products, and minimising illicit drug use; recommends legal, taxation, and other measures for the implementation and monitoring of the national policy on tobacco and alcohol, encourages research; monitors economic and health issues, monitors the progress of all investigations; and liaises with local, regional, and international organisations on issues related to tobacco and alcohol. Over and above these functions, NATA also operates a helpline "1948" for support and counselling of substance users and their families.

Alcohol and Drug Information Centre (ADIC)

ADIC is a resource centre that promotes the demand reduction of alcohol, tobacco, and other drugs (ATOD). It also advocates for effective policies to control ATOD both nationally and internationally. ADIC provides technical help, promotional material, resource persons, and information in this regard. ADIC's vision is to make everyone realise that the use of drugs at whatever level is an impediment to happiness. ADIC aims to achieve the prevention of substance use through social change and education (Alcohol and Drug Information Centre (ADIC) 2024).

There are several other organisations such as the Social Services Department, the Ministry of Justice, Prison Affairs, Constitutional Reforms, the Department of Community-based corrections, Police Narcotics Bureau, and the Narcotics Control Unit of Sri Lanka Customs that contribute to the control of substances and assist with the legal processes related to the substance users.

8.4.11 Negative Aspects of the Substance Use Treatment Facilities, and the Infrastructure

Specialised substance use disorders clinics or dual diagnosis clinics are currently not widely available to substance-abusing patients in Sri Lanka. Plans to launch subspecialisation in addiction psychiatry have not worked out so far in a context the country is struggling to fill the general psychiatrists posts this year with the rapid brain drain of trained psychiatrists leaving for greener pastures (Hettiarachchi 2024). This has happened in the background of the forex crisis, increase of tax, recent adverse economic and political situation in Sri Lanka, and global shortage of health workforce. The loss of highly trained specialists to out-migration is a real issue when it comes to service development and subspecialisation (D de Silva and Sunil de Alwis 2022).

The lack of a well-organised general practitioner network that is best placed to follow up with substance users and ensure their engagement with the services is another hindrance to success.

The noteworthy absence of clinical psychologists in the teams makes the delivery of the psychological interventions which is the mainstay of treatment for addictions more challenging. Recruitment of psychologists to the public health service has not happened over the years, and occupational therapists, psychiatric social workers, nurses, and doctors were involved in delivering psychological interventions in some clinics.

It has been reported that between 75 and 80% of the individuals who have completed in-patient rehabilitation relapse in this setting, which may indicate the inadequacy of the current services (Fernando 2019).

Current treatment practices that take place in drug rehabilitation centres for offenders are criticised by human rights organisations as rigid and unhelpful. Stigma towards the drug users may discourage the drug users to seek help from family and their close network. A more user-friendly approach is therefore desirable.

Substance abuse seems to be a problem of the lower socio-economic standing in Sri Lanka. People from those strata are very vulnerable to take up drug habits due to bad neighbourhoods, substance-using peers, poor educational achievements, and labouring jobs that are underpaid that often require moving away from their villages, e.g., jobs at building sites, poverty, and lack of opportunities to progress. The effect of young people using substances will be felt by their wives, children, and the elderly (Sri Lanka: Stop Abusive Anti-Drug Operation and Release Those Arbitrarily Detained 2024). Most of the drug-related arrests are in the lower social classes and big fish seem to escape (Sri Lanka: Stop Abusive Anti-Drug Operation and Release Those Arbitrarily Detained 2024). Citizens have no confidence that the future will be different (Sri Lanka: Stop Abusive Anti-Drug Operation and Release Those Arbitrarily Detained 2024).

Disadvantaged communities such as women in urban slum areas who have migrated to the cities, with fragmented family structures, have become a new target for the drug vendors putting them in high-risk situations such as prostitution. More and more newborn babies of these mothers are diagnosed with substance withdrawal at birth.

News about arrests of corrupt officials who are supposed to control the drug trafficking shows a lack of strong law enforcement and governance which is a serious threat to the country's future (Arrests of Narcotics Police Highlight Sri Lanka's Drug Menace 2020).

The country's geographical location is posing a major threat due to the potential of Sri Lanka becoming a transshipment hub between the Asian opium fields and the rest of the world (Hettiarachchi 2024). Sri Lanka has become a convenient transit port for heroin traffickers from the Golden Triangle and the Golden Crescent increasing the availability of heroin in the country. It has been recognised as a threat to the national security of the country due to the increase of substance availability within the country and other related illegal operations that may come with it (CLCM Patabendige). Availability of the substances in the communities and neighbourhoods influences the take up of the habit. Cannabis is easily available in Sri Lanka due to the illegal cultivation of the plants.

8.4.12 Lessons that Can Be Learnt from Sri Lanka

Sri Lanka provides many interesting experiments on reducing the harm from substance use. These stem from several decades of activity by various community groups as well as state and non-state agencies. Some small-scale experiments have fizzled out while others have led to good results and become incorporated in more widely applied interventions. The main pillar on which these unique approaches rests is that of questioning the so-called positive effects of alcohol, tobacco, and other such substances, instead of focussing only on the negatives as a reason to reduce or quit. This includes recognising the media and other influences that incessantly glamourise substance use and attribute magical chemically induced states to their use. Another important component is getting citizens involved in these efforts rather than interventions being conducted by "authorities" only.

On alcohol, the approaches by a national-level NGO (Alcohol and Drug Information Centre; ADIC) have led to the application of little-known science in real-life settings. These so-called community actions have generated a good deal of public awareness about the chemical versus other influences that render alcohol use pleasurable. They have also addressed the question of how far "alcohol-induced" behaviours are stimulated by alcohol itself—as opposed to the social approval, permission, and expectation of certain kinds of behaviour after alcohol consumption. Such understanding has led to changes in real-life settings, on which the validation of the theory rests.

A factor that has been found influential in mobilising communities to take action is the hitherto unnoticed level of economic impact of alcohol and tobacco use. People are startled to learn how much they spend when they themselves do the calculations. A policy stimulus too has been the recognition of the proportion of income spent on alcohol by low-income families.

A second front of progress on alcohol interventions is the national policy arena. Sri Lanka has a unique national policy that applies to alcohol the same control measures that are widely applied in other countries to tobacco alone (NATA Act 2006).

Another approach, specific to alcohol, has been the questioning of the alleged health benefits of consuming small amounts of alcohol. The understanding has prevailed long before the current scientific community has moved to recognising that all levels of alcohol are harmful. This fact was recognised and applied by lay communities for a few decades now, despite the medically backed claims of alcohol's protective effect on health. These were based on understanding the spurious basis on which claims of health benefits were made (Fekjær and Fekjær 2012), long before results from more recent epidemiological evidence challenged mainstream medical views (Zhao et al. 2023; Biddinger et al. 2022).

On tobacco, general approaches that reduce the attractiveness were applied from around the mid-1990s. Sri Lanka's strong commitment to control tobacco has resulted in a significant decline in the smoking rate. The national policy approaches leading to the adoption of the "National Alcohol and Tobacco Authority" act and other measures have helped sustain the trend.

On illicit substance use too, how the attribution of magical subjective states to chemical intoxication has successfully been challenged should interest individuals and relevant agencies outside Sri Lanka. This has implications for the treatment sector too. A view seen among some in the treatment field is that addiction to the alleged ecstatic states generated by substances such as opiates is so overpowering that overcoming these must rely on providing medications that substitute for them. The ability of dependent persons to challenge through their own experience some of the tenets of mainstream therapeutic approaches may interest some readers.

Substance use is quite low among females and they act as a main source of help in seeking treatment for substances for their family members and supporting them through the journey out of the substance habit. Close family support and female empowerment act as resilience factors against substance use disorders. Similarly high literacy rate in the country and a large majority of children completing their school education are protective against substance use. Health promotion and primary prevention have been incorporated into school and university curriculums showing promise that the same line of work will be continued in the future.

8.5 Laws and Policies Related to Substance Abuse

8.5.1 Illicit Drug Control

Sri Lanka has committed to all three United Nations Conventions addressing drug abuse and trafficking: the Single Convention on Narcotic Drugs 1961, the Convention on Psychotropic Substances 1971, and the United Nations Convention Against Illicit Traffic in Narcotic Drugs and Psychotropic Substances 1988.

The primary legal framework governing drug control in Sri Lanka includes the Poisons, Opium, and Dangerous Drugs Act; the Penal Code; the Cosmetic, Devices, and Drugs Act; the Customs Ordinance; and the Indigenous Medical Act.

The commencement date of the Poisons, Opium, and Dangerous Drugs Ordinance of 1935 was 1st January 1936 and since then has undergone a number of amendments of which the latest one was the act No. 41 of 2022. It serves as the primary statutory legislation overseeing the mentioned illicit drugs within the country. The Customs Ordinance (Ordinance No. 17 of 1869) plays a pivotal role by imposing prohibitions and restrictions on both the import and export of substances prohibited under the above Ordinance.

Additional statutes incorporating provisions related to drugs include the Penal Code (Ordinance No. 2 of 1983, subsequently amended), with Chap. 14 specifically addressing aspects related to public health and safety.

The Cosmetics, Devices, and Drugs Act (Act No. 27 of 1980, amended by Act No. 38 of 1984) governs the manufacturing, sale, distribution, labelling, and advertising of all commercial drugs. Moreover, the Ayurveda Act (Act No. 31 of 1961, amended by Act No. 5 of 1962) grants ayurvedic physicians the authority to procure opium and cannabis for the manufacture of their medicinal preparations.

In addition, the other related legislation includes the Prevention of Narcotic drugs and Psycotropic Substance Ordinance No. 14 of 1984, Rehabilitation of persons, places and Articles Act No. 9 of 1987, and Drug Dependent Persons (Treatment And Rehabilitation) Act, No. 54 of 2007.

8.5.2 Tobacco Control

Sri Lanka officially ratified the Framework Convention on Tobacco Control on November 11, 2003. Notably, Sri Lanka holds the distinction of being the first country in Asia and the fourth globally to accomplish this significant milestone.

In 2006, Sri Lanka enacted the National Authority on Tobacco and Alcohol (NATA) Act 27, a comprehensive legislative measure aimed at safeguarding public health. This law rendered it illegal to distribute tobacco or alcohol products to individuals below the age of 21, mandated the incorporation of health warnings on labels, imposed higher taxes on cigarettes, limited advertising of mass media, and enforced a ban on smoking in all public spaces.

Additionally, the NATA Act established the National Authority on Tobacco and Alcohol, defining its organisational structure, powers, and operational mechanisms. Provisions within the document extended to the prohibition of vending machines for dispensing tobacco or alcohol products, as well as the restriction of advertisements and sponsorships related to these substances. The law further prohibited the free distribution of tobacco products and the use of tobacco product trademarks on non-tobacco items.

Crucially, the legislation introduced stringent tests for the constituents of tobacco products, ensuring a more rigorous regulatory framework. The NATA Act 27 represented a significant step towards promoting public health and curbing the harmful effects of tobacco and alcohol consumption in Sri Lanka.

In July 2012, NATA issued the Tobacco Products (Labelling and Packaging) Regulations, No. 01 of 2012, addressing concerns related to false, misleading, or deceptive messages on tobacco product packaging. The regulations stipulate the incorporation of pictorial health warnings, encompassing 80% of the total area of a packet, package, or carton. Additionally, the regulations mandate the inclusion of information on constituents and emissions to be printed on tobacco packages.

Moreover, the regulations specify that each cigarette manufacturer must ensure the inclusion of only one type of pictorial health warning from each category, as outlined in the Schedule to the regulations, on any packet, package, or carton containing cigarette products. These warnings were originally intended to be changed every six months. However, facing industry opposition, a legal challenge ensued, resulting in a directive from the Sri Lanka Court of Appeal in May 2014 instructing the Ministry to amend the regulations. Consequently, the size of the warning was reduced to 50–60% of the package.

On July 11, 2014, the Supreme Court of Sri Lanka endorsed revised regulations, directing the Ceylon Tobacco Company to exhibit pictorial health warnings covering 60% of the front and back panels of all packages by January 1, 2015. However, in February 2015, a parliamentary bill was passed, amending the National Authority on Tobacco and Alcohol Act No. 27 of 2006, and elevating pictorial warnings to 80%. These warnings, including pictorials printed on both sides, became mandatory for every cigarette packet, package, or carton, with changes required every six months. A grace period until June 1, 2015, was granted to manufacturers and importers of existing tobacco product stocks to comply with the provisions. Subsequently, cigarette packages in Sri Lanka are obligated to display health warnings covering 80% of the larger sides.

In 2016, Sri Lanka has implemented all aspects of the MPOWER package.

Smoke-free laws have proven to be effective in various settings, including healthcare, educational institutions, government facilities, indoor offices, workplaces, and public transport. These regulations contribute to creating environments that promote better public health by reducing exposure to second-hand smoke and supporting the well-being of individuals in these spaces. Enforcement is supported by relevant funds, with fines imposed on both smokers and establishments for non-compliance. Smoking cessation assistance is available through a toll-free quit-line/helpline, and healthcare facilities provide support, including prescription options like NRT and bupropion.

Tobacco advertising activities were largely banned in 2006, with further restrictions in 2016, extending to most media channels, except for international ones (Sri Lanka: Overview of Tobacco Use, Tobacco Control Legislation, and Taxation 2017).

8.5.3 Alcohol Control

Concerning alcohol control, Sri Lanka has a National Policy on Alcohol Control (2016), with the vision to achieve the best practice in alcohol control. It spells out the objectives of eliminating the promotion of alcohol products and alcohol use; enforcing pricing, trade, andinvestment policies to control alcohol trade; reducing availability and accessibility of alcohol; protecting the population from the consequences of alcohol use; eliminating injuries related to alcohol use; creating a social milieu to prevent initiation and discourage alcohol use; promoting surveillance and research on alcohol-related issues; strengthening the supportive services and rehabilitation; preventing alcohol industry interference on national policy on alcohol control as well as implementing and monitoring the national policy on the alcohol control with the provisions of NATA act.

In the view of achieving these objectives, the main strategies included to control alcohol consumption are (1) pricing and taxation, (2) regulating physical availability, (3) altering the drinking context, (4) education and persuasion, (5) regulating alcohol promotion, (6) drinking-driving countermeasures, and (7) treatment and early intervention.

8.6 Research on Substance Use and Substance Use Disorders

Substance use and related research in Sri Lanka have gained prominence in the recent past as the country grapples with the escalating challenges posed by various forms of substance abuse. To gain a comprehensive understanding of the specific challenges related to substance use within the country, it is imperative to conduct scientifically rigorous and nationally representative studies.

8.6.1 Epidemiological Studies on Prevalence and Associated Factors

Researchers in Sri Lanka have conducted epidemiological studies to assess the prevalence of substance use across different demographics. These studies encompass a range of substances, including alcohol, tobacco, and illicit drugs.

Findings often reveal variations based on age, gender, socio-economic status, and geographical locations, providing crucial insights for targeted interventions. These studies have been conducted among community-based samples as well as in specific populations. In assessing the magnitude of the issue community-based samples have been used more frequently for alcohol use and tobacco use in comparison to substance use.

For instance, community/population-based studies have been carried out assessing alcohol use in selected geographic areas (Zavos et al. 2015; De Silva et al. 2009), as well as defined populations including military personnel (Hanwella et al. 2012), undergraduates (Perera and Torabi 2012), college students, and family members such as spouses (Ariyasinghe et al. 2015) and children (Laslett et al. 2020).

In addition, community-based studies on the prevalence of tobacco use have been conducted in selected geographic locations (De Silva et al. 2009); institutionalised patients (Sumithrarachchi et al. 2024), youth groups (Dhanapriyanka et al. 2022a, b), and school children (CDC 2008). Furthermore, second-hand smoking in pregnant women (Perera et al. 2021) and school children (Alagiyawanna et al. 2018) has also been assessed.

On the other hand, substance use has been assessed among adolescents (Dissanayake et al. 2023), institutionalised patients (Jayamaha et al. 2022, 2023; Hapangama et al. 2013), Navy personnel (De Silva et al. 2016) as well as school children (Liyanage et al. 2013). Further, there are evidence generated from multi-centre studies on illicit drugs (Darshana et al. 2022) in this regard.

Exploration of context-specific factors associated with substance use is fundamental to developing effective preventive strategies. Research in Sri Lanka has explored various determinants such as socio-economic disparities, peer influences, mental health issues, and familial dynamics. Most of the epidemiological studies discussed above on alcohol, tobacco as well as substance use have either described or analysed associated factors. In addition, qualitative research approach has been also used to delve into social implications associated with alcohol use in rural settings (Sørensen et al. 2020).

8.6.2 Studies on Impact on Physical and Mental Health

The intricate relationship between substance use and mental health is another important aspect assessed in related research in Sri Lanka. Studies delve into the simultaneous occurrence of substance use disorders together with other mental health conditions, shedding light on the interconnected challenges faced by individuals. This research helps inform integrated treatment approaches that address both substance abuse and mental health issues simultaneously.

Effects on mental and social health in relation to alcohol use in special populations such as spouses (Ariyasinghe et al. 2015) and children (Laslett et al. 2020) have been studied. Furthermore, alcohol use, its related problems including psychological health in college students (Perera et al. 2011), and social factors associated with alcohol use (Sørensen et al. 2017) were other researched areas in the local context.

Several epidemiological studies have strengthened the local evidence base on tobacco and mental health (Wijesundera et al. 2014) as well as drug use and mental health (Dharmawardene and Menkes 2017). Apart from that, local studies have elucidated the Sociological factors related to smoking (Mahees et al. 2021).

Given the important and consistent associations of substance use with different cancers, few studies have been conducted shedding important evidence in the local context such as cancer burden with alcohol use (Edirisinghe et al. 2023) and tobacco use and oral cancer (Edirisinghe et al. 2022). In addition, there have been studies assessing the tobacco use and chronic non-communicable disease associations (Herath et al. 2022). Other than the non-communicable diseases, there are a few studies focussed on injury association with alcohol use among hospitalised patients (Schölin et al. 2022).

8.6.3 Economic Burden

The economic burden of substance abuse in Sri Lanka is a pressing concern that necessitates thorough research to quantify and understand its impact on the macro as well as micro-economy. Substance abuse contributes significantly to direct and indirect costs, encompassing healthcare expenses, loss of productivity, legal consequences, and social welfare expenditures.

Even though limited in number in comparison to other epidemiological aspects studies in Sri Lanka, it is noteworthy to mention the studies such as large-scale economic burden assessment in relation to alcohol use in Sri Lanka (Ranaweera et al. 2018) and household economic burden assessment in rural settings (Perera et al. 2017).

8.6.4 Intervention Studies

Researchers in Sri Lanka have examined the effectiveness of different interventions and treatment modalities for substance use disorders. This includes pharmacological interventions, behavioural therapies, and community-based rehabilitation programmes. Evaluating the outcomes of such interventions contributes to refining treatment protocols and enhancing the overall effectiveness of substance abuse interventions.

For instance, studies related to alcohol use include community-based education interventions (Pearson et al. 2023) as well as behaviour change interventions (Sørensen et al. 2023a, b). Similarly, an evaluation of successful capacity building programmes was carried out about tobacco use (Jayasinghe et al. 2021).

8.6.5 Policy and Control Strategies Related to Research

Research efforts extend to assessing the impact of existing policies and legal frameworks on substance use in Sri Lanka. Studies that focus on evaluating the efficacy of regulatory measures and strategies provide valuable insights into areas of improvement and addressing potential gaps.

Among the studies with regard, the majority are focussed on tobacco use. Tobacco control strategies (Rajapaksa et al. 2021) as well as control policies (Perera et al. 2020; Athauda et al. 2019) have been the focus of some of the recently conducted local studies.

8.6.6 Challenges and Future Research

While substance use research in Sri Lanka has made significant strides especially during the recent past, challenges persist. Limited funding, stigma associated with substance abuse, and the rapidly evolving nature of the drug landscape pose ongoing challenges for researchers.

Future directions should prioritise longitudinal studies to elicit potential causal relationships of identified associations in the local context, collaborative research initiatives for attracting more funding for research and expertise, and the integration of technology for more robust data collection and analysis involving sensitive data appropriately.

Furthermore, it is crucial to employ mixed method research approaches to delve into the intricate interplay of social, economic, and cultural factors that contribute to substance use in different settings.

Investing in well-designed, comprehensive studies that are both scientifically rigorous and nationally representative is essential to develop a better understanding of substance use challenges, which would guide informed policy decisions and facilitate the implementation of effective interventions aimed at promoting public health and mitigating the impact of substance use within the country.

8.7 Future Directions

Current evidence suggests prison sentence for using drugs is not an effective strategy as they often resume the drug habit on release. People affected by substance use should be able to receive more acceptable and personalised treatment programmes that are sensitive to socio-cultural beliefs and practices. While the suitability of an opioid substitution therapy such as a methadone programme is being debated in the country, employing other pharmacological strategies to manage withdrawals and to prevent relapse and improving focus on harm reduction strategies are immediately doable. Scrutiny of the currently practised psychological interventions such as counselling, and re-designing the approach to include better identification of patients for treatment programmes, early preparation for the detoxification using evidence-based psychological interventions, and vigorous follow-up therapy will be essential in order to make a difference in this client group. Capacity building that includes staff training, recruitment of psychologists, and developing addiction psychiatry as a subspeciality will be a good starting point in this battle (Nawaratne and Vidanapathirana 2023). Although individual institutions in Sri Lanka are weak in the resources, a coordinated approach that will pool the resources from all the organisations that are involved may overcome some of the difficulties we are facing at present.

Policy and law reforms regarding the handling of substance users and looking at ways to allocate better funding for a coordinated treatment programme should facilitate the protection of human rights and upliftment of the quality of life for the patients and families affected by substance habits. Opportunities for service users and their family members to feedback about the care received and their participation in designing treatment programmes need to be put in place. Barriers to seek treatment such as stigma and discrimination needs to be actively combated using staff education and training programmes in health and criminal justice services and less intensive interventions to reduce stigma and improve health literacy related to substance use should also be given to the society at large.

Sri Lanka currently has strict media rules and it is crucial that positive portrayal of substance use by celebrities as well as substance pro-advertisements continue to be barred in the movies and media. It is commendable that Sri Lanka does not allow sports events to be sponsored by alcohol or tobacco companies. Scrutiny of social media for promoting substances and regulation of such practices is a new challenge that needs to be focussed on now.

Effective and culture sensitive interventions to prevent substance use among adolescents need to be developed that include empowering parents to improve parenting practices, enabling schools and other community organisations to engage young people, increasing awareness about various social influences that promote substance use and teaching resistance skills, imparting them with correct knowledge, and improving their social competence and life skills (Griffin and Botvin 2010). Promoting such activities that are already taking place and thinking of ways to provide a better coverage to involve all schools and youth organisations is necessary

(Madhumadawa et al. 2019). Profile of the health promotion activities in the communities and universal, selected, and indicated prevention activities in the country need to be elevated and incorporated to become routine practices and the norms of the Sri Lankan society (Guruge et al. 2021).

Strict enforcement of laws that control access of substances to young people and ensuring the measures that generally reduce or restrict the availability of substances in the community need to be upscaled in parallel with other individual and community measures. Promoting research to identify helpful practices that are suitable in the Sri Lankan context, taking proactive steps to handle new substances entering the country, and uniting with neighbouring countries to handle the substance use problem in the region are other necessary steps towards a secure future for the young people of South-East Asia.

8.8 Conclusion

Widespread use of psychoactive substances is a serious threat to the citizens' health as well as the development of the Sri Lankan economy. People using substances are often ostracised from the society making them and their families helpless and causing unnecessary suffering, inadvertently putting the society in an even more dangerous situation. The need for interventions to prevent substance-related harm should be recognised immediately. Better accountability and responsibility need to be taken in providing care for the affected persons, and opportunities to breach human rights need to be minimised in this process. Adequate resource allocation, ensuring correct policies and guidelines are in place to direct resources and treatment strategies, recruitment and training of correct staff categories, and coordination of services are urgently needed to prevent harm to young people and citizens who can otherwise contribute to the productivity of the Sri Lankan society.

References

Abayaratna, S., & Krishnarasa, K. (1997). National Oral Health Survey 1994/95: Ministry of Health, Sri Lanka.

Abeysundara, D. (2016). What's Your Poison? Alcohol Consumption + Content A Major Problem Among Sri Lankan Tea Workers. The Catamaran. https://thecatamaran.org/?p=2960

Alagiyawanna, A. M. A. A. P., Veerasingam, E. Q., & Townsend, N. (2018). Prevalence and correlates of exposure to second hand smoke (SHS) among 14 to 15 year old schoolchildren in a medical officer of health area in Sri Lanka. BMC public health, 18, 1–8. https://doi.org/10.1186/s12889-018-6148-4

Alcohol and drug information centre (ADIC); 2024. https://adicsrilanka.org/

Alcohol and Drug Information Centre. (2021). Annual Trend Survey on Alcohol consumption in Sri Lanka, 2022. https://adicsrilanka.org/wp-content/uploads/2023/10/Alcohol-Trend-Survey-2022-designed.pdf

Alcohol, Sri Lanka country profile, WHO. (2018). https://www.who.int/publications/m/item/alcohol-lka-2019

Ariyasinghe, D., Abeysinghe, R., Siriwardhana, P., & Dassanayake, T. (2015). Prevalence of major depressive disorder among spouses of men who use alcohol in a rural community in Central Sri Lanka. Alcohol and Alcoholism, 50(3), 328–332. https://doi.org/10.1093/alcalc/agu105

Arrests of narcotics police highlight Sri Lanka's drug menace. (2020). AlJazeera News. https://www.aljazeera.com/news/2020/9/17/arrests-of-narcotics-police-highlight-sri-lankas-drug-menace

Athauda, L. K., Pathiraja, C. K., Pathirana, A. C., Pathiraja, S. K., Nonis, W. M., & Nimrod, D. (2019). Adherence to tobacco control policy implementation: a cross sectional study in a selected area in Ragama town, Sri Lanka. https://doi.org/10.4038/cmj.v64i1.8826

Baklien, B., & Samarasinghe, D. (2005). Alcohol and poverty in Sri Lanka. Forut. https://forut.no/alcohol-and-poverty-in-sri-lanka/#:~:text=The%20research%20report%20%C2%ABAlcohol%20and,on%20Alcohol%2C%20Drugs%20and%20Development.

Biddinger, K. J., Emdin, C. A., Haas, M. E., Wang, M., Hindy, G., Ellinor, P. T., & Kathiresan, S. (2022). Association of Habitual Alcohol Intake With Risk of Cardiovascular Disease. 5(3), 1–12. https://doi.org/10.1001/jamanetworkopen.2022.3849

Centers for Disease Control and Prevention (CDC). (2008). Tobacco use among students aged 13–15 years—Sri Lanka, 1999–2007. MMWR. Morbidity and mortality weekly report, 57(20), 545–549.

Darshana, N., Wijesinghe, C. J., & De Silva, P. V. (2022). Assessment of characteristics and exposure to vulnerable factors for drug use among male illicit drug users in Sri Lanka: A multicenter cross-sectional study. Indian Journal of Community Medicine: Official Publication of Indian Association of Preventive & Social Medicine, 47(2), 285. https://doi.org/10.4103/ijcm.ijcm_712_21

De Silva, V., Samarasinghe, D., & Gunawardena, N. (2009). Alcohol and tobacco use among males in two districts in Sri Lanka. Ceylon Med J, 54(4), 119–124. https://doi.org/10.4038/cmj.v54i4.1452

De Silva, V. A., Jayasekera, N., & Hanwella, R. (2016). Cannabis use among Navy personnel in Sri Lanka: a cross sectional study. BMC research notes, 9(1), 1–6. https://doi.org/10.1186/s13104-016-1988-4

de Silva, D., Sunil de Alwis, P. A. (2022). Update on critical issues faced by the health sector in Sri Lanka. Sri Lanka Journal of Health Research, 2(1). gov.lk/wp-content/uploads/2022/08/Sri-Lanka-Journal-of-Health-Research-Vo.02-Iss.-01-December-2022-1.pdf https://doi.org/10.4038/sljhr.v2i1.47

Dhanapriyanka, M., Kanthi, R. D. F. C., Jayasekara, P., & Ha, D. H. (2022a). Tobacco chewing and associated factors among a vulnerable youth population in Sri Lanka. BMC Public Health, 22(1), 1–7. https://doi.org/10.1186/s12889-022-14704-6

Dhanapriyanka, M., Kanthi, R. D. F. C., Jayasekara, P., & Ha, D. H. (2022b). Tobacco chewing and associated factors among a vulnerable youth population in Sri Lanka. BMC Public Health, 22(1), 2209. https://doi.org/10.1186/s12889-022-14704-6

Dhanarisi, H. J., Gawarammana, I. B., Mohamed, F., & Eddleston, M. (2018). Relationship between alcohol co-ingestion and outcome in profenofos self-poisoning–a prospective case series. PLoS one, 13(7), e0200133. https://doi.org/10.1371/journal.pone.0200133

Dharmawardene, V., & Menkes, D. B. (2017). Violence and self-harm in severe mental illness: inpatient study of associations with ethnicity, cannabis and alcohol. Australasian psychiatry, 25(1), 28–31. https://doi.org/10.1177/1039856216671650

Dissanayake, L., Jabir, S., Shepherd, T., Helliwell, T., Selvaratnam, L., Jayaweera, K., ... & Sumathipala, A. (2023). The aftermath of war; mental health, substance use and their correlates with social support and resilience among adolescents in a post-conflict region of Sri Lanka. Child and adolescent psychiatry and mental health, 17(1), 101. https://doi.org/10.1186/s13034-023-00648-1

Edirisinghe, S. T., Weerasekera, M., De Silva, D. K., Liyanage, I., Niluka, M., Madushika, K., ... & Yasawardene, S. (2022). The risk of oral cancer among different categories of exposure to tobacco smoking in Sri Lanka. Asian Pacific Journal of Cancer Prevention: APJCP, 23(9), 2929–2935. https://doi.org/10.31557/APJCP.2022.23.9.2929

Edirisinghe, S. T., Devmini, T., Pathmaperuma, S., Weerasekera, M., De Silva, K., Liyanage, I., ... & Yasawardene, S. (2023). Risk Assessment of Alcohol Consumption for Oral Cancer: A Case-Control Study in Patients Attending the National Cancer Institute (Apeksha Hospital, Maharagama) of Sri Lanka. Asian Pacific Journal of Cancer Prevention: APJCP, 24(4), 1181. https://doi.org/10.31557/APJCP.2023.24.4.1181

Fekjær, H. O., & Fekjær, H. O. (2012). Alcohol — a universal preventive agent ? A critical analysis. 2051–2057. https://doi.org/10.1111/add.12104

Fernando, R., Senannayake, B., & Darshana, T. (2017). Trends, Patterns and Prevalence of Injecting Drug Users (IDUs) in Sri Lanka. National Dangerous Drugs Control Board. http://www.nddcb.gov.lk/Docs/research/IDU_SL.pdf

Fernando, A. (2019). More than 75% of rehabilitated drug users return to habit. The Sunday Times, Sri Lanka. https://www.sundaytimes.lk/190120/news/more-than-75-of-rehabilitated-drug-users-return-to-habit-331229.html#:~:text=View(s)%3A,of them relapsing%2C experts said. https://doi.org/10.1177/11782218221100823

Griffin, K. W., & Botvin, G. J. (2010). Evidence Based Interventions for Preventing Substance Use Disorders in Adolescents. Child Adolesc Psychiatr Clin N Am, 19(3), 505–526. https://doi.org/10.1016/j.chc.2010.03.005

Guruge, N., Rathnayake, N., Perera, S., Kumara, S., Thilakarathna, U., Young, S., & Kithalawaarachchi, S. (2021). Empowering government field officers on tobacco control using health promotion interventions: examples from Anuradhapura district, Sri Lanka. 15th Asia Pacific Conference on Tobacco on Health.

Hand book of drug abuse information in Sri Lanka, National Dangerous Drug Control Board Sri Lanka. (2023). https://www.nddcb.gov.lk/Docs/research/Final_Handbook_2023.pdf

Hanwella, R., de Silva, V. A., & Jayasekera, N. E. (2012). Alcohol use in a military population deployed in combat areas: a cross sectional study. Substance abuse treatment, prevention, and policy, 7(1), 1–7. https://doi.org/10.1186/1747-597x-7-24

Hapangama, A., Kuruppuarachchi, K. A. L. A., & Pathmeswaran, A. (2013). Substance use disorders among mentally ill patients in a General Hospital in Sri Lanka: prevalence and correlates. The Ceylon Medical Journal. 58(3), 111–115. https://doi.org/10.4038/cmj.v58i3.6103

Herath, P., Wimalasekera, S., Amarasekara, T., Fernando, M., & Turale, S. (2022). Effect of cigarette smoking on smoking biomarkers, blood pressure and blood lipid levels among Sri Lankan male smokers. Postgraduate Medical Journal, 98(1165), 848–854. https://doi.org/10.1136/postgradmedj-2021-141016

Hettiarachchi, K. (2024). Sri Lanka short of 630 medical specialists this year, State sector peripheral hospitals in grave danger and patients in jeopardy. The Sunday Times, Sri Lanka.

Jayamaha, A. R., Herath, N. D., Dharmarathna, N. D., Sandakumari, H. S., Ranadeva, N. D., Fernando, M. M., ... & Fernando, N. (2023). Health-related quality of life in patients with substance use disorders enrolled to the residential treatment in Sri Lanka: a retrospective cross-sectional study. Quality of Life Research, 32(2), 435–445. https://doi.org/10.1007/s11136-022-03270-4

Jayamaha, A. R., Dharmarathna, N. D., Herath, N. D., Ranadeva, N. D., Fernando, M. M., Samarasinghe, K. L., ... & Fernando, N. (2022). The pattern of substance use and characteristics of the individuals enrolled in residential treatment at selected rehabilitation centers in Sri Lanka: A descriptive cross-sectional study. Substance Abuse: Research and Treatment, 16, 11782218221100823. https://doi.org/10.1177/11782218221100823

Jayasinghe, R. D., Jayasooriya, P. R., Amarasinghe, H., Hettiarachchi, P. V. K. S., Siriwardena, B. S. M. S., Wijerathne, U. K. Y. G. D. M., ... & Tilakaratne, W. M. (2021). Evaluation of successfulness of capacity building programmes on smokeless tobacco and areca nut cessation. Asian Pacific journal of cancer prevention: APJCP, 22(4), 1287. https://doi.org/10.31557/apjcp.2021.22.4.1287

Laslett, A. M., Stanesby, O., Graham, K., Callinan, S., Karriker-Jaffe, K. J., Wilsnack, S., ... & Room, R. (2020). Children's experience of physical harms and exposure to family violence from others' drinking in nine societies. Addiction research & theory, 28(4), 354–364. https://doi.org/10.1080/16066359.2019.1704272

Liyanage, I. K., Wickramasinghe, K., Ratnayake, H. E., Palmer, P., Matthews, D. R., & Katulanda, P. (2013). Use of illicit substances among schoolchildren in Colombo District, Sri Lanka. Substance abuse, 34(2), 137–142. https://doi.org/10.1080/08897077.2012.726961

Madhumadawa, J., Neranjana, R., Airawansha, N., Baduge, F., Wijesundara, W., Ranapathy, R., Gunerathne, H., Manamperi, M., Madhubashini, B., Rasiah, G., Anojan, S., Rathnayake, N., & Guruge, G. (2019). Empowering adolescents to identify media and company strategies that target youth through health promotion interventions in Kothmale, Nuwara Eliya District, Sri Lanka. World Conference on Child and Youth 2019.

Mahees, M., Amarasinghe, H. K., Usgodaarachchi, U., Ratnayake, N., Tilakaratne, W. M., Shanmuganathen, S., ... & Abeykoon, P. (2021). A sociological analysis and exploration of factors associated with commercial preparations of smokeless tobacco use in Sri Lanka. Asian Pacific journal of cancer prevention: APJCP, 22(6), 1753. https://doi.org/10.31557/apjcp.2021.22.6.1753

National Authority on Tobacco and Alcohol (NATA). 2024, https://nata.gov.lk/web/index.php?lang=en

National Authority on Tobacco and Alcohol Act, No. 27 of 2006. https://www.nddcb.gov.lk/Docs/acts/NATA%20Act%20English.pdf

National Dangerous Drug Control Board (NDDCB), Sri Lanka. (2018). https://www.nddcb.gov.lk/index.php

National Prevalence Survey on Drugs Use 2019, NDDCB Presidential task force on Drug prevention, Sri Lanka Police. (2019). https://www.nddcb.gov.lk/Docs/research/National%20Prevalence%20Survey%20on%20Drugs%20Use%202019.pdf

Nawaratne, S., & Vidanapathirana, J. (2023). Improving substance use disorder care: Service providers' perceptions on barriers to drug use treatment in the Western Province Sri Lanka. Asian Journal of Interdisciplinary Research, 6(4), 1–9. https://doi.org/10.54392/ajir2341

Pearson, M., Dawson, A., Raubenheimer, J., Senerathna, L., Conigrave, K., Lee, K. K., ... & Glozier, N. (2023). Community-based alcohol education intervention (THEATRE) study to reduce harmful effects of alcohol in rural Sri Lanka: design and adaptation of a mixed-methods stepped wedge cluster randomised control trial. BMJ open, 13(6), e064722. https://doi.org/10.1136/bmjopen-2022-064722

Perera, B., & Torabi, M. R. (2012). Alcohol use behavior among undergraduates: A cross-cultural comparison between the United States and Sri Lanka. Southeast Asian J Trop Med Public Health, 43(4), 1025–1034. https://doi.org/10.1016/j.jobcr.2021.05.001

Perera, K. M. N., Guruge, G. D., & Jayawardana, P. L. (2017). Household expenditure on tobacco consumption in a poverty-stricken rural district in Sri Lanka. Asia Pacific Journal of Public Health, 29(2), 140–148. https://doi.org/10.1177/1010539517690225

Perera, A. S., Jayasinghe, R. M., Rajapakse, A., Ratnayake, R. M. H. E., & Jayasinghe, R. D. (2021). Second hand smoking and tobacco use among pregnant women in Yatinuwara Medical Officer of Health (MOH) area in Sri Lanka. Journal of Oral Biology and Craniofacial Research, 11(3), 442–446. https://doi.org/10.1016/j.jobcr.2021.05.001

Perera, S. K., Vaikuntam, B. P., John, D., & Senanayake, B. (2020). Designing an optimum fiscal policy for tobacco to maximise the tax revenue, social savings and the net monetary benefits in Sri Lanka. International Journal of Health Policy and Management, 9(6), 250. https://doi.org/10.15171/ijhpm.2019.114

Punyadasa, D., & Samarakkody, D. (2016). Community-based study on family-related contributory factors for childhood unintentional injuries in an urban setting of Sri Lanka. Asia-Pacific Journal of Public Health, 28(Suppl. 1), 102S–110S. https://doi.org/10.1177/1010539515616454

Rajapaksa, S. W., Vidanapathirana, J., Nawaratne, S., & Suranga, M. A. (2021). Tobacco Control Strategies Enrich the National Strategic Plan on Prevention and Control of Cancer in Sri Lanka.

Asian Pacific Journal of Cancer Prevention, 22(S2), 45–50. https://doi.org/10.31557/apjcp.2021.22.s2.45

Rajapaksa, Lalini Silva, Padmal de, Abeykoon, Palitha, Somatunga, Lakshmi, Sathasivam, S. (2021). Sri Lanka health system review. In Health Systems in Transition (Vol. 10, Issue 1). https://iris.who.int/handle/10665/342323.

Ranaweera, S., Amarasinghe, H., Chandraratne, N., Thavorncharoensap, M., Ranasinghe, T., Karunaratna, S., … & De Silva, A. (2018). Economic costs of alcohol use in Sri Lanka. PLoS One, 13(6), e0198640. https://doi.org/10.1371/journal.pone.0198640

Raveendran, S., & Hulathduwa, S. R. (2021). Changing Patterns in the Types and Methods of Abuse of Illegal Drugs in Sri Lanka: A Study Based on Five Recent Case Series. Medico-Legal Journal of Sri Lanka, 9(1), 37. https://doi.org/10.4038/mljsl.v9i1.7439

Reitsma, M. B., Kendrick, P. J., Ababneh, E., Abbafati, C., Abbasi-Kangevari, M., Abdoli, A., … & Gorini, G. (2021). Spatial, temporal, and demographic patterns in prevalence of smoking tobacco use and attributable disease burden in 204 countries and territories, 1990–2019: a systematic analysis from the Global Burden of Disease Study 2019. The Lancet, 397(10292), 2337–2360. https://doi.org/10.1016/s2468-2667(21)00102-x

Satkunanathan, A. (2021). A Broken System: Drug Control, Detention and Treatment of People Who Use Drugs in Sri Lanka. https://www.hri.global/files/2021/08/03/HRI_Report_-_Sri_Lanka_Drug_Control.pdf

Schölin, L., Weerasinghe, M., Agampodi, S., Chathurange, U., Rajapaksha, S., Holloway, A., … & Pearson, M. (2022). Involvement of alcohol in injury cases in rural Sri Lanka: prevalence and associated factors among in-patients in three primary care hospitals. BMC public health, 22(1), 514. https://doi.org/10.1186/s12889-022-12958-8

Sehgal, R. (2024). Travel to Sri lanka-"The Pearl of the Indian Ocean". Thomas Cook India Travel Blog. https://www.thomascook.in/blog/travel-to-sri-lanka

Somatunga, L. C., Sinha, D. N., Sumanasekera, P., Galapatti, K., Rinchen, S., Kahandaliyanage, A., Mehta, F. R., & Jayasuriya-Dissanayake, N. L. (2012). Smokeless tobacco use in Sri Lanka. Indian Journal of Cancer, 49(4), 357–363. https://doi.org/10.4103/0019-509X.107729

Sørensen, J. B., Konradsen, F., Agampodi, T., Sørensen, B. R., Pearson, M., Siribaddana, S., & Rheinländer, T. (2020). A qualitative exploration of rural and semi-urban Sri Lankan men's alcohol consumption. Global public health, 15(5), 678–690. https://doi.org/10.1080/17441692.2019.1642366

Sørensen, J. B., Lee, K. K., Dawson, A., Dawson, A., Senarathna, L., Pushpakumara, P. J., … & Pearson, M. (2023a). Evaluating the programme and behavior change theories of a community alcohol education intervention in rural Sri Lanka: a study protocol. Global Health Action, 16(1), 2273625. https://doi.org/10.1080/16549716.2023.2273625

Sørensen, J. B., Pearson, M., Pushpakumara, J., Leth-Sørensen, D., Buhl, A., Konradsen, F., & Senarathna, L. (2023b). Alcohol use, self-harm and suicide: a scoping review of its portrayal in the Sri Lankan literature. Heliyon. https://doi.org/10.1016/j.heliyon.2023.e17566

Sørensen, J. B., Agampodi, T., Sørensen, B. R., Siribaddana, S., Konradsen, F., & Rheinländer, T. (2017). 'We lost because of his drunkenness': the social processes linking alcohol use to self-harm in the context of daily life stress in marriages and intimate relationships in rural Sri Lanka. BMJ global health, 2(4). https://doi.org/10.1136/bmjgh-2017-000462

South Asia Regional Profile—Sri Lanka. https://www.unodc.org/pdf/india/publications/south_Asia_Regional_Profile_Sept_2005/13_srilanka.pdf

Sri Lanka: Stop Abusive Anti-Drug Operation and Release Those Arbitrarily Detained. (2024). Human Rights Watch. https://www.hrw.org/news/2024/01/15/sri-lanka-stop-abusive-anti-drug-operation-and-release-those-arbitrarily-detained

Subramaniam, P., & Sivayogan, S. (2001). The prevalence and pattern of wife beating in the Trincomalee district in eastern Sri Lanka. *Southeast Asian Journal of tropical medicine and public health, 32*(1), 186–195.

Sumithrarachchi, S., Athukorala, I., Rumy, F., & Jayasinghe, R. (2024). Prevalence of tobacco and areca-nut use among patients attending dental teaching hospital in the central province of Sri

Lanka and its association with oral mucosal lesions; a cross sectional study. Journal of Oral Biology and Craniofacial Research, 14(1), 39–43. https://doi.org/10.1016/j.jobcr.2023.11.006
United Nations Country profile: Sri Lanka. (2006). In country profile.
Welagedara, L. (2020). Country Statement—Sri Lanka 63 rd Session of the Commission on Narcotic Drugs (CND) National Dangerous Drugs Control Board, Sri Lanka.
WHO Alcohol Sri Lanka 2019 country profile. https://cdn.who.int/media/docs/default-source/country-profiles/substances-abuse/lka.pdf?sfvrsn=c64ecc99_3&download=true
WHO report on the global tobacco epidemic, 2023: protect people from tobacco smoke. (2023). https://www.who.int/publications/i/item/9789240077164
Wijesundera, H., Hanwella, R., & de Silva, V. A. (2014). Antipsychotic medication and tobacco use among outpatients with schizophrenia: a cross-sectional study. Annals of general psychiatry, 13, 1–5. https://doi.org/10.1186/1744-859x-13-7
World Bank Group Global Tobacco Control Program Country Brief. (2017). Sri Lanka Overview of Tobacco Use, Tobacco Control Legislation, and Taxation. https://documents1.worldbank.org/curated/en/478361561398136333/pdf/Sri-Lanka-Overview-of-Tobacco-Use-Tobacco-Control-Legislation-and-Taxation.pdf
World Health Statistics. (2023). In Monitoring health for the SDGs. https://www.who.int/data/stories/world-health-statistics-2023-a-visual-summary/
www.unodc.org/documents/commissions/CND/CND_Sessions/CND_63/Statements63_02.03.2020/Country_02.03.2020/Sri_LAnka.pdf
Zavos, H. M., Siribaddana, S., Ball, H. A., Lynskey, M. T., Sumathipala, A., Rijsdijk, F. V., & Hotopf, M. (2015). The prevalence and correlates of alcohol use and alcohol use disorders: a population based study in Colombo, Sri Lanka. BMC psychiatry, 15, 1–8. https://doi.org/10.1186/s12888-015-0549-z
Zhao, J., Stockwell, T., Naimi, T., Churchill, S., Clay, J., & Sherk, A. (2023). Association Between Daily Alcohol Intake and Risk of All-Cause Mortality A Systematic Review and Meta-analyses. 6(3), 1–17. https://doi.org/10.1001/jamanetworkopen.2023.6185

Chapter 9
Substance Use Disorder in South Asia: Challenges and Ways Ahead

Arpit Parmar, Dibyendu Mohanty, Arghya Pal, and Amit Singh

9.1 Introduction

Substance use is a major public health concern across the world. As per the World Health Organization (WHO), around 22.3% of the population of the world used tobacco in 2020. On the other hand, the use of drugs is reported by one in every 17 people worldwide (World Drug Report 2023a). Cannabis continues to be the most common illicit drug use, with an estimated prevalence of 4.3% globally. This translates to 219 million cannabis users globally. Around 60 million people reported non-medical recreational use of various opioids in 2021. During the last decade, there has been a 23% increase in the use of drugs. Finally, around 2.348 billion of the world's population drink alcohol, as per the WHO Global Status Report on Alcohol and Health (2018). Around 1.5% of the global burden of disease (as measured by DALYs) is attributable to substance use conditions. Substance use disorders (SUDs) account for 3.1% of the Years of Healthy Life lost due to Disability (YLDs) (World Health Organization 2022).

A. Parmar (✉) · D. Mohanty
All India Institute of Medical Sciences, Bhubaneswar, Odisha 751019, India
e-mail: dr.arpitparmar@gmail.com

A. Pal
All India Institute of Medical Sciences, Kalyani, West Bengal, India

A. Singh
King George Medical University, Lucknow, Uttar Pradesh, India

S. M. Y. Arafat and S. K. Kar (eds.), *Current Perspectives on Substance Use Disorders in South Asia*, https://doi.org/10.1007/978-981-97-6619-2_9

9.2 Drug Use in South Asia

The regional office for South Asia of the United Nations Office on Drugs and Crime (UNODC) covers six countries: Bangladesh, Bhutan, India, Maldives, Nepal, and Sri Lanka (UNODC 2023b). It comprises one-quarter of the world's population. An estimated 150–200 million population is affected by psychiatric disorders in this region, ranging from mood and anxiety disorders to a significant burden of SUD. A recent study has found the prevalence of common mental disorders to be 14.2%, which is slightly higher compared to the worldwide prevalence of 13.4%. When it comes to SUD, alcohol abuse was most prominent, with a 13% prevalence (Naveed et al. 2020). This was followed by cannabis at 3% and opioid and stimulant use at 1.84% and 0.48%, respectively. Tobacco, as a culturally acceptable behavior, is used more commonly in the form of chewable form compared to smoking. The prevalence of opiate use in South Asian countries is around 1.1%, almost double the estimated global average of 0.6% in 2021 (WHO 2023).

The South Asian region faces significant challenges in terms of substance use control. Such challenges exist in all aspects of substance use control, including supply reduction, demand reduction, and harm reduction. The chapter aims to discuss such issues in detail.

9.3 Challenges in Managing Substance Use in South Asia

Key challenges in South Asia in terms of managing substance use and related problems have been listed in Box 9.1.

Box 9.1: Key challenges in South Asian countries

- Easy availability and accessibility to illicit substances
- Unrecorded alcohol consumption
- Primarily criminal justice response (which is essentially ineffective) to drug use with less emphasis on public health aspects
- Criminalization of drug use
- No/poor support to harm reduction services in principle in national policies (harm reduction is often seen as supporting/encouraging drug use)
- Huge treatment gap
- Poor access to evidence-based treatment for SUDs
- Poor access to harm reduction services (low coverage of OAT and NSP)
- Poorly regulated private addiction treatment facilities
- Sociocultural factors, including faith healing practices
- High level of stigma and discrimination
- Poor awareness and understanding of the medical model of SUDs in general public and healthcare workers (including doctors)

- Limited trained manpower, budget, and resource allocation
- Poor integration of SUDs treatment services into mental health care and primary care
- Poor surveillance/research data on the epidemiology of substance use, their trends, and patterns, as well as other aspects of SUDs
- High prevalence of smokeless tobacco use, betel nut use, and country-made/home-brewed liquor

Supply Reduction

Alcohol-related policies

As per the WHO Global Status Report on Alcohol and Health 2014, only the WHO South-East Asia Region (contains all South Asian countries and the Democratic People's Republic of Korea, Indonesia, Myanmar, Thailand, and Timor-Leste) and the WHO Western Pacific region showed an increase in alcohol consumption (WHO 2018). All other WHO regions reported a decrease in consumption. Compared to other WHO regions (except the Eastern Mediterranean Region), this region had a lower percentage of the population with AUD. One of the unique features of alcohol use in the region is that more than 77% of alcohol consumption in the region is in the form of spirits (as compared to 50.1% worldwide). The per capita consumption among male users is also quite high in the region.

From the policy perspective, various factors that could be important in terms of increasing alcohol consumption in the region include (1) innovative methods of promotion of alcohol use in the region, such as social media promotions, product placements, movie storylines, and pop/music videos, (2) introduction of different types of alcohol products, and (3) interference from alcohol industry in policy development. Alcohol policies also vary significantly from complete prohibition in Maldives to regulation in India. In a country like India, where almost 1.42 billion people reside and contribute to huge numbers of people who use alcohol, there is no national policy on alcohol use. Considering that alcohol is a state subject in the country, alcohol regulations vary dramatically from one state to another (Parmar et al. 2023a, b).

Another great challenge in this region is the use of unrecorded alcohol. Unrecorded alcohol is usually produced, distributed, and sold outside the government-controlled channels. This includes traditional drinks that are produced in the homes or community, such as fermented products from wheat, maize, and rice. This also includes smuggled alcohol as well as alcohol bought from cross-border trafficking. In a country like Nepal, the unrecorded alcohol consumption is at least five times the recorded consumption. In India, unrecorded alcohol consumption stands at around 50% (World Health Organization 2018). These types of "home-brewed" liquor are, at times, part of socio-cultural practices and are part of normal day-to-day activities. Also, such alcohol is not produced by criminal syndicates or is not made in illegal alcohol facilities, thus making the issue more complex. Simple strengthening of alcohol-related laws and their enforcement does not impact such practices.

Trafficking, cultivation, and availability of drugs

There is a high rate of drug trafficking between countries in this region, especially opioids. This is largely due to two major factors. First, Afghanistan is the world's largest illicit opium producer, which supplies over 90% of the world's demand (UNODC 2023a). Secondly, this region is sandwiched between the Golden Crescent and the Golden Triangle, two of the world's most heroin-producing regions (Mandal et al. 2023). This makes the region fertile and more conducive for the drug to reach different countries across borders. In 2002, 20% of the global total of opioid users resided in this region. The number increased to 39% in 2021 (roughly 12 million people) (UNODC 2023a). Also, plants like opium poppy and cannabis are traditionally grown in this region. For example, cannabis grows as a wild plant in these countries. Illicit cultivation of opium is also a major concern, although the same has declined over the past two decades. The majority of heroin found in these countries originates from Southeast Asian countries, mainly Afghanistan.

Not just opium, even methamphetamine and Amphetamine type stimulants (ATS) are part of the drug trade, which is on the rise. More recently, methamphetamine laboratories have also been detected in South Asia. There are signs that there is increasing trafficking of methamphetamine through South Asia for markets in Oceania and Europe (UNODC 2023a). Some local manufacturing of such drugs has also been reported in these countries. At the same time, large seizures of precursor chemicals like ephedrine and pseudoephedrine are reported from this region. Based on the seizure data, the UNODC suggests that Bangladesh is the largest methamphetamine market in South Asia.

Criminalization of drug use

Criminalization of drug use continues across the world, including in South Asian countries. South Asian governments prefer primarily a criminal justice system approach for drug control and not a public health approach. All South Asian countries impose criminal and administrative penalties for drug consumption. At the same time, there are certain exceptions. For example, Indian law prohibits the use of any cannabis product (except Bhang—a cannabis leaves product) (Parmar et al. 2024). Death penalties for drug-related offenses exist in South Asian countries like Bangladesh and India (Girelli et al. 2022). Such criminalization stigmatizes those who use drugs and adds to the stigma of drug use, deterring them from seeking help and treatment. People who use drugs (PWUD) report various kinds of abuses, including abusive law enforcement practices, coercive treatment, and discriminatory access to healthcare, even denial of health services at times. To control drug use, mass arrests and human rights violations of PWUD have also been reported in South Asian countries like Sri Lanka and Bangladesh. It has been previously seen that the punitive laws and actions against PWUD impede efforts to reach them with harm and demand reduction measures such as OAT (Murphy et al. 2021).

Compulsory detention centers for PWUD

In line with the "war on drugs" approach, PWUDs are commonly detained in detention centers for "treatment and rehabilitation" in Asian countries. As per one Lancet study (Wegman et al. 2017), around 6 lakh PWUD are confined in such centers across the Asian continent. Such compulsory, abstinence-based approaches are found to be ineffective for the treatment and prevention of drug use after release. Though such centers are not reported in South Asian countries, there are some reports that NGO-based, faith-based, or private rehabilitation centers where human rights violations are reported are operational in countries like India, Pakistan, and Nepal. As per some reports, hundreds of such centers exist in South Asian countries. On the other hand, there are punitive systems of mandatory treatment in countries like Bangladesh, Bhutan, Maldives, and Sri Lanka. There are no sustained benefits of admission in such compulsory detention centers. However, studies report negative consequences, including health complications, increased HIV risk-taking behaviors, compounded stigma and discrimination, and violations of many basic human rights.

Demand reduction

Investment in healthcare and political commitment

Lack of investment in healthcare is another troubling phenomenon persisting in these parts. Compared to European countries and the USA, where more than 8% of GDP is generally spent on healthcare, the figures are at a discouraging 2% in South Asian countries except for Bhutan and Maldives, where the expenditure stands at 3.3% and 6.4%, respectively. Mental illnesses and SUDs are not a priority area for most governments in this region. Hence, the expenditure on mental health and SUDs is even lower. Less than 1% of the health budget is allocated to mental health in India.

Non-availability of regular epidemiological data to inform policy

Epidemiological surveys documenting the trends and patterns of substance use are the cornerstone for informing substance use policies and programs. Various monitoring systems exist in the western countries. For example, the Drug Abuse Warning Network (DAWN) of the Substance Abuse and Mental Health Services Administration (SAMHSA), USA, is a nationwide surveillance system that provides annual data about emergency department visits due to substance use-related issues. Such a system provides timely data on trends in substance use, especially related to novel substances of use (such as vaping and NPS). Similarly, the SAMSHA, USA, has been conducting the National Survey on Drug Use and Health (NSDUH) annually since 1971. NSDUH provides national-level data on the use of psychoactive substances, SUDs, mental health issues, and treatment. Such robust systems of documenting substance use trends and patterns are nonexistent in South Asian countries. For example, nationwide surveys on substance use in India have been conducted only twice till now (Parmar et al. 2023b). The trend of substance use in the region continues to change. The new nationwide survey from India reported heroin to be the most used opioid, as compared to opium, as seen during the first nationwide survey during the

2000s. Within a decade, the number of PWID jumped from 1.75 lakh to around 8.5 lakhs in India. Anecdotal evidence suggests increasing use of newer psychoactive substances in the region (UNODC 2023a). Thus, there is an urgent need to capture the extent of the ever-evolving market of drug use in the region.

Use of smokeless forms of tobacco and betel quid

An important difference from the Western countries in terms of substance use is the high prevalence of smokeless forms of tobacco use in South Asia. Though these smokeless products are used in more than 140 countries across the globe, their use is mainly concentrated in South Asian countries. Out of 356 million users from across the world, India is home to around 67% of users (Sinha et al. 2018). The use of smokeless tobacco among women is another major concern. In South Asia, drug and alcohol use is primarily a male phenomenon. However, the smokeless tobacco use is quite common in women of South Asia. As per one study, the prevalence of such use in women in Bangladesh was 33%, followed by 18.4% in India (Suliankatchi et al. 2019). Smoking cessation interventions have not been adequately assessed for smokeless tobacco users in the South Asian context. The findings of effectiveness for smoking, as well as studies on smokeless forms of tobacco from other Western countries, might not be readily applicable here.

Another substance that is commonly used in South Asian countries is betel quid. It is the fourth most common psychoactive substance used worldwide. Almost 600 million people use betel quid in the Asia Pacific region. The prevalence of its use ranges from 8.4 to 40% in countries of India, Pakistan, Nepal, and Sri Lanka (Lee et al. 2011). Despite its high prevalence and carcinogenic potential, the use of betel quid remains an orphan addiction. Very little research has been conducted to date on various addiction-related aspects of betel quid (Vashney et al. 2020). Furthermore, the availability of evidence-based treatment approaches is limited. Unlike tobacco use, there are no targeted cessation therapies. Only during the last decade have various countries enacted public health policies to deal with betel quid use's individual and public health costs (Dhingra and Jhanjee 2023).

Limited availability of trained workforce and resources

There is a shortage of psychiatrists, psychologists, nurses, and social workers to meet these regions' huge demand for care. The teaching in medical institutes regarding mental health and addiction is often abysmal. Medical students generally have minimal exposure to mental health practices, and the curriculum does not emphasize these postings and teachings (The Global Health Observatory 2023). Other non-mental health professionals play a significant role in identifying and referring such patients. These include community health workers, teachers, key community members, community volunteers, and religious leaders. However, the awareness and skills to deal with such problems in the community among these populations are inadequate. Although the bulk of cases with common mental disorders and SUDs are expected to present in primary care, integration of mental health and SUD care at such levels is almost negligible in the South Asian region. Primary care physicians are often not ready to treat such patients (Thara and Padmavati 2013).

In such a scenario, telepsychiatry could help overcome some of the system's shortcomings. The COVID-19 pandemic provided an opportunity to scale up such efforts to provide mental healthcare through teleservices. Of all the South Asian countries, India, Bangladesh, and Nepal have published their telemedicine guidelines after the onset of the COVID-19 pandemic. However, certain limitations still exist when it comes to SUD treatment (Mohan & Ambekar 2020; Parmar et al. 2020). All these countries prohibit prescriptions of medications that are either narcotic or psychotropic (such as buprenorphine, methadone, and benzodiazepines). Such medicines are of paramount importance for acute and long-term treatment of various SUDs.

There is also a lack of medications and equipment, with shortage being the norm rather than the exception. Medications for SUD, like naltrexone, acamprosate, buprenorphine, etc., are costly and are generally not affordable by the poor patient population. Also, the resources available are seldom used judicially and in line with evidence-based practices (Table 9.1).

Policy initiatives to improve accessibility and availability of SUD medicines

The World Health Organization (WHO) releases a list of medicines that are considered essential to satisfy the priority public health needs of the country/population. The selection is based on the prevalence of the disease and its public health relevance, evidence base, safety, and cost-effectiveness. Countries are supposed to make these medicines (or similar medicines) essential based on their own public health priorities. These are intended to be made available at all health system levels all the time, in assured quality, and at prices the health system can afford. In the latest list released in 2023, WHO EML has medications for all major SUDs (alcohol, tobacco, and opioids). However, most Asia Pacific countries do not include any SUD medicines in their national EML lists. All six South Asian countries have their own EML. However, the inclusion of SUD medicines is limited (Parmar et al. 2023). Recently released Indian EML added buprenorphine to their list, but it does not contain any alcohol-use medicine (Parmar et al. 2023a, b, c) (Table 9.2).

Table 9.1 Mental health workforce in South Asian countries (The Global Health Observatory 2023)

	Psychiatrists*	Mental health nurse*	Social workers in psychiatry*	Psychologists*
Bangladesh	0.13	0.87	NA	0.12
Bhutan	0.51	0.13	NA	NA
India	0.29	0.80	0.065	0.069
Maldives	2.39	NA	0.48	2.15
Nepal	0.36	0.56	NA	0.52
Pakistan	NA	NA	NA	NA
Sri Lanka	0.52	3.28	0.28	0.25

* per 1,00,000 population

Table 9.2 Inclusion of SUD medicines in the national EML of South Asian countries (UNODC 2023a)

	Buprenorphine	Methadone	Naltrexone	Varenicline	Bupropion	Nicotine replacement therapy	Acamprosate	Disulfiram
Bangladesh	No	No	No	No	No	No	No	No
Bhutan	No	No	No	No	No	No	No	No
India	Yes	No	No	No	No	Yes	No	No
Maldives	No	No	Yes	No	No	Yes	No	No
Nepal	Yes	Yes	No	No	No	No	No	Yes
Pakistan	No	Yes	No	No	No	Yes	No	No
Sri Lanka	No	Yes	Yes	Yes	No	Yes	No	No
WHO (2023)	Yes	Yes	Yes	Yes	Yes	Yes	Yes	No

Understanding of the medical model of addiction

In South Asian countries, addiction is generally viewed as a psychosocial issue rather than a biopsychosocial problem that requires treatment. These countries generally follow the conventional approach of drug demand reduction that centers around prevention, abstinence, and rehabilitation. The management focuses primarily on short-term withdrawal management, followed by rehabilitation. Addiction-related interventions are generally provided by the NGOs with some support from the government. The limited availability of treatment services in this region has been attributed to the limited understanding of the concept of addiction. This chronic, relapsing, remitting illness requires long-term treatment. However, there has been a recent increase in government addiction treatment centers in countries like India. Such poor understanding is highly reflected in the policies that control the use of narcotic and psychotropic drugs like buprenorphine and methadone—a cornerstone of treatment in opioid addiction, ultimately leading to meager availability of such drugs even for other chronic medical issues such as cancer and palliative care in the region.

Socio-cultural factors

The use of psychotropic substances for recreational and spiritual purposes has been prevalent since ancient times and is a socially acceptable behavior in many parts of the region. Tobacco use is highly prevalent in almost all countries in South Asia, and it is one of the largest producers and consumers of tobacco products in the world. Chewable tobacco is more prevalent in these parts as compared to smoking tobacco. Alcohol use is culturally acceptable in countries like India, Nepal, Bhutan, and Sri Lanka. There is a long-standing tradition of cannabis among sadhus in India, and it is associated with worshipping Lord Shiva. Bhang, a preparation of cannabis leaves, is often consumed in festivals like Holi (Balhara et al. 2020). Opium (such as poppy husk and after) is one of the most common forms of opioid use in India. Its use is socio-culturally sanctioned in the north/northwestern parts of the country (Parmar et al. 2017b, 2018). Government-sponsored bhang shops are legal in a few states of India. Muslim countries are stricter when it comes to alcohol and other psychotropics secondary to religious beliefs.

Faith healing practices

Faith healing practices are fairly prevalent in South Asian countries. This can be attributed to the lack of robust healthcare infrastructure and cultural acceptance of such practices, among other reasons. Various faith healing practices, including *puja*, prayers, the use of *tabeez*, specific rings, branding with rods, chaining in temples, and exorcism, are prevalent in the region for patients with various mental illnesses and SUDs. Some of these practices may be not just ineffective but can also be downright dangerous. Involvement in such practices may impede treatment seeking for SUDs. Apart from ethical issues with some of these faith healing practices in the case of SUDs, involvement in prolonged faith healing practices may unnecessarily delay the appropriate medical care and may cause the disease to progress further. This is especially important in cases like AUD, where not providing adequate medical treatment might be fatal (Sarkar 2014; Parmar et al. 2017a).

Stigma and discrimination

Stigma is another crucial determinant of treatment-seeking and outcomes among patients with mental illnesses and SUD. Diagnosis of SUD leads to experiencing various personal and professional barriers as well as discrimination. PWUDs suffer from multiple types of stigma, including internalized/self-stigma, structural stigma, and public stigma (Lowe et al. 2022; Balhara et al. 2016). Research suggests that PWUDs in South Asia have more pronounced self-stigma as compared to those with mental illnesses. Greater stigma is associated with poorer help-seeking as well as quality of life. Such stigma is significantly higher among women with SUDs. Interestingly, some studies have reported lower stigma with culturally sanctioned drugs such as opium (Gupta et al. 2019). At the same time, some other studies report no difference in stigma between legal and illegal substances (Manthey et al. 2022). Further, those with dual diagnosis suffer from more stigma than either of these illnesses alone and hence, they have more barriers in seeking treatment. Some evidence attributes this higher stigma to the presence of SUD, which is more stigmatized (especially in the South Asian context). The stigma is not only faced by PWUD but also extends to their family members and children (Herath and Ambekar 2018). Finally, other special populations such as women, sexual and gender minorities, the elderly, and homeless people with SUD suffer from more stigma and have more severe consequences of SUD (Sarkar et al. 2015).

Harm reduction

Harm reduction services have indeed improved in the South Asian region over the last decade. As per the recent report by Harm Reduction International, opioid agonist treatment (OAT) is available in India, Bangladesh, Maldives, and Bhutan. The rest of the countries do not have operational OAT. On the other hand, all the South Asian countries, except Maldives and Sri Lanka, have Needle Syringe Exchange Programs operational in their countries. Although more than 212 sites provide OAT in India, there is weak support for harm reduction in general and OAT in particular in national policy (Parmar et al. 2023a, 2024). An OAT pilot has been conducted in Pakistan, yet OAT is not currently available at any sites. Similarly, OAT is supported in Bhutan's national policy, but it is not yet available in the country. Table 9.3 provides an overview of the availability of harm reduction services in South Asia.

Even in the countries where harm reduction services are available, the coverage is abysmally low. For example, as per a recent systematic review, the global coverage for OAT per 100 PWID is 18. The corresponding figure in South Asian countries varies from 1 to 3 per 100 PWID who predominantly inject opioids (Colledge-Frisby et al. 2023). The number of sites providing OAT services is also grossly insufficient. Similarly, the coverage of NSEP services is limited too. A recent systematic review shows that 34 (95% UI 31–38) needles and syringes are distributed per PWID per year. The figures for other South Asian countries are as Bangladesh: 33 (95% UI 31–36) needles and syringes per PWID per year, Nepal: 68 (95% UI 65–72) needles and

Table 9.3 Availability of harm reduction services in South Asian countries

Country	Support to harm reduction services in national policy	At least one OAT operational	At least one NSP operational	At least one OAT in prison	At least one NSP in prison	Naloxone distribution or take-home naloxone	At least one drug consumption room
Bangladesh	Yes	Yes	Yes	No	No	No	No
Bhutan	No	No	No	No	No	No	No
India	Yes	Yes	Yes	Yes	No	Yes	No
Maldives	Yes	Yes	No	No	No	No	No
Nepal	Yes	Yes	Yes	No	No	No	No
Pakistan	Yes	No	Yes	No	No	No	No
Sri Lanka	No	No	No	No	No	No	No

Adapted from Global State of Harm Reduction Report (2022)

syringes per PWID per year, and Pakistan: 12 (95% UI 10–14) needles and syringes per PWID per year. The number of sites providing NSEP services ranged from 30 (in Pakistan) to 277 (in India) in 2016. Thus, the coverage of both OAT and NSEP is low (as per WHO indicators) in South Asian countries where such services are available.

Other issues also exist at the country level regarding expanding coverage of harm reduction interventions. In India, harm reduction is limited to the prevention of blood-borne virus infections such as HIV and HCV, as per the national policy (Ambekar et al. 2013). Hence, OAT is primarily available for PWUD. OAT has been elevated to the status of a national program in Nepal and is being provided by government hospitals and NGOs. However, as the country is heavily reliant on international support with little contribution from the government, the sustainability of such a program is still being determined (Stone and Shirley-Beavan 2018; Ambekar et al. 2013).

9.4 Recommendations and Ways Forward

Substance use and SUDs are still major public health concerns in South Asian countries. A lot needs to be done in South Asia. The following set of recommendations should be considered.

1. South Asian countries have signed the three UN conventions, namely the Single Convention on Narcotic Drugs 1961, the Convention on Psychotropic Substances 1971, and the Convention against Illicit Traffic in Narcotic Drugs and Psychotropic Substances 1988. These conventions focus on regulating precursors and pharmaceutical products along with legislation to tackle illicit drug

trafficking directly. However, the implementation of these policies has been quite challenging. Poor precursor control regimes, variability of laws and bylaws pertaining to drug regulation and cybercrimes, lack of uninhibited sharing of data, and well-coordinated actions owing to regional conflicts are the major roadblocks. Therefore, it is prudent to focus on bridging these gaps not just within countries but between countries as well.

2. There is an urgent need to apply national and subnational alcohol policies in the South Asian region that focus on (1) reducing affordability, (2) restricting the availability, (3) addressing alcohol promotions, (4) regulating newer types of alcohol products, and (5) counteracting the industry influence on alcohol policies. There is a need to address the cultural and social norms surrounding unrecorded alcohol consumption at the individual, social, and community levels. Community pressure, and not legal enforcement methods, should be adopted to eliminate illegal alcohol production. More regular surveillance of alcohol use and related harms should be conducted in the region. Such surveillance mechanisms should also include other proximal determinants of alcohol consumption (such as alcohol availability, affordability, cultural norms, and media types) apart from patterns, morbidity, and mortality.
3. Apart from alcohol policy reforms, drug policy reforms are also need of the hour. The drug policies in the region are heavily skewed towards supply reduction. There is little emphasis on demand reduction aspects. In view of this, the countries should make policies that support and provide evidence-based interventions and treatment for PWUD. As can be seen, the number of healthcare facilities that provide such treatment is limited. There is also a severe crunch of trained workforce. In such a scenario, better integration of mental health and SUD care into general healthcare is the need of the hour.
4. Evidence-based harm reduction interventions such as OAT, NSP, and naloxone distribution should be instituted and scaled up to reach the desired level of coverage. These interventions are highly effective and, at the same time, are cost-effective and do not lead to an increase in drug use. Considering that heroin use is common among PWUD in these countries, they remain at risk of transitioning to injecting drug use (Herath and Ambekar 2018; Ambekar et al. 2019). Thus, harm reduction interventions must be scaled up in the region. The countries must include buprenorphine and methadone in their respective national EMLs and make them available at the appropriate healthcare levels. This should be done cautiously, keeping in mind the risk of diversion of buprenorphine, which has been reported from across the world (Balhara et al. 2023; Ghosh et al. 2018).
5. Demand reduction efforts for alcohol use should also be scaled up. In the context of South Asian countries, one of the most cost-effective and evidence-based approaches is brief interventions. This intervention tries to identify alcohol-related problems and provides motivational counseling to help the client quit alcohol use. Such an approach can be scaled up at the community level to identify and link the problem users to treatment. Similarly, including medications for AUD treatment in the national EML and making them widely available is another important step.

6. The capacity building of relevant stakeholders is another critical area in dealing with SUD-related problems. Such an approach should target all levels—from the top levels, which make policies, to the community level, which implements various activities in the field. This is one of the pressing needs in South Asian countries and should be prioritized. As alcohol and drug control goes beyond healthcare workers, capacity building of policymakers, legal professionals, and bureaucracies should also be prioritized.
7. One area where South Asian countries require urgent attention is data and evidence generation. Epidemiological surveys are usually one-off studies in the region. Regular data collection, monitoring, surveillance, and evaluation mechanisms should be established in the countries to take the initiatives forward and analyze the impact of various policies.
8. There is a need to scale up evidence-based programs for the prevention of substance use targeting the young population in the region. Such programs should involve working with individuals, families, communities, and schools. Only spreading awareness about substance use and related harms does not work as a prevention strategy. Such programs should ensure that the risk and protective factors for SUDs are considered while formulating policies and that the young population is provided with an environment where they can grow and stay healthy into adulthood.
9. Finally, the stigma of SUD needs to be addressed in the South Asian context. Stigma reduction interventions and public awareness campaigns should be conducted regularly. Interventions such as contact-based training programs, communication of positive stories of people with SUDs, and education programs targeting medical students and professionals such as police and counselors may be incorporated into drug demand reduction efforts of the countries.

9.5 Conclusion

The challenges associated with substance use in South Asia are unique compared to other parts of the world owing to its geography and large diversity in ethnicity, religion, and socio-economic conditions. Regardless, it needs urgent attention owing to its rapid rise and social and healthcare implications. Dissemination of evidence-based treatments, conducive policies, demand, and supply reduction strategies, regularizing the laws, healthcare capacity building, creating awareness and reducing stigma, regional cooperation to tackle drug trafficking, and generating valuable data are a few of the ways that can be utilized to tackle this complex issue. The member nations need to commit to harmonized efforts at policy, legislative, and operational levels to bring a positive outcome aligned with international conventions and human rights goals.

References

Ambekar, A., Rao, R., & Agrawal, A. (2013). India's national narcotic drugs and psychotropic substances policy, 2012: A 20th century document in the 21st century. *International Journal of Drug Policy, 24*(4), 374–375.

Ambekar, A., Rao, R., Pun, A., Kumar, S., & Kishore, K. (2013). The trajectory of methadone maintenance treatment in Nepal. *International Journal of Drug Policy, 24*(6), e57–e60. https://doi.org/10.1016/j.drugpo.2013.06.001

Ambekar, A., Mishra, A., Parmar, A., Kumar, R., Kumar, M., Rao, R., & Agrawal, A. (2019). Are non-injecting opioid users at risk of transition to injecting drug use? A multi-site study from India. *Asian Journal of Psychiatry, 42*, 79–84. https://doi.org/10.1016/j.ajp.2019.03.017

Balhara, Y., Parmar, A., Sarkar, S., & Verma, R. (2016). Stigma in dual diagnosis: A narrative review. *Indian Journal of Social Psychiatry, 32*, 128. https://doi.org/10.4103/0971-9962.181093

Balhara, Y. P. S., Parmar, A., Modak, T., & Vikram, V. (2020). From "Bhang Shops" to "Cannabis in Coffee Shops": Time to Debate the Option? *Indian Journal of Psychological Medicine, 44*(3), 285–289. https://doi.org/10.1177/0253717620957501

Balhara, Y. P. S., Saha, P., Mathew, M., Kumar, M., Parmar, A., Lal, R., & Sarkar, S. (2023). Nonprescription use of buprenorphine tablets among patients at a tertiary care addictive disorder treatment center in India: Observa-tions and implications. *Journal of Opioid Management, 19*(5), 403–411. https://doi.org/10.5055/jom.0814

Colledge-Frisby, S., Ottaviano, S., Webb, P., Grebely, J., Wheeler, A., Cunningham, E. B., Hajarizadeh, B., Leung, J., Peacock, A., Vickerman, P., Farrell, M., Dore, G. J., Hickman, M., & Degenhardt, L. (2023). Global coverage of interventions to prevent and manage drug-related harms among people who inject drugs: A systematic review. *The Lancet Global Health, 11*(5), e673–e683. https://doi.org/10.1016/S2214-109X(23)00058-X

Dhingra, K., & Jhanjee, S. (2023). A Review of Intervention Strategies for Areca Nut Use Cessation. *Indian Journal of Psychological Medicine, 45*(2), 117–123. https://doi.org/10.1177/02537176221144711

Ghosh, A., Basu, D., & Avasthi, A. (2018). Buprenorphine-based opioid substitution therapy in India: A few observations, thoughts, and opinions. *Indian Journal of Psychiatry, 60*(3), 361–366. https://doi.org/10.4103/psychiatry.IndianJPsychiatry_218_17

Girelli, G., Jofré, M., & Larasati, A. (2022). *The Death Penalty for Drug Offences: Global Overview 2022.*

Gupta, P., Panda, U., Parmar, A., & Bhad, R. (2019). Internalized stigma and its correlates among treatment seeking opium users in India: A cross-sectional observational study. *Asian Journal of Psychiatry, 39*, 86–90. https://doi.org/10.1016/j.ajp.2018.12.004

Global State of Harm Reduction Report (2022). Harm Reduction International. The global state of harm reduction 2022. https://hri.global/wpcontent/uploads/2022/11/HRI_GSHR-2022_Full-Report_Final.pdf. (Accessed on Oct 10, 2024)

Herath, S., & Ambekar, A. (2018). Cross-sectional study of drug-use patterns (RADUP) to inform risk-reduction interventions for people who use/inject drugs (PWUD/PWID) in Sri Lanka. *Journal of Virus Eradication, 4*, 21. https://doi.org/10.1016/S2055-6640(20)30420-9

Lee, C.-H., Ko, A. M.-S., Warnakulasuriya, S., Yin, B.-L., Sunarjo, Zain, R. B., Ibrahim, S. O., Liu, Z.-W., Li, W.-H., Zhang, S.-S., Kuntoro, null, Utomo, B., Rajapakse, P. S., Warusavithana, S. A., Razak, I. A., Abdullah, N., Shrestha, P., Kwan, A.-L., Shieh, T.-Y., … Ko, Y.-C. (2011). Intercountry prevalences and practices of betel-quid use in south, southeast and eastern Asia regions and associated oral preneoplastic disorders: An international collaborative study by Asian betel-quid consortium of south and east Asia. *International Journal of Cancer, 129*(7), 1741–1751. https://doi.org/10.1002/ijc.25809

Lowe D. J.E, Simpkin E, & George T.P. (2022, May 30). Dual Diagnosis: Double the Stigma, Double the Trouble. *Psychiatric Times, 39*(5).

Mandal, P., Mittal, S., & Chadda, R. K. (2023). Polysubstance use in South Asia. *Current Opinion in Psychiatry, 36*(4), 269. https://doi.org/10.1097/YCO.0000000000000869

Manthey, J., Benegal, V., Kilian, C., Mahadevan, J., Mejía-Trujillo, J., Morojele, N., Murthy, P., Neufeld, M., Pérez-Gómez, A., & Rehm, J. (2022). International Perspectives on Stigma toward People with Substance Use Disorders. In G. Schomerus & P. W. Corrigan (Eds.), *The Stigma of Substance Use Disorders* (pp. 107–143). Cambridge University Press. https://doi.org/10.1017/9781108936972.007

Mohan, A., & Ambekar, A. (2020). Telepsychiatry and addiction treatment. *Indian Journal of Psychological Medicine, 42*(5_suppl), 52S–56S.

Murphy, E. & Cliff, V. (Eds.). (2021). *Legal and policy trends impacting people living with HIV and key populations in Asia and the Pacific 2014–2019.* UNAIDS.

Naveed, S., Waqas, A., Chaudhary, A. M. D., Kumar, S., Abbas, N., Amin, R., Jamil, N., & Saleem, S. (2020). Prevalence of Common Mental Disorders in South Asia: A Systematic Review and Meta-Regression Analysis. *Frontiers in Psychiatry, 11*, 573150. https://doi.org/10.3389/fpsyt.2020.573150

Parmar, A., Chakraborty, R., & Balhara, Y. P. (2024). Current status of harm reduction in India: Are we doing enough?. *Indian Journal of Psychiatry, 66*(4), 388–391.

Parmar, A., Pal, A., & Sharma, P. (2023). National list of essential Medicines 2022 of India: Perspectives from Psychiatrists. *Indian Journal of Psychological Medicine, 45*(4), 411–414.

Parmar, A., Patil, V., & Sarkar, S. (2017a). Ethical management of substance use disorders: The Indian scenario. *Indian Journal of Medical Ethics*, 2(4), 265–270. https://doi.org/10.20529/IJME.2017.051

Parmar, A., Patil, V., & Sarkar, S. (2017b). Natural opioid use in elderly in India: A case series. *Journal of Substance Use, 22*(2), 156–158. https://doi.org/10.3109/14659891.2016.1162211

Parmar, A., Patil, V., Sarkar, S., & Rao, R. (2018). An Observational Study of Treatment Seeking Users of Natural Opiates from India. *Substance Use & Misuse, 53*(7), 1139–1145. https://doi.org/10.1080/10826084.2017.1400564

Parmar, A., Nath, S., & Bhatia, G. (2022). Essential substance use disorder medications in Asia Pacific countries: An observational study. *Asian Journal of Psychiatry, 78*, 103276. https://doi.org/10.1016/j.ajp.2022.103276

Parmar, A., Balhara, Y. P. S., & Singh, A. (2023a). Toward a national policy on Alcohol: A complex public health issue in need of urgent action. *Indian Journal of Psychiatry, 65*(9), 974. https://doi.org/10.4103/indianjpsychiatry.indianjpsychiatry_440_23

Parmar, A., Bhatia, G., Sharma, P., & Pal, A. (2023b). Understanding the epidemiology of substance use in India: A review of nationwide surveys. *Indian Journal of Psychiatry, 65*(5), 498–505. https://doi.org/10.4103/indianjpsychiatry.indianjpsychiatry_791_22

Parmar, A., Narasimha, V. L., & Nath, S. (2023c). National Drug Laws, Policies, and Programs in India: A Narrative Review. *Indian Journal of Psychological Medicine*, 025371762311705. https://doi.org/10.1177/02537176231170534

Parmar, A., Narasimha, V. L., & Nath, S. (2024). National Drug Laws, Policies, and Programs in India: A Narrative Review. *Indian Journal of Psychological Medicine, 46*(1), 5–13.

Parmar, A., Rina, K., & Padhy, S. K. (2020). COVID-19 pandemic and people who use opioids in India: Opportunities and evolutions. *Indian Journal of Psychological Medicine, 42*(6), 566–568.

Sarkar, S., Parmar, A., & Chatterjee, B. (2015). Substance use disorders in the elderly: A review. *Journal of Geriatric Mental Health Care, 2*, 74–82. https://doi.org/10.4103/2348-9995.174271

Sarkar, S. (2014). Ethical Issues Relating to Faith Healing Practices in South Asia: A Medical Perspective. *Journal of Clinical Research & Bioethics, 05*(04). https://doi.org/10.4172/2155-9627.1000190

Sinha, D. N., Gupta, P. C., Kumar, A., Bhartiya, D., Agarwal, N., Sharma, S., Singh, H., Parascandola, M., & Mehrotra, R. (2018). The Poorest of Poor Suffer the Greatest Burden From Smokeless Tobacco Use: A Study From 140 Countries. *Nicotine & Tobacco Research: Official Journal of the Society for Research on Nicotine and Tobacco, 20*(12), 1529–1532. https://doi.org/10.1093/ntr/ntx276

Stone K., & Shirley-Beavan S. (2018). *The Global State of Harm Reduction 2018—Harm Reduction International* (6th ed.). Harm Reduction International. https://hri.global/flagship-research/the-global-state-of-harm-reduction/global-state-of-harm-reduction-2018/

Suliankatchi, R. A., Sinha, D. N., Rath, R., Aryal, K. K., Zaman, M. M., Gupta, P. C., Karki, K. B., & Venugopal, D. (2019). Smokeless Tobacco Use is 'Replacing' the Smoking Epidemic in the South-East Asia Region. *Nicotine & Tobacco Research: Official Journal of the Society for Research on Nicotine and Tobacco, 21*(1), 95–100. https://doi.org/10.1093/ntr/ntx272

Thara, R., & Padmavati, R. (2013). Community mental health care in South Asia. *World Psychiatry, 12*(2), 176–177. https://doi.org/10.1002/wps.20042

The Global Health Observatory. (2023). *Mental health service availability.*

UNODC. (2023a). *World Drug Report 2023.* United Nations publication.

UNODC. (2023b, May 17). *Regional programme for South Asia.*

Vashney, M., Parmar, A., & Mishra, A. K. (2020). The Past, Present and Future of Literature Pertaining to Betel (Areca) Nut: A Citation Analysis. *Substance Use & Misuse, 55*(9), 1403–1412. https://doi.org/10.1080/10826084.2019.1660677

Wegman, M. P., Altice, F. L., Kaur, S., Rajandaran, V., Osornprasop, S., Wilson, D., Wilson, D. P., & Kamarulzaman, A. (2017). Relapse to opioid use in opioid-dependent individuals released from compulsory drug detention centres compared with those from voluntary methadone treatment centres in Malaysia: A two-arm, prospective observational study. *The Lancet Global Health, 5*(2), e198–e207. https://doi.org/10.1016/S2214-109X(16)30303-5

WHO. (2018). *Epidemiology of alcohol use in the WHO South-East Asia Region.*

WHO. (2023). *World Drug Report 2023—Statistical Annex.* United Nations: Office on Drugs and Crime. www.unodc.org/unodc/en/data-and-analysis/wdr2023_annex.html

World Health Organization. (2018). *Global status report on alcohol and health 2018.* World Health Organization. https://iris.who.int/handle/10665/274603

World Health Organization. (2022). *World mental health report: Transforming mental health for all.*

Chapter 10
Policy, Legalisation and Programs Related to Substance Use Disorders in South Asia

Nandhini Bojappen and Prabhat Chand

10.1 Introduction

Peninsular India and the Indo-Gangetic Plain comprise the South Asian Region (SAR), a section of Asia. This region is made up of countries including Bhutan, Bangladesh, Sri Lanka, Pakistan, Nepal, and India; Afghanistan and the Maldives are also commonly included. For this book, we are considering all eight countries. Currently one of the world's most densely inhabited regions, SAR was home to one of the oldest known civilisations, the Indus civilisation. Though their history has been characterised by political, linguistic, and ethnic differences, the people in the region are united by a shared ethical and cultural outlook (Arafat and KAR 2024). In many countries and regions across the world, substance use has long been ingrained in both ancient and modern societies.

Opium and cannabis are the two types of narcotics that the subcontinents have been exposed to throughout their long history. Opium was grown over time as a cash crop for global trade. After the colonial administration, the production of opium poppies was further increased as a source of income and a vehicle for both domestic and international trade.

With invasions and constant political unrest, in turn, bringing unrest in identity and socio-political stability, drugs did become a regular means of relaxation in vulnerable populations, further bringing colonial Government monopoly, leading to further marginalisation and an increase in substance use. Effects of the same continue to persist; SARs still lag in terms of development, mental health care, growth, and drug use continues to be a problem.

N. Bojappen · P. Chand (✉)
Department of Psychiatry, National Institute of Mental Health and Neurosciences (NIMHANS), Bangalore, India
e-mail: prabhat@vknnimhans.in

S. M. Y. Arafat and S. K. Kar (eds.), *Current Perspectives on Substance Use Disorders in South Asia*, https://doi.org/10.1007/978-981-97-6619-2_10

10.2 Drug Use Burden

SAR still faces numerous drug-related issues, some of which are made worse by the region's proximity to the Golden Triangle and Golden Crescent, the world's two principal hubs for the production and trafficking of illegal opiates.

Data that is now available suggests that a sizable portion of the population in SAR, particularly the young, productive male section, abuses drugs despite variations in their availability and quality. Additionally, a sizable percentage of drug users fall into the category of chronically dependent users. According to the 2022 World Drug Report, over a third of the world's opiate users reside in SAR, where almost 25% of the world's population resides (UNODC, World Drug Report 2022 (United Nations Publication) 2022). As per the United Nations Office on Drugs and Crime's World Drug Report 2021 Annex, the estimated prevalence of drug usage in South Asia's general population is 0.7%. Yet, there is a gap in a synthesised overview of the prevalence of mental disorders in this region (World Drug Report 2021 (United Nations Publication) 2021).

The drug markets in the region have changed over time, and current issues comprise the large-scale production and trafficking of methamphetamine as well as the smuggling of pharmaceutical medicines containing narcotic and psychotropic drugs. SARs continue to be at risk of illicit ATS production because of their proximity to significant methamphetamine supply countries. The diversion of controlled substances from legal to illegal channels and the lack of coordination among the region's drug enforcement agencies. The rise in ATS abuse, trafficking, and the establishment of covert laboratories are contemporary trends in the area (South Asia: The Emerging Threat of Synthetic Drugs 2010).

10.3 Need for Policies and Programs

Considering the pressing need to bring things under control, government policies and programs are in place. Legislation and regulations express the commitments that we as a society have decided to abide by, known as policies. They shape our ethical standards and societal morals. The many policy alternatives available to lessen the public health burden of drug consumption have been divided into three broad categories: population-based policies, problem-directed policies, and direct intervention. Programs, on the other hand, are targeted efforts or actions done to carry out a specified objective or put a policy into effect. However, the range of national policies and programs enacted, as well as the potency and efficacy of these policies' execution, differ greatly among nations. Numerous elements, including politics, ideology, morals, and perceived public opinion, influence policy decisions, and programs executed.

In SARs, views, and policies towards drugs have taken a transition in line with the Western libertarian approaches to the drug problem to medical and criminal views of the problem, policies framed accordingly. Policies shape the course of drug use in any nation and, in turn, the youth and lives of human inhabitants in these countries. This brings in a pressing need to critically evaluate the policy frame of countries.

This chapter will discuss policies and programs for drug control and give an overview of the legalisation of drugs in these countries.

10.4 Policies

10.4.1 Alcohol

Countries in the WHO's SAR, which have historically had low rates of alcohol use, are gradually beginning to drink alcohol more often. It is commonly known that a rise in alcohol use within a community or a country is associated with a higher percentage of individuals suffering from alcohol use disorders, which encompass hazardous use, abuse, dependence, or addiction.

Countries like Sri Lanka, Bhutan, and Nepal have national policies on alcohol on the one end, with countries like Pakistan and Afghanistan, which have banned alcohol on the other end of the spectrum. The WHO Global Alcohol Action Plan has provided a strategic plan for a national policy for harm reduction—except for Bhutan, Sri Lanka, and Nepal other nations do not have a nationally framed policy of alcohol use as per the WHO strategic plan. Hence, policies are being viewed through the lens of the SAFER alcohol control strategy brought by the WHO.

- Strengthening the restriction on availability
- Advance and ensure countermeasures against drunk and driving
- Facilitate treatment
- Enforce restriction on advertising
- Raise excise taxes.

Advance and Enforce Drunk Driving Countermeasures

Restrictions on Consumption and Availability

Legal Age for Drinking

Restrictions have been reducing access to alcohol to certain ages, ensuring nonavailability at certain places and for certain ages. Most SARs have specified 18 years as standard with various states taking different stances in India (ages ranging from 18 to 25 years).

It is evident that different countries have used various strategies to bring in WHO's proposed plan, most SARs have banned advertisements, drink and driving policies are in place, excise taxes have been imposed on alcohol, and awareness activities are being initiated. On record, initiatives have been taken in all SARs (except Afghanistan where following Taliban rule, clear information regarding recent policy changes and intricacies of the same is not available), but even where there are clear policies in place, there are major questions as to the implementation and enforcement of these regulations considering the growing prevalence of alcohol use disorders in these nations.

Secondly, the following are—effective intervention strategies mentioned by WHO/Europe

- Change in taxes (specifically excise tax)
- Restricts on advertisement
- Ensure restriction on availability.

The above-mentioned are vastly underused in SARs, same is reflected in Table 10.1 where complete countermeasures have not been enforced and many countries have internal variability among states due to policies; for instance, in India, the excise tax is completely handled by states, which varies across states. If it is being used adequately to bring down alcohol use, it is questionable. Most countries do not have functioning monitoring systems to improvise with feedback raising the need for change in policy and approach.

10.4.2 Tobacco Policies

Tobacco policies taken up by countries have predominantly been based on the Framework convention on Tobacco Control (FCTC) brought in by WHO. Countries have ratified it at various time points from 2003 to 2006 (Geneva 2003).

The key demand reduction strategies are contained in Articles 6–14, and supply reduction strategies are contained in Articles 15–17. WHO unveiled the MPOWER initiatives. These actions are meant to support the effective country-level implementation of the WHO FCTC's tobacco demand reduction interventions. In Table 10.2, we have summarised MPOWER for various SARs.

Despite decades after FCTC (as mentioned in Table 10.2) in majority of the countries, tobacco use continues to be rampant. There is an evident lack of consistent application of FCTC tactics and articles in South Asian counties, they are falling behind in enacting some anti-tobacco laws while concentrating more on enacting others, with a lack of collaboration between the clinical and public policy levels.

This can be secondary to cultural acceptance of tobacco use and the perceived safer nature of tobacco in comparison with other addictive agents thirdly, socioeconomic constraints in SARs that impede the successful implementation of FCTC articles.

To lessen the prevalence of cigarette smoking in South Asian regions, regulations pertaining to higher taxes, smoke-free areas, health warnings, and visuals must be implemented effectively at the policy level. There is a pressing Substantial national cooperation is required between politicians, researchers, educators, and anti-tobacco organisations. Furthermore, an updated surveillance system for tobacco prevalence

Table 10.1 Blood alcohol content (BAC) and penalty for offenses across SAR nations

Country	Setting BAC limits	Penalties that reflect the seriousness of offence	Enforcement of BAC levels (RBT, sobriety check points)	Offender management alcohol ignition interlocks, alcohol rehabilitation, and/or treatment programs
Bhutan	Limit for driving in Bhutan is 0.8% for most drivers or 0% for commercial drivers	Yes	Yes	Yes
India	0.03% no variability based on groups	Yes	Certain states have implemented	No
Pakistan	0.08% or higher is illegal and punishable by imprisonment for up to three years or a fine up to 50,000 rupees or both BAC of 0.15% or higher is considered reckless and negligent driving and punishable by imprisonment for up to seven years or a fine up to 100,000 rupees or both	Yes	No	No
Afghanistan	0.0% No variability based on groups	Yes	No	No
Myanmar	0.05% No variability based on groups	Yes	Yes	No
Nepal	0.08% No variability based on groups	Yes	No	No
Sri Lanka	0.05% No variability based on groups	Yes	Not yet, pilot studies going on	No
Maldives	0.0% No variability based on groups	Yes	Data not available	No

"GHO|By Category|BAC Limit—Data by Country" (2020)

Table 10.2 WHO MPOWER status in South Asian countries

		Bangladesh	Bhutan	Sri Lanka	Maldives	Pakistan	India	Afghanistan
M	Monitoring cigarettes less affordable since 2010	Complete	Complete	Moderate	Moderate	Minimal	Moderate	Minimal
P	Smoke-free environments	Moderate (6)	Moderate (8)	Moderate	Minimal	Complete	Moderate	Complete
O	Cessation programmes	Minimal	Moderate	Moderate	Cessation programmes	Moderate	Complete	Minimal
W	Health warnings	Complete	No/weak measure	Complete	Moderate	Complete	Complete	Minimal
	Mass media	Moderate	No/weak measure	No/weak measure	No/weak measure	No/weak measure	Moderate	No/weak measure
E	Advertising bans	Moderate	Complete measure	Moderate	Moderate	Moderate	Moderate	No/weak measure
R	Taxation (%)	73.0	8.1	77.0	29.9	51.8	Moderate	20.7
	Cigarettes less affordable since 2010	Yes	No change	Yes	Yes	No change	Yes	Yes

A policy package to reverse the tobacco epidemic (2008)

and rates of tobacco cessation and reduction is required with the inclusion of context-based treatments with special attention to local facilitators and impediments.

10.4.3 Narcotics and Psychotropics

Most SARs, except for Afghanistan (following Taliban rule), have ratified the UN treaties on psychotropic and narcotic drugs considering shared issues of transnational organised crime, including the trafficking of illicit narcotics such as heroin, synthetic drugs, cannabis, and medicinal preparations containing narcotic chemicals pressing the need for policy.

Policies regarding narcotic and psychotropic substances have changed over time in several jurisdictions, as it has been said that the present laws regarding narcotics and psychotropic substances are predominantly prohibitionary. They have been found to provide minimal room and opportunity for corrective action when it comes to the use of opioids and psychoactive substances. There has been a gradual paradigm shift in approach towards narcotics and psychotropic agents among South Asian countries that have worked to outlaw the manufacturing, selling, and usage of certain psychoactive substances, giving a prohibitionistic perspective to a humanistic approach.

Below (Table 10.3), we have outlined major facets of policies on narcotics and psychotropics.

Regrettably, despite all of this work, wholesale markets have not been able to be tightly controlled as desired. The three primary plant-based psychoactive products with the largest global markets are cannabis, cocaine, and heroin. Notable expansions of these chemicals' new markets and distribution channels, especially in SARs, and the concurrent rise of markets for various synthetically generated substitutes.

In India, opioid use is three times more common than the global norm. The total amount of opioids used has increased since 2004, and heroin consumption has overtaken opium use (Atul et al. 2019). Similarly, in Bangladesh, seizures of yaba increased 50 times in less than ten years, from about 8 lakh to almost 4.5 crore pieces. The prohibitionist approach has not yielded dramatic changes in other southern countries as well, wherein there has been a steady increase in narcotic use rate (Panthee et al. 2017; Suzana et al. 2021).

From failing to control drug production to substance use disorder, the war against drugs has turned into a ward against the deprived. According to information released by the Maldives Correctional Service (MCS), 55% of individuals given prison sentences last month were admitted for drug-related offences; also noted was a steady increase in arrests from 11,380 to 18,346 from 2015 to 2019 in Bangladesh (Huge Increase in Transnational Crime and Synthetic Drugs in SE Asia Requires Cross-Border Cooperation|UN News, n.d.; South Asia: Understanding and Addressing the Threat of Opiate Trafficking 2024).

Other South Asian countries like Sri Lanka, Maldives, and India have taken up a very similar pattern (India: Persons Prosecuted for Drug Trafficking|Statista 2024).

Table 10.3 Summary of policies on narcotics and psychotropics

Country		Death penalty for drug-related offenses	Mandatory death penalty	Classification based on quantity	Consideration of drug addicts as patient	Asset forfeiture	Drug trafficking	Grading of penalty
Sri Lanka	Conventions against illicit traffic in narcotic drugs and psychotropic substances act	+	–	+	+	+	+	+
Bhutan	Narcotic drugs, psychotropic substance and substance abuse act of Bhutan	–	–	+	+	+	+	+
Nepal	Narcotics drugs (control) act		–	+	+	+	+	+
Pakistan	CNSA	+	+	+	–		+	+
Afghanistan	–	+	+	–	–	–	–	–
Bangladesh	Narcotics control act	+	–	+	+	+	+	+
Maldives	Narcotics drug act	–	–	+	+	+	+	+
India	NDPS	+	–	+	+	+	+	+

Means Any Establishment for the Manufacture of Alcohol (n.d.); Narcotic Drugs Psychotropic Substances and Substance Abuse Act of Bhutan 2015 (n.d.); Parliament of the democratic socialist republic of Sri Lanka conventions against illicit traffic in narcotic drugs and psychotropic substances act, no. 1 of 2008, *National Drugs and Psychotropics Act* (1985), *Drugs Act 2020, Maldives* (2020)

As a result, prison overcrowding has become a severe problem in Bangladesh, India, Sri Lanka, and Pakistan; one of the main causes of subpar jail conditions is prison overcrowding, which can have potentially fatal results.

The application of drug control strategies has led to numerous violations of human rights, such as the excessive use of force and extrajudicial killings; the elimination of many farmers' primary sources of income, the harm done to the environment from crop eradication programmes, the abuse of drug users under the pretext of drug treatment, and the violations of the right to health resulting from the enforcement of laws that discriminate against drug users, women, minorities, and children; the denial of drug users access to necessary painkillers and treatment for drug dependence; and the application of harsh penalties, such as life in prison and the death penalty, for drug-related offences.

One of the most significant consequences is the growth of crime networks. These groups operate across nations and continents, in turn controlling the globe; they are involved in the manufacture of newer substances from the precursor. Based on a widely used law enforcement community rule of thumb for seizures, which states that seizures account for 10% of all trafficking, Sri Lanka and the Maldives are identified as centres of opium distillation, with an estimated 3.5 tonnes of heroin smuggled into Sri Lanka annually.

This would be considerably in excess of the requirements of drug-dependent persons in the country.

There is general agreement that during the time of a control regime that had eradication and reduction as its goals, the extent of drug use and drug markets have expanded dramatically, with continued violence and extrajudicial acts against persons suspected of drug-related activities. The war on drugs did become a war on people. Despite the gradual change from a prohibitionist to a humanistic approach, change has been very slow, continuing to marginalise vulnerable populations.

Most of these laws were abstract and administrative in nature. Many policies mention the rehabilitation and treatment of patients who are brought under the Narcotics Act. However, there is still a lack of clarity regarding the specific range of services provided, as well as the nature and approach towards patients with addictive illnesses. The effectiveness of these policies in helping individuals suffering from addiction and subsequently engaging in criminal activities is questionable. This is due to the fact that these individuals often become entangled in a lengthy criminal justice system. Additionally, most SARs have limited financial resources allocated to the judiciary system, which further marginalises patients under the Narcotics Act and their families.

Secondly, most of these nations are still developing. Illegal drug markets thrive in areas with socio-economic disparity in terms of lack of education, poor housing, lack of basic amenities, and social security are rampant (Lupton and Power 2004). Even though law enforcement authorities remove hundreds of acres of opium plants every year, government survey reports indicate that opium cultivation is widespread throughout the SARs, with Myanmar competing with Afghanistan in maximum illicit opium cultivation (Myanmar Opium Survey 2022 Cultivation, Production, and Implications 2023).

There are very few alternatives to illegal poppy farming that could offer growers chances for economic sustainability and inducement to abandon the practice. A few more benefits of growing poppies over other crops are that they can be grown practically anywhere and are a reasonably high-value commodity with a guaranteed market, which stresses the need for policies to ensure need-based, economically viable alternatives.

Thirdly, despite shared ethnical origin, there occurs minimal sharing of information between SARs, which has been stressed by UNODC (Regional programme for South Asia (2018–2021) Background and Context 2021). There is a need for nations to strike transnational and transcontinental collaboration to improve international cooperation and mutual legal aid arrangements for better control of organised crime.

10.5 Programs

To mitigate and reduce the issue of drug addiction, a country needs policies and initiatives that address supply management as well as demand-reduction medicines. Each nation's policy formulations refer to supply and demand reduction initiatives. The significance of demand reduction initiatives has just come to light with the slower and steadier shift to demand reduction from mere supply reduction. Measures to reduce supply imply taking legal action. Conversely, primary prevention, treatment, and reintegration into society are a few demand reduction strategies.

10.5.1 Bangladesh

The following table summarises various programme.

Supply reduction:
The Narcotics Control Act of 1990
Demand reduction:
CAP—comprehensive action plan
Awareness programmes
Intersectoral corroboration
Harm reduction:
National harm reduction policy
Committees:
National narcotics control advisory committee
National anti-drug committee
District narcotics control and publicity committee
Upazila narcotics control and publicity committee
Comprehensive action plan

Department of Narcotics recently launched a comprehensive action plan (Annual Drug Report 2020; Department of Narcotics Control, Bangladesh 2020; Ray 2018) to comply with

(1) Meeting to implement the zero-tolerance policy drug offence
(2) To identify the drug offenders and routes used to traffic drugs, to conduct a raid and searches based on real-time information sharing against drug traffickers
(3) Commitment to creating treatment opportunities and facilities for substance abusers to render doorstep services
(4) Conducting workshops with concerned prisons to implement the above activities and monitoring through apps
(5) Anti-drug awareness meetings, posters, distribution of souvenirs, anti-drug discussion meetings in prison, anti-drug campaigning on TV and print media, creating mentors in educational institutes, anti-narcotics class lectures, and narcotics drug committees in schools and colleges.

Objectives:

(1) To create awareness among people of all walks of life across the country and to build strong social movements/resistance against drugs
(2) Creation of anti-drug attitude among all, including students
(3) Organizing concerned citizens against drugs to raise their voices against drug offenders
(4) To identify drug traffickers and take strict legal action to reduce social influence and prestige
(5) Identifying drug addicts across the country and providing treatment
(6) To take the initiative to control drug crime through mutual communication and coordination of all government and non-government officials and employees.

10.5.2 Bhutan

Since its founding in 2006, the Bhutan Narcotics Control Authority (BNCA) has undertaken several initiatives aimed at reducing both supply and demand (Royal Government of Bhutan the National Policy and Strategic Framework to Reduce Harmful Use of Alcohol 2018).

Collaboration with

- Stakeholders,
- Royal Bhutan Police,
- Ministry of Education,
- Youth Development Fund.

Drug demand reduction:

- Focuses on carrying out awareness activities specifically targeting youth through IEC materials, treat and rehabilitate patients with substance use disorders by

offering medical and therapeutic management along with rehabilitation and community support initiatives.
- To ensure help at community level through drop in centres.

Also to work on capacity building to improve the quality of services provided.

Drug supply reduction:

- To improve collaboration with capable regional and global organisations in the fight against drug abuse, its causes, and associated crimes.
- Provide suitable controls to stop money related to illegal drugs and substances from being laundered.
- Bolster law enforcement organisations' ability to stop the illegal trafficking of psychoactive substances and narcotics.
- Collaborate with international, sub-international, and regional intergovernmental organisations to provide financial and technical support for research.
- To enhance capacity development.
- Establish mandated, arbitrary, or ad hoc drug testing programmes in ministries, organisations, and other settings.
- Create instructional materials and train law enforcement officers' trainers.
- Facilitate and issue import permits for controlled substances and precursor compounds.
- Ensure monitoring of the programme.

NGOs have also been part of activities.

Youth Development Fund (YDF) is a non-governmental agency through treatment and rehabilitation services, has been addressing drug problems, specifically vulnerable populations like women and youth with substance use.

Program Activities

YDF's Drug Education and Rehabilitation Services (DEARS) ensures demand reduction, specifically with vulnerable populations. It acts through awareness campaigns and capacity building, also engages in grant writing reporting to bring in changes, and concurrently ensures community-based treatment and rehabilitation through drop-in centres. The same is achieved by collaboration with national and international stakeholders to ensure the needs of the population are addressed comprehensively.

10.5.3 India

Supply and demand reduction is provided by the Narcotic Drugs and Psychotropic Substances (NDPS) Act (1985). It took the place of previous laws regarding the matter. The Act primarily addresses supply-reduction initiatives.

Supply Reduction:

- NDPS
- State alcohol-related policies.

Demand Reduction:

NAPDDR—National action plan for drug demand reduction

Central sector scheme for prevention of alcoholism and drug abuse.

Harm Reduction:

NACP—National AIDS Control Programme

National Viral hepatitis control programme.

National Action Plan for Drug Demand Reduction

Focal points:

- The Ministry of Health and Family Welfare
- The Ministry of Welfare
- Ministries of Human Resources and other Information and Broadcasting
- Resource Development (Department of Youth Affairs, Education).

Objectives:

- Focus on improving awareness, reducing stigma, and improvising early intervention through identification, treatment, and counselling of drug use population—this has been implemented through improving community services and capacity building through intersectoral collaborative efforts of central and state governments and NGOs.
- To bring awareness about drug effects across the population and reduce stigma.
- To bring in programs for demand reduction activities.
- Facilitate research.
- Improvise capacity for community work, Whole capacity recovery of patients with addiction.

In addition to framing policies also provides financial assistance for awareness, capacity building, Improving quality, Focused interventions for the population in vulnerable areas, Programmes for Drug Demand Reduction by States/UTs, and Any other activity or item that will augment/strengthen the implementation of NAPDDR—National action plan for drug demand reduction, rehabilitation of ex-drug addicts, research and scientific activities under the scheme and also activities for raising awareness in schools, colleges, and universities; parent workshops and seminars; community-based peer-led interactions; and intervention programs for at-risk adolescents and young people.

The primary Focus has been on bringing together the Indian government, state and union governments, and implementing entities such as trusts, NGOs, autonomous organizations, hospitals, and technical forums.

Secondarily, the community has been brought together in preventive aspects—Community-based Intervention for Early Drug Use Prevention among Adolescents (CPLI)—Through this curriculum, young people will receive training to become peer educators, enabling them to oversee peer-led community interventions and provide early prevention education, particularly to the community's most vulnerable adolescents and young people. For drug addicts detected in the community, this system would also offer referrals and connections to counselling, treatment, and rehabilitation facilities.

Finally, Outreach and Drop in Centres (ODIC) offer a safe and secure location for community drug users to drop in. These clinics will offer counselling, evaluation, and screening services.

10.5.4 Maldives

The National Drug Agency has been the predominant body that has helped in designing programmes in addition to national policy, which has aimed at supply reduction predominantly; there have been demand reduction initiatives in the form of

(A) Halfway Home: Halfway House is a semi-residential centre providing treatment for people with substance use disorder in a family milieu concept. It offers treatment for males and females above 18 years of age.

   1. Semi-residential treatment (Male and female).
   2. Community Reintegration Treatment (Male and female).

(B) Drug Detoxification and Community Rehabilitation Center.
(C) Women's special drug rehabilitation centres.

Predominantly, Maldives has focused on supply reduction and treatment aspects rather than preventive ones (Mortimore and Stimson 2010).

10.5.5 Pakistan

Focal Points:

- Anti-Narcotics Force (ANF) (Ministry of Narcotics Control)
- Frontier Corps—Khyber Pakhtunkhwa (KP)
- Frontier Corps—Balochistan
- Home Departments of Khyber Pakhtunkhwa and Balochistan provinces.

Objectives:

- Supply reduction
- Demand reduction
- Disrupt supply from Pakistan.

Strategy:

- Crop control
- Training, operational, and commodity support
- Demand reduction (rehabilitation, job skills training, and educational opportunities, increase public awareness)
- Increase in private and public clinics
- Increase counter—narcotics training among officials.

10.5.6 Sri Lanka

Demand Reduction:

National Dangerous Drugs Control Board

- Treatment and Rehabilitation Division
- Designated and Private Treatment Centres
- Preventive Education and Training Unit.

Supply Reduction:

National Policy for the Prevention and Control of Drug Abuse

National Dangerous Drugs Control Board—PCA Division

- Issuing of Licenses
- Registration of Premises
- Monitoring and Examination.

The preventive Education and Training unit under the National Dangerous Drugs Control Board handles preventive aspects; Sri Lanka has taken up school-based preventive programs, Vocational Training Centres and Tertiary Education Institutions, Family-based prevention, Larger workplace-based prevention, Community Programmes focusing on prevention, treatment, rehabilitation to ensure reintegration and sustainable livelihood, innovative educational initiatives aimed at government, non-government, and commercial sector workers as well as schoolchildren, teenagers, and college students. Youth-based prevention.

Skills-building exercises with college students to ensure a positive outlook and coping skills that can prevent indulgence in substance and, in turn, pave the way to substance use disorder. Collaborative, developmentally appropriate learning techniques to assist kids in mastering the abilities that have been demonstrated to prevent substance abuse attempts have been made to incorporate the same through programs.

Peer-led intervention has also been done by training trainers sessions for chosen youth leaders. Under the direction of preventive education and training youth leaders with training have been leading drug prevention initiatives in their communities.

Outreach Division:

Aims at reaching the general public through community programs—raises awareness, provides treatment and rehabilitation. This helps in reaching the high-risk population who end up being below the iceberg in terms of treatment. It ensures collaboration between Divisional Secretaries, Grama Niladaries, field Officers, community leaders, and civil society organisations.

10.6 Legalisation

Drug legalisation enables the regulation of substances by enacting laws that remove penalties and ensure that the production and marketing of these substances are under legal control. However, criminal or civil penalties may still be imposed if production, marketing, or use occurs outside of these regulations (Abbott et al. n.d.).

Following is the list of substances legalised in various South Asian countries.

Many factors, such as politics, ideology and morality, and public opinion perception, influence policy decisions regarding legalisation. From table it is evident that SARs have managed to legalise soft drugs and legalising or decriminalizing agents like cannabis seems a distant issue. South Asian countries, being at the whims of Western nations secondary to poor economic development, had usually taken up the route taken up by the predecessor (Table 10.4).

Legalisation should be looked at through two lenses:

(a) Did it achieve what is supposed to achieve
(b) Can other "hard" drugs be legalised too.

Unfortunately patients who require treatment of substance use disorders end up getting imprisoned and populate prisons worldwide. Prisoners, in turn, have much higher rates of drug use, especially injection drug use, than the general population, they pave way for shift from softer drugs to hard drugs—legalising agents like alcohol

Table 10.4 Substance legalized in SAR

Country	Legalised substance
India	Alcohol, tobacco
Pakistan	Tobacco, medical use of cannabis (CBD)
Afghanistan	Tobacco
Sri Lanka	Tobacco, alcohol
Maldives	Tobacco
Nepal	Tobacco, alcohol
Bhutan	Tobacco, alcohol
Bangladesh	Tobacco

Countries Where Alcohol Is Illegal 2024 (2024)

and tobacco indeed have prevented them from being part of conducive environments and a slower criminal judicial system.

It serves as an enabler to bringing in people with addictive disorders to the treatment loop. Tobacco has been the agent that has been regulated across South Asian regions. Did we eradicate tobacco users? Not, but we have been able to bring in gradual changes. Had every South Asian nation prohibited it, the situation must have been very similar to Bhutan, wherein tobacco once prohibition had to be withdrawn following COVID, there were a whopping 26 million tobacco users who had been smuggling tobacco all along, further reiterating the point that regulation is always better than prohibition—thus, criminalisation only increased crime and reduced treatment opportunities for the user.

10.7 Conclusion

The substance use and policy in South Asia has multifaceted dynamics, underscoring the urgent need for a nuanced approach to address the complex issue. It becomes evident that a singular focus on prohibition has a limited impact. There is a need for a balanced strategy that encompasses both harm reduction and supply reduction, emphasising the importance of legal reform, enhanced law enforcement, and international cooperation. Also, there is a requirement for a comprehensive policy overhaul, integrating evidence-based demand reduction strategies with social and health services to support individuals affected by drug use. Recognising the diversity of the South Asian context, it is necessary to have policies that are not only culturally sensitive but also adaptable to the evolving drug use landscape. Ultimately, it posits that addressing the drug problem in South Asia requires a concerted effort from all stakeholders, leveraging regional insights and global best practices.

References

A policy package to reverse the tobacco epidemic (2008).

Abbott, K. W., Keohane, R. O., Moravcsik, A., Slaughter, A.-M., & Snidal, D. (n.d.). *The Concept of Legalization.*

Ambekar Atul, Agrawal Alok, & Rao Ravindra. (n.d.). *Magnitude of Substance Use in India. New Delhi: Ministry of Social Justice and Empowerment, Government of India: 2019 on behalf of Group of Investigators for the National Survey on Extent and Pattern of Substance Use in India.*

Annual Drug Report, 2020, Department of Narcotics control, Bangladesh. (2020).

Arafat, S., & Kar, S. (2024). Epidemiology of psychiatric disorders and overview of access to mental health care in South Asia. In: S. M. Y. Arafat, S. K. Kar, *Access to mental health care in South Asia.* Springer Nature Singapore. https://doi.org/10.1007/978-981-99-9153-2_1

Countries Where Alcohol Is Illegal 2024. (n.d.). Retrieved February 7, 2024, from https://worldpopulationreview.com/country-rankings/countries-where-alcohol-is-illegal

Drugs Act. (n.d.).

Drugs Act 2020, Maldives. (2020).

Geneva. (2003). *4. Who framework convention on tobacco control.*

GHO|By category|BAC limit—Data by country. (n.d.). *WHO.*

Huge increase in transnational crime and synthetic drugs in SE Asia requires cross-border cooperation|UN News. (n.d.). Retrieved February 7, 2024, from https://news.un.org/en/story/2023/06/1137182

India: persons prosecuted for drug trafficking|Statista. (n.d.). Retrieved February 7, 2024, from https://www.statista.com/statistics/983816/india-persons-prosecuted-for-drug-trafficking/

Means any establishment for the manufacture of alcohol. (n.d.).

Mortimore, G., & Stimson, G. (2010). *A process and systems evaluation of the drug treatment and rehabilitation services in the Maldives a project undertaken for the ministry of health and family, Republic of Maldives, with support from world bank, South Asia and the bank-Netherlands partnership program 71288.*

Myanmar Opium Survey 2022 Cultivation, Production, and Implications. (2023). www.unodc.org/roseap

Narcotic Drugs Psychotropic Substances and Substance Abuse Act of Bhutan 2015. (n.d.).

National drugs and Psychotropics Act. (1985).

Panthee, B., Panthee, S., Gyawali, S., & Kawakami, N. (2017). Prevalence and correlates of substance use among health care students in Nepal: A cross sectional study. *BMC Public Health, 17*(1). https://doi.org/10.1186/s12889-017-4980-6

Parliament of the democratic socialist republic of Sri Lanka conventions against illicit traffic in narcotic drugs and psychotropic substances act, no. 1 of 2008. (2008).

Ray, R. (2018). *UNODC, National Drug Demand Reduction Programme.*

Regional Programme for South Asia (2018–2021) Background and Context. (n.d.).

South Asia: The emerging threat of synthetic drugs. (n.d.). Retrieved February 7, 2024, from https://www.unodc.org/southasia/frontpage/2011/january/emerging-threat-of-synthetic-drugs-in-south-asia.html

South Asia: Understanding and Addressing the Threat of Opiate Trafficking. (n.d.). Retrieved February 7, 2024, from https://www.unodc.org/southasia//frontpage/2023/May/south-asia_-understanding-and-addressing-the-threat-of-opiate-trafficking.html

Suzana, M., Zoona, A., Director, M., & Shujau, M. (2021). *Disclaimer.*

UNODC, World Drug Report 2022 (United Nations Publication 2022). (2022).

World Drug Report 2021 (United Nations publication). (n.d.).

Chapter 11
Public Health Aspects and Interventions for Substance Use Disorders in South Asia

Ravi Philip Rajkumar

11.1 Introduction

11.1.1 The Public Health Approach to Substance Use Disorders

Substance use disorders (SUD) are a group of conditions characterized by the excessive or problematic use of psychoactive drugs or substances. These substances may be legally available and sold in the open market, as in the case of alcohol or tobacco, or illegal, as in the case of heroin. Substance misuse can also occur with prescription such as benzodiazepines or opioid analgesics. Approximately 300 million individuals have used substances at least occasionally. About 8% of these users, or over 35 million adults, go on to develop a substance use disorder (World Health Organization and United Nations Office on Drugs and Crime 2020). Substance use disorders are associated with significant health, interpersonal, social, and economic costs. For example, alcohol use disorder (AUD) can lead to medical problems such as hepatic failure; it is one of the chief risk factors for road traffic accidents (RTA), and it can lead to relational and social problems such as marital disharmony, family violence, and unemployment (Klostermann 2006). The families of persons with alcohol dependence are at an elevated risk of psychological distress, physical or sexual abuse, and economic adversity (Rossow et al. 2016). Injecting drug users (IDUs) are a special subset of substance users with a distinctive profile of risks. IDUs often obtain substances illegally and inject them using shared or unsterile equipment. This leads to criminality, involvement with law enforcement agencies, and the transmission of blood-borne infections (Tavitian-Exley et al. 2015). Both licit and illicit SUD impose

R. P. Rajkumar (✉)
Department of Psychiatry, Jawaharlal Institute of Postgraduate Medical Education and Research (JIPMER), Puducherry, India
e-mail: ravi.psych@gmail.com

S. M. Y. Arafat and S. K. Kar (eds.), *Current Perspectives on Substance Use Disorders in South Asia*, https://doi.org/10.1007/978-981-97-6619-2_11

substantial health, social, and economic costs on communities and nations beyond their direct effects on users (Degenhardt et al. 2013; Bhattacharya 2017; Miller et al. 2017; GBD Alcohol and Drug Use Collaborators 2018).

Substance use disorders are a multifaceted problem, and societies have attempted to manage them in various ways. Traditionally, substance misuse has been seen as a moral weakness or "bad habit" (Goldstein and Engwall 1992; Morse 2004; Henden et al. 2013). This has led to interventions such as moral exhortation, involvement in support groups, and judicial or extra-judicial punishments for drug use. Early treatment approaches for substance abuse involved a "patchwork" of law enforcement, social services, self-help movements, with medical intervention limited to the treatment of overdoses or medical complications (Rawson et al. 2013).

The past five decades have seen a paradigm shift in our understanding of SUDs. It is now understood that they have significant biological underpinnings, involving genetic vulnerability, gene–environment interactions, and dysregulation of specific neural circuits and neurotransmitter pathways (Compton et al. 2022; Olsen 2022). This has led to the development of pharmacological treatments for SUD, such as drugs to reduce craving for alcohol (Kiefer and Mann 2005) or methadone maintenance for those with opioid dependence (Connock et al. 2007).

Medical treatments for substance use disorders are efficacious in controlled conditions. In real-world settings, their effectiveness is limited if they are not linked to appropriate psychosocial interventions and regular follow-ups (Ray et al. 2020; McPheeters et al. 2023; Wen et al. 2023). Ensuring the continuity of multidisciplinary care for SUD is a significant challenge in low- and middle-income countries (Belete et al. 2019; Kalmin et al. 2023). Substance use disorders are also associated with a significant level of social stigma, which acts as a barrier to treatment-seeking (Kiriazova et al. 2017). In the case of illicit substance misuse, stringent laws and policies may lead to the harassment or incarceration of those with SUD, limiting their ability to access health care (Otiashvili et al. 2016; Lasco 2018).

Due to the shortcomings of purely medical and legal approaches, here is an urgent need to address SUD from a broader, biopsychosocial perspective. This would entail combining pharmacological therapies, psychological and social interventions, and the judicious formulation and application of laws related to substance misuse. Ideally, this would facilitate harmonious interaction between the health care, social welfare, and criminal justice systems, and allow for a broad-based approach to SUDs that involves prevention, early intervention, case finding, treatment, and rehabilitation. Such a framework is provided by the public health approach to substance use.

The term "public health approach" (PHA) has been used in various ways with reference to substance use disorders. A recent thematic review found that descriptions of PHA varied according to the substance being considered (Crepault et al. 2023). For "licit" substances such as alcohol and tobacco, the term PHA was used synonymously with regulation—that is, with policies related to taxation and restrictions based on pricing. For "illicit" drugs, PHA referred to the minimization of harsh penalties and excessive criminalization, and emphasized medical treatment and psychosocial rehabilitation. For opioids, the term PHA was used to describe medical treatments, such as agonist substitution and other harm reduction strategies (Crepault et al. 2023).

However, this is a somewhat narrow perspective, and the broader meaning of a PHA should also be considered. In general discussions of social and preventive medicine, a PHA is considered to have four components: descriptive epidemiology, analytical epidemiology, planning, and implementation and evaluation of interventions (Satcher and Higginbotham 2008).

On this basis, a public health approach to SUD could involve the following steps:

- data collection on the prevalence of specific SUDs in a given population;
- identification of risk and protective factors for SUDs;
- the use of this data to plan preventive and treatment programmes that are appropriate for a given country or community; and
- evaluation of these programmes to ensure that they are effective, accessible, and accountable to the communities they serve (Todd et al. 2012; Crofts and Azim 2015; Saeed and Taj 2017).

In this context, "prevention" should be defined as broadly as possible, including strategies to reduce substance use in communities, to prevent progression to SUD in those using or experimenting with substances, and to prevent relapses in those with SUD (Winer et al. 2022; Carter et al. 2023).

In summary, a PHA is a multifaceted and long-term approach. It is not limited to medical or psychological interventions, but considers the cultural, economic, and political realities of a given situation, and incorporates them into the planning and implementation of health services for those with SUD, while adhering to evidence-based practices (World Health Organization and United Nations Office on Drugs and Crime 2020; Blum et al. 2022). It should adapt itself to the needs and vulnerabilities of specific populations, such as adolescents, women, or persons living with HIV/AIDS (Amin and Douaihy 2018; Ghosh et al. 2023a). To be truly effective and acceptable, such an approach should be sustainable, inclusive, comprehensive, culturally appropriate, and focussed equally on prevention, treatment, and harm reduction (Todd et al. 2012). This chapter will examine the principles, potential, realities, and challenges of a public health approach to SUD in the South Asian context.

11.1.2 Domains and Principles of a Public Health Approach to Substance Use Disorders

Public health encompasses prevention, treatment, and rehabilitation. Several experts in the field have highlighted the "vital" role of prevention in a PHA to substance use disorders (Todd et al. 2012; Chadi et al. 2018; Malick 2018; Johnson et al. 2022). Based on a synthesis of existing data and guidelines, a PHA for SUD could be seen as involving:

- Preventive services at multiple levels.
- Short- and long-term treatment, both pharmacological and psychosocial, which should be integrated with treatment for comorbid illnesses.

- A recovery-friendly approach aimed at rehabilitation and reintegration into communities.
- Changes in governmental policies related to substance use.

As policies related to substance use disorders are the subject of a separate chapter in this volume (Bojappen and Chand 2024), they will be discussed only briefly in this chapter.

Certain guiding principles are important when designing, implementing, and assessing public health programmes for substance use. These can be seen as providing an internal coherence to public health approaches, ensuring that they work in an integrated manner. A recent review by Blanco et al. (2020) has clearly enumerated these principles. These are outlined in Table 11.1.

These domains and principles are important when appraising the current state of PHA to SUDs in a country or region, and in planning or modifying public health programmes. They will be used when discussing barriers to the management of substance use in South Asia, and how they can be overcome using public health principles and methods.

Table 11.1 Guiding principles of a public health approach to substance use disorders (based on Blanco et al. 2020)

Principle	Description
Concern for social factors	The course and outcome of substance use is strongly influenced by social, cultural, and economic factors. A public health approach should address these, and not focus only on short-term medical or psychological treatments. Modifying social vulnerabilities is also important for prevention of SUDs
Person-centred approach	Persons with SUDs require medical and psychosocial care and rehabilitation, and their families require psychosocial support. They are often subjected to stigmatization or discrimination. A public health approach should protect the rights of SUDs, reject punitive or unhelpful interventions, and ensure equitable access to care tailored to each person's needs and circumstances
Bridging the gap between evidence and practice	A public health approach should be data-driven and adapted to variables such as the prevalence of SUD, the most common substances used, psychosocial risk factors, and comorbid illnesses requiring treatment. Care for SUDs should be integrated with the broader healthcare system as well as with social welfare measures, and treatment should be based on the best available evidence
Data collection	Periodic national and regional surveys of the pattern of SUDs in a country should be carried out and used to design or modify health planning. The functioning of existing programmes should be evaluated objectively, thereby enabling the healthcare system to "learn from experience"

11.2 Public Health and Substance Use in the South Asian Context

11.2.1 Substance Use in South Asia: A Public Health-Based Overview

The South Asian region encompasses eight countries: Afghanistan, Bangladesh, Bhutan, India, the Maldives, Nepal, Pakistan, and Sri Lanka. Nearly two billion people reside in South Asia. These countries are classified as low- and middle-income countries according to the World Bank (Arafat and Kar 2024). According to Global Burden of Disease (GBD) estimates, the point prevalence of AUDs in South Asian countries in 2019 ranges from 0.4 to 2.4% and the prevalence of other substance use disorders ranges from 0.4 to 0.6% (Global Burden of Disease Collaborative Network 2019).

South Asia is one of the regions with the highest number of drug-related Disability-Adjusted Life Years (DALYs), with alcohol and drug use together accounting for approximately 3.3% of all DALYs. This disability is not only due to SUDs themselves, but also to the various diseases associated with them, including tuberculosis, hepatitis B and C, HIV/AIDS, cancer, cardiovascular and cerebrovascular disease, as well as accidental injuries, self-harm and violence against others (GBD 2016 Alcohol and Drug Use Collaborators 2018).

The results of epidemiological research in South Asia suggest that the GBD data may slightly underestimate the prevalence of SUDs in this region. National surveys of SUD have been conducted in all South Asian countries, yielding prevalence estimates of at least 2–9% for SUD and 0.4–1% for IDU (United Nations Office on Drugs and Crime 2013; Cottler et al. 2014; Sivapuram et al. 2020; Rather et al. 2021; Rasheed et al. 2022). SUDs are commonly encountered in primary care settings in South Asia (Luitel et al. 2018).

Geographically, South Asia is located in between the "Golden Triangle" and the "Golden Crescent", which are among the world's largest heroin-producing regions (Mandal et al. 2023). This has led to high levels of illicit opioid use in Afghanistan and some regions of Pakistan, which are adjacent to these zones (Islam 2020; Nafeh et al. 2022). The use of captagon, an illicit amphetamine derivative, is also likely to increase in these regions (Mohaddes Ardabili et al. 2022).

Policies regarding alcohol vary in South Asia: it is legal in Bhutan, Nepal, Sri Lanka, and most states of India, but prohibited or restricted in the Islamic countries of Afghanistan, Bangladesh, Maldives, and Pakistan. However, even in countries or regions where the sale of alcohol is restricted, it is often produced and sold illegally (Subramanian et al. 2005; Mir et al. 2012). Likewise, in countries where laws exist to prevent adolescents from purchasing alcohol, these are not strictly enforced by retailers (Gyeltshen et al. 2021). Rates of use and misuse vary considerably in countries where alcohol is legal. Overall, about 20–30% of adults use alcohol in countries where restrictions are not in place (National Dangerous Drugs Control Board 2019; Wangdi and Jamtsho 2019; Parmar et al. 2023).

When considering tobacco use disorders, it is important to note that smokeless tobacco (SLT) is often the predominant form used in South Asian countries. It is usually marketed as a socially acceptable substance, in combination with other products such as the areca nut and betel leaf (Thavarajah et al. 2019; Naznin et al. 2021). However, smoking is also common, and involves both commercially available cigarettes and locally produced alternatives, such as *bidis*. Current tobacco use has been reported in 15–32% of adults from South Asian countries (National Dangerous Drugs Control Board 2019; Parmar et al. 2023).

Patterns of SUD have evolved over time in South Asia. For example, AUD became more common in patients from higher socioeconomic strata in Afghanistan in the 1970s (Gobar 1976), while the use of methamphetamine ("crystal meth", "ice", "white crystal") has increased in Pakistan in the past decade (Islam 2020; Khalid et al. 2020). In Nepal, on the other hand, the use of illicit opioids was associated with an increased influx of users or dealers from other countries and of cross-border trafficking during the 1960s and 70s. This led to an increase in heroin use among urban youth in subsequent decades (Shrestha 1992; Chatterjee et al. 1996). The most used substances in individuals seeking treatment in Bangladesh were amphetamines, cannabis, alcohol, "cough syrup", opioids (heroin and "cough syrup"), and "sleeping pills", suggesting that both illicit and prescription drug misuse are common (Hawlader et al. 2020). Urban–rural variations can also be seen in several South Asian countries. For example, the consumption of home-made "country liquor" and of hand-rolled cigarettes (bidis) may be higher in rural areas (Singh et al. 2021; Balhara et al. 2023). "Preferred" substances may vary according to age, gender, and comorbidity. In a study of youth from Afghanistan, misuse of sedative-hypnotics was more common in girls, while experimentation with tobacco, cannabis, alcohol, and stimulants was more common in boys (Momand et al. 2020).

Misuse of prescription drugs such as buprenorphine, dextropropoxyphene, nitrazepam, and "cough syrup" has also been documented extensively in research from Bangladesh, Bhutan, Nepal and Pakistan (Chatterjee et al. 1996; Choki et al. 2014; Hemel et al. 2021; Nawaz et al. 2023). Up to 15–30% of those seeking treatment for SUDs have been found to utilize these substances.

Social, economic, and political circumstances contribute to variations in the severity and distribution of SUDs in South Asia. For example, in Afghanistan and Sri Lanka, civil unrest, insurgency, and migration have contributed to an increase in IDU and in comorbid HIV infection, necessitating collaboration between the health care, law enforcement, and social welfare sectors (Jayasuriya 1995; Griffin and Khoshnood 2010). Civil unrest can have effects on patterns of substance use even in neighbouring countries. For example, the war in Afghanistan in 2001 was associated with disruptions in the supply chain of opioids and increased policing in neighbouring Pakistan. This led to an increase in needle sharing in Pakistani IDUs (Strathdee et al. 2003).

The impact of the recent COVID-19 pandemic on patterns of substance use and misuse also requires consideration. Available evidence from the region suggests that the lifting of movement restrictions was associated with increased binge drinking and relapse in persons with SUDs (Murthy and Narasimha 2021).

The social consequences of SUDs in South Asian countries can be severe, particularly in the case of illicit substance use. In a representative survey of over 900 patients recruited from over a hundred drug treatment centres, SUDs were associated with high rates of familial problems and dissolution (>75%), stigmatization by others in the community (>70%), bullying or mistreatment by others (60%), incarceration (49%), and divorce (8%) (Hawlader et al. 2020). High levels of enacted and perceived stigma may lead to self-stigma in persons with SUDs, which can lead to depression and hinder treatment-seeking (Khalid et al. 2020). Other social difficulties faced by persons with SUDs in South Asia include disruptions of education, poor work adjustment, impaired relationships with peers and family members, and reduced social competence (Poudel et al. 2016).

SUDs impose a substantial cost on the health and prosperity of South Asian nations. Estimates based on data from India suggest that alcohol use alone is associated with a loss of 258 million life years, and a loss of around 1.5% of India's gross domestic product per year (Jyani et al. 2019).

11.2.2 *The Course of Substance Use in South Asia: A Public Health Perspective*

To prevent SUDs effectively, and to offer timely interventions for them, it is essential to understand the psychosocial factors associated with the initiation and maintenance and substance use, as well as the predictors of treatment outcome for SUDs in South Asian settings. This process is depicted graphically in Fig. 11.1 and described from a public health perspective below.

In patients seeking medical treatment for SUDs in Afghanistan, peer pressure (37%) and stress reduction (22%) were cited as the leading reason for initiating the use of heroin, opium, or cannabis (Farook et al. 2022). A survey of adolescents from Bangladesh found that reduced family influence and increased smartphone use were associated with higher rates of experimentation with substances (Moonajilin et al. 2021), while both peer pressure and teachers' tobacco use were associated with smoking (Rahman et al. 2011). Peer pressure was reported to be the factor responsible for initiation of substances in 92% of a sample of Nepali adolescents (Chapagain et al. 2020). Apart from peer pressure, curiosity and a desire to have "fun" or to "escape" from unfavourable living circumstances have also been cited as frequent reasons for initiating substance use in South Asian patients (Maruf et al. 2016; Darshana et al. 2022; Madill et al. 2023). In the case of SLT, cultural beliefs about positive health benefits and social acceptability combine with aggressive marketing practices to influence initial use (Thavarajah et al. 2019). Witnessing regular substance use by family members or elders in the community may double the risk of tobacco, alcohol, or drug use in adolescents, suggesting a role for social learning and imitation

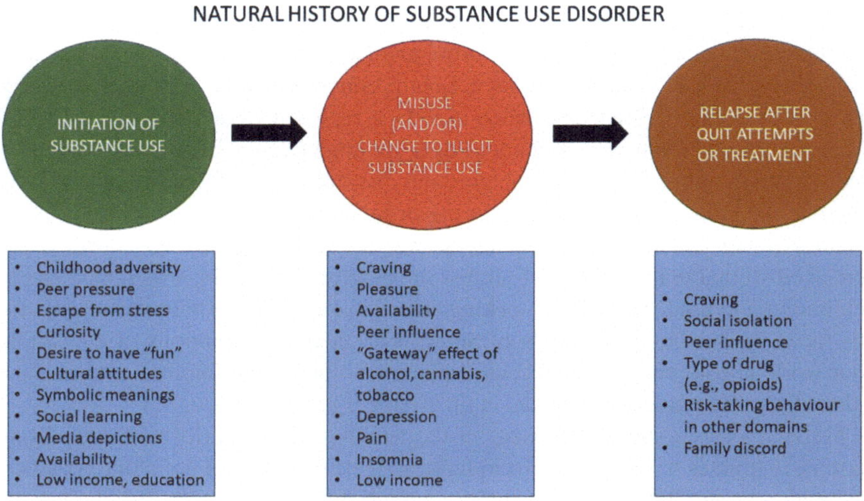

Fig. 11.1 Factors associated with initiation, continuation, and relapse of substance use in South Asian countries

(Srivastava et al. 2021). Exposure to childhood adversity at the family or community level has also been associated with a four- to six-fold increase in the risk of SUDs in this region (Fernandes et al. 2021). Cultural attitudes regarding the "tolerability" or "acceptability" of alcohol or tobacco, and "positive" portrayals of their use in media, can also lead youth to initiate the use of these substances (Bhandari et al. 2021a, b). Youth may consume certain substances due to their symbolic association with a "modern" or "Western" lifestyle (Sørensen et al. 2020). From a broader sociological perspective, men with lower educational attainment, lower standards of living, and/or belonging to disadvantaged castes or communities are more likely to initiate and continue alcohol consumption (Subramanian et al. 2005). Finally, substance use also depends on supply: those substances that are readily available in local shops or markets are the ones most likely to be tried, especially by adolescents (Chapagain et al. 2020; Bhandari et al. 2021a, b; Darshana et al. 2022).

Moving from occasional to heavy use of a substance is an indication of progression to an SUD. In a survey of smokers from India and Bangladesh, 7.2% of men and 0.4% of women who smoked developed a "hardcore" pattern of use, characterized by increased consumption, difficulty in quitting, and low motivation to change. Male gender, older age, and lower income were associated with this type of smoking (Kishore et al. 2013). A typological study of alcohol use in Sri Lanka found evidence for two patterns: *moderate consumption*, which was socially acceptable and occurred in specific settings, and *heavy consumption*, which involved a loss of control and failure to conform to social norms (Sørensen et al. 2020). A qualitative study of youth from Assam found that the transition from illicit drug use to addiction evolved an initial phase characterized by fluctuating use, craving, and feelings of relaxation and pleasure (the "relaxation phase"). Later, these were replaced by more marked functional impairment and unsuccessful attempts to quit (the "chaotic phase"), and finally by more purposeful drug-seeking behaviour and failed treatment attempts (the "strategic phase") (Madill et al. 2023). The presence of symptoms of mental illness, such as depression, anxiety, and aggression, has been found to predict sustained alcohol use in adolescents (Shahzad et al. 2020). In adults, symptoms of pain, depression, and disturbed sleep have been associated with progression to prescription drug misuse (Nawaz et al. 2023). Easy access to specific substances and the presence of friends using the same substance are associated with continued use of illicit drugs (Jayamaha et al. 2022).

Progression from one form of substance to another—particularly from non-injecting to injecting drug use—is also important from a preventive standpoint. A study of IDUs from Bangladesh found that many of these patients initially used cannabis before progressing to injectable opioids, suggesting that cannabis may act as a "gateway" drug in these cases (Hossain and Nandi 2015). Similar "gateway" effects have been observed with tobacco and alcohol in Sri Lanka (Darshana et al. 2022). The non-availability of illicit drugs may lead patients to seek alternatives in the form of prescription drugs: users unable to obtain heroin may substitute it with buprenorphine or pentazocine (Nawaz et al. 2023).

Knowledge of the factors associated with relapse or treatment discontinuation is important in planning long-term treatment and rehabilitation. A cohort study of Bangladeshi patients with SUD found that over 72% of treated users relapsed. Living alone or with other users, prior treatment failure, higher income, high-risk sexual behaviour, and the use of opioids predicted poor treatment outcomes (Maehira et al. 2013). A nation-wide study from the same country found that family discord, peer pressure, depression, and craving were the most cited reasons for relapse. Respondents in this sample were mainly users of amphetamines, cannabis, or alcohol (Nabi et al. 2022).

Data on medium- and long-term outcomes is lacking. A prospective study of patients with nicotine use disorder in Nepal found that 37% of patients were able to successfully quit tobacco at 3 months (Elsey et al. 2016). A cohort study from Sri Lanka followed 188 patients with alcohol dependence over 3 years, and found that 73 (39%) maintained sobriety. Mortality was 14% in those who relapsed, but only 3% in abstainers, and almost all the deaths in the relapse group were alcohol-related (De Silva and Ellawala 1994). Another study from the same country followed up users who were unsuccessfully treated in a hospital and admitted at a residential care centre for 6 weeks. At 2 years, 36% maintained abstinence from alcohol, which was comparable to the best outcomes reported in developed countries (De Silva et al. 1992).

11.2.3 Issues Related to Comorbidity

A detailed discussion of comorbidities in persons with SUDs is provided in Chap. 12 (Bhad and Shukla 2024). The following section will provide a brief overview of key comorbidities from a preventive medicine and public health perspective.

11.2.3.1 Communicable Diseases

SUDs are associated with high rates of comorbid infectious diseases, particularly among IDUs. These include HIV/AIDS, viral hepatitis (HBV and HCV), and reproductive tract infections (Shrestha et al. 1996; Reza et al. 2019). Public health experts from South Asia have warned that this could lead to local epidemics unless proper preventive measures are instituted among IDUs (Azim et al. 2008; Sahibzada et al. 2022). Currently, over one-third of new HIV infections in some South Asian countries occur in relation to IDU and associated risk behaviours (Khan et al. 2019). Recent South Asian data suggests that the prevalence of these infections in IDUs is 7–21% for HIV/AIDS, 3–7% for HBV, 34–40% for HCV, and 5–11% for other sexually transmitted infections (Ruiseñor-Escudero et al. 2014; Hossain and Nandi 2015; Asif et al. 2019; Khan et al. 2019; Rahman et al. 2019; Ganesh et al. 2020). Risk behaviours associated with these diseases are related to a lack of knowledge regarding disease transmission. These include unsterile needles, needle sharing, and unprotected sexual contacts with multiple partners (Lucy et al. 2005; Neupane and Mishra 2014; Pachuau et al. 2022). Apart from these infections, SUDs in South Asia are associated with an increased risk and greater severity of pulmonary tuberculosis (Rumi et al. 2000; Kan et al. 2020) and COVID-19 (Murthy and Narasimha 2021). Though these disorders are treatable, treatment facilities for IDUs may be lacking or inaccessible in South Asian countries, and users may be non-adherent to prescribed antiviral medication (Petersen et al. 2013). Effective prevention and treatment of these infections in IDUs requires continued outreach, education, and harm reduction (Rahman et al. 2019).

11.2.3.2 Non-communicable Diseases

SUDs are highly comorbid with a variety of non-infectious diseases that are associated with elevated morbidity and mortality and impaired quality of life. These include musculoskeletal, gastrointestinal, cardiorespiratory, genitourinary, and neuropsychiatric disorders, as well as malignant neoplasms (Ali et al. 2023; Bhatt et al. 2023; Singh et al. 2023). There are high levels of comorbidity between SUDs and mental disorders (Rahman et al. 2015; Gyawali et al. 2016). Around 30–70% of persons with SUDs have symptoms of depression or anxiety (Hossain et al. 2012; Gyawali et al. 2016; Stanikzai and Wahidi 2023), and about 40% of those with alcohol, opioid, or cannabis use disorder have major depression (Neupane and Bramness 2013; Ghazal

2019). Despite these patients being extensive users of mental health services, there is poor integration between mental health care and SUD treatment in South Asian countries (Pelzang 2012; Hapangama et al. 2013).

Suicide is also a frequent outcome of SUDs. SUDs may increase the risk of suicidal ideas or attempts almost ten-fold (Armstrong and Samson 2016; Dema et al. 2019; Wadood et al. 2021). Persons with SUDs also frequently contact suicide helplines when in a personal crisis related to their disorder (Iqbal et al. 2019), and engage in non-suicidal self-injury (Hemel et al. 2021). There is evidence that substance-related suicides are increasing in some South Asian countries, particularly in younger adults (Menon et al. 2023). Thus, integrating SUD screening and treatment into national suicide prevention strategies is essential from a public health perspective.

Medical emergencies due to overdoses of certain substances are often encountered in hospital settings. In a survey of 109 patients with opioid use disorder, 45% had overdosed at least once in their lifetime, and one-fourth of them had overdosed in the last year (Saini et al. 2020). Likewise, emergencies related to alcohol withdrawal, such as delirium or seizures, are frequently encountered in medical settings (Bhalla et al. 2006).

Accidents and trauma related to SUDs are also common in South Asian countries. A survey of commercial bus and truck drivers from Pakistan found that up to 10% use alcohol and 30% consume cannabis while driving. The use of these substances is associated with a higher risk of road traffic accidents (RTAs) (Mir et al. 2012). In Sri Lanka, alcohol-related injuries were seen in 15% of patients hospitalized for injuries, 33% of these patients were using alcohol at the time of the accident, and 19% were dependent on alcohol. Most of these injuries occurred because of RTAs (Schölin et al. 2022), highlighting the need for effective public health measures to prevent such accidents.

11.2.4 Substance Use in High-Risk and Vulnerable Populations in South Asia

Apart from patients with comorbid diagnoses, there are certain subgroups that pose specific challenges regarding the prevention and treatment of SUDs in South Asian countries (Gupta and Mehrotra 2021). As these "high-risk" groups require targeted public health interventions, they are briefly reviewed in Table 11.2. More detailed coverage of vulnerable populations in South Asia is provided in Chap. 14 (Singh et al. 2024).

Table 11.2 Substance use in high-risk and vulnerable populations in South Asia from a public health perspective

Group	Public health concerns
Adolescents	• Difficulty in engagement for prevention and treatment programmes (Petrosino et al. 2002; Shackleton et al. 2016) • High rates of tobacco and alcohol use in South Asian youth (Rahman et al. 2011; Chapagain et al. 2020; Moonajilin et al. 2021; Srivastava et al. 2021) • Evidence of significant numbers of adolescents misusing cannabis or prescription drugs (Bhandari et al. 2021b) • Risk of transition from experimentation to SUD (Ghazal 2019; Shahzad et al. 2020) • Possible increase in injecting drug use in youth (Biswas et al. 2020) Adolescence provides a public health "window of opportunity" for education, prevention, and early intervention (Jiloha 2017)
Women	• Higher rates of mistreatment by spouses, families, and members of the community (Abadi et al. 2012) • Involvement in sex work (Baral et al. 2013) • Lack of social and economic freedom when requiring or seeking treatment (Irfan et al. 2021) • High risk of HIV/AIDS (Ghimire et al. 2013; Pachuau et al. 2023) • "Socially acceptable" SUD (e.g. SLT), with acceptance of myths about the "positive" effects of these substances (Sreenivasan et al. 2022) Despite these risks, women have better treatment outcomes when engaged in treatment for SUD, especially if provided in a gender-sensitive manner, and are more adherent to legal restrictions on alcohol use (Abadi et al. 2015; Schweinhart et al. 2022; Balhara et al. 2023)
Injecting drug users (IDUs)	• Higher risk of infections and other medical comorbidities, with poor adherence to prescribed treatments (Dolan and Larney 2009; Ali et al. 2018; Nafeh et al. 2022) • Complex psychosocial difficulties (Pant et al. 2023) • Risk of criminality or incarceration (Nafeh et al. 2022) • Victimization by law enforcement (Khan et al. 2021) • Involvement in high-risk behaviours (Hemel et al. 2021; Capelastegui et al. 2023) • Multiple substance misuse (Ojha et al. 2014) This population is of key public health and epidemiological significance, and requires adequate outreach measures and access to harm reduction programmes (Todd et al. 2012)

(continued)

Table 11.2 (continued)

Group	Public health concerns
Families of persons with SUD	• Risk of physical, emotional, or sexual abuse (Laslett et al. 2017; Naved et al. 2018; Iversen et al. 2021) • Imitation of fathers' substance use by sons (Srivastava et al. 2021; Nattala et al. 2022) • Risk of stress-related mental disorders (Srivastava et al. 2021; Nattala et al. 2022) • Elevated risk of HIV/AIDS and related infections (Reza et al. 2023) It is crucial from a public health standpoint to engage with these families, screen them for physical or mental illness, and offer them treatment and psychosocial support
Other vulnerable populations	• Tribal and indigenous communities—high rates of "licit" SUDs, inadequate outreach, lack of access to treatment (Sadath et al. 2022) • Prison inmates—high rates of SUD and high-risk behaviours, inadequate access to treatment (Dissabandara et al. 2009; Kumar et al. 2014; Jamal et al. 2022) • Healthcare workers and students—easy access to prescription drugs, risk of misuse due to workplace, or academic stress (Panthee et al. 2017) These groups would benefit from public health interventions centred on education, outreach, and improved coordination with other sectors

11.3 Existing Public Health Programmes for Substance Use Disorders in South Asia

Initiatives aimed at the prevention or treatment of SUDs have been launched in all South Asian countries, though their functioning and effective coverage vary widely both across countries and over time. A complete overview of these programmes is beyond the scope of this chapter: only those aspects relevant to a public health approach will be covered. Such initiatives are often hampered by logistic factors common to all low- and middle-income countries, and by a lack of planning at the primary or community level (Baron et al. 2018). Table 11.3 summarizes national policies on the treatment of SUDs in South Asian countries from a public health perspective. Sri Lanka and India have passed legislation on the treatment of SUDs independent of law enforcement, while Bhutan has amended existing laws to address public health. However, regulatory authorities are not always fully functional, and implementation of policies is inconsistent.

Care for SUDs in South Asia has been envisaged in terms of a stepped-care model, with milder and uncomplicated cases managed at the primary level. In practice, this does not happen: as few as 2% of smokers are accurately identified at the primary level, due to patients' reluctance to disclose substance use and staff's lack of motivation and familiarity with screening or brief interventions (Elsey et al. 2016).

An overview of the scenario in Nepal 30 years ago found that the capacity of both governmental and non-governmental treatment facilities was unable to handle the growing number of users, particularly those with relapses (Shrestha 1992). A more recent study in the same country found that nearly half of patients with AUD did not

Table 11.3 National programmes and legislation related to substance use disorders in South Asia

Country	Programmes for the prevention and treatment of SUDs	Relevant legislation
Afghanistan (Todd et al. 2012; Noroozi et al. 2024)	National Harm Reduction Policy launched in 2005, but not fully functional. SUDs mentioned briefly in National Mental Health Strategy (2019)	Counter Narcotics Drug Law, 2005: emphasis on supply reduction and law enforcement, minimal integration with public health
Bangladesh (Rahman 2019)	Private Treatment and Rehabilitation Centre Rules (2005) provide government oversight of private facilities for the treatment of SUDs	Narcotics Control Act, 1990: emphasis on supply reduction and law enforcement, minimal integration with public health. Amendment planned in 2018
Bhutan (Bhutan Narcotics Control Authority 2020)	Demand Reduction Division of Bhutan Narcotics Control Authority in charge of education, prevention, treatment, and rehabilitation as per 2015 legislation	Narcotic Drugs, Psychotropic Substances and Substance Use Act, 2015: emphasis on supply reduction and law enforcement, partial integration with public health. Amended to address education, prevention, and treatment in 2018
India (Avasthi and Ghosh 2019)	Programmes for prevention and reduction of alcohol and drug abuse launched by the Ministry of Social Justice and Empowerment in 2015 and 2018, but not integrated with Mental Health Action Plan (2014)	Narcotic Drugs and Psychotropic Substances (NDPS) Act, 1985: emphasis on supply reduction and law enforcement, partial integration with public health. Amended in 2014 to improve linkage with treatment and harm reduction Mental Health Care Act (MHCA), 2017: incorporates care for SUDs including protection of human rights, right to treatment, and rehabilitation
Maldives (United Nations Office on Drugs and Crime 2013)	National Drug Rehabilitation Centre opened in 1997; provides treatment and community-based rehabilitation, but no nation-wide programme	Law on Narcotic Drugs and Psychotropic Substances (Law No. 17/77), 1977: emphasis on supply reduction and law enforcement, partial integration with public health
Nepal (Tandon 2021)	National Policy for Drug Control (2006) mentions right to treatment and treatment in private facilities. Public–private partnership for treatment and rehabilitation centres initiated in 2021	Narcotic Drugs (Control) Act, 1976: emphasis on supply reduction and law enforcement, no integration with public health

(continued)

Table 11.3 (continued)

Country	Programmes for the prevention and treatment of SUDs	Relevant legislation
Pakistan	Ministry of Narcotics Control (created 2017) oversees education, prevention, treatment, and harm reduction, but no nation-level programme	Control of Narcotic Substances Act (1997): emphasis on supply reduction and law enforcement, no integration with public health
Sri Lanka (National Dangerous Drugs Control Board 2021)	Treatment and Rehabilitation Division of National Dangerous Drugs Control Board in change of treatment, rehabilitation, and support to family members	Poisons, Opium and Dangerous Drugs Act (1984): emphasis on supply reduction and law enforcement, amended in 2022 Drug Dependent Persons (Treatment and Rehabilitation) Act, 2007: addresses public health, treatment, and protection of human rights of persons with SUDs

access treatment (Jordans et al. 2017). More recent initiatives, involving community volunteers and the integration with primary health care, have significantly improved detection, retention in treatment, and symptomatic improvement in persons with AUDs (Jordans et al. 2019a, 2020). This provides an example of how a public health approach can improve case finding and treatment outcomes in a South Asian setting over time, especially when there is collaboration between healthcare services and local communities.

Outreach measures are even more important when dealing with populations such as IDUs, who are socially marginalized and less likely to engage with clinical services. For example, a "street-based" programme based on non-confrontational counselling, education, and harm reduction was effective than in reducing HIV infection and needle sharing in patients from Nepal. Such programmes may be more "expensive" in terms of manpower and financial requirements, but may be more effective—and, ultimately, more cost-effective—than "routine" care (Singh 1998).

In populations with socioeconomic vulnerabilities, public health approaches to substance use may be more effective when integrated with broader measures aimed at social security and empowerment. For example, the CHILD intervention, an integrated programme for high-risk Afghan youth, includes not only drug-related education but interventions aimed at improving literacy and numeracy, personal safety, communication skills, and coping with traumatic situations. This programme had a positive impact on drug-free behaviour over time (Momand et al. 2017).

Harm reduction programmes in South Asia have had a chequered history. Due to culturally conditioned attitudes about addiction, they may lack societal support and acceptance. They are often accorded a low priority in health budgets, and may experience hostility from more expensive private treatment facilities (Ambekar et al. 2013). Nevertheless, the available evidence suggests that these programmes are efficacious in reducing the risk of infectious diseases. For example, the CARE-SHAKTI intervention, based on reduction of high-risk injecting and sexual behaviour, was cost-effective and halved the rate of HIV infections even when baseline HIV prevalence in IDUs was high (Guinness et al. 2010). Similarly, a harm reduction package based on education and needle provision through a non-governmental organization (NGO), the Lifesaving and Lifegiving Society, reduced the seroprevalence of HIV to nearly zero in clients (Peak et al. 1995). Targeted interventions by outreach workers can improve the outcome of such programmes, particularly in terms of reducing high-risk behaviours (Sahu et al. 2022).

The measures taken by South Asian countries to address the problems of licit substance use, and particularly tobacco use disorder, should also be recognized. Starting with India in 2003, all South Asian nations have enacted legislation aimed at reducing tobacco consumption, restricting advertising, and placing public health warnings on tobacco products (Gupta et al. 2022). There is evidence that such measures have been effective in reducing tobacco use disorders in some South Asian countries, such as India and Bangladesh (see Sect. 5.2). Smoking cessation interventions have also been implemented in several South Asian countries, though their effectiveness varies significantly based on public awareness and availability (Iqbal et al. 2022).

11.4 Challenges and Barriers to a Public Health Approach for Substance Use Problems in South Asia

11.4.1 Socioeconomic Barriers

Several social factors may stand in the way of a public health approach to SUDs in the South Asian context. These include stigmatization of substance users due to cultural or religious values and beliefs, denial or minimization of SUDs, and a lack of social support. Social stigmatization and hostility from family members is associated with worse treatment outcomes in patients with any form of SUD (Shahid and Asmat 2023). The cost of treatment is also an important barrier to care. In a study of patients with AUDs from Nepal, financial barriers, rather than stigma, cultural attitudes, or lack of support were significantly correlated with low help-seeking behaviour (Luitel et al. 2019). Financial constraints are especially likely when primary or publicly funded treatment for SUDs is inadequate, forcing patients to pay for treatment "out-of-pocket" in the private sector (Ambekar et al. 2013). Cultural taboos against substance use are also associated with significant delays in receiving treatment (Neupane and Bramness 2014). These social and economic barriers may be especially severe in the case of women with SUDs (Al-Ghafri et al. 2023).

11.4.2 Barriers to Outreach and Engagement

A public health approach to SUDs requires the recognition of the humanity and dignity of users, and the need to engage with them in appropriate ways without undue coercion or violence (Blanco et al. 2020) (Table 11.1). Certain aspects of the healthcare and law enforcement systems can limit attempts to reach out to persons with SUD or to engage them in treatment. These include a lack of trust in existing treatment facilities, a perceived lack of confidentiality and privacy, and negative attitudes on the part of physicians and other healthcare workers (Al-Ghafri et al. 2023). In addition, harsh or punitive laws related to substance possession or use can create a conflict between legal and person-centred approaches. Users in such settings may avoid seeking help due to a fear of legal repercussions or punishment, or may be prevented from accessing existing treatment programmes (Gobar 1976; Al-Ghafri et al. 2023). This was vividly illustrated in a study of injecting drug users' experiences during a governmental "anti-drug drive" in Bangladesh. This initiative was associated with experiences of violence, harassment, and forced relocation. As a result, many users were unable to access treatment facilities or harm reduction programmes during this period (Khan et al. 2021). Harm reduction facilities, which are often the most humane form of intervention for IUDs, may be the victims of societal disapproval and shortages in funding (Ambekar et al. 2013).

Mixed or negative attitudes towards persons with SUD and their treatment can be seen even among medical professionals (Narasimha et al. 2022). This can interfere with the provision of adequate care for SUDs, even when individuals are motivated to quit. Data from the National Family Health Surveys in India suggest that over 30% of smokers try to quit (International Institute of Population Sciences and ICF 2021; Parmar et al. 2023), but few have access to appropriate advice or to tobacco cessation facilities.

A lack of appropriate facilities for treatment and harm reduction has led to the proliferation of unregulated "deaddiction centres" which claim to treat or even cure SUDs. Users and caregivers may resort to admission in such facilities out of desperation. These often function more as detention centres than as treatment facilities, and their users incur high costs and often run into debts (Singh and Rao 2021).

Finally, engagement with persons with SUDs in the community requires the involvement of primary or community healthcare workers. Such workers are often overburdened with responsibilities for other national health programmes, and may not have received adequate training in identifying and managing SUDs. This can lead to a lack of motivation in implementing SUD-related initiatives (Elsey et al. 2016; Rabbani et al. 2023).

11.4.3 Barriers in Translating Evidence to Practice

Perhaps the largest barrier in translating evidence on prevention and treatment of SUDs into practice is the lack of, or inadequate functioning of, existing treatment systems. In a study of IDUs in Afghanistan, 94% reported the need for better treatment than what was available to them, and 56% reported an inability to access treatment. Most of these users also experienced difficulties in accessing harm reduction interventions such as needle sharing (Todd et al. 2009a, b) due to a lack of funding; negative societal attitudes towards this approach; and a fear that certain harm reduction measures, such as opioid substitution, will be misused. In a survey of IDUs in Bangladesh, only 3% reported being able to access opioid agonist therapy (Khan et al. 2019). A similar shortfall was observed in a multi-country survey involving Afghanistan, Bangladesh, and India. While needle-sharing programmes were functioning reasonably well in Bangladesh and India (>200 syringes distributed per user in 1 year), they were rudimentary in Afghanistan. Opioid substitution therapy was documented in only 0.3% of patients from Bangladesh, 0.4% from Afghanistan, and 3% from India (Petersen et al. 2013). In some cases, initial treatment facilities produce good outcomes, but there is a lack of continuity of care. A review of records from three rehabilitation centres in Nepal found that they all achieved good results in terms of short-term abstinence; however, only one of them had a functioning harm reduction programme, and one did not have facilities for long-term rehabilitation. This could lead to high relapse rates in spite of a good initial response to treatment (Niraula et al. 2006).

Psychological interventions developed in other cultural contexts may not be effective if they are used without modification in South Asian clients. A study of therapists attempting to use cognitive-behavioural therapy (CBT) for patients with SUD in Pakistan identified a number of barriers to the use of this therapy, including cultural, familial and religious attitudes and beliefs, lower patient self-awareness, and unrealistic expectations of the outcome of therapy. This can lead to resistance on the part of clients, and eventually to their dropping out of treatment (Azad et al. 2022).

Lacunae in medical education can also stand in the way of public health measures. A review of the medical curriculum in Nepal found that there was good coverage of the theoretical aspects of SUDs. However, clinical exposure was inadequate, and trainees' knowledge and skills regarding SUDs were not sufficiently assessed (Marahatta et al. 2021). This could lead to difficulties when new medical graduates from South Asian countries are involved in programmes for the prevention and treatment of substance use. This problem may be more acute in the case of non-medical healthcare workers in South Asia. Curricula for these staff may contain little meaningful knowledge or practical training related to SUDs (Rabbani et al. 2023). Besides, much healthcare education is based on a biomedical model of illness and may not address the psychosocial aspects of SUDs. This was observed in a qualitative study of therapists treating patients with SUDs in Pakistan, who encountered a lack of comprehension and cooperation from medically trained psychiatrists (Azad et al. 2022).

An issue of particular concern regarding prescription drug misuse is the lack of trained personnel in pharmacies and drugstores. A study of two hundred pharmacies in Punjab, Pakistan, found that only 5% were run by qualified pharmacists. The remainder were run by non-qualified staff, who were willing to sell prescription drugs such as opioids, benzodiazepines, and amphetamines "over the counter" to investigators posing as patients (Bashir et al. 2021). Such hazardous practices can lead to an increase in SUDs related to prescription drugs over time, even if the use of illicit substances is curtailed.

11.4.4 Other Barriers

Public health approaches are most effective when based on accurate data. However, conducting large-scale surveys on a personally sensitive and culturally stigmatized topic is challenging in South Asian countries, particularly when there is a lack of research personnel and infrastructure. Though all South Asian countries except Pakistan have conducted national surveys on the prevalence of SUDs, accurate information on the burden of SUD in vulnerable populations is lacking. Moreover, the findings of these surveys have not been fully incorporated into public health initiatives, leading to a large treatment gap (Balan et al. 2023).

Issues related to priority and integration with other aspects of health care represent another substantial barrier. SUDs may be seen as a relatively low-priority area for public health initiatives when compared to communicable diseases or cardiovascular diseases in a South Asian context, leading to reduced budgetary allocation and reduced service availability. This can be compounded by negative cultural attitudes related to SUD and pessimism regarding treatment outcomes (Schroeder 2005). Though SUDs are extensively comorbid with many diseases that are prioritized in public health, integrated care for these conditions is not available. Thus, for example, tobacco cessation services may not be readily available to patients seeking treatment for tobacco-related cardiovascular or respiratory diseases (Bhatt et al. 2023).

Though religion is sometimes cited as a protective factor against SUD, certain religious beliefs and taboos can act as a barrier to effective treatment and rehabilitation. For example, in Afghanistan, there are strong religious prohibitions against the use of alcohol. This can lead to clandestine use and difficulty in seeking treatment, with some users of alcohol reporting that they experience greater stigmatization than opioid users (Al-Ghafri et al. 2023).

The implementation of public health programmes for SUDs requires a certain amount of social, economic, and political stability. In countries with high levels of civil unrest, insurgency, and terrorism, measures for the prevention and treatment of SUDs may be an early casualty, as has been observed in Afghanistan (Stepanova 2012) and Sri Lanka (Jayasuriya 1995). Internal conflict may also be associated with higher rates of substance use and drug trafficking, creating a situation where the number of persons with SUDs increases while treatment becomes less accessible

(Strathdee et al. 2003). In some cases, a criminal nexus may link terrorism and the illicit drug trade, causing a "spillover" effect to neighbouring countries (Myers 2013).

A lack of political will may impede the development and implementation of a PHA aimed at preventing or treating SUD, even if social and economic conditions are otherwise favourable. This is particularly likely to happen for substances which are culturally tolerated or provide a source of revenue for governments. In South Asia, this problem has been observed in the context of smokeless tobacco use (Mackay et al. 2013).

11.5 Strategies to Overcome Existing Barriers

11.5.1 Building on Existing Psychosocial Strengths and Protective Factors

The preceding sections have painted a somewhat bleak picture of the prospects for a public health approach for SUDs in South Asia. However, despite a wide range of social, cultural, economic, and systemic barriers, certain strengths of South Asian societies and cultures also need to be emphasized. These are valuable in ensuring that persons with SUDs receive appropriate preventive, therapeutic, and harm reduction interventions. A recent study of drug users from Afghanistan found that 73% reported good levels of social support (Stanikzai and Wahidi 2023). Higher levels of social and familial support may explain why disulfiram therapy, considered a second-line treatment in Europe and North America, is acceptable and effective in preventing relapses in Indian patients with AUD (Bharadwaj et al. 2018). Family support has also been positively associated with treatment outcomes during opioid substitution therapy in India (Kermode et al. 2020) and with treatment outcomes for SUDs in general (Shahid and Asmat 2023).

The motivation of South Asian clients to change their own behaviour should not be underestimated. For example, 68% of patients admitted for alcohol-related problems in Nepal expressed a desire to be treated for AUD and to maintain sobriety. However, they also expressed a wish for concurrent treatment of their physical and psychological comorbidities, such as depression and sexual dysfunction. Integrated models of care may be particularly effective in such patients (Pandey et al. 2012).

Leveraging existing protective factors is particularly important for the prevention of SUDs. Evidence suggests that adolescents' coping skills are an important determinant of their experimentation with substances. Therefore, apart from specific education on the harms associated with alcohol, tobacco, or drugs, more general training in life skills or positive coping may reduce the risk of substance misuse in youth (Bhandari et al. 2021a).

Understanding South Asian users' perspectives on addiction and recovery is also important, as these are important in engaging with and retaining patients in treatment and rehabilitation. For example, users from an Indian state found that meaningful engagement with a counsellor, personal commitment to change, altering prior lifestyles, and finding meaning through helping other users (e.g. through participating in awareness programmes) could aid recovery (Madill et al. 2023).

Though most laws related to SUDs are focussed on penalties, there is encouraging evidence that this trend is changing. As seen in Table 11.2, specific legislation on the care of persons with SUDs has been enacted in India and Sri Lanka, and amendments to existing law have been made in Bhutan and are in process in Bangladesh.

11.5.2 Working with Communities and Existing Systems

Certain positive trends in patterns of substance use in South Asia over the past decade should be acknowledged. For example, a study of smoking behaviour in India and Bangladesh showed significant decreases in both daily and "heavy" smoking (Sreeramareddy and Aye 2021). Awareness of the adverse effects of tobacco has increased over time, with over 60% of a sample of Indian respondents displaying good level knowledge on this topic. This has been associated with a delay in initiation of tobacco use (Kankaria et al. 2021; Verma et al. 2023). Likewise, national survey data suggests that alcohol consumption in India has reduced significantly over the past decade, except in men with heavy alcohol use (Balhara et al. 2022; Parmar et al. 2023). These findings suggest that existing national policies and programmes have reduced effect on the consumption of licit substances, and that men with increased consumption could be a focus for targeted interventions. Similarly, the gains seen regarding nicotine have been less pronounced for SLT use: this should lead to an emphasis on preventing and treating this form of tobacco use (Verma et al. 2023).

Negative attitudes towards persons with SUDs have been documented in most South Asian countries, even among healthcare professionals. However, these attitudes are not unchangeable. In a report from Afghanistan, positive attitudes towards providing support to drug users and towards harm reduction improved significantly among medical staff over a period of 2 years (2007–2009) during which harm reduction and counselling programmes were expanded (Todd et al. 2016). Medical professionals' negative attitudes towards SUD tend to decrease with clinical experience, making them more ready to provide brief interventions in a primary care setting (Narasimha et al. 2022). Likewise, healthcare workers' reluctance to involve themselves in programmes such as tobacco cessation can be overcome through appropriate training and leadership (Elsey et al. 2016).

Encountering and assisting users in a natural, non-clinic setting can also be helpful, particularly in terms of prevention and early treatment. A school-based programme of this sort is under development and evaluation in India, and aims to address not just SUD but the physical, mental, and sexual health of adolescents (Guthold et al. 2023). Another project of this sort in Sri Lanka aims to engage with the parents of children attending preschool. Its aims include training volunteers from among parents and teachers, educating families about substance misuse, providing treatment to affected parents, and protecting mothers from IPV (Lokuge et al. 2018).

A shortage of manpower can, in some cases, be circumvented with the help of motivated volunteers from the community (Samarasinghe 1989). In a trial of home-based detoxification and counselling by lay health workers, up to 40% of Indian patients with alcohol dependence completed treatment and experienced a resolution of withdrawal symptoms. Improvement in a global measure of alcohol-related problems—but not in daily or heavy drinking—was also observed. Such an approach is promising in low-resource settings, but may need fine-tuning to address issues such as craving and lapses (Nadkarni et al. 2020). Brief counselling by trained laypersons may also be useful and cost-effective for persons with AUDs in this context (Nadkarni et al. 2017). Likewise, the involvement of parents, school teachers, and other key members of local communities is being evaluated as a strategy to prevent or reduce adolescent SUDs (Guthold et al. 2023).

Psychosocial interventions for SUDs should be adapted to the social and cultural context of patients from South Asian countries. If this is not done, even "evidence-based" therapies such as CBT may be ineffective. Such adaptations are both feasible and practical, and attempts to evaluate these modified therapies in South Asia are ongoing. For example, a culturally sensitive adaptation of techniques such as motivational intervening and mindfulness-based CBT is being tested for relapse prevention in patients with SUD in Pakistan (Asif et al. 2023).

Integration of SUD treatment with care for other disorders is already being implemented in some South Asian countries. In India, certain centres offer integrated care for IDU and HIV/AIDS, using a combination of ART, opioid substitution with buprenorphine, and counselling: over 50–60% of patients are retained in treatment at these centres and achieve good outcomes (Ganapathi et al. 2023). Likewise, the experience of an opioid substitution centre in an Indian state with high rates of opioid use disorder suggests that over 65% of patients can be retained in treatment, with significant reductions in needle sharing, substance use, and criminality, and improvements in physical and mental health, relationships, and hope (Kermode et al. 2020).

Though public health is the responsibility of local and national governments, effective public health approaches to SUDs require collaboration between the public and private sectors and affected communities. NGOs may plan an important role in certain aspects of SUD treatment, particularly harm reduction strategies for IDUs (Jayasuriya 1995; Peak et al. 1995; Maguet and Majeed 2010). The regulation of prescription drug abuse also requires the cooperation of stakeholders from the private sector, particularly those involved in the supply and distribution of these drugs. Retailers should be educated about the risks of misuse associated with certain drugs, particularly benzodiazepines and opioids, and should be instructed not to dispense them without a valid prescription (Upadhaya et al. 2018).

Substance use affects not just individuals but entire communities; in other words, members of a community affected by alcohol or drug use are key stakeholders, and their experiences and perspectives should be respected and valued from a public health standpoint. In an example of such an initiative, youth from Assam were invited to "co-create" educational materials such as posters and videos addressing substance use, addiction, and recovery. These materials were perceived as culturally acceptable and useful for SUD prevention by youth in the community (Duara et al. 2022). A similar community-based educational initiative for AUD, the THEATRE study, is ongoing in Sri Lanka. This programme involves the use of drama and culturally appropriate educational materials (Pearson et al. 2023).

Religion and spirituality (R/S) play an important role in the personal and social lives of South Asians. The incorporation of psychotherapeutic strategies based on R/S principles may be effective in the management of SUDs in this context (Jayasuriya 1995). A study of an integrative mind–body–spirit therapy for Indian patients with alcohol dependence found significant reductions in use, relapse rates, and craving, and improvements in well-being and motivation that were sustained for up to 6 months (Rentala et al. 2022). It has also been observed that yoga-based interventions are useful in reducing substance consumption and craving in this context (Kuppili et al. 2018). In Pakistan, a pilot trial of an R/S-based therapy, involving religious reading, prayer, meditation, and methods influenced by 12-step programmes, found a positive effect on psychological well-being in persons with SUD (Bano et al. 2019).

11.5.3 Leveraging Novel Technologies and Approaches

Limitations in manpower, infrastructure, and funding can constitute a significant barrier to the prevention and treatment of SUDs in South Asia. However, these limitations can be circumvented in some cases through novel technologies that enable capacity building and task-shifting, such as mobile health (mHealth). A mobile-based learning programme was found to be potentially useful in improving knowledge related to SUDs in rural Afghan healthcare providers (Tirmizi et al. 2017). A survey of healthcare workers in Nepal revealed high levels of motivation and interest in the use of mHealth for SUDs and related problems, provided that certain needs—such as translation into the vernacular, adequate Internet connectivity, and measures to ensure patient confidentiality—could be met (Pokhrel et al. 2021). A telemedicine-based mentoring programme for primary care physicians in India found good improvements in knowledge regarding SUD; 32% of participants reported being more confident in handling these disorders at their level (Sagi et al. 2018).

mHealth interventions can also be provided directly to persons with SUD. A pilot study conducted in Indian college students evaluated the usefulness of web-based screening and brief intervention for alcohol or drug use. Digital screening was useful in identifying those with possible SUDs, and was found to be acceptable and useful by 70–80% of those with AUD and 50% of those with drug use disorders (Ghosh et al. 2023b; Sharma et al. 2023a). An Android-based mobile application ("app") developed by the same group achieved good levels of acceptability and user-friendliness (65–80%) and significantly reduced alcohol consumption for up to 3 months in urban patients seeking treatment for alcohol dependence (Sharma et al.

2023b). Simple interventions of this sort, if adapted for use in the vernacular, could be useful in addressing less severe forms of SUD at the primary care level. Similar app-based interventions for SUDs, based on the World Health Organization's Mental Health Gap Action Programme (mhGAP), are under development and evaluation in Nepal (Taylor Salisbury et al. 2021).

Telemedicine-based interventions may be particularly useful for patients in rural or remote areas. In a pilot study from India, conducted during the COVID-19 pandemic, treatment for SUDs was offered using a stepped-care model. The first step consisted of brief assessment and brief interventions over the telephone, the second step was a more detailed evaluation and medication prescription using a video call, and the third was in-person assessment. Preliminary data suggests that about two-thirds of patients with SUDs could be handled using the telephonic or video-based treatments (Ghosh et al. 2021).

11.5.4 Improving Validity and Accountability

Apart from the measures discussed above, an honest appraisal of the impact of existing policies and programmes aimed at curtailing SUDs should be carried out in each South Asian country. Policies that seem "ideal" at reducing the use of substances, such as the prohibition of alcohol, often have mixed effects in real-world settings. Such measures, whether implemented in Western or Asian countries, are often motivated by moral and cultural considerations rather than accurate evidence (Unnithan 1985). An evaluation of prohibition measures in the Indian state of Bihar did find an overall reduction in alcohol consumption, but this was much more significant in women users, and was associated with an increase in "home-brewed" illicit liquor consumption in men (Balhara et al. 2023). Some authors have even suggested that prohibition has little impact on drinking patterns in men (Subramanian et al. 2005).

Accurate assessment of outcomes can also help in identifying ineffective interventions, allowing for greater streamlining and cost-effectiveness of SUD care. For example, data from Nepal suggests that the addition of psychological interventions, such as counselling, problem-solving, or behavioural techniques, adds little to mhGAP-based care for AUD in primary care settings (Jordans et al. 2019b, 2020). Therefore, such interventions need not be provided to all persons with alcohol misuse, and can be reserved for use in selected patients at the secondary or tertiary level.

Changes in patterns of use should be tracked at both the national and regional levels, as there are marked variations in inter-regional or inter-state SUD prevalence within South Asian countries (Singh et al. 2021). Nation-wide surveys of alcohol, tobacco, or drug use should be methodologically sound and acceptable to users; otherwise, they may underestimate the burden of SUDs and their comorbidities (Rai et al. 2020). Inter-regional variations in SUDs should be considered when planning prevention strategies. For example, IDU is common among youth in the Indian state of Mizoram, but is more common in older adults in the nearby states of Manipur and Meghalaya: the interventions required in each region should be tailored to the demographic profile of users (Biswas et al. 2020). Where accurate statistics are available, services should be scaled in accordance with them.

Similar caveats apply to national legislation regarding drug possession and use. While such laws may be well-intentioned and aimed at curtailing the illicit drug trade, they often suffer from a lack of integration with health care and limitations in transparency. As a result, populations such as IDUs may face stringent punishments instead of receiving SUD treatment, harm reduction, and medical care for their comorbid illnesses (Singh Balhara and Singh 2020). Amending such laws to incorporate the best evidence and practice on the rehabilitation of persons with SUDs could reduce unnecessary incarceration or ill-treatment, and would facilitate a more person-centred approach to these disorders.

11.5.5 Integrated Care for Substance Use Disorders

From a public health perspective, the high levels of comorbidity between SUD and other disorders offer countless opportunities for screening, treatment, and integrated health care. Moreover, patients may find treatments easier to access and experience less stigmatization if care is delivered in an integrated or "general" setting than in a "deaddiction centre".

An illustrative example of such integrated care can be drawn from the link between SLT use, which is frequent in South Asia, and oral pre-malignant or malignant lesions. Patients with oral pre-malignant lesions can be offered combined treatment for tobacco cessation and for the respective local pathology, and tobacco cessation clinics can be co-located with dental or surgical services. Moreover, patients with non-malignant lesions presenting to these services could be educated about the risks of cancer associated with tobacco or alcohol use, and offered treatment as appropriate. Likewise, patients presenting to an emergency setting with substance-related problems should be evaluated for other comorbidities, and their treatment should not stop at the management of acute symptoms.

Such integrated programmes are being developed and tested in many South Asian countries. For example, an integrated trial of pharmacotherapy and behavioural interventions for tobacco cessation, given as part of general care for persons with pulmonary tuberculosis, is in progress in Bangladesh and Pakistan (Boeckmann et al. 2018).

At a higher level, integration is required at the level of planning and health policy. For example, screening and brief interventions for tobacco and alcohol use should be part of national plans for cardiorespiratory diseases and cancer, and treatment for IDU should be a routine component of care for HIV/AIDS and other blood-borne infections. Ultimately, integrated care involves not just collaboration between different healthcare specialties, but inter-sectoral collaborations with social welfare, human development, and law enforcement departments and agencies. Persons with SUDs can certainly benefit from pharmacological and psychological interventions in a medical setting. However, they often have marked impairments in functioning and quality of life across multiple domains. Their rehabilitation and reintegration into the community depends on several other factors, including vocational skills, social skills, secure housing, education, and protection from violence or harassment. Achieving this requires the concerted efforts of multiple sectors of civil society and not the healthcare system alone (Armstrong and Samson 2016; Islam 2020; Pant et al. 2023).

11.6 Conclusion

Substance use disorders are a significant cause of morbidity, disability, and socioeconomic difficulty in South Asian countries. The public health approach represents the most promising and broad-based strategy for the prevention and treatment of substance use disorders at various levels in this context. In spite of the existence of cultural, economic, and systemic barriers, the public health research reviewed in this chapter offers hope for substantial improvements in the prevention, detection, and treatment of SUDs in South Asia. Available evidence suggests that public health-based strategies can be combined with biomedical and technological advances to reduce the treatment gap; to build healthcare capacity; and ultimately to develop sustainable, humane, and socially responsible programmes that will benefit persons with SUDs, their families, and their communities.

References

Abadi, M. H., Shamblen, S. R., Johnson, K., Thompson, K., Young, L., Courser, M., Vanderhoff, J., & Browne, T. (2012). Examining human rights and mental health among women in drug abuse treatment centers in Afghanistan. *International journal of women's health*, 4, 155–165. https://doi.org/10.2147/IJWH.S28737

Abadi, M. H., Shamblen, S. R., Courser, M., Johnson, K. W., Thompson, K., Young, L., & Browne, T. (2015). Gender differences in Afghan drug-abuse treatment: an assessment of treatment entry characteristics, dropout, and outcomes. *Ethnicity & health*, 20(5), 453–473. https://doi.org/10.1080/13557858.2014.921898

Al-Ghafri, Q., Radcliffe, P., & Gilchrist, G. (2023). Barriers and facilitators to accessing inpatient and community substance use treatment and harm reduction services for people who use drugs in the Muslim communities: A systematic narrative review of studies on the experiences of people who receive services and service providers. *Drug and alcohol dependence*, 244, 109790. https://doi.org/10.1016/j.drugalcdep.2023.109790

Ali, B., Nisar, N., & Nawab, F. (2018). Adherence to antiretroviral therapy in HIV-positive, male intravenous drug users in Pakistan. *Eastern Mediterranean health journal*, 24(3), 237–242. https://doi.org/10.26719/2018.24.3.237

Ali, M., Siddiq, M. A. B., Pranto, N. K., Amran, N. H., Akter, M., Munny, M. A., Hossain, M. I., Khan, S. S., & Mehedi, M. M. H. (2023). Prevalence and predictors of musculoskeletal health complaints among sedentary, monotonous urban workers: A survey in Bangladesh. *PloS one*, 18(4), e0282922. https://doi.org/10.1371/journal.pone.0282922

Ambekar, A., Rao, R., Pun, A., Kumar, S., & Kishore, K. (2013). The trajectory of methadone maintenance treatment in Nepal. *The International journal on drug policy*, 24(6), e57–e60. https://doi.org/10.1016/j.drugpo.2013.06.001

Amin, P., & Douaihy, A. (2018). Substance use disorders in people living with human immunodeficiency virus/AIDS. *The Nursing clinics of North America*, 53(1), 57–65. https://doi.org/10.1016/j.cnur.2017.10.007

Arafat, S., & Kar, S. (2024). Epidemiology of psychiatric disorders and overview of access to mental health care in South Asia. In: S. M. Y. Arafat, S. K. Kar, *Access to mental health care in South Asia*. Springer Nature Singapore. https://doi.org/10.1007/978-981-99-9153-2_1

Armstrong, G., & Samson, L. (2016). The imperative to integrate suicide prevention within community-based harm reduction programs for people who inject drugs: Informed by the situation in Delhi, India. *The International journal on drug policy*, 28, 133–135. https://doi.org/10.1016/j.drugpo.2015.08.014

Asif, A., Ayub, S., Komal, A., Noor, S., & Jalal, U. (2019). Prevalence of human immunodeficiency virus and Hepatitis (B & C) among drug users in a tertiary care public hospital. *Pakistan journal of medical sciences*, 35(2), 459–463. https://doi.org/10.12669/pjms.35.2.500

Asif, M., Khoso, A. B., Husain, M. A., Shahzad, S., Van Hout, M. C., Rafiq, N. U., Lane, S., Chaudhry, I. B., & Husain, N. (2023). Culturally adapted motivational interviewing with cognitive behavior therapy and mindfulness-based relapse prevention for substance use disorder in Pakistan (CAMAIB): protocol for a feasibility factorial randomised controlled trial. *Pilot and feasibility studies*, 9(1), 67. https://doi.org/10.1186/s40814-023-01296-0

Avasthi, A., & Ghosh, A. (2019). Drug misuse in India: Where do we stand & where to go from here? *The Indian journal of medical research*, 149(6), 689–692. https://doi.org/10.4103/ijmr.IJMR_548_19

Azad, A. H., Khan, S. A., Ali, I., Shafi, H., Khan, N. A., & Umar, S. A. (2022). Experience of psychologists in the delivery of cognitive behaviour therapy in a non-western culture for treatment of substance abuse: a qualitative study. *International journal of mental health systems*, 16(1), 55. https://doi.org/10.1186/s13033-022-00566-3

Azim, T., Khan, S. I., Haseen, F., Huq, N. L., Henning, L., Pervez, M. M., Chowdhury, M. E., & Sarafian, I. (2008). HIV and AIDS in Bangladesh. *Journal of health, population, and nutrition*, 26(3), 311–324. https://doi.org/10.3329/jhpn.v26i3.1898

Bhad, R., & Shukla, S. (2024). Understanding Substance Use Disorder and Comorbidities: Insights from South Asia. In: Arafat, S. M. Y., Kar, S. K. *Access to Mental Health Care in South Asia—Current status, potential challenges, and ways out.* Springer Nature Singapore.

Balan, A., Kannekanti, P., & Khanra, S. (2023). Pathways to care for substance use treatment among tribal patients at a psychiatric hospital: A comparative study. *Journal of neurosciences in rural practice*, 14(3), 432–439. https://doi.org/10.25259/JNRP_30_2023

Balhara, Y. P. S., Singh, P. K., Sarkar, S., Chattopadhyay, A., & Singh, S. (2022). How and What are Indians Drinking? Findings from the National Family Health Survey. *Alcohol and alcoholism*, 57(6), 674–677. https://doi.org/10.1093/alcalc/agac035

Balhara, Y. P. S., Sarkar, S., Singh, P. K., Chattopadhyay, A., & Singh, S. (2023). Impact of three years of prohibition on extent and pattern of alcohol use in Bihar: Observations and insights from the National Family Health Survey. *Asian journal of psychiatry*, 82, 103479. https://doi.org/10.1016/j.ajp.2023.103479

Bano, Z., Naz, I., Leghari, N., & Ahmed, I. (2019). Psychological well-being of substance use patient: Role of religious therapy as the treatment. *Pakistan journal of medical sciences*, 35(5), 1376–1381. https://doi.org/10.12669/pjms.35.5.561

Baral, S., Todd, C. S., Aumakhan, B., Lloyd, J., Delegchoimbol, A., & Sabin, K. (2013). HIV among female sex workers in the Central Asian Republics, Afghanistan, and Mongolia: contexts and convergence with drug use. *Drug and alcohol dependence*, 132 Suppl 1, S13–S16. https://doi.org/10.1016/j.drugalcdep.2013.07.004

Baron, E. C., Rathod, S. D., Hanlon, C., Prince, M., Fedaku, A., Kigozi, F., Jordans, M., Luitel, N. P., Medhin, G., Murhar, V., Nakku, J., Patel, V., Petersen, I., Selohilwe, O., Shidhaye, R.,

Ssebunnya, J., Tomlinson, M., Lund, C., & De Silva, M. (2018). Impact of district mental health care plans on symptom severity and functioning of patients with priority mental health conditions: the Programme for Improving Mental Health Care (PRIME) cohort protocol. *BMC psychiatry*, 18(1), 61. https://doi.org/10.1186/s12888-018-1642-x

Bashir, I., Ahmad, M., Jamshaid, M., & Zaman, M. (2021). Illicit sale of controlled drugs at community pharmacy/medical stores of Punjab, Pakistan: A road to demolition of public health. *Heliyon*, 7(5), e07031. https://doi.org/10.1016/j.heliyon.2021.e07031

Belete, H., Mekonen, T., Fekadu, W., Legas, G., & Getnet, A. (2019). Help seeking behavior for problematic substance uses in north-West Ethiopia. *Substance abuse treatment, prevention, and policy*, 14(1), 25. https://doi.org/10.1186/s13011-019-0202-9

Bhalla, A., Dutta, S., & Chakrabarti, A. (2006). A profile of substance abusers using the emergency services in a tertiary care hospital in Sikkim. *Indian journal of psychiatry*, 48(4), 243–247. https://doi.org/10.4103/0019-5545.31556

Bhandari, T. R., Khatiwada, B., Rajbhandari, B., Bestman, A., Mistry, S. K., Rayamajhee, B., Rawal, L. B., & Yadav, U. N. (2021a). A qualitative study to understand drivers of psychoactive substance use among Nepalese youth. *PloS one*, 16(11), e0259021. https://doi.org/10.1371/journal.pone.0259021

Bhandari, T. R., Paudel, G., Bestman, A., Thapa, T. B., Gwayali, C. P., Ghimire, B., Sharma, S., & Yadav, U. N. (2021b). Use of Psychoactive Substance and its Associated Factors among School Adolescents in Rupandehi District of Nepal. Journal of Nepal Health Research Council, 19(3), 474–480. https://doi.org/10.33314/jnhrc.v19i3.3405

Bharadwaj, B., Selvakumar, N., & Kuppili, P. P. (2018). Pharmacotherapy for relapse prevention of alcohol use disorder in the Indian setting: A systematic review. *Industrial psychiatry journal*, 27(2), 163–171. https://doi.org/10.4103/ipj.ipj_79_17

Bhatt, G., Goel, S., Kiran, T., Grover, S., Medhi, B., Singh, G., & Singh Gill, S. (2023). Estimating the Cost of Delivering Tobacco Cessation Intervention Package at Noncommunicable Disease Clinics in Two Districts of North India. *Nicotine & tobacco research: official journal of the Society for Research on Nicotine and Tobacco*, 25(11), 1727–1735. https://doi.org/10.1093/ntr/ntad105

Bhattacharya, A. (2017). Which cost of alcohol? What should we compare it against? *Addiction*, 112(4), 559-565. https://doi.org/10.1111/add.13335

Bhutan Narcotics Control Agency. (2020). Demand Reduction Division. Available online at: https://bnca.gov.bt/divisions/demand-reduction-division/

Biswas, S., Ghosh, P., Chakraborty, D., Kumar, A., Aggarwal, S., & Saha, M. K. (2020). Variation in injecting drug use behavior across different North-eastern States in India. *Indian journal of public health*, 64(Supplement), S71–S75. https://doi.org/10.4103/ijph.IJPH_73_20

Blanco, C., Wiley, T. R. A., Lloyd, J. J., Lopez, M. F., & Volkow, N. D. (2020). America's opioid crisis: the need for an integrated public health approach. *Translational psychiatry*, 10, 167. https://doi.org/10.1038/s41398-020-0847-1

Bojappen, N., Chand, P., (2024). Policy, Legalisation and Programs Related to Substance Use Disorders in South Asia. In: Arafat, S. M. Y., Kar, S. K. (eds) Current Perspectives on Substance Use Disorders in South Asia. Springer Nature Singapore.

Blum, K., Bowirrat, A., Gomez, L. L., Downs, B. W., Bagchi, D., Barh, D., Modestino, E. J., Baron, D., McLaughlin, T., Thanos, P., Ceccanti, M., Elman, I., Badgaiyan, R. D., Dennen, C., Gupta, A., Braverman, E. R., & Gold, M. S. (2022). Why haven't we solved the addiction crisis? *Journal of the neurological sciences*, 442, 120404. https://doi.org/10.1016/j.jns.2022.120404

Boeckmann, M., Nohavova, I., Dogar, O., Kralikova, E., Pankova, A., Zvolska, K., Huque, R., Fatima, R., Noor, M., Elsey, H., Sheikh, A., Siddiqi, K., Kotz, D., & TB & Tobacco Project Consortium (2018). Protocol for the mixed-methods process and context evaluation of the TB & Tobacco randomised controlled trial in Bangladesh and Pakistan: a hybrid effectiveness-implementation study. *BMJ open*, 8(3), e019878. https://doi.org/10.1136/bmjopen-2017-019878

Capelastegui, F., Trickey, A., Thompson, L. H., Reza, T., Emmanuel, F., Cholette, F., Blanchard, J. F., Archibald, C., Vickerman, P., & Lim, A. G. (2023). Risk factors of HIV and variation in access to clean needles among people who inject drugs in Pakistan. *Pathogens and global health*, 117(8), 696–707. https://doi.org/10.1080/20477724.2023.2191234

Carter, T., Heaton, K., Merlo, L. J., Roche, B. T., & Puga, F. (2023). Relapse prevention and prediction strategies in substance use disorder: a scoping review. *Journal of addictions nursing*, 34(2), 146–157. https://doi.org/10.1097/jan.0000000000000527

Chadi, N., Bagley, S. M., & Hadland, S. E. (2018). Addressing adolescents' and young adults' substance use disorders. *The Medical clinics of North America*, 102(4), 603–620. https://doi.org/10.1016/j.mcna.2018.02.015

Chapagain, K., Rai, D., Koirala, B., & Rauniyar, G. P. (2020). Exploring the Prevalence and Correlates of Substance Abuse Amongst the Adolescents of Dharan, Eastern Nepal. *Journal of Nepal Health Research Council*, 18(2), 263–267. https://doi.org/10.33314/jnhrc.v18i2.2484

Chatterjee, A., Uprety, L., Chapagain, M., & Kafle, K. (1996). Drug abuse in Nepal: a rapid assessment study. *Bulletin on narcotics*, 48(1–2), 11–33.

Choki, S., Dorji, T., & Choden, T. (2014). Psychoactive substance use by psychiatric patients in the National Referral Hospital, Bhutan: a retrospective analysis. *WHO South-East Asia journal of public health*, 3(2), 186–189. https://doi.org/10.4103/2224-3151.206735

Compton, W. M., Wargo, E. M., & Volkow, N. D. (2022). Neuropsychiatric model of addiction simplified. *The Psychiatric clinics of North America*, 45(3), 321–334. https://doi.org/10.1016/j.psc.2022.05.001

Connock, M., Juarez-Garcia, A., Jowett, S., Frew, E., Liu, Z., Taylor, R. J., Fry-Smith, A., Day, E., Lintzeris, N., Roberts, T., Burls, A., & Taylor, R. S. (2007). Methadone and buprenorphine for the management of opioid dependence: a systematic review and economic evaluation. *Health technology assessment*, 11(9), 1–iv. https://doi.org/10.3310/hta11090

Cottler, L. B., Ajinkya, S., Goldberger, B. A., Ghani, M. A., Martin, D. M., Hu, H., & Gold, M. S. (2014). Prevalence of drug and alcohol use in urban Afghanistan: epidemiological data from the Afghanistan National Urban Drug Use Study (ANUDUS). *The Lancet. Global health*, 2(10), e592–e600. https://doi.org/10.1016/S2214-109X(14)70290-6

Crepault, J.-F., Russell, C., Watson, T. M., Strike, C., Bonato, S., & Rehm, J. (2023). What is a public health approach to substance use? A qualitative systematic review and thematic synthesis. *International journal of drug policy*, 112, 103958. https://doi.org/10.1016/j.drugpo.2023.103958

Crofts, N., & Azim, T. (2015). Harm reduction in Asia and the Pacific: an evolving public health response. *Harm reduction journal*, 12, 47. https://doi.org/10.1186/s12954-015-0074-x

Darshana, N., Wijesinghe, C. J., & De Silva, P. V. (2022). Assessment of Characteristics and Exposure to Vulnerable Factors for Drug use among Male Illicit Drug Users in Sri Lanka: A Multicenter Cross-Sectional Study. *Indian journal of community medicine*, 47(2), 285–291. https://doi.org/10.4103/ijcm.ijcm_712_21

de Silva, H. J., Peiris, M. U., Samarasinghe, D. S., & Ellawala, N. S. (1992). A two-year follow-up study of alcohol dependent men rehabilitated at a special unit in a developing country. *British journal of addiction*, 87(10), 1409–1414. https://doi.org/10.1111/j.1360-0443.1992.tb01920.x

De Silva, H. J., & Ellawala, N. S. (1994). Influence of temperance on short-term mortality among alcohol-dependent men in Sri Lanka. *Alcohol and alcoholism*, 29(2), 199–201.

Degenhardt, L., Whiteford, H. A., Ferrari, A. J., Baxter, A. J., Charlson, F. J., Hall, W. D., Freedman, G., Burstein, R., Johns, N., Engell, R. E., Flaxman, A., Murray, C. J., & Vos, T. (2013). Global burden of disease attributable to illicit drug use and dependence: findings from the Global Burden of Disease Study 2010. *Lancet*, 382(9904), 1564–1574. https://doi.org/10.1016/S0140-6736(13)61530-5

Dema, T., Tripathy, J. P., Thinley, S., Rani, M., Dhendup, T., Laxmeshwar, C., Tenzin, K., Gurung, M. S., Tshering, T., Subba, D. K., Penjore, T., & Lhazeen, K. (2019). Suicidal ideation and

attempt among school going adolescents in Bhutan—a secondary analysis of a global school-based student health survey in Bhutan 2016. *BMC public health*, 19(1), 1605. https://doi.org/10.1186/s12889-019-7791-0
Dissabandara, L. O., Dias, S. R., Dodd, P. R., & Stadlin, A. (2009). Patterns of substance use in male incarcerated drug users in Sri Lanka. *Drug and alcohol review*, 28(6), 600–607. https://doi.org/10.1111/j.1465-3362.2009.00062.x
Dolan, K., & Larney, S. (2009). A review of HIV in prisons in Nepal. *Kathmandu University medical journal (KUMJ)*, 7(28), 351–354. https://doi.org/10.3126/kumj.v7i4.2753
Duara, R., Chowdhury, D., Dey, R., Goswami, S., & Madill, A. (2022). Using cocreated visually informed community mental health education in low- and middle-income countries: A case study of youth substance misuse in Assam, India. *Health expectations*, 25(4), 1930–1944. https://doi.org/10.1111/hex.13550
Elsey, H., Khanal, S., Manandhar, S., Sah, D., Baral, S. C., Siddiqi, K., & Newell, J. N. (2016). Understanding implementation and feasibility of tobacco cessation in routine primary care in Nepal: a mixed methods study. *Implementation science: IS*, 11, 104. https://doi.org/10.1186/s13012-016-0466-7
Farook, M. İ., İlhan, M. N., & Koçak, C. (2022). Determination of epidemiological characteristics of addicts treated in drug addiction clinics in Kabul. *Journal of ethnicity in substance abuse*, 21(3), 1063–1082. https://doi.org/10.1080/15332640.2020.1824842
Fernandes, G. S., Spiers, A., Vaidya, N., Zhang, Y., Sharma, E., Holla, B., Heron, J., Hickman, M., Murthy, P., Chakrabarti, A., Basu, D., Subodh, B. N., Singh, L., Singh, R., Kalyanram, K., Kartik, K., Kumaran, K., Krishnaveni, G., Kuriyan, R., Kurpad, S., … Benegal, V. (2021). Adverse childhood experiences and substance misuse in young people in India: results from the multisite cVEDA cohort. *BMC public health*, 21(1), 1920. https://doi.org/10.1186/s12889-021-11892-5
Ganapathi, L., McFall, A. M., Greco, K. F., Srikrishnan, A. K., Kumar, M. S., Mayer, K. H., O'Cleirigh, C., Mehta, S. H., Lucas, G. M., & Solomon, S. S. (2023). Buprenorphine treatment receipt characteristics and retention among people who inject drugs at Integrated Care Centers in India. *Drug and alcohol dependence*, 246, 109839. https://doi.org/10.1016/j.drugalcdep.2023.109839
Ganesh, B., Mosoniro, K., Vasna, J., Elangovan, A., Santhakumar, A., & Shobini, R. (2020). Factors associated with human immunodeficiency virus infection and self-assessed risk to human immunodeficiency virus among injecting drug users in Manipur, India. *Indian journal of public health*, 64(Supplement), S61–S66. https://doi.org/10.4103/ijph.IJPH_61_20
GBD 2016 Alcohol and Drug Use Collaborators (2018). The global burden of disease attributable to alcohol and drug use in 195 countries and territories, 1990–2016: a systematic analysis for the Global Burden of Disease Study 2016. *The Lancet. Psychiatry*, 5(12), 987–1012. https://doi.org/10.1016/S2215-0366(18)30337-7
Ghazal P. (2019). Rising trend of substance abuse in Pakistan: a study of sociodemographic profiles of patients admitted to rehabilitation centres. *Public health*, 167, 34–37. https://doi.org/10.1016/j.puhe.2018.10.020
Ghimire, B., Suguimoto, S. P., Zamani, S., Ono-Kihara, M., & Kihara, M. (2013). Vulnerability to HIV infection among female drug users in Kathmandu Valley, Nepal: a cross-sectional study. *BMC public health*, 13, 1238. https://doi.org/10.1186/1471-2458-13-1238
Ghosh, A., Mahintamani, T., B N, S., Pillai, R. R., Mattoo, S. K., & Basu, D. (2021). Telemedicine-assisted stepwise approach of service delivery for substance use disorders in India. *Asian journal of psychiatry*, 58, 102582. https://doi.org/10.1016/j.ajp.2021.102582
Ghosh, A., Jerkovic, D., Ignjatova, L. A., Bruguera, C., Ibrahim, D. I., Okulicz-Kozaryn, K., Maphisa, J. M., Martinelli, T. F., Neto, A., Canedo, J., & Gordon, R. (2023a). Drug policies' sensitivity towards women, pregnancy, and motherhood: a content analysis of national policy and programs from nine countries and their adherence to international guidelines. *Addiction science & clinical practice*, 18, 53. https://doi.org/10.1186/s13722-023-00410-0

Ghosh, A., Krishnan, N. C., Kathirvel, S., Pillai, R. R., Basu, D., George, B. B., P V, A., Sharma, K., & Kumar, A. (2023b). Digital screening and brief intervention for alcohol misuse in college students: A pilot, mixed-methods, cluster randomized controlled trial from a low-resourced setting. *Asia-Pacific psychiatry*, 15(2–3), e12527. https://doi.org/10.1111/appy.12527

Global Burden of Disease Collaborative Network (2019). Global Burden of Disease Study 2019 (GBD 2019) Results. Seattle, United States: Institute for Health Metrics and Evaluation (IHME), 2020. Available online at: https://vizhub.healthdata.org/gbd-results/

Gobar, A. H. (1976). Drug abuse in Afghanistan. *Bulletin on narcotics*, 28(2), 1–11.

Goldstein, M. B., & Engwall, D. B. (1992). The politics of prevention: changing definitions of substance use/abuse. *Journal of health & social policy*, 3(3), 69–83. https://doi.org/10.1300/J045v03n03_05

Griffin, N., & Khoshnood, K. (2010). Opium trade, insurgency, and HIV/AIDS in Afghanistan: relationships and regional consequences. *Asia-Pacific journal of public health*, 22(3 Suppl), 159S–167S. https://doi.org/10.1177/1010539510374524

Guinness, L., Vickerman, P., Quayyum, Z., Foss, A., Watts, C., Rodericks, A., Azim, T., Jana, S., & Kumaranayake, L. (2010). The cost-effectiveness of consistent and early intervention of harm reduction for injecting drug users in Bangladesh. *Addiction*, 105(2), 319–328. https://doi.org/10.1111/j.1360-0443.2009.02755.x

Gupta, A. K., & Mehrotra, R. (2021). Increasing use of flavoured tobacco products amongst youth. *The Indian journal of tuberculosis*, 68S, S105–S107. https://doi.org/10.1016/j.ijtb.2021.07.020

Gupta, P. C., Puntambekar, N., & Assunta, M. (2022). South Asia's evolving tobacco hydra: moving from quandary to hope. *Tobacco control*, 31(2), 142–145. https://doi.org/10.1136/tobaccocontrol-2021-057013

Guthold, R., Kann, L., Bhatti, L., Abduvahobov, P., Ansong, J., Atkinson, U., Baltag, V., Caffe, S., Caixeta, R., Diallo, C. B., Fouad, H., Haddad, S., Hachri, H., Jaggi, J. A., Joshi, P., Karna, P., Louazani, S. A., Mbola Mbassi, S., Mehta, R., Mudgal, Y., … Riley, L. M. (2023). Effectiveness of a participatory approach to develop school health interventions in four low resource cities: study protocol of the 'empowering adolescents to lead change using health data' cluster randomised controlled trial. *BMJ open*, 13(7), e071353. https://doi.org/10.1136/bmjopen-2022-071353

Gyawali, B., Choulagai, B. P., Paneru, D. P., Ahmad, M., Leppin, A., & Kallestrup, P. (2016). Prevalence and correlates of psychological distress symptoms among patients with substance use disorders in drug rehabilitation centers in urban Nepal: a cross-sectional study. *BMC psychiatry*, 16(1), 314. https://doi.org/10.1186/s12888-016-1003-6

Gyeltshen, T., Penjor, T., Dorji, L., Tshering, L., Dorji, K., Subedi, B. N., Tshering, D., Xu, Y. Y., Dorji, G., & Gueye, G. N. (2021). Alcohol policy compliance among retailers in Bhutan: a multisite community intervention study. *BMC public health*, 21(1), 1893. https://doi.org/10.1186/s12889-021-11932-0

Hapangama, A., Kuruppuarachchi, K. A., & Pathmeswaran, A. (2013). Substance use disorders among mentally ill patients in a General Hospital in Sri Lanka: prevalence and correlates. *The Ceylon medical journal*, 58(3), 111–115. https://doi.org/10.4038/cmj.v58i3.6103

Hawlader, M. D. H., Nabi, M. H., Hussain, A., Al Amin, S. U., Zaman, S., & Masud, I. (2020). Legal and social consequences of substance use: Results from a nationwide study in Bangladesh. *Journal of ethnicity in substance abuse*, 21(4), 1327–1337. https://doi.org/10.1080/15332640.2020.1846008

Hemel, M. M., Reza, M. M., Shafiq, T. K., Kabir, M. I., Rana, A. M., & Khan, S. I. (2021). Correlates of sharing of needles and syringes among people who inject drugs in Dhaka city, Bangladesh. *Journal of infection in developing countries*, 15(10), 1497–1506. https://doi.org/10.3855/jidc.13629

Henden, E., Melberg, H. O., & Rogeberg, O. J. (2013). Addiction: choice or compulsion? *Frontiers in psychiatry*, 4, 77. https://doi.org/10.3389/fpsyt.2013.00077

Hossain, K. J., Nandi, A. K., Karim, M. R., Haque, M. M., & Kamal, M. M. (2012). Pattern of mental illness on substance abusers. *Mymensingh medical journal: MMJ*, 21(2), 251–258.

Hossain, K. J., & Nandi, A. K. (2015). Hepatitis-B Infections among the Injection Drug Abusers: An Emerging Risk in Public Health, Bangladesh. *Mymensingh medical journal: MMJ*, 24(4), 813–824.

International Institute for Population Sciences (IIPS) and ICF. (2021). National Family Health Survey (NFHS-5), 2019–2021: India. Mumbai: IIPS.

Iqbal, Y., Jahan, R., & Matin, M. R. (2019). Descriptive characteristics of callers to an emotional support and suicide prevention helpline in Bangladesh (first five years). *Asian journal of psychiatry*, 45, 63–65. https://doi.org/10.1016/j.ajp.2019.09.005

Iqbal, S., Barolia, R., Petrucka, P., Ladak, L., Rehmani, R., & Kabir, A. (2022). Smoking cessation interventions in South Asian Region: a systematic scoping review. *BMC public health*, 22(1), 1096. https://doi.org/10.1186/s12889-022-13443-y

Irfan, S. D., Khan, M. N. M., & Khan, S. I. (2021). Tales of gender-based oppression and violence: Risks and vulnerabilities of women who inject drugs (WWID) in Dhaka, Bangladesh. *The International journal on drug policy*, 92, 103144. https://doi.org/10.1016/j.drugpo.2021.103144

Islam, M. (2020). State of the art treatment options for Pakistan's opioid, alcohol and methamphetamine crisis. *JPMA. The Journal of the Pakistan Medical Association*, 70(6), 1063–1068. https://doi.org/10.5455/JPMA.29284

Iversen, J., Ul H Qureshi, S., Zafar, M., Busz, M., & Maher, L. (2021). HIV incidence and associated risk factors in female spouses of men who inject drugs in Pakistan. *Harm reduction journal*, 18(1), 51. https://doi.org/10.1186/s12954-021-00497-1

Jamal, M., Waheed, S., & Shakoor, A. (2022). The prevalence of substance abuse and associated factors among male prisoners in Karachi jails, Pakistan. *Journal of Taibah University Medical Sciences*, 17(6), 929–935. https://doi.org/10.1016/j.jtumed.2022.05.001

Jayamaha, A. R., Dharmarathna, N. D., Herath, N. D., Ranadeva, N. D., Fernando, M. M., Samarasinghe, K. L., Amarabandu, P. N., Senanayake, B., Darshana, T., Renuka, N., Rajapakse, I. H., Gunasekara, C. P., Meegoda, L., & Fernando, N. (2022). The Pattern of Substance Use and Characteristics of the Individuals Enrolled in Residential Treatment at Selected Rehabilitation Centers in Sri Lanka: A Descriptive Cross-Sectional Study. *Substance abuse: research and treatment*, 16, 11782218221100823. https://doi.org/10.1177/11782218221100823

Jayasuriya D. C. (1995). The drug abuse problem in Sri Lanka. *Medicine and law*, 14(1–2), 37–43.

Jiloha R. C. (2017). Prevention, early intervention, and harm reduction of substance use in adolescents. *Indian journal of psychiatry*, 59(1), 111–118. https://doi.org/10.4103/0019-5545.204444

Johnson, K., Pinchuk, I., Melgar, M. I. E., Agwogie, M. O., & Salazar Silva, F. (2022). The global movement towards a public health approach to substance use disorders. *Annals of medicine*, 54(1), 1797–1808. https://doi.org/10.1080/07853890.2022.2079150

Jordans, M. J., Kohrt, B. A., Luitel, N. P., Lund, C., & Komproe, I. H. (2017). Proactive community case-finding to facilitate treatment seeking for mental disorders, Nepal. *Bulletin of the World Health Organization*, 95(7), 531–536. https://doi.org/10.2471/BLT.16.189282

Jordans, M. J. D., Luitel, N. P., Kohrt, B. A., Rathod, S. D., Garman, E. C., De Silva, M., Komproe, I. H., Patel, V., & Lund, C. (2019a). Community-, facility-, and individual-level outcomes of a district mental healthcare plan in a low-resource setting in Nepal: A population-based evaluation. *PLoS medicine*, 16(2), e1002748. https://doi.org/10.1371/journal.pmed.1002748

Jordans, M. J. D., Luitel, N. P., Garman, E., Kohrt, B. A., Rathod, S. D., Shrestha, P., Komproe, I. H., Lund, C., & Patel, V. (2019b). Effectiveness of psychological treatments for depression and alcohol use disorder delivered by community-based counsellors: two pragmatic randomised controlled trials within primary healthcare in Nepal. *The British journal of psychiatry*, 215(2), 485–493. https://doi.org/10.1192/bjp.2018.300

Jordans, M. J. D., Garman, E. C., Luitel, N. P., Kohrt, B. A., Lund, C., Patel, V., & Tomlinson, M. (2020). Impact of integrated district level mental health care on clinical and functioning outcomes of people with depression and alcohol use disorder in Nepal: a non-randomised controlled study. *BMC psychiatry*, 20(1), 451. https://doi.org/10.1186/s12888-020-02832-5

Jyani, G., Prinja, S., Ambekar, A., Bahuguna, P., & Kumar, R. (2019). Health impact and economic burden of alcohol consumption in India. *The International journal on drug policy*, 69, 34–42. https://doi.org/10.1016/j.drugpo.2019.04.005

Kalmin, M. M., Nicolo, C., Long, W., Bodden, D., Van Nunen, L., Shoptaw, S., & Ipser, J. (2023). A systematic review of the efficacy of contingency management for substance use disorders in low- and middle-income countries. *International journal of behavioral medicine*, https://doi.org/10.1007/s12529-023-10197-8. Advance online publication. https://doi.org/10.1007/s12529-023-10197-8

Kan, C. K., Ragan, E. J., Sarkar, S., Knudsen, S., Forsyth, M., Muthuraj, M., Vinod, K., Jenkins, H. E., Horsburgh, C. R., Salgame, P., Roy, G., Ellner, J. J., Jacobson, K. R., Sahu, S., & Hochberg, N. S. (2020). Alcohol use and tuberculosis clinical presentation at the time of diagnosis in Puducherry and Tamil Nadu, India. *PloS one*, 15(12), e0240595. https://doi.org/10.1371/journal.pone.0240595

Kankaria, A., Sahoo, S. S., & Verma, M. (2021). Awareness regarding the adverse effect of tobacco among adults in India: findings from secondary data analysis of Global Adult Tobacco Survey. *BMJ open*, 11(6), e044209. https://doi.org/10.1136/bmjopen-2020-044209

Kermode, M., Choudhurimayum, R. S., Rajkumar, L. S., Haregu, T., & Armstrong, G. (2020). Retention and outcomes for clients attending a methadone clinic in a resource-constrained setting: a mixed methods prospective cohort study in Imphal, Northeast India. *Harm reduction journal*, 17(1), 68. https://doi.org/10.1186/s12954-020-00413-z

Khalid, F., Jaan, A., Aslam, M. M. S., Ahmed, Z., Raheem, A., Bodla, Z. H., Basit, A., Hussain, B., Iftikhar, A., Tayyeb, M., Khalid, A., & Rehman, U. (2020). Social Stigmatization of Drug Abusers in a Developing Country: A Cross-Sectional Study. *Cureus*, 12(9), e10661. https://doi.org/10.7759/cureus.10661

Khan, S. I., Reza, M. M., Crowe, S. M., Rahman, M., Hellard, M., Sarker, M. S., Chowdhury, E. I., Rana, A. K. M. M., Sacks-Davis, R., Banu, S., & Ross, A. G. (2019). People who inject drugs in Bangladesh—The untold burden!. *International journal of infectious diseases*, 83, 109–115. https://doi.org/10.1016/j.ijid.2019.03.009

Khan, S. I., Irfan, S. D., & Khan, M. N. M. (2021). "I held on to the police's leg for mercy": experiences of adversity, risk and harm among people who inject drugs during an anti-drug drive in Dhaka, Bangladesh. *International journal of drug policy*, 92, 103299. https://doi.org/10.1016/j.drugpo.2021.103299

Kiefer, F., & Mann, K. (2005). New achievements and pharmacotherapeutic approaches in the treatment of alcohol dependence. *European journal of pharmacology*, 526(1–3), 163–171. https://doi.org/10.1016/j.ejphar.2005.09.028

Kiriazova, T., Lunze, K., Raj, A., Bushara, N., Blokhina, E., Krupitsky, E., Bridden, C., Lioznov, D., Samet, J. H., & Gifford, A. L. (2017). "It is easier for me to shoot up": stigma, abandonment, and why HIV-positive drug users in Russia fail to link to HIV care. *AIDS Care*, 29(5), 559–563. https://doi.org/10.1080/09540121.2016.1259451

Kishore, J., Jena, P. K., Bandyopadhyay, C., Swain, M., Das, S., & Banerjee, I. (2013). Hardcore smoking in three South-East Asian countries: results from the global adult tobacco survey. *Asian Pacific journal of cancer prevention*, 14(2), 625–630. https://doi.org/10.7314/apjcp.2013.14.2.625

Klostermann, K. C. (2006). Substance abuse and intimate partner violence: treatment considerations. *Substance abuse treatment, prevention and policy*, 1, 24. https://doi.org/10.1186/1747-597x-1-24

Kumar, D., Viswanath, B., Sebestian, A., Holla, B., Konduru, R., Chandrashekar, C. R., & Math, S. B. (2014). Profile of male forensic psychiatric inpatients in South India. *The International journal of social psychiatry*, 60(1), 55–62. https://doi.org/10.1177/0020764012461334

Kuppili, P. P., Parmar, A., Gupta, A., & Balhara, Y. P. S. (2018). Role of Yoga in Management of Substance-use Disorders: A Narrative Review. *Journal of neurosciences in rural practice*, 9(1), 117–122. https://doi.org/10.4103/jnrp.jnrp_243_17

Lasco G. (2018). Kalaban: Young drug users' engagements with law enforcement in the Philippines. *The International journal on drug policy*, 52, 39–44. https://doi.org/10.1016/j.drugpo.2017.11.006

Laslett, A. M., Rankin, G., Waleewong, O., Callinan, S., Hoang, H. T., Florenzano, R., Hettige, S., Obot, I., Siengsounthone, L., Ibanga, A., Hope, A., Landberg, J., Vu, H. T., Thamarangsi, T., Rekve, D., & Room, R. (2017). A Multi-Country Study of Harms to Children Because of Others' Drinking. *Journal of studies on alcohol and drugs*, 78(2), 195–202. https://doi.org/10.15288/jsad.2017.78.195

Lokuge, K., Wallace, P., Subasinghe, K., Thurber, K., De Silva, T., Clarke, N., Waas, D., Liyanage, N., Attygalle, U., Carron-Arthur, B., Rodrigo, K., Banks, E., D'Este, C., & Rajapakse, T. (2018). Protocol for a cluster-randomised controlled trial evaluating the impact of a preschool-based capacity building intervention on intimate partner violence and substance misuse in Sri Lanka. *BMC public health*, 18(1), 572. https://doi.org/10.1186/s12889-018-5423-8

Luitel, N. P., Baron, E. C., Kohrt, B. A., Komproe, I. H., & Jordans, M. J. D. (2018). Prevalence and correlates of depression and alcohol use disorder among adults attending primary health care services in Nepal: a cross sectional study. *BMC health services research*, 18(1), 215. https://doi.org/10.1186/s12913-018-3034-9

Luitel, N. P., Garman, E. C., Jordans, M. J. D., & Lund, C. (2019). Change in treatment coverage and barriers to mental health care among adults with depression and alcohol use disorder: a repeat cross sectional community survey in Nepal. *BMC public health*, 19(1), 1350. https://doi.org/10.1186/s12889-019-7663-7

Lucy, R. H., Akter, S. F., Hussain, S. Z., Haque, M., & Islam, M. A. (2005). Trend of selected risk factors for hepatitis B infection among the drug addicts in Bangladesh: a five year statistics. *Bangladesh Medical Research Council bulletin*, 31(3), 110–116.

Mackay, J., Ritthiphakdee, B., & Reddy, K. S. (2013). Tobacco control in Asia. *Lancet*, 381(9877), 1581–1587. https://doi.org/10.1016/S0140-6736(13)60854-5

Madill, A., Duara, R., Goswami, S., Graber, R., & Hugh-Jones, S. (2023). Pathways to recovery model of youth substance misuse in Assam, India. *Health expectations: an international journal of public participation in health care and health policy*, 26(1), 318–328. https://doi.org/10.1111/hex.13658

Maehira, Y., Chowdhury, E. I., Reza, M., Drahozal, R., Gayen, T. K., Masud, I., Afrin, S., Takamura, N., & Azim, T. (2013). Factors associated with relapse into drug use among male and female attendees of a three-month drug detoxification-rehabilitation programme in Dhaka, Bangladesh: a prospective cohort study. *Harm reduction journal*, 10, 14. https://doi.org/10.1186/1477-7517-10-14

Maguet, O., & Majeed, M. (2010). Implementing harm reduction for heroin users in Afghanistan, the worldwide opium supplier. *The International journal on drug policy*, 21(2), 119–121. https://doi.org/10.1016/j.drugpo.2010.01.006

Malick, R. (2018). Prevention of substance use disorders in the community and workplace. *Indian journal of psychiatry*, 60 (Suppl. 4), S559-S563. https://doi.org/10.4103/psychiatry.indianjpsychiatry_24_18

Mandal, P., Mittal, S., & Chadda, R. K. (2023). Polysubstance use in South Asia. *Current opinion in psychiatry*, 36(4), 269–276. https://doi.org/10.1097/YCO.0000000000000869

Marahatta, K., Pant, S. B., Basnet, M., Sharma, P., Risal, A., & Ojha, S. P. (2021). Mental health education in undergraduate medical curricula across Nepalese universities. *BMC medical education*, 21(1), 304. https://doi.org/10.1186/s12909-021-02743-3

Maruf, M. M., Khan, M. Z., & Jahan, N. (2016). Pattern of Substance Use: Study in a De-addiction Clinic. *Oman medical journal*, 31(5), 327–331. https://doi.org/10.5001/omj.2016.66

McPheeters, M., O'Connor, E. A., Riley, S., Kennedy, S. M., Voisin, C., Kuznacic, K., Coffey, C. P., Edlund, M. D., Bobashev, G., & Jonas, D. E. (2023). Pharmacotherapy for Alcohol Use Disorder: A Systematic Review and Meta-Analysis. *JAMA*, 330(17), 1653–1665. https://doi.org/10.1001/jama.2023.19761

Menon, V., Cherian, A. V., Gnanadas, J., Kar, S. K., & Vijayakumar, L. (2023). NCRB Indian suicide data 2021: The key trends and their implications. *Asian journal of psychiatry*, 84, 103568. https://doi.org/10.1016/j.ajp.2023.103568

Miller, T. R., Nygard, P., Gaidus, A., Grube, J. W., Ponicki, W. R., Lawrence, B. A., & Gruenewald, P. J. (2017). Heterogeneous costs of alcohol and drug problems across cities and counties in California. *Alcoholism: clinical and experimental research*, 41(4), 758–768. https://doi.org/10.1111/acer.13337

Mir, M. U., Khan, I., Ahmed, B., & Abdul Razzak, J. (2012). Alcohol and marijuana use while driving--an unexpected crash risk in Pakistani commercial drivers: a cross-sectional survey. *BMC public health*, 12, 145. https://doi.org/10.1186/1471-2458-12-145

Mohaddes Ardabili, H., Akbari, A., Rafei, P., Butner, J. L., Khan, R., Khazaal, Y., Arab, A. Z., Qazizada, M. R., Al-Ansari, B., & Baldacchino, A. M. (2022). Tramadol, captagon and khat use in the Eastern Mediterranean Region: opening Pandora's box. *BJPsych international*, 19(3), 58–62. https://doi.org/10.1192/bji.2021.53

Momand, A. S., Mattfeld, E., Morales, B., Ul Haq, M., Browne, T., O'Grady, K. E., & Jones, H. E. (2017). Implementation and Evaluation of an Intervention for Children in Afghanistan at Risk for Substance Use or Actively Using Psychoactive Substances. *International journal of pediatrics*, 2017, 2382951. https://doi.org/10.1155/2017/2382951

Momand, A. S., Mattfeld, E., Gerra, G., Morales, B., Browne, T., Haq, M. U., O'Grady, K. E., & Jones, H. E. (2020). Implementation and Evaluation of a Psychoactive Substance Use Intervention for Children in Afghanistan: Differences Between Girls and Boys at Treatment Entry and in Response to Treatment. *Global journal of pediatrics & neonatal care*, 2(1), 527. https://doi.org/10.33552/gjpnc.2020.02.000527

Moonajilin, M. S., Kamal, M. K. I., Mamun, F. A., Safiq, M. B., Hosen, I., Manzar, M. D., & Mamun, M. A. (2021). Substance use behavior and its lifestyle-related risk factors in Bangladeshi high school-going adolescents: An exploratory study. *PloS one*, 16(7), e0254926. https://doi.org/10.1371/journal.pone.0254926

Morse, S. J. (2004). Medicine and morals, craving and compulsion. *Substance use and misuse*, 39(3), 437–460. https://doi.org/10.1081/ja-120029985

Murthy, P., & Narasimha, V. L. (2021). Effects of the COVID-19 pandemic and lockdown on alcohol use disorders and complications. *Current opinion in psychiatry*, 34(4), 376–385. https://doi.org/10.1097/YCO.0000000000000720

Myers, C. (2013). Insurgency, terrorism, and the drug trade. International Institute for Counter-Terrorism. Available online at: https://www.ict.org.il/UserFiles/Insurgency,%20Terrorism,%20and%20the%20Drug%20Trade.pdf

Nabi, M. H., Masud, I., Humaira, T., Hussain, A., Naz, F., Chakraborty, P. A., & Hawlader, M. D. H. (2022). Reasons of relapse and pattern of drug use among the substance users in Bangladesh: A nationwide study. *Journal of ethnicity in substance abuse*, 21(3), 876–885. https://doi.org/10.1080/15332640.2020.1801549

Nadkarni, A., Weobong, B., Weiss, H. A., McCambridge, J., Bhat, B., Katti, B., Murthy, P., King, M., McDaid, D., Park, A. L., Wilson, G. T., Kirkwood, B., Fairburn, C. G., Velleman, R., & Patel, V. (2017). Counselling for Alcohol Problems (CAP), a lay counsellor-delivered brief psychological treatment for harmful drinking in men, in primary care in India: a randomised controlled trial. *Lancet*, 389(10065), 186–195. https://doi.org/10.1016/S0140-6736(16)31590-2

Nadkarni, A., Velleman, R., Bhatia, U., Fernandes, G., D'souza, E., & Murthy, P. (2020). Home-detoxification and relapse prevention for alcohol dependence in low resource settings: An exploratory study from Goa, India. *Alcohol*, 82, 103–112. https://doi.org/10.1016/j.alcohol.2019.08.006

Nafeh, F., Fusigboye, S., & Sornpaisarn, B. (2022). Understanding injecting drug use in Afghanistan: A scoping review. *Substance abuse treatment, prevention, and policy*, 17(1), 65. https://doi.org/10.1186/s13011-022-00491-1

Narasimha, V. L., Arvind, B. A., Holla, B., Tadepalli, R., Kandasamy, A., & Murthy, P. (2022). Practice and attitude of doctors towards patients with substance use: A study from south India. *Asian journal of psychiatry*, 77, 103247. https://doi.org/10.1016/j.ajp.2022.103247

National Dangerous Drugs Control Board (2019). National Prevalence Survey on Drug Use 2019. Available online at: https://www.nddcb.gov.lk/Docs/research/National%20P%20New.pdf

National Dangerous Drugs Control Board. (2021). Policy & Regulation Documents. Available online at: https://www.nddcb.gov.lk/policy-regulation-documents.php

Nattala, P., Murthy, P., Weiss, M. G., Leung, K. S., Christopher, R., V, J. S., & S, S. (2022). Experiences and reactions of adolescent offspring to their fathers' heavy drinking: A qualitative study from an urban metropolis in India. *Journal of ethnicity in substance abuse*, 21(1), 284–303. https://doi.org/10.1080/15332640.2020.1747041

Naved, R. T., Mamun, M. A., Parvin, K., Willan, S., Gibbs, A., Yu, M., & Jewkes, R. (2018). Magnitude and correlates of intimate partner violence against female garment workers from selected factories in Bangladesh. *PloS one*, 13(11), e0204725. https://doi.org/10.1371/journal.pone.0204725

Nawaz, A., Nielsen, S., Mehmood, T., Abdullah, A., Ahmed, A., Ullah, W., & Khan, A. (2023). Prescription drug dependence with and without concurrent illicit drug use: a multicenter cross-sectional survey among an addiction treatment seeking population. *Frontiers in psychiatry*, 14, 1133606. https://doi.org/10.3389/fpsyt.2023.1133606

Naznin, E., Wynne, O., George, J., Denham, A. M. J., Hoque, M. E., Milton, A. H., Bonevski, B., & Stewart, K. (2021). Smokeless tobacco policy in Bangladesh: A stakeholder study of compatibility with the World Health Organization's Framework Convention on Tobacco Control. Drug and alcohol review, 40(5), 856–863. https://doi.org/10.1111/dar.13243

Neupane, S. P., & Bramness, J. G. (2013). Prevalence and correlates of major depression among Nepalese patients in treatment for alcohol-use disorders. *Drug and alcohol review*, 32(2), 170–177. https://doi.org/10.1111/j.1465-3362.2012.00487.x

Neupane, S. P., & Bramness, J. G. (2014). Who seeks treatment for alcohol problems? Demography and alcohol-use characteristics of patients in taboo and non-taboo drinking groups attending professional alcohol services in Nepal. *Asian journal of psychiatry*, 12, 82–87. https://doi.org/10.1016/j.ajp.2014.06.017

Neupane, S. R., & Mishra, S. R. (2014). Knowledge about human immunodeficiency virus infection and sexual behavior among drug users: a cross sectional study in Pokhara submetropolitan city, Nepal. *HIV/AIDS*, 6, 1–7. https://doi.org/10.2147/HIV.S57176

Niraula, S. R., Chhetry, D. B., Singh, G. K., Nagesh, S., & Shyangwa, P. M. (2006). Role of rehabilitation centres in reducing drug abuse problem in a town of Eastern Nepal. *Kathmandu University medical journal (KUMJ)*, 4(4), 448–454.

Noroozi, A., De Lara, M., & Abouzeid, A. (2024). Drug policies and responses in Afghanistan. *The lancet. Psychiatry*, 11(2), 90–91. https://doi.org/10.1016/S2215-0366(23)00390-5

Ojha, S. P., Sigdel, S., Meyer-Thompson, H. G., Oechsler, H., & Verthein, U. (2014). 'South Asian cocktail'—the concurrent use of opioids, benzodiazepines and antihistamines among injecting drug users in Nepal and associations with HIV risk behaviour. *Harm reduction journal*, 11, 17. https://doi.org/10.1186/1477-7517-11-17

Olsen, Y. (2022). What is addiction? History, terminology, and core concepts. *The Medical clinics of North America*, 106(1), 1–12. https://doi.org/10.1016/j.mcna.2021.08.001

Otiashvili, D., Tabatadze, M., Balanchivadze, N., & Kirtadze, I. (2016). Policing, massive street drug testing and poly-substance use chaos in Georgia—a policy case study. *Substance abuse treatment, prevention, and policy*, 11, 4. https://doi.org/10.1186/s13011-016-0049-2

Pachuau, L. N., Tannous, C., Dhami, M. V., & Agho, K. E. (2022). HIV among people who inject drugs in India: a systematic review. *BMC public health*, 22(1), 1529. https://doi.org/10.1186/s12889-022-13922-2

Pachuau, L. N., Tannous, C., Chawngthu, R. L., & Agho, K. E. (2023). Changes in and Predictors of HIV among People Who Inject Drugs in Mizoram, Northeast India, from 2007 to 2021.

International journal of environmental research and public health, 20(10), 5871. https://doi.org/10.3390/ijerph20105871

Pandey, A. K., Sapkota, N., Tambi, A., & Shyangwa, P. M. (2012). Clinico-demographic profile, sexual dysfunction and readiness to change in male alcohol dependence syndrome inpatients in a tertiary hospital. *Nepal Medical College journal: NMCJ*, 14(1), 35–40.

Pant, S. B., Thapa, S. B., Howard, J., Ojha, S. P., & Lien, L. (2023). Psychological distress and quality of life among Opioid Agonist Treatment service users with a history of injecting and non-injecting drug use: A cross-sectional study in Kathmandu, Nepal. *PloS one*, 18(2), e0281437. https://doi.org/10.1371/journal.pone.0281437

Panthee, B., Panthee, S., Gyawali, S., & Kawakami, N. (2017). Prevalence and correlates of substance use among health care students in Nepal: a cross sectional study. *BMC public health*, 17(1), 950. https://doi.org/10.1186/s12889-017-4980-6

Parmar, A., Bhatia, G., Sharma, P., & Pal, A. (2023). Understanding the epidemiology of substance use in India: A review of nationwide surveys. *Indian journal of psychiatry*, 65(5), 498–505. https://doi.org/10.4103/indianjpsychiatry.indianjpsychiatry_791_22

Peak, A., Rana, S., Maharjan, S. H., Jolley, D., & Crofts, N. (1995). Declining risk for HIV among injecting drug users in Kathmandu, Nepal: the impact of a harm-reduction programme. *AIDS (London, England)*, 9(9), 1067–1070. https://doi.org/10.1097/00002030-199509000-00013

Pearson, M., Dawson, A., Raubenheimer, J., Senerathna, L., Conigrave, K., Lee, K. S. K., Rajapakse, T., Pushpakumara, P. H. G. J., Siribaddana, S., Soerensen, J. B., Konradsen, F., Jan, S., Dawson, A. J., Buckley, N., Abeysinghe, R., Siriwardhana, P., Priyadarshana, C., Haber, P. S., Dzidowska, M., Abeykoon, P., … Glozier, N. (2023). Community-based alcohol education intervention (THEATRE) study to reduce harmful effects of alcohol in rural Sri Lanka: design and adaptation of a mixed-methods stepped wedge cluster randomised control trial. *BMJ open*, 13(6), e064722. https://doi.org/10.1136/bmjopen-2022-064722

Pelzang R. (2012). The pattern of psychiatric admissions in a referral hospital, Bhutan. *WHO South-East Asia journal of public health*, 1(1), 52–58. https://doi.org/10.4103/2224-3151.206914

Petersen, Z., Myers, B., van Hout, M. C., Plüddemann, A., & Parry, C. (2013). Availability of HIV prevention and treatment services for people who inject drugs: findings from 21 countries. *Harm reduction journal*, 10, 13. https://doi.org/10.1186/1477-7517-10-13

Petrosino, A., Turpin-Petrosino, C., & Buehler, J. (2002). "Scared Straight" and other juvenile awareness programs for preventing juvenile delinquency. *The Cochrane database of systematic reviews*, (2), CD002796. https://doi.org/10.1002/14651858.CD002796

Pokhrel, P., Karmacharya, R., Taylor Salisbury, T., Carswell, K., Kohrt, B. A., Jordans, M. J. D., Lempp, H., Thornicroft, G., & Luitel, N. P. (2021). Perception of healthcare workers on mobile app-based clinical guideline for the detection and treatment of mental health problems in primary care: a qualitative study in Nepal. *BMC medical informatics and decision making*, 21(1), 21. https://doi.org/10.1186/s12911-021-01386-0

Poudel, A., Sharma, C., Gautam, S., & Poudel, A. (2016). Psychosocial problems among individuals with substance use disorders in drug rehabilitation centers, Nepal. *Substance abuse treatment, prevention, and policy*, 11(1), 28. https://doi.org/10.1186/s13011-016-0072-3

Rabbani, F., Akhtar, S., Nafis, J., Khan, S., Siddiqi, S., & Merali, Z. (2023). Addition of mental health to the lady health worker curriculum in Pakistan: now or never. *Human resources for health*, 21(1), 29. https://doi.org/10.1186/s12960-023-00814-8

Rahman, M. M., Ahmad, S. A., Karim, M. J., & Chia, H. A. (2011). Determinants of smoking behaviour among secondary school students in Bangladesh. *Journal of community health*, 36(5), 831–838. https://doi.org/10.1007/s10900-011-9382-6

Rahman, M., Nakamura, K., Seino, K., & Kizuki, M. (2015). Do tobacco smoking and illicit drug/alcohol dependence increase the risk of mental disorders among men? Evidence from a national urban Bangladeshi sample. *Perspectives in psychiatric care*, 51(1), 16–27. https://doi.org/10.1111/ppc.12058

Rahman, K. F. (2019). Prevention Of Drug Addiction In Bangladesh: Challenges and A Way Forward. Indian Society of Criminology Conference 2019, 4–14 https://doi.org/10.2139/ssrn.3936819

Rahman, M., Janjua, N. Z., Shafiq, T. K. I., Chowdhury, E. I., Sarker, M. S., Khan, S. I., Reza, M., Faruque, M. O., Kabir, A., Anis, A. H., & Azim, T. (2019). Hepatitis C virus treatment in people who inject drugs (PWID) in Bangladesh. *The International journal on drug policy*, 74, 69–75. https://doi.org/10.1016/j.drugpo.2019.09.002

Rai, S. K., Ahamed, F., Kant, S., Haldar, P., Jha, S., & Rajan, S. (2020). Did Inclusion of informed consent affect the observed HIV prevalence rate among injecting drug users during HIV sentinel surveillance 2017 in Delhi, Uttar Pradesh, Uttarakhand, and Jharkhand States of Central Zone of India?. *Indian journal of public health*, 64(Supplement), S67–S70. https://doi.org/10.4103/ijph.IJPH_35_20

Rasheed, A., Sharifi, H., Wesson, P., Pashtoon, S. J., Tavakoli, F., Ghalekhani, N., Haghdoost, A. A., Atarud, A., Banehsi, M. R., Hamdard, N., Sadaat, S. I., McFarland, W., & Mirzazadeh, A. (2022). Mapping and population size estimates of people who inject drugs in Afghanistan in 2019: Synthesis of multiple methods. *PloS one*, 17(1), e0262405. https://doi.org/10.1371/journal.pone.0262405

Rather, Y. H., Bhat, F. R., Malla, A. A., Zahoor, M., Ali Massodi, P. A., & Yousuf, S. (2021). Pattern and prevalence of substance use and dependence in two districts of Union Territory of Jammu & Kashmir: Special focus on opioids. *Journal of family medicine and primary care*, 10(1), 414–420. https://doi.org/10.4103/jfmpc.jfmpc_1327_20

Rawson, R. A., Rieckmann, T., & Gust, S. W. (2013). Addiction Science: A Rationale and Tools for a Public Health Response to Drug Abuse. *Public health reviews*, 35, 6. https://doi.org/10.1007/BF03391705

Ray, L. A., Meredith, L. R., Kiluk, B. D., Walthers, J., Carroll, K. M., & Magill, M. (2020). Combined Pharmacotherapy and Cognitive Behavioral Therapy for Adults With Alcohol or Substance Use Disorders: A Systematic Review and Meta-analysis. *JAMA network open*, 3(6), e208279. https://doi.org/10.1001/jamanetworkopen.2020.8279

Rentala, S., Ng, S. M., Chan, C. L. W., Bevoor, P., Nayak, R. B., & Desai, M. (2022). Effect of holistic relapse prevention intervention among individuals with alcohol dependence: a prospective study at a mental health care setting in India. *Journal of ethnicity in substance abuse*, 21(2), 687–707. https://doi.org/10.1080/15332640.2020.1793867

Reza, M., Faruque, M. O., Kabir, A., Anis, A. H., & Azim, T. (2019). Hepatitis C virus treatment in people who inject drugs (PWID) in Bangladesh. *The International journal on drug policy*, 74, 69–75. https://doi.org/10.1016/j.drugpo.2019.09.002

Reza, M. M., Rana, A. K. M. M., Morshed Khan, M. N., Safiullah Sarker, M., Chowdhury, S., Uddin, M. Z., Rahman, L., Chowdhury, M. E. I., Taher, M. A., & Khan, S. I. (2023). Prevalence of HIV, risk behaviours and vulnerabilities of female sex partners of the HIV positive people who inject drugs (PWID) in Dhaka city, Bangladesh. *PloS one*, 18(6), e0286673. https://doi.org/10.1371/journal.pone.0286673

Rossow, I., Felix, L., Keating, P., & McCambridge, J. (2016). Parental drinking and adverse outcomes in children: A scoping review of cohort studies. *Drug and alcohol review*, 35(4), 397–405. https://doi.org/10.1111/dar.12319

Ruiseñor-Escudero, H., Wirtz, A. L., Berry, M., Mfochive-Njindan, I., Paikan, F., Yousufi, H. A., Yadav, R. S., Burnham, G., & Vu, A. (2014). Risky behavior and correlates of HIV and Hepatitis C Virus infection among people who inject drugs in three cities in Afghanistan. *Drug and alcohol dependence*, 143, 127–133. https://doi.org/10.1016/j.drugalcdep.2014.07.022

Rumi, M. A., Siddiqui, M. A., Salam, M. A., Iqbal, M. R., Azam, M. G., Chowdhury, A. K., Khan AYM, Hasan, K. N., & Hassan, M. S. (2000). Prevalence of infectious diseases and drug abuse among Bangladeshi workers. *The Southeast Asian journal of tropical medicine and public health*, 31(3), 571–574.

Sadath, A., Jose, K., Jiji, K. M., Mercy, V. T., Ragesh, G., & Arensman, E. (2022). Prevalence and Determinants of Substance Use Among Indigenous Tribes in South India: Findings from a

Tribal Household Survey. *Journal of racial and ethnic health disparities*, 9(1), 356–366. https://doi.org/10.1007/s40615-021-00964-2

Saeed, K., & Taj, M. (2017). A regional framework for action on substance use and public health. *Eastern Mediterranean health journal*, 23(3), 129–130.

Sagi, M. R., Aurobind, G., Chand, P., Ashfak, A., Karthick, C., Kubenthiran, N., Murthy, P., Komaromy, M., & Arora, S. (2018). Innovative telementoring for addiction management for remote primary care physicians: A feasibility study. *Indian journal of psychiatry*, 60(4), 461–466. https://doi.org/10.4103/psychiatry.IndianJPsychiatry_211_18

Sahibzada, K. I., Ganova-Raeva, L., Dimitrova, Z., Ramachandran, S., Lin, Y., Longmire, G., Arthur, L., Xia, G. L., Khudyakov, Y., Khan, I., & Sadaf, S. (2022). Hepatitis C virus transmission cluster among injection drug users in Pakistan. *PloS one*, 17(7), e0270910. https://doi.org/10.1371/journal.pone.0270910

Sahu, D., Ranjan, V., Chandra, N., Nair, S., Kumar, A., Arumugam, E., & Rao, M. V. V. (2022). Analysis of a Targeted Intervention Programme on the Risk Behaviours of Injecting Drug Users in India: Evidence From the National Integrated Biological and Behavioural Surveillance Survey. *Journal of preventive medicine and public health*, 55(4), 407–413. https://doi.org/10.3961/jpmph.22.150

Saini, R., Rao, R., Parmar, A., Mishra, A. K., Ambekar, A., Agrawal, A., & Dhingra, N. (2020). Rates, knowledge and risk factors of non-fatal opioid overdose among people who inject drugs in India: A community-based study. *Drug and alcohol review*, 39(1), 93–97. https://doi.org/10.1111/dar.13016

Samarasinghe D. (1989). Treating alcohol problems in Sri Lanka. *British journal of addiction*, 84(8), 865–867. https://doi.org/10.1111/j.1360-0443.1989.tb00758.x

Satcher, D., & Higginbotham, E. J. (2008). The public health approach to eliminating disparities in health. *American journal of public health*, 98(3), 400–403. https://doi.org/10.2105/AJPH.2007.123919

Schölin, L., Weerasinghe, M., Agampodi, S., Chathurange, U., Rajapaksha, S., Holloway, A., Norrie, J., Mohamed, F., Eddleston, M., & Pearson, M. (2022). Involvement of alcohol in injury cases in rural Sri Lanka: prevalence and associated factors among in-patients in three primary care hospitals. *BMC public health*, 22(1), 514. https://doi.org/10.1186/s12889-022-12958-8

Schroeder S. A. (2005). An agenda to combat substance abuse. *Health affairs*, 24(4), 1005–1013. https://doi.org/10.1377/hlthaff.24.4.1005

Schweinhart, A., Shamblen, S., Shepherd, C., Courser, M. W., Young, L., Morales, B., & Redpath, B. (2022). Gender differences in patient outcomes following drug abuse treatment in Afghanistan: Results from a new evaluation. *Journal of substance abuse treatment*, 134, 108475. https://doi.org/10.1016/j.jsat.2021.108475

Shackleton, N., Jamal, F., Viner, R., Dickson, K., Hinds, K., Patton, G., & Bonell, C. (2016). Systematic review of reviews of observational studies of school-level effects on sexual health, violence and substance use. *Health & place*, 39, 168–176. https://doi.org/10.1016/j.healthplace.2016.04.002

Shahid, A., & Asmat, A. (2023). Stigmatisation and perceived social support as predictor of treatment of substance use disorder (SUD): A systematic review. *JPMA. The Journal of the Pakistan Medical Association*, 73(4), 848–852. https://doi.org/10.47391/JPMA.6478

Shahzad, S., Kliewer, W., Ali, M., & Begum, N. (2020). Different risk factors are associated with alcohol use versus problematic use in male Pakistani adolescents. *International journal of psychology*, 55(4), 585–589. https://doi.org/10.1002/ijop.12617

Sharma, K., Ghosh, A., Krishnan, N. C., Kathirvel, S., Basu, D., Kumar, A., & George, B. B. (2023a). Digital screening and brief intervention for illicit drug misuse in college students: A mixed methods, pilot, cluster, randomized trial from India. *Asian journal of psychiatry*, 81, 103432. https://doi.org/10.1016/j.ajp.2022.103432

Sharma, A. K., Shadakshari, D., Chand, P., & Murthy, P. (2023b). Design, development and pilot testing of 'Quest', a smartphone-based relapse prevention app for patients with alcohol dependence. *Asian journal of psychiatry*, 83, 103572. https://doi.org/10.1016/j.ajp.2023.103572

Shrestha N. M. (1992). Alcohol and drug abuse in Nepal. *British journal of addiction*, 87(9), 1241–1248. https://doi.org/10.1111/j.1360-0443.1992.tb02733.x

Shrestha, S. M., Shrestha, D. M., Gafney, T. E., Maharjan, K. G., Tsuda, F., & Okamoto, H. (1996). Hepatitis B and C infection among drug abusers in Nepal. *Tropical gastroenterology: official journal of the Digestive Diseases Foundation*, 17(4), 212–213.

Singh M. (1998). Harm reduction and street-based program: looking into Nepal. *Substance use & misuse*, 33(5), 1069–1074. https://doi.org/10.3109/10826089809062207

Singh, A., Joshi, M., & Parmar, A. (2024). Substance Use Disorder among Women and Children in South Asia. In: Arafat, S. M. Y., Kar, S. K. *Access to Mental Health Care in South Asia—Current status, potential challenges, and ways out.* Springer Nature Singapore.

Singh, B., & Rao, R. (2021). Perspectives: Is there an opioid epidemic in India?. *Journal of public health*, 43(Suppl 2), ii43–ii50. https://doi.org/10.1093/pubmed/fdab322

Singh, L., Jain, P., Kumar, C., Singh, A., Lal, P., Yadav, A., Singh, P. K., & Singh, S. (2023). Trends in age of tobacco use initiation over time in Bangladesh, India and Pakistan: analysis of cross-sectional nationally representative surveys. *BMJ open*, 13(12), e067875. https://doi.org/10.1136/bmjopen-2022-067875

Singh, P. K., Singh, N., Jain, P., Sinha, P., Kumar, C., Singh, L., Singh, A., Yadav, A., Singh Balhara, Y. P., Kashyap, S., Singh, S., & Subramanian, S. V. (2021). Mapping the triple burden of smoking, smokeless tobacco and alcohol consumption among adults in 28,521 communities across 640 districts of India: A sex-stratified multilevel cross-sectional study. *Health & place*, 69, 102565. https://doi.org/10.1016/j.healthplace.2021.102565

Singh Balhara, Y. P., & Singh, S. (2020). Provisions for Health Sector Response to Substance Use Disorders in the Indian Policy: A Critique of the National Policy on Narcotic Drugs and Psychotropic Substances. *Journal of psychoactive drugs*, 52(1), 93–100. https://doi.org/10.1080/02791072.2019.1709000

Sivapuram, M. S., Nagarathna, R., Anand, A., Patil, S., Singh, A., & Nagendra, H. R. (2020). Prevalence of Alcohol and Tobacco Use in India and Implications for COVID-19—Niyantrita Madhumeha Bharata Study Projections. *Journal of medicine and life*, 13(4), 499–509. https://doi.org/10.25122/jml-2020-0079

Sørensen, J. B., Konradsen, F., Agampodi, T., Sørensen, B. R., Pearson, M., Siribaddana, S., & Rheinländer, T. (2020). A qualitative exploration of rural and semi-urban Sri Lankan men's alcohol consumption. *Global public health*, 15(5), 678–690. https://doi.org/10.1080/17441692.2019.1642366

Sreenivasan, S. T., Nattala, P., Rao, G. N., & Sridaramurthy, M. K. (2022). "So what if I use tobacco or alcohol? It won't hurt me!" How women perceive substance use: insights from a community study in India. *Archives of women's mental health*, 25(1), 129–136. https://doi.org/10.1007/s00737-021-01180-x

Sreeramareddy, C. T., & Aye, S. N. (2021). Changes in adult smoking behaviours in ten global adult tobacco survey (GATS) countries during 2008–2018—a test of 'hardening' hypothesis'. *BMC public health*, 21(1), 1209. https://doi.org/10.1186/s12889-021-11201-0

Srivastava, S., Kumar, P., Rashmi, Paul, R., & Dhillon, P. (2021). Does substance use by family members and community affect the substance use among adolescent boys? Evidence from UDAYA study, India. *BMC public health*, 21(1), 1896. https://doi.org/10.1186/s12889-021-11911-5

Stanikzai, M. H., & Wahidi, M. W. (2023). Bio-psycho-social profile of people with substance use disorders treated in locally assigned treatment facilities in Kandahar, Afghanistan. *Substance abuse and rehabilitation*, 14, 89–98. https://doi.org/10.2147/SAR.S412821

Stepanova, E. (2012). Illicit drugs and insurgency in Afghanistan. Perspectives on terrorism, 6(2), 4–18.

Strathdee, S. A., Zafar, T., Brahmbhatt, H., Baksh, A., & ul Hassan, S. (2003). Rise in needle sharing among injection drug users in Pakistan during the Afghanistan war. *Drug and alcohol dependence*, 71(1), 17–24. https://doi.org/10.1016/s0376-8716(03)00072-3

Subramanian, S. V., Nandy, S., Irving, M., Gordon, D., & Davey Smith, G. (2005). Role of socioeconomic markers and state prohibition policy in predicting alcohol consumption among men and women in India: a multilevel statistical analysis. *Bulletin of the World Health Organization*, 83(11), 829–836.

Tandon T. (2021). Human rights and drug policies in Nepal. London, United Kingdom: International Drug Policy Consortium. Available online at: https://idpc.net/publications/2021/12/human-rights-and-drug-policies-in-nepal

Tavitian-Exley, I., Vickerman, P., Bastos, F. I., & Boily, M-C. (2015). Influence of different drugs on HIV risk in people who inject: systematic review and meta-analysis. *Addiction*, 110(4), 572–584. https://doi.org/10.1111/add.12846

Taylor Salisbury, T., Kohrt, B. A., Bakolis, I., Jordans, M. J., Hull, L., Luitel, N. P., McCrone, P., Sevdalis, N., Pokhrel, P., Carswell, K., Ojagbemi, A., Green, E. P., Chowdhary, N., Kola, L., Lempp, H., Dua, T., Milenova, M., Gureje, O., & Thornicroft, G. (2021). Adaptation of the World Health Organization Electronic Mental Health Gap Action Programme Intervention Guide App for Mobile Devices in Nepal and Nigeria: Protocol for a Feasibility Cluster Randomized Controlled Trial. JMIR research protocols, 10(6), e24115. https://doi.org/10.2196/24115

Thavarajah, R., Ranganathan, K., Joshua, E., & Rao, U. K. (2019). Areca nut use disorder: A dynamic model map. Indian journal of dental research. *Official Publication of Indian Society for Dental Research*, 30(4), 612–621. https://doi.org/10.4103/ijdr.IJDR_947_18

Tirmizi, S. N., Khoja, S., Patten, S., Yousafzai, A. W., Scott, R. E., Durrani, H., Khoja, W., & Husyin, N. (2017). Mobile-based blended learning for capacity building of health providers in rural Afghanistan. *mHealth*, 3, 14. https://doi.org/10.21037/mhealth.2017.04.01

Todd, C. S., Abed, A. M. S., Scott, P. T., Safi, N., Earhart, K. C., & Strathdee, S. A. (2009a). A cross-sectional assessment of utilization of addiction treatment among injection drug users in Kabul, Afghanistan. *Substance use and misuse*, 44(3), 416–430. https://doi.org/10.1080/10826080802347669

Todd, C. S., Stibich, M. A., Stanekzai, M. R., Rasuli, M. Z., Bayan, S., Wardak, S. R., & Strathdee, S. A. (2009b). A qualitative assessment of injection drug use and harm reduction programmes in Kabul, Afghanistan: 2006–2007. *The International journal on drug policy*, 20(2), 111–120. https://doi.org/10.1016/j.drugpo.2007.11.022

Todd, C. S., Macdonald, D., Khoshnood, K., Mansoor, G. F., Eggerman, M., & Panter-Brick, C. (2012). Opiate use, treatment, and harm reduction in Afghanistan: recent changes and future directions. *The International journal on drug policy*, 23(5), 341–345. https://doi.org/10.1016/j.drugpo.2012.05.004

Todd, C. S., Stanekzai, M. R., Nasir, A., Fiekert, K., Orr, M. G., Strathdee, S. A., & Vlahov, D. (2016). Change in attitudes and knowledge of problem drug use and harm reduction among a community cohort in Kabul, Afghanistan. *Eastern mediterranean health journal*, 22(3), 183–192. https://doi.org/10.26719/2016.22.3.183

United Nations Office on Drugs and Crime. (2013). National Drug Use Survey: Maldives – 2011/2012. Available online at: http://www.unodc.org/documents/southasia//reports/National_Drug_Use_Survey_-_Report.pdf

Unnithan N. P. (1985). A cross-national perspective on the evolution of alcohol prohibition. *The International journal of the addictions*, 20(4), 591–604. https://doi.org/10.3109/10826088509044938

Upadhaya, N., Jordans, M. J. D., Gurung, D., Pokhrel, R., Adhikari, R. P., & Komproe, I. H. (2018). Psychotropic drugs in Nepal: perceptions on use and supply chain management. *Globalization and health*, 14(1), 10. https://doi.org/10.1186/s12992-018-0322-4

Verma, M., Rana, K., Bhatt, G., Sharma, N., & Lal, P. (2023). Trends and determinants of tobacco use initiation in India: analysis of two rounds of the Global Adult Tobacco Survey. *BMJ open*, 13(9), e074389. https://doi.org/10.1136/bmjopen-2023-074389

Wadood, A., Karim, R., Hussain, A. A. M., Rana, M., & Hossain, G. (2021). Risk factors of suicidality among married adults: A cross-sectional survey in Rajshahi City, Bangladesh. PloS one, 16(5), e0251717. https://doi.org/10.1371/journal.pone.0251717

Wangdi, K., & Jamtsho, T. (2019). Prevalence and Correlates of Current Alcohol Use among Bhutanese Adults: A Nationally Representative Survey Data Analysis. *Indian journal of psychological medicine*, 41(1), 38–45. https://doi.org/10.4103/IJPSYM.IJPSYM_412_18

Wen, H., Xiang, X., Jiang, Y., Zhang, H., Zhang, P., Chen, R., Wei, X., Dong, Y., Xiao, S., & Lu, L. (2023). Comparative efficacy of psychosocial interventions for opioid-dependent people receiving methadone maintenance treatment: A network meta-analysis. *Addiction*, 118(6), 1029–1039. https://doi.org/10.1111/add.16167

Winer, J. M., Yule, A. M., Hadland, S. E., & Bagley, S. M. (2022). Addressing adolescent substance use with a public health prevention framework: the case for harm reduction. *Annals of medicine*, 54(1), 2123–2136. https://doi.org/10.1080/07853890.2022.2104922

World Health Organization & United Nations Office on Drugs and Crime. (2020). International standards for the treatment of drug use disorders. Geneva: World Health Organization and United Nations Office on Drugs and Crime. Available online at: https://www.who.int/publications/i/item/international-standards-for-the-treatment-of-drug-use-disorders

Chapter 12
Understanding Substance Use Disorder and Comorbidities: Insights from South Asia

Roshan Bhad and Shreya Shukla

12.1 Introduction

South Asia is one of the most populous regions with India, Pakistan, and Bangladesh figuring in the ten most populated countries of the world. Among the WHO regions, the South East Asian region holds a key position by being home to more than 25% of the world's population. Out of the eleven member countries of this region, eight countries are part of South Asia, namely, Afghanistan, Bangladesh, Bhutan, India, Maldives, Nepal, Pakistan, and Sri Lanka. These countries share common geo-political and economic aspects since all these countries are low- and middle-income countries (Arafat and Kar 2024). They also bear striking similarities between their respective health issues including mental health needs and access to services. The area being rife with conflict and natural disasters also leaves its occupants vulnerable to their impact. Apart from this what binds these countries together is the largest number of alcohol and drug-attributable Disability-Adjusted Life Years (DALYs) regions in the world according to the Global Burden of Diseases Study (Collaborators 2022). Not only this, there is a paucity of mental health professionals in this region with national expenditure on mental health being less than 1% of the national budget except in Afghanistan (Mental Health ATLAS 2020 n.d.; Murthy 2017; Trivedi et al. 2007). According to the WHO, except for Maldives, all the other countries have less than 1 psychiatrist per 100,000 population (Mental Health ATLAS 2020 n.d.).

Tobacco and Alcohol are the major public health problems and risk factors for preventable deaths due to non-communicable diseases in the region. However, opioids and stimulants are emerging substance use problems as per the recent world drug reports. This area is home to two important areas known as the "Golden Triangle" comprising of Thailand, Laos, and Myanmar, and the "Golden Crescent" including Iran, Pakistan, and Afghanistan. Both these areas constitute the highest

R. Bhad (✉) · S. Shukla
National Drug Dependence Treatment Centre (NDDTC), AIIMS, New Delhi, India
e-mail: drroshansindia@gmail.com

S. M. Y. Arafat and S. K. Kar (eds.), *Current Perspectives on Substance Use Disorders in South Asia*, https://doi.org/10.1007/978-981-97-6619-2_12

illicit opium-producing regions in the world. Afghanistan is the leading producer of opium in the world and with the evolution of the drug market, there is a rise in the production and trafficking amphetamine-type stimulants as well. The member states share porous borders with the rest of the South Asian countries leading to easy availability and drug trafficking of opium across these states. Trafficking of opium and heroin from Pakistan and Afghanistan to India and further to the neighboring South Asian nations and other countries of Europe and America poses a challenge to drug control all over the world.

Contrary to the trends in other geographical areas, opioids contribute to about 58% of the population in addiction treatment facilities followed by cannabis (33%) among illicit drugs (Fig. 12.1), whereas other substances such as amphetamine-type stimulants, cocaine, and sedative-hypnotic use comprise of less than 5% of the given population. The smallest population of females in drug-related treatment facilities is seen in Asia. Similarly, the number of people who inject drugs is lower than the global average of 0.26% by about a third; the lowest prevalence of PWID is found only in the Far and Middle East region at 0.08% with prevalence in South Asia at a close 0.09% (UNODC 2023). The South East Asian region accounts for about 81% of all smokeless tobacco users and 22% of adult smokers globally (*Tobacco Control in the South-East Asia Region* n.d.). Rise in the use of stimulants, e.g., Amphetamine-Type Stimulants (ATSs) is an emerging problem in the region.

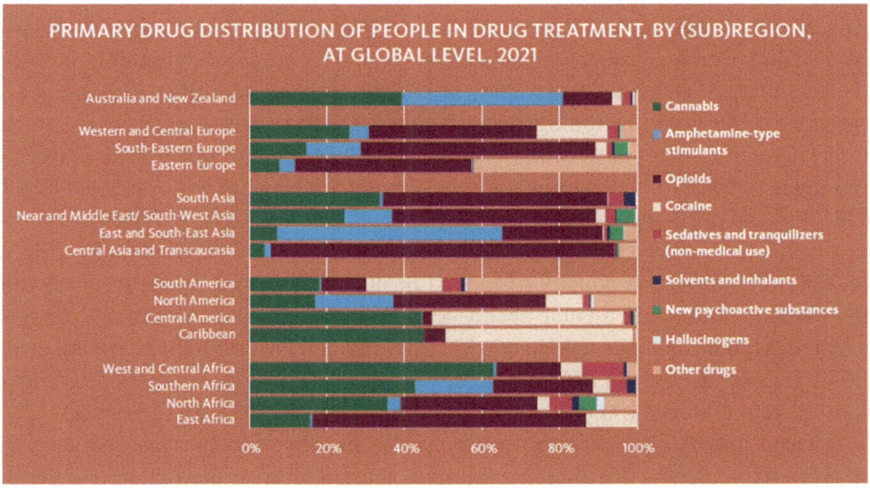

Fig. 12.1 Primary drug distribution in drug treatment (UNODC 2023)

12.2 Prevalence of Substance Use Disorder in South Asian Countries

Magnitude of substance use in the eight countries of South Asia has been studied by their national surveys with alcohol, cannabis, and opioids making up the most common substances of use in this area (Table 12.1). The prevalence has been discussed in Chapter One of this book (Choudhury et al. 2024).

12.2.1 Tobacco Use

Smokeless tobacco is the major form used in most of the South Asian countries that include Bangladesh, Nepal, Afghanistan, Bhutan, Sri Lanka, and India. Pakistan and Maldives being the only nations in this region that have smoking as the major route of tobacco use (GATS Report Final-2017_20 MB.Pdf n.d.; Tobacco-Fact-Sheet-1.Pdf n.d.; Vltwo5kq.Pdf n.d.; Alemi et al. 2021; Global-Adult-Tobacco-Survey-Second-Round-India-2016-2017.Pdf n.d.; Gurung et al. 2016; Steps-2015-Survey-Tobacco-Fact-Sheet-Sri-Lanka.Pdf n.d.). It is consumed in the form of *gul* and *naswar* which are indigenous to this region.

12.2.2 Alcohol Use

Alcohol use varies across different countries in the area mainly influenced by the religious majority. For instance, in the countries of Afghanistan and Pakistan, the prevalence of alcohol use is less than 1% since they have an Islamic majority (*Pak.Pdf* n.d.). In the rest of the South Asian member states, the prevalence of alcohol use

Table 12.1 Prevalence of substance use in South Asian countries as per the latest National Survey

Sl. No.	Countries	Alcohol	Cannabis	Opioids	ATS
1	Afghanistan	<1%	2.2%	4.9%	0.3%
2	Bangladesh (among drug users)	Up to 30% of drug users	42.7%	5.4%	15.2%
3	Bhutan	30%	–	–	–
4	India	15%	2.8%	2.1%	0.18%
5	Nepal (among drug users)	1.5–25%	90.5%	93.5%	5.2%
6	Maldives (among drug users)	Up to 50% of drug users	38–71%	67–40%	1–4%
7	Pakistan	<1%	3.6%	1%	0.08%
8	Sri Lanka	17.8%	1.98%	0.61%	N/A

ranges from anywhere between 1.5 and 30% (Ambekar et al. 2019; Organization 2019; *National_Drug_Use_Survey_-_Report.Pdf* n.d.; *2015 STEPS Fact Sheet Sri Lanka* n.d.; Wangdi and Jamtsho 2019; *Pak.Pdf* n.d.; Rathod et al. 2018).

12.2.3 Opioids

Opioid use is major problem in South Asia due to its proximity to Myanmar and Afghanistan which are the largest producers of opium. Opioids are the most common substance of abuse in Afghanistan with prevalence in other countries ranging from anywhere between 0.3 and 5.4%. (Global 2015; Ambekar et al. 2019; crime (Vienna) 2009; *Nepal Drug Users Survey: 2076* 2020; *National_Drug_Use_Survey_-_Report.Pdf* n.d.).

12.2.4 Cannabis

Cannabis use via oral and inhaled routes is common in the South Asian region due to the rampant wild as well as illicit growth of the plant. In India alone, oral use of cannabis in the form of bhang is rampant with about 4 million users compared to 5 million users of charas or ganja which are predominantly inhaled.

12.2.5 Stimulants

Methamphetamine use, manufacture, and trafficking are on the rise around the world especially in non-traditional markets of South Asia. Production of methamphetamine mainly in Afghanistan in the west and Myanmar in the east sandwiches the region between the two hubs. Use of amphetamine-type stimulants is a problem in the north-eastern states of India and Bangladesh. Amphetamine is the predominant stimulant of use in the states of India. Pakistan, Bangladesh, and Bhutan have use of pharmaceutical products containing amphetamines while methamphetamine is used in Sri Lanka and Nepal (UNODC 2023).

12.3 Comorbidities

12.3.1 Psychiatric Comorbidities

Substance use disorders and psychiatric illnesses share a complicated relationship. The emergence, course and prognosis of these conditions are intertwined such that the co-occurrence of these conditions is known as "dual disorder" or "dual diagnosis" (Wittchen 1996). Psychiatric illness can play a part in the initiation of substance use as explained by the self-medication hypothesis. It can also be a consequence of substance use disorders or can just co-exist with substance use due to common vulnerabilities (Mueser et al. 1998). Patients with dual diagnosis have poorer prognosis, more lapses and relapses for substance use, more frequent hospitalization, higher risk of suicide, and medical illnesses with higher rates of non-adherence (Batki et al. 2009; Buckley 2006; Gupta et al. 1996; Kerfoot et al. 2011).

In a retrospective chart review spanning over 11 years in a center for addiction treatment in North India, 13.2% of patients registered were found to have comorbid psychiatric disorder. Mood disorder accounted for about 42.2% of these cases, while psychotic disorders, anxiety disorders, and personality disorder were diagnosed in about 27.5%, 16.7%, and 10.1% cases, respectively (Basu et al. 2013). A prospective study albeit with a much lesser sample size of 79 cases reported the prevalence of dual diagnosis to be 32.4% with mood, anxiety, and psychotic disorders being the most common in this order (Subodh et al. 2017). A study including 289 patients seeking treatment from the dual diagnosis clinic of a tertiary care center for the treatment of substance use disorder found that schizophrenia, major depressive disorder, bipolar disorder, and anxiety disorder were the most common comorbid conditions. Patients diagnosed with psychotic disorder and Major Depressive Disorders (MDD) mostly had comorbid alcohol use disorder, while most of those with bipolar affective disorder had comorbid cannabis dependence (Balhara et al. 2016). Another retrospective study in India posited that use of sedative-hypnotics and opioids had greater odds of being associated with depression, use of alcohol with anxiety disorders, while cannabis with psychotic disorders (Balhara et al. 2017).

In an Indian study exploring the pathway to care in dual-diagnosis cases, it was found that treatment seeking for substance use disorders in dual-diagnosis cases is delayed than the time to seek treatment for psychiatric illness. A study exploring outcomes in 307 patients of dual diagnosis in terms of onset of substance use was undertaken in a tertiary care center in North India. In addition, patients with dual diagnosis with early age of initiation of substance use (less than 18 years age of onset) have been found to have a poorer prognosis for both psychiatric disorders and substance use along with higher risky sexual behavior, poorer adherence to treatment, and more need for inpatient care (Subodh et al. 2019).

The prevalence of comorbid mood and anxiety disorders in patients with alcohol use disorders was found to range between 6 and 65% for affective disorders and 0 and 30% for anxiety disorders in a systematic review of 22 Indian studies (Hendrickson et al. 2019). Similar rates of comorbid anxiety disorder of 28.62% was found in a study conducted in Pakistan among 156 substance-using participants between February 2021 and January 2023 (Awan et al. 2023). A cross-sectional study among 541 patients with substance use disorder in Afghanistan revealed that about 87.1% patients had symptoms of depression, 91.6% had symptoms of anxiety with the estimates of severe anxiety and depression being 34.8% and 65.8%, respectively (Stanikzai and Wahidi 2023). In 5 OAT (Opioid Agonist Treatment) centers in Nepal, 231 participants were included in a study out of which 16.5% reported a history of mental disorder. Using M.I.N.I. (Mini International Neuropsychiatric Interview) lifetime MDD was noted in 24.2% and lifetime suicidality in 26% (Pant et al. 2022). A cross-sectional survey was carried out among 188 patients with alcohol use disorder who consecutively sought inpatient care in a residential treatment center for Alcohol Use Disorders (AUDs) in Nepal. It reported that the 12-month and lifetime prevalence of major depressive disorder was 36% and 45%, respectively. There was no statistically significant difference in the prevalence of depression in groups on the basis of social stigma (Neupane 2011).

In a community-based cross-sectional study in India, it was seen that out of 104 participants using drugs via injecting route comorbid tobacco use was reported by all the patients. Lifetime use of alcohol and cannabis use was found in 90.4% and 89.4%, respectively, with lifetime sedative/hypnotic use and use of inhalants to be about 61.5 and 46.2%. Among comorbid psychiatric illness, antisocial personality disorder, and suicidality was found to be the most common comorbidity present in 25 and 23.1% of the participants, respectively, with about 13.5% of participants having a history of major depressive episodes and 13.4% with anxiety disorders (Saini et al. 2021).

Among Indian women seeking treatment for alcohol use disorders with a sample size of 35, a majority of them were found to have comorbid Axis I disorders such as major depressive disorder and anxiety disorder with borderline personality disorder co-occurring in 17% of cases (Malik et al. 2017). Similarly in a study in Nepal, among 100 patients (86 males and 14 females) seeking treatment for substance use disorder at a tertiary care center, about 63% of the patients had a history of one or more personality disorders as per the International Personality Disorder Examination module interview schedule (Mahara Rawal et al. 2021). Among 325 patients registered in a tertiary care psychiatric setup in Sri Lanka, prevalence of substance use disorders was found to be 45% (Hapangama et al. 2013). Similarly, in Bhutan, a cross-sectional study lasting a year, including 155 patients with substance use disorders the rate of major depressive disorder was 38% according to Patient Health Questionnaire-9 (PHQ-9) when patients with mild depression were excluded (Chhetri et al. 2023).

Substance use among adolescents is a reason for concern worldwide since early onset of substance use is responsible for higher morbidity. Among adolescents, comorbidity is more often the rule. A study was conducted in Bangladesh with the aim of studying the pattern and frequency of comorbidities among adolescents with substance use disorders. It included a total of 70 adolescents with a mean age of 13.2 ± 2.1 years with an age range of 11–17 years. More than half were diagnosed with tobacco use disorder (51.4%) with cannabis use disorder accounting for about 47.1% of cases. 77.1% of the cases also had a comorbid psychiatric condition, while almost 45% of cases were diagnosed with more than one psychiatric condition. Conduct disorder (30.4%) was the most common comorbid condition followed by attention deficit hyperactivity disorder (21.4%), oppositional defiant disorder (18.5%), and depressive disorders (17.1%) (Khan et al. 2021). In another Indian study, 240 adults seeking treatment for substance use disorders were screened for ADHD (Attention Deficit Hyperactivity Disorder) on ADHD self-report rating scale (ASRS). They found that 56.25% of the patients screened positive for "likely ADHD" and 21.7% for "highly likely ADHD" (Ganesh et al. 2017). Similarly, a study in Nepal was conducted to study the association between substance use and behavioral and emotional issues among adolescents. It included 408 adolescents aged 12–18 years and found that depressive symptoms, internalizing or externalizing problems were associated with substance use disorder (Karki et al. 2019). There is a dearth of literature in the South Asian region with regards to dual diagnosis with only a handful of studies shedding light on the situation.

12.3.2 Pain and Other Medical Comorbidities

Pain is a common comorbid medical condition encountered among people using substances. Pain is either cause of initiation of substance use and development of addictive behaviors or can develop as its consequence leading to chronic painful conditions or even hyperalgesia.

Prevalence of opioid use disorder in patients with chronic non-cancer pain or cancer pain. An Indian study shed light on the rates of opioid use disorder in patients receiving palliative care on prescription opioids. The sample consisted of over 40 patients who were receiving opioids with a mean dose of 159.50 ± 327.90 mg/day of morphine for a cumulative period of 1479 months. Out of these only six patients screened positive for inappropriate use of the opioids and none were diagnosed to have opioid use disorder.

Chronic medical conditions are also known to be associated with substance use. In a study of electronic health records of 211,880 patients in North Carolina, USA, the prevalence of substance use disorder was found to be 13.3% and the prevalence increased as the number of comorbidities increased in the patients. The rate of substance use disorders was 4.3% among patients with one medical condition, which increased to 21.2 and 32.5% in patients having two to three and four to nine conditions, respectively, thus leading to the conclusion that chronic medical conditions were associated with increased rates of substance use (Wu et al. 2018).

In India, 20% of all patients diagnosed to have any kind of liver pathology, notwithstanding the etiology are alcohol users. Not only this, it is the most common cause of cirrhosis of liver contributing to about 35% of all cases (Mukherjee et al. 2017). An Indian study was conducted in a tertiary care center to study drinking patterns in a cohort of patients with and without liver cirrhosis. Among patients with heavy drinking, about 38.3% of cases were found to have liver cirrhosis (Sharma et al.

2023). Secondary analysis of the data from the Study on Global Ageing and Adult Health revealed that about 17% of the population consumed alcohol and moderate drinking was associated with hypertension and higher body mass index (Patel et al. 2020). Similarly, acute pancreatitis is a complication arising as a result of alcohol use. A cross-sectional observational study conducted in a tertiary care center in India including 88 patients with acute pancreatitis found that 38.8% of these patients had alcohol use disorder (Bajwa et al. 2023). Significant proportion of victims of road traffic accidents had history of alcohol use. About 2–33% of injured and 6–48% of killed Road Traffic Accidents (RTA) in India were attributable to driving under influence of alcohol and other drugs (Das et al. 2012).

In Sri Lankan studies rates of pancreatic calcification among chronic alcohol users is almost 2.4%, while, that in patients of cancer of liver, alcohol use was seen among 70% of the cases (Nagaratnam et al. 1984; Nagaratnam and Gunawardene 1972). Seven to ten percent of hospital admissions in Sri Lanka were in some way linked to alcohol use (Ramachandran et al. 1986).

In a retrospective chart review among patients admitted to a tertiary care center in Nepal during a 4 month period, 332 patients were of non-communicable diseases. The study reports that a total of 17% of these patients were admitted with alcohol-related complications including esophageal varices, ascites, cirrhosis, and acute pancreatitis (Amundsen et al. 2016). The etiological factors of severe acute pancreatitis among patients admitted in a tertiary level ICU included gallstones followed by alcohol use in 28.8% of the cases out of 52 cases recruited (Khanal et al. 2023). Even though rates of hepatocellular carcinoma attributable to alcohol is quite low in Asian countries as compared to the west, however a low level of aldehyde dehydrogenase renders them more susceptible to the harmful consequences of alcohol intake (Setshedi et al. 2010).

A systematic review and meta-analysis aiming to study the prevalence of Chronic Obstructive Pulmonary Disease (COPD) among population above 30 years in India was conducted. It included 22 cross-sectional and 1 cohort study and concluded that 5.6–100% of patients with COPD had been exposed to some form of tobacco either smoking or smokeless. Three studies denied the exposure to smoke among the participants and one study did not comment on the same (Verma et al. 2021). In a similar study in Nepal, the pooled prevalence of former smokers, non-smokers, and current smokers among COPD patients was 28.5%, 25.8%, and 59.4% respectively (Budhathoki et al. 2022). Tobacco smoking was reported as a major risk factor for the development of COPD in Bangladesh as well. One-fifth of the tobacco-attributable deaths in the world are in the South East Asian region. The population attributable fraction in the world is almost 3.8%, however, that in the South East Asian region is more than twice that at 8.7%. About 16 and 1% of deaths due to non-communicable diseases in India are attributable to tobacco among males and females, respectively (Thakur et al. 2011).

12.3.3 *Blood-Borne Viral Diseases and Other Infections*

Though sexual route is the main mode of HIV transmission in India, but according to the Integrated Biological and Behavioural Surveillance (IBBS) 2014–15, the prevalence of HIV among IDUs is about 9.9%. As the world's largest opium producer, most of Afghanistan's HIV cases are from injecting drug users amounting to 4.4%. National estimates of HIV according to national surveys in South Asian countries varies from 2.4% to as high as 21% (Table 12.2). According to the World Drug Report 2023, the prevalence of HIV among people who inject drugs worldwide is 11.9% however that among South Asian countries is 9.01% (Fig. 12.2).

Among all the regions, East and South East Asia have the highest number of PWID with Hepatitis C (Grebely et al. 2019). In a systematic review of 327 Indian studies, community based seroprevalence rates of hepatitis C among injecting drug users was found to be 44.7% (Goel et al. 2019). As many as 80% of PWID in Nepal are had HCV infection, however, Maldives has less than 1% of injecting drug users diagnosed to have HCV (Martinello et al. 2016; Crime United Nations Office on Drugs 2013).

Needless to say, other infections such as Hepatitis B and tuberculosis are also a cause of concern in the population using drugs. The prevalence of Hepatitis B among people who inject drugs among South Asian countries varies from 5 to 10% as per a recent study (Fig. 12.3). Other sexually transmitted infections such as genital ulcers are rampant among IDUs.

12.4 Treatment Needs and Gap

South Asia as a region lacks far behind in terms of provision of treatment services for mental health and substance use disorders. Poor financial allocation, governance, and human resources plague the region, especially in delivering effective mental healthcare. According to WHO, four out of five people with mental illnesses residing in low- and middle-income countries such as countries in South Asian region receive

Table 12.2 HIV prevalence in PWID in the South Asian countries (2021) (*Final_SAARC-Epidemiological-Response-on-HIVAIDS-_2022.Pdf* n.d.)

Sl. No.	Country	HIV prevalence in PWID
1	Afghanistan	4.4
2	Bangladesh	2.4
3	Bhutan	N/A
4	India	9
5	Maldives	N/A
6	Nepal	2.7
7	Pakistan	21
8	Sri-Lanka	N/A

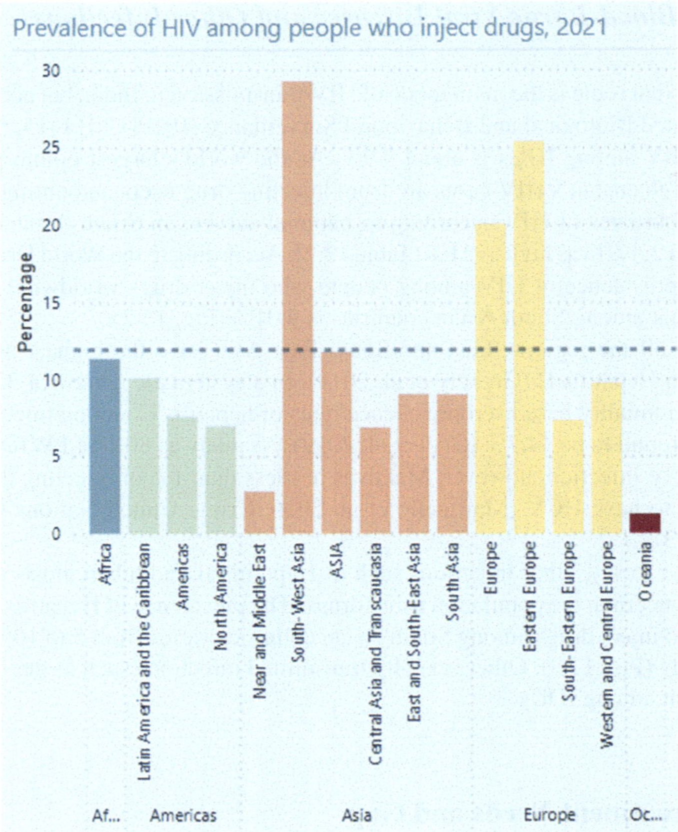

Fig. 12.2 Prevalence of HIV among PWID (UNODC 2023)

no treatment for the same. Median number of psychiatrists in these countries stood at 0.05 per 100,000 population which is much less than the 8.9 per 100,000 population seen in developed countries. In the National Mental Health Survey of India, 2016 the treatment gap ranged from 28 to 83% for mental disorders with 86% for alcohol use disorders. Similarly, the GATS-2 survey in India reported that less than 50% of current smokers and about 31.7% of those using smokeless tobacco were even advised by healthcare providers to quit tobacco use.

Similarly, Nepal has about a fourth of its psychiatrists working overseas and over 1.5 beds per 100,000 population designated to meet the mental health needs of its population (Luitel et al. 2015). Pakistan has a high prevalence of suicide and other psychiatric disorders along with substance use disorders with 6.45 million people using illegal drugs. Less than 500 psychiatrists with only 654 psychiatric units and 4 psychiatric hospitals cater to this huge a population. Currently, there are 2.1 psychiatric beds per 100,000 people with mental and substance use disorders creating a treatment gap of almost 90% in Pakistan (Shah et al. 2022). The prevalence

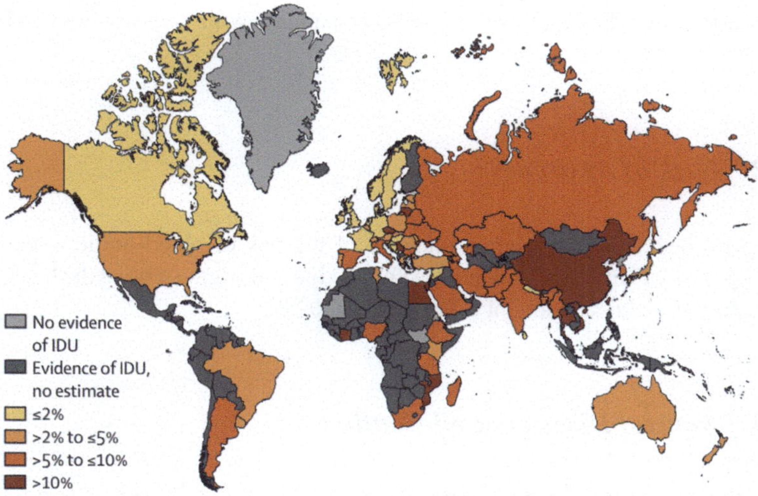

Fig. 12.3 Prevalence of hepatitis B infection among PWID in South Asia as compared to the rest of the world reported to be 6.6% (Degenhardt et al. 2023)

of mental, neurological and substance use disorders is almost 32.5% in Bhutan with treatment gap reaching almost 90% (*Mental Health for All* n.d.). Afghanistan has only 0.23 psychiatrists, 0.10 mental health nurses, and 0.3 psychologists per 100,000 population which is quite low by global standards (Kovess-Masfety et al. 2021). The country's population is catered by only one mental hospital and four GHPUs in addition to community-based and mental health outpatient facilities. Similarly, the country of Sri Lanka has 100 psychiatrists catering to the mental health needs of the whole population spanning across 24 districts. The tally in each of the South Asian countries is lower than the WHO recommended standards (Kathriarachchi et al. 2019). The specialized training program in addiction psychiatry is currently available only in India. Workforce development in the field of addiction psychiatry/ medicine will be key for reducing treatment gap in the region (Tripathi et al. 2020).

12.5 Challenges in Addressing Substance Use Problem

12.5.1 Stigma

Stigma among people with mental health issues has always been a roadblock to seeking health care. Literature posits that self-stigma in people with substance use disorder is even higher than that found in people with other psychiatric illnesses including schizophrenia (Modi et al. 2018; Garg et al. 2012). Stigma is a significant deterrent among the South Asians, especially females for seeking treatment for substance use disorders and even more so in patients with comorbidities (Murthy 2017).

12.5.2 Lack of Awareness

People who inject drugs are often unaware of the risk of blood-borne infection it poses, especially Hepatitis C. Deficits in knowledge and stigma among the healthcare workers further delays treatment (Ghosh et al. 2023).

12.5.3 Natural Disasters and Conflict

The South Asian region is strife with both natural disasters and conflict over the past few decades which affect the availability of good health care systems. Immigration due to conflict has also added to the mental health burden and contributed to poor mental healthcare services. Forced displacement is one of the key risk factors for substance use disorders (Elkholy et al. 2023).

12.5.4 Poor Policy Implementation

The implementation of national programs and policies is quite poor in these South Asian countries. In the absence of any monitoring and evaluation of the national programs, the implementation goes unchecked and the dismal condition of these services continues. Careful policy evaluation and integration of existing healthcare services is the need of the hour in these countries along with resource allocation and more specialized drug dependence treatment centers.

12.5.5 Participation and Collaboration

Intersectoral collaboration between various policies and national programs is needed to face the challenge of substance use disorders. Components of mental health programs need to be integrated with other national programs for a better coverage and addressal of substance use disorders.

12.6 Treatment Models for Substance Use Disorders and Comorbidities

12.6.1 Dual Diagnosis Treatment Models

There is limited literature from South Asia describing the different treatment models in this area for dual diagnosis. In an Indian study, members of the Dual Diagnosis India Network were approached to share the service models provided by their centers for dual diagnosis cases. An analysis revealed that these models can be grouped into five different subtypes which included a specialized dual diagnosis clinic for cases presenting with a substance use disorder as well as psychiatric illness. Along with this within general psychiatry setups, specialized substance use treatment is offered, dual-diagnosis clinic within general psychiatry setup, dual-diagnosis clinic within substance use services, and dual-disorder clinic combined with treatment of substance use disorder offered in general psychiatry services (Balhara et al. 2022).

12.6.2 Consultation–Liaison Services in Addiction Psychiatry

A subspecialty of clinical psychiatry that deals with the clinical, teaching, and research activities of mental healthcare workers in the non-psychiatric divisions of a general hospital (Lipowski 1983). It has further been subdivided into consultation liaison addiction psychiatry that deals with the management of substance use disorders in patients admitted in GHPU setting with other medical issues. This treatment model deals with management of substance use disorders with medical comorbidities. It is still an emerging branch and there is little literature about the availability of these services in the region (Rao et al. 2020). However, an Indian survey reported that about 75% of the 90 training centers provide consultation liaison services as "on-call services" (Grover and Avasthi 2018). Only a third of these have a dedicated consultation liaison psychiatry team with a faculty member, senior and junior residents being a part of the three-tier system of care. Similarly, a handful of studies suggest that consultation liaison services exist in other South Asian countries such as Nepal, Bangladesh, and Pakistan as well however low utilization of these services are a major challenge. Specialized consultation liaison services for addiction psychiatry are lacking in most South Asian countries.

12.6.3 Linkage with Blood-Borne and Other Infections

The Revised National Tuberculosis Control Programme (RNTCP) of India guidelines in 2016 mandated the documentation and linkage of patients with tuberculosis with use of tobacco or alcohol to tobacco cessation clinics or treatment services for alcohol use. It also requires assessment of the status of substance use at the end of treatment of TB (*National-Framework-for-Joint-TB-Tobacco-Collaborative-Activities.Pdf* n.d.).

Integrated Care Centers have been set up in six Indian districts that provide testing and management of HIV, screening of TB and HCV testing along with linkage to government hospitals for management of the same. Opioid agonist treatment (OAT) and needle and syringe exchange is also offered at the same venue (Solomon et al. 2016). Similarly, OST services have been included in the Pakistan AIDS Strategy IV owing to its evidence in improving adherence to ART (*Strategies—National AIDS Control Programme* n.d.).

12.7 South Asian Collaborative Programs for Substance Use Problem

The Colombo plan has been one of the forerunners in the field of social and economic development in the Asia pacific region since 1951. It included Canada, Australia, the United Kingdom, and the South Asian countries of India, Sri Lanka, and Pakistan. It has expanded its reach to include a total of 26 states including all SAARC countries. The Drug Advisory Program under the overarching umbrella of the Colombo Plan was launched with the focus of demand reduction and mutual help in development. The DAP targets drug use through focus on eight networks encompassing prevention, treatment and rehabilitation, special services for children, youth, supply reduction and law enforcement, curriculum development as well as expert committee and publications. These network services are open for collaboration with non-member countries as well (*Colombo Plan|International Society of Substance Use Professionals* n.d.).

Since the inception of the South Asian Association for Regional Cooperation (SAARC) in 1987 with the eight member countries mentioned, these countries have collaborated on various fronts including drug use and trafficking in the area. The common interest of combating drug use in the area gave rise to a regional strategy and the SAARC Convention on Narcotic Drugs and Psychotropic Substances came into being in November of 1990. It was ratified by the eight member countries and came into force about 3 years later. It aims at prevention, treatment, and rehabilitation of drug use and combat drug trafficking by capacity building through a joint effort between the law enforcement agencies. Information and intelligence about drug-related offences can be exchanged between the member nations through the SAARC Drug Offences Monitoring Desk (SDOMD) in Colombo. It also coordinates seminars and workshops focusing on prevention, mobilization of community, and treatment and relapse prevention methods. Monitoring of the implementation of the convention is the role of the Technical Committee on Prevention of Drug Trafficking and Drug Abuse during the SAARC annual meeting to ensure better regulation.

The United Nations Office on Drugs and Crime is the UN organization established to keep in check the organized crime across nations, and terrorism and is the forerunner in the global fight against illicit drugs. It also acts as the guardian of the international drug control conventions. The UNODC has a Regional Program for South Asia (2018–2023) to respond to the challenges faced by the region by building partnerships and bringing in place tailor-made pragmatic interventions which are result-oriented (*Regional Programme for South Asia (2018–2022)* n.d.).

Asia–Pacific Society for Alcohol and Addiction Research (APSAAR) is another foundation with 17 member countries in the Asia–Pacific region including India that endeavors to promote regional cooperation, information exchange, and research in the field of alcohol use and other substance use disorders (*Mission|APSAAR* n.d.).

12.8 Conclusions

The exploration of substance use and comorbidities in South Asia unveils a complex interplay of factors that significantly impact public health in the region. The multi-faceted nature of substance use coupled with its intricate relationship with various psychiatric and physical comorbid conditions, poses a substantial challenge for healthcare systems and policymakers alike. Factors such as poverty, lack of education, political unrest, and conflict along with challenges like immigration exacerbate the individual's vulnerability to substance use and other psychiatric conditions. The bi-directional relationship between substance use and comorbidities underscores the importance of adopting a wholesome approach that addresses both the conditions. Stigma and poor healthcare infrastructure complicate the South Asian landscape. Poor implementation of public health policies calls for a holistic plan of action on the part of national and regional agencies to combat the issue by promoting increased mental healthcare expenditure, comprehensive public health policies, and community-based interventions. Acknowledging and addressing the nuances of substance use in this region, the region should work towards building a healthier and resilient society, where nations as well as individuals are empowered to overcome the challenges posed by substance use and its comorbid conditions.

References

2015 STEPS Fact Sheet Sri Lanka. (n.d.). Retrieved January 1, 2024, from https://www.who.int/publications/m/item/2015-steps-fact-sheet-sri-lanka

Alemi, Q., Stempel, C., & Montgomery, S. (2021). Prevalence and social determinants of tobacco use in Afghanistan. *International Health, 13*(1), 3–12. https://doi.org/10.1093/inthealth/ihaa010

Ambekar, A., Agrawal, A., Rao, R., Mishra, A. K., Khandelwal, S. K., & Chadda, R. K. (2019). Magnitude of substance use in India. *New Delhi: Ministry of Social Justice and Empowerment, Government of India*.

Amundsen, M. S., Kirkeby, T. M. G., Giri, S., Koju, R., Krishna, S. S., Ystgaard, B., Solligård, E., & Risnes, K. (2016). Non-communicable diseases at a regional hospital in Nepal: Findings of a high burden of alcohol-related disease. *Alcohol (Fayetteville, N.Y.)*, *57*, 9–14. https://doi.org/10.1016/j.alcohol.2016.10.008

Awan, N., Noureen, S., & Saher, A. (2023). Prevalence of Co-Occurring Physical and Mental Health Problems in People with Drug Addiction in Pakistan. *Journal of Professional & Applied Psychology*, *4*, 478–487. https://doi.org/10.52053/jpap.v4i3.176

Bajwa, M. K., Chauhan, V. S., Nath, S., Singh, K. R., Banyal, N., & Panjrattan, C. (2023). Prevalence of alcohol dependence syndrome in the patients of acute pancreatitis: A cross-sectional study. *Industrial Psychiatry Journal*, *32*(Suppl 1), S59. https://doi.org/10.4103/ipj.ipj_195_23

Balhara, Y. P. S., Ghosh, A., Sarkar, S., Mahadevan, J., Pal, A., Narasimha, V. L., Kattula, D., Prasad, S., Parmar, A., Kathiresan, P., Basu, A., Bhatia, G., Shah, R., Dhagudu, N. K., Tripathi, R., & Bharadwaj, B. (2022). Clinical care of patients with dual disorders in India: Diverse models of care delivery. *Advances in Dual Diagnosis*, *15*(4), 227–243. https://doi.org/10.1108/ADD-09-2022-0025

Balhara, Y. P. S., Gupta, R., & Lal, R. (2016). Time trend for substance use disorder and psychiatric disorders among patients seeking treatment from a dual diagnosis clinic of a tertiary care substance use disorder treatment centre in India. *ASEAN Journal of Psychiatry*, *17*(2), 1–5. https://www.aseanjournalofpsychiatry.org/abstract/time-trend-for-substance-use-disorder-andrnpsychiatric-disorders-among-patientsrnseeking-treatment-from-a-dual-diagnosis-53464.html

Balhara, Y. P. S., Sarkar, S., Bera, S. C., Gupta, R., Chawla, N., & Lal, R. (2017). Who Seeks Treatment for Dual Disorders? Observations from a Dual Disorder Clinic at the National Drug Dependence Treatment Centre in India Over a 12 Year Period. *International Journal of High Risk Behaviors and Addiction*, *6*(1), Article 1. https://doi.org/10.5812/ijhrba.32501

Basu, D., Sarkar, S., & Mattoo, S. K. (2013). Psychiatric Comorbidity in Patients With Substance Use Disorders Attending an Addiction Treatment Center in India Over 11 Years: Case for a Specialized "Dual Diagnosis Clinic." *Journal of Dual Diagnosis*, *9*(1), 23–29. https://doi.org/10.1080/15504263.2012.749557

Batki, S. L., Meszaros, Z. S., Strutynski, K., Dimmock, J. A., Leontieva, L., Ploutz-Snyder, R., Canfield, K., & Drayer, R. A. (2009). Medical comorbidity in patients with schizophrenia and alcohol dependence. *Schizophrenia Research*, *107*(2–3), 139–146. https://doi.org/10.1016/j.schres.2008.10.016

Buckley, P. F. (2006). Prevalence and consequences of the dual diagnosis of substance abuse and severe mental illness. *The Journal of Clinical Psychiatry*, *67 Suppl 7*, 5–9.

Budhathoki, P., Shrestha, D. B., Sedhai, Y. R., Baniya, R., Bhatt, A., Chaudhary, K., Acharya, A., Rajkarnikar, R., Basnet, M., & Atreya, A. (2022). Prevalence and Risk Factors of COPD in Nepal: A Systematic Review and Meta-Analysis. *Journal of Nepal Health Research Council*, *19*(4), 652–660. https://doi.org/10.33314/jnhrc.v19i04.3543

Chhetri, B., Dem, U., Letho, Z., Tshering, K., & Skodlar, B. (2023). Prevalence of major depressive disorder in adult patients with alcohol use disorder admitted in the psychiatric ward at the Jigme Dorji Wangchuck National Referral Hospital, Thimphu, Bhutan. *Population Medicine*, *5*(May), 1–8. https://doi.org/10.18332/popmed/166187

Collaborators, G. 2019 M. D. (2022). Global, regional, and national burden of 12 mental disorders in 204 countries and territories, 1990–2019: A systematic analysis for the Global Burden of Disease Study 2019. *The Lancet Psychiatry*, *9*(2), 137–150.

Colombo Plan | International Society of Substance Use Professionals. (n.d.). Retrieved January 12, 2024, from https://www.issup.net/about-issup/international-partners/colombo-plan

Crime United Nations Office on Drugs. (2013). *National drug use survey: Maldives 2011/2012*.

Crime (Vienna), U. N. O. on drugs and. (2009). *2008 World drug report*.

Das, A., Gjerde, H., Gopalan, S. S., & Normann, P. T. (2012). Alcohol, drugs, and road traffic crashes in India: A systematic review. *Traffic Injury Prevention*, *13*(6), 544–553. https://doi.org/10.1080/15389588.2012.663518

Degenhardt, L., Webb, P., Colledge-Frisby, S., Ireland, J., Wheeler, A., Ottaviano, S., Willing, A., Kairouz, A., Cunningham, E. B., Hajarizadeh, B., Leung, J., Tran, L. T., Price, O., Peacock,

A., Vickerman, P., Farrell, M., Dore, G. J., Hickman, M., & Grebely, J. (2023). Epidemiology of injecting drug use, prevalence of injecting-related harm, and exposure to behavioural and environmental risks among people who inject drugs: A systematic review. *The Lancet. Global Health, 11*(5), e659–e672. https://doi.org/10.1016/S2214-109X(23)00057-8

Elkholy, H., Tay Wee Teck, J., Arunogiri, S., Asaad, M. R., Baessler, F., Bhad, R., Borghi, E. N., Busse, A., Ekhtiari, H., & Dave, S. (2023). Substance Use Disorders Among Forcibly Displaced People: A Narrative Review. *Current Addiction Reports*, 1–12. https://doi.org/10.1007/s40429-023-00467-6

Final_SAARC-Epidemiological-Response-on-HIVAIDS-_2022.pdf. (n.d.). Retrieved January 14, 2024, from https://www.saarctb.org/wp-content/uploads/2022/12/Final_SAARC-Epidemiological-Response-on-HIVAIDS-_2022.pdf

Ganesh, S., Kandasamy, A., Sahayaraj, U. S., & Benegal, V. (2017). Adult Attention Deficit Hyperactivity Disorder in Patients with Substance Use Disorders: A Study from Southern India. *Indian Journal of Psychological Medicine, 39*(1), 59–62. https://doi.org/10.4103/0253-7176.198945

Garg, R., Chavan, B., & Arun, P. (2012). Stigma and discrimination: How do persons with psychiatric disorders and substance dependence view themselves. *Indian Journal of Social Psychiatry, 28*, 3–4.

GATS Report Final-2017_20 MB.pdf. (n.d.). Retrieved January 1, 2024, from https://ntcc.gov.bd/ntcc/uploads/editor/files/GATS%20Report%20Final-2017_20%20MB.PDF

Ghosh, A., Mahintamani, T., Premkumar, M., Basu, D., Singh, V., Duseja, A., Subodh Bn, null, Mohindra, R., Sharma, A., & Arora, S. K. (2023). Multidisciplinary and Integrated Treatment for Substance Use Disorders and Hepatitis C in an Addiction Treatment Service in India. *Indian Journal of Psychological Medicine, 45*(2), 193–197. https://doi.org/10.1177/02537176221086013

Global, L. (2015). Afghanistan National Drug Use Survey. *Afghanistan National Drug Use Survey*.

Global-Adult-Tobacco-Survey-Second-Round-India-2016–2017.pdf. (n.d.). Retrieved January 1, 2024, from https://ntcp.mohfw.gov.in/assets/document/surveys-reports-publications/Global-Adult-Tobacco-Survey-Second-Round-India-2016-2017.pdf

Goel, A., Seguy, N., & Aggarwal, R. (2019). Burden of hepatitis C virus infection in India: A systematic review and meta-analysis. *Journal of Gastroenterology and Hepatology, 34*(2), 321–329.

Grebely, J., Larney, S., Peacock, A., Colledge, S., Leung, J., Hickman, M., Vickerman, P., Blach, S., Cunningham, E. B., & Dumchev, K. (2019). Global, regional, and country-level estimates of hepatitis C infection among people who have recently injected drugs. *Addiction, 114*(1), 150–166.

Grover, S., & Avasthi, A. (2018). Consultation-liaison psychiatry services: A survey of medical institutes in India. *Indian Journal of Psychiatry, 60*(3), 300–306. https://doi.org/10.4103/psychiatry.IndianJPsychiatry_256_17

Gupta, S., Hendricks, S., Kenkel, A. M., Bhatia, S. C., & Haffke, E. A. (1996). Relapse in schizophrenia: Is there a relationship to substance abuse? *Schizophrenia Research, 20*(1–2), 153–156. https://doi.org/10.1016/0920-9964(95)00108-5

Gurung, M. S., Pelzom, D., Dorji, T., Drukpa, W., Wangdi, C., Chinnakali, P., & Goel, S. (2016). Current tobacco use and its associated factors among adults in a country with comprehensive ban on tobacco: Findings from the nationally representative STEPS survey, Bhutan, 2014. *Population Health Metrics, 14*, 28. https://doi.org/10.1186/s12963-016-0098-9

Hapangama, A., Kuruppuarachchi, K. a. L. A., & Pathmeswaran, A. (2013). Substance use disorders among mentally ill patients in a General Hospital in Sri Lanka: Prevalence and correlates. *The Ceylon Medical Journal, 58*(3), 111–115. https://doi.org/10.4038/cmj.v58i3.6103

Hendrickson, R., Nishanth, J. H., & Michael, S. (2019). Diagnostic prevalence of common psychiatric comorbidities of alcohol use disorders in India: A systematic review. *International Journal of Mental Health and Addiction, 17*, 1268–1296. https://doi.org/10.1007/s11469-018-9951-3

Karki, S., Laukkanen, E., Länsimies, H., Tuomainen, T.-P., & Pietilä, A.-M. (2019). Substance use and associated emotional and behavioral problems in Nepalese adolescents. *Journal of Substance Use*, *24*(3), 300–308. https://doi.org/10.1080/14659891.2018.1562576

Kathriarachchi, S., Seneviratne, V., & Amarakoon, L. (2019). Development of mental health care in Sri Lanka: Lessons learned. *Taiwanese Journal of Psychiatry*, *33*, 55. https://doi.org/10.4103/TPSY.TPSY_15_19

Kerfoot, K. E., Rosenheck, R. A., Petrakis, I. L., Swartz, M. S., Keefe, R. S. E., McEvoy, J. P., Stroup, T. S., & CATIE Investigators. (2011). Substance use and schizophrenia: Adverse correlates in the CATIE study sample. *Schizophrenia Research*, *132*(2–3), 177–182. https://doi.org/10.1016/j.schres.2011.07.032

Khan, N. M., Mullick, M., & Hussain, S. (2021). Psychiatric Comorbidity Among Adolescents with Substance Use Disorder. *American Journal of Psychiatry and Neuroscience*, *9*, 98. https://doi.org/10.11648/j.ajpn.20210903.14

Khanal, K., Poudel, S., Ghimire, A., Regmi, A., Khadka, B., Bist, M., Shrestha, S. K., Sharma, R., & Shrestha, U. K. (2023). A study on demographic and clinicopathological characteristics of severe acute pancreatitis in a tertiary-level intensive care unit in Nepal. *Journal of Advances in Internal Medicine*, *12*(1), Article 1. https://doi.org/10.3126/jaim.v12i1.56675

Kovess-Masfety, V., Karam, E., Keyes, K., Sabawoon, A., & Sarwari, B. A. (2021). Access to Care for Mental Health Problems in Afghanistan: A National Challenge. *International Journal of Health Policy and Management*, *11*(8), 1442–1450. https://doi.org/10.34172/ijhpm.2021.46

Luitel, N. P., Jordans, M. J., Adhikari, A., Upadhaya, N., Hanlon, C., Lund, C., & Komproe, I. H. (2015). Mental health care in Nepal: Current situation and challenges for development of a district mental health care plan. *Conflict and Health*, *9*(1), 3. https://doi.org/10.1186/s13031-014-0030-5

Mahara Rawal, N., Pradhan, M., Prasad Adhikari, S., & Manandhar, P. (2021). Personality Disorders among Patients with Mental and Behavioral Disorders due to Psychoactive Substance Use in a Tertiary Care Center of Nepal: A Descriptive Cross-sectional Study. *JNMA; Journal of the Nepal Medical Association*, *59*(234), 184–187. https://doi.org/10.31729/jnma.6176

Malik, K., Chand, P. K., Marimuthu, P., & Suman, L. N. (2017). Addiction severity and comorbidity among women with alcohol use disorders: A hospital-based study from India. *Asian Journal of Psychiatry*, *28*, 67–72. https://doi.org/10.1016/j.ajp.2017.03.028

Martinello, M., Amin, J., Matthews, G. V., & Dore, G. J. (2016). Prevalence and Disease Burden of HCV Coinfection in HIV Cohorts in the Asia Pacific Region: A Systematic Review and Meta-Analysis. *AIDS Reviews*, *18*(2), 68–80.

Mental Health ATLAS 2020. (n.d.). Retrieved January 1, 2024, from https://www.who.int/publications-detail-redirect/9789240036703

Mental Health for All: Leaving no one behind. (n.d.). Retrieved January 10, 2024, from https://www.unicef.org/bhutan/press-releases/mental-health-all-leaving-no-one-behind

Mission | APSAAR. (n.d.). Retrieved January 13, 2024, from https://www.apsaar.org/mission.html

Modi, L., Gedam, S. R., Shivji, I. A., Babar, V., & Patil, P. S. (2018). Comparison of Total Self-Stigma Between Schizophrenia and Alcohol Dependence Patients. *International Journal of High Risk Behaviors and Addiction*, *7*(3), Article 3. https://doi.org/10.5812/ijhrba.61043

Mueser, K. T., Drake, R. E., & Wallach, M. A. (1998). Dual diagnosis: A review of etiological theories. *Addictive Behaviors*, *23*(6), 717–734.

Mukherjee, P. S., Vishnubhatla, S., Amarapurkar, D. N., Das, K., Sood, A., Chawla, Y. K., Eapen, C. E., Boddu, P., Thomas, V., Varshney, S., Hidangmayum, D. S., Bhaumik, P., Thakur, B., Acharya, S. K., & Chowdhury, A. (2017). Etiology and mode of presentation of chronic liver diseases in India: A multi centric study. *PloS One*, *12*(10), e0187033. https://doi.org/10.1371/journal.pone.0187033

Murthy, R. S. (2017). National mental health survey of India 2015–2016. *Indian Journal of Psychiatry*, *59*(1), 21.

Nagaratnam, N., & Gunawardene, K. R. W. (1972). Aetiological factors in pancreatic calcification in Ceylon. *Digestion*, *5*(1), 9–16.

Nagaratnam, N., Ramachandra, V., Jiffry, A. J., & Bhuvanendran, N. (1984). Primary liver cancer in Sri Lanka. *The Journal of Tropical Medicine and Hygiene, 87*(4), 185–187.

National_Drug_Use_Survey_-_Report.pdf. (n.d.). Retrieved January 1, 2024, from https://www.unodc.org/documents/southasia/reports/National_Drug_Use_Survey_-_Report.pdf

National-Framework-for-Joint-TB-Tobacco-Collaborative-Activities.pdf. (n.d.). Retrieved January 13, 2024, from https://ntcp.mohfw.gov.in/assets/document/surveys-reports-publications/National-Framework-for-Joint-TB-Tobacco-Collaborative-Activities.pdf

Nepal Drug Users Survey: 2076. (2020). Government of Nepal, Ministry of Home Affairs. https://books.google.co.in/books?id=wt_XzwEACAAJ

Neupane, S. P. (2011). *Prevalence and correlates of major depression and anxiety disorders among patients with alcohol-use disorders in Nepal.*

Organization, W. H. (2019). *National mental health survey of Bangladesh, 2018–19: Provisional fact sheet.*

Pak.pdf. (n.d.). Retrieved January 1, 2024, from https://cdn.who.int/media/docs/default-source/country-profiles/substances-abuse/pak.pdf?sfvrsn=a5d212f2_3&download=true

Pant, S. B., Thapa, S. B., Howard, J., Ojha, S. P., & Lien, L. (2022). Mental disorders and suicidality among Opioid Agonist Treatment service users in Nepal: A cross sectional study. *SSM - Mental Health, 2*, 100165. https://doi.org/10.1016/j.ssmmh.2022.100165

Patel, S., Ram, F., Parry, C., & Patel, S. K. (2020). Associations of alcohol consumption with chronic diseases, lifestyle behaviors and socioeconomic-demographic characteristics in India. *International Journal of Alcohol and Drug Research, 8*(1), Article 1. https://doi.org/10.7895/ijadr.259

Ramachandran, S., Lahie, Y. K. M., Herath, C. A., & Thenabadu, P. N. (1986). Recent aspects of alcoholism in Sri Lanka—An increasing health hazard. *Alcohol and Alcoholism, 21*(4), 397–402. https://doi.org/10.1093/oxfordjournals.alcalc.a044647

Rao, R., George, A. B., & Chadda, R. K. (2020). Consultation Liaison Addiction Psychiatry: An Evolving Discipline. *Cover Designed by Dr Koushik Sinha Deb*, 139.

Rathod, S. D., Luitel, N. P., & Jordans, M. J. D. (2018). Prevalence and correlates of alcohol use in a central Nepal district: Secondary analysis of a population-based cross-sectional study. *Global Mental Health (Cambridge, England), 5*, e37. https://doi.org/10.1017/gmh.2018.28

Regional Programme for South Asia (2018–2022). (n.d.). Retrieved January 12, 2024, from https://www.unodc.org/southasia/en/topics/frontpage/2009/regional-programme-for-south-asia-2018-2021.html

Saini, R., Parmar, A., Rao, R., Mishra, A. K., Ambekar, A., & Agrawal, A. (2021). Psychiatric and Substance Use Comorbidities among People who Inject Drugs in India: A Cross-Sectional, Community-Based Study. *World Social Psychiatry, 3*(3), 195–202.

Setshedi, M., Wands, J. R., & de la Monte, S. M. (2010). Acetaldehyde adducts in alcoholic liver disease. *Oxidative Medicine and Cellular Longevity, 3*(3), 178–185. https://doi.org/10.4161/oxim.3.3.3

Shah, S. M., Sun, T., Xu, W., Jiang, W., & Yuan, Y. (2022). The mental health of China and Pakistan, mental health laws and COVID-19 mental health policies: A comparative review. *General Psychiatry, 35*(5), e100885. https://doi.org/10.1136/gpsych-2022-100885

Sharma, M., Gora, B. A., Kulkarni, A., Soumya, T. R., Shaik, S., Jagtap, N., Alla, M., Gupta, R., Archana, C., & Qadri, S. (2023). The Pattern of Alcohol Use in Alcohol-Related Cirrhosis in Indian Patients: AUDIT Indian Liver Study. *Journal of Clinical and Experimental Hepatology, 13*(3), 437–446.

Solomon, S. S., Lucas, G. M., Celentano, D. D., McFall, A. M., Ogburn, E., Moulton, L. H., Srikrishnan, A. K., Kumar, M. S., Anand, S., Solomon, S., & Mehta, S. H. (2016). Design of the Indian NCA study (Indian national collaboration on AIDS): A cluster randomized trial to evaluate the effectiveness of integrated care centers to improve HIV outcomes among men who have sex with men and persons who inject drugs in India. *BMC Health Services Research, 16*(1), 652. https://doi.org/10.1186/s12913-016-1905-5

Stanikzai, M. H., & Wahidi, M. W. (2023). Bio-Psycho-Social Profile of People with Substance Use Disorders Treated in Locally Assigned Treatment Facilities in Kandahar, Afghanistan. *Substance Abuse and Rehabilitation, 14*, 89–98. https://doi.org/10.2147/SAR.S412821

Steps-2015-survey-tobacco-fact-sheet-sri-lanka.pdf. (n.d.). Retrieved January 1, 2024, from https://cdn.who.int/media/docs/default-source/ncds/ncd-surveillance/data-reporting/sri-lanka/steps/steps-2015-survey-tobacco-fact-sheet-sri-lanka.pdf?sfvrsn=23f7c803_5&download=true

Strategies—National AIDS Control Programme. (n.d.). Retrieved January 13, 2024, from https://nacp.gov.pk/howwework/strategies.html

Subodh, B. N., Hazari, N., Elwadhi, D., & Basu, D. (2017). Prevalence of dual diagnosis among clinic attending patients in a de-addiction centre of a tertiary care hospital. *Asian Journal of Psychiatry, 25*, 169–174. https://doi.org/10.1016/j.ajp.2016.10.020

Subodh, B. N., Sahoo, S., Basu, D., & Mattoo, S. K. (2019). Age of onset of substance use in patients with dual diagnosis and its association with clinical characteristics, risk behaviors, course, and outcome: A retrospective study. *Indian Journal of Psychiatry, 61*(4), 359–368. https://doi.org/10.4103/psychiatry.IndianJPsychiatry_454_18

Thakur, J. S., Garg, R., Narain, J. P., & Menabde, N. (2011). Tobacco Use: A Major Risk Factor for Non Communicable Diseases in South-East Asia Region. *Indian Journal of Public Health, 55*(3), 155. https://doi.org/10.4103/0019-557X.89943

Tobacco Control in the South-East Asia Region. (n.d.). Retrieved December 31, 2023, from https://www.who.int/southeastasia/health-topics/tobacco/tobacco-control-in-the-south-east-asia-region

Tobacco-Fact-Sheet-1.pdf. (n.d.). Retrieved January 1, 2024, from https://nhrc.gov.np/wp-content/uploads/2019/11/Tobacco-Fact-Sheet-1.pdf

Tripathi, R., Singh, S., & Bhad, R. (2020). The need, scope, challenges, and potential solutions for enhancing addiction psychiatry training in India. *Indian Journal of Psychiatry, 62*(6), 728–731. https://doi.org/10.4103/psychiatry.IndianJPsychiatry_355_19

Trivedi, J. K., Goel, D., Kallivayalil, R. A., Isaac, M., Shrestha, D. M., & Gambheera, H. C. (2007). Regional cooperation in South Asia in the field of mental health. *World Psychiatry, 6*(1), 57. https://www.ncbi.nlm.nih.gov/pmc/articles/PMC1805715/

Verma, A., Gudi, N., Yadav, U. N., Roy, M. P., Mahmood, A., Nagaraja, R., & Nayak, P. (2021). Prevalence of COPD among population above 30 years in India: A systematic review and meta-analysis. *Journal of Global Health, 11*, 04038. https://doi.org/10.7189/jogh.11.04038

Vltwo5kq.pdf. (n.d.). Retrieved January 1, 2024, from https://health.gov.mv/storage/uploads/2ywDEKYN/vltwo5kq.pdf

Wangdi, K., & Jamtsho, T. (2019). Prevalence and Correlates of Current Alcohol Use among Bhutanese Adults: A Nationally Representative Survey Data Analysis. *Indian Journal of Psychological Medicine, 41*(1), 38–45. https://doi.org/10.4103/IJPSYM.IJPSYM_412_18

Wittchen, H. U. (1996). Critical issues in the evaluation of comorbidity of psychiatric disorders. *The British Journal of Psychiatry. Supplement, 30*, 9–16.

Wu, L.-T., Zhu, H., & Ghitza, U. E. (2018). Multicomorbidity of chronic diseases and substance use disorders and their association with hospitalization: Results from electronic health records data. *Drug and Alcohol Dependence, 192*, 316–323. https://doi.org/10.1016/j.drugalcdep.2018.08.013

Chapter 13
Addiction Research in South Asia

Aishwariya Jha, Abhishek Kumar Sharma, and Jayant Mahadevan

13.1 Introduction

South Asia is a region of unparalleled diversity in terms of geography, history, culture, and traditions (Wadley 2014). Politically, it has governance models ranging from democratic to authoritarian regimes. Economically, it has some of the world's fastest-growing economies, but also areas of significant underdevelopment and poverty (Smith 2015). The definition of the South Asian region varies across different literature sources. However, for this discussion, we will define the nations of South Asia as those that are members of the South Asian Association for Regional Cooperation (SAARC). This includes Afghanistan, Bangladesh, Bhutan, India, Maldives, Nepal, Pakistan, and Sri Lanka, which together constitute close to one-fourth of the world's population (Arafat and Kar 2024).

There is a long history of the use of psychoactive substances, such as alcohol, cannabis, and opium among the countries of South Asia, for recreational, religious, and medicinal purposes (Murthy 2015; Touw 1981). It is also a hub for heroin trafficking due to its proximity to the Golden Crescent and the Golden Triangle, the world's largest cultivators of illicit opium (UNODC 2005) and has also seen a rise in the production and trafficking of amphetamine-type stimulants (United Nations Office on Drugs and Crime 2022). In recent years, it has also seen a trend of synthetic drugs replacing natural and semi-synthetic ones and an increase in the misuse of pharmaceutical drugs diverted from legal sources.

The public spending on health in South Asia is low and the public spending on mental health and addictions is less than 1% of health budgets. A minuscule proportion of this goes to research on mental health and addictions, as evidenced by the research output when compared to the rest of the world (Grover 2023). Several studies

A. Jha · A. K. Sharma · J. Mahadevan (✉)
Department of Psychiatry, NIMHANS, Bangalore, India
e-mail: jayantmahadevan@gmail.com

S. M. Y. Arafat and S. K. Kar (eds.), *Current Perspectives on Substance Use Disorders in South Asia*, https://doi.org/10.1007/978-981-97-6619-2_13

have noted the dearth of research in the region making it difficult for policymakers to make informed policy decisions (Lemon et al. 2023; Murthy et al. 2010).

With this background, this chapter will summarize key findings of research from South Asia on SUD. While the majority of studies are from India, the chapter will try to focus more on studies from other South Asian countries.

13.2 Epidemiological Research on Substance Use Disorders in South Asian Countries

There are several studies from the region on the prevalence and patterns of use, although nationally representative estimates are not available in all cases. The rates of substance use disorders surpass many global averages, indicating a substantial burden in this region. A recent systematic review and meta-analysis in South Asia reported the rates of alcohol use, tobacco smoking, tobacco chewing, cannabis use, opioid use, IV drug use, and stimulant use to be 12.9%, 18.6%, 21%, 3.4%, 0.8%, 2.5%, and 0.9%, respectively (Naveed et al. 2020). However, the studies included for review were heterogeneous in their type of settings, methods, and instruments. Table 13.1 lists a selection of recent population-level epidemiological research on addiction from South Asia.

Alcohol and tobacco are the most commonly used substances in India, Nepal, Bhutan, and Sri Lanka, while cannabis and opioids are seen to be more prevalent in Afghanistan, Pakistan, Bangladesh, and Maldives, where there is a strong cultural proscription of alcohol use. Polysubstance use, characterized by the consumption of more than one psychoactive substance, has emerged as a significant public health concern in South Asia (Mandal et al. 2023). Studies have found that a significant proportion of injecting drug users (IDU) in countries like India, Pakistan, and Nepal engage in polysubstance use, often combining opioids with benzodiazepines, cannabis, and other substances. This practice not only increases the risk of overdose but also exacerbates the potential for spreading infectious diseases such as HIV and hepatitis (Bertholet et al. 2023). In many instances, users combine drugs to enhance the desired effects, manage the adverse effects of withdrawal, or self-medicate for underlying psychiatric conditions (Boileau-Falardeau et al. 2022). Studies have also shown that the combination of alcohol and tobacco is quite common, with many users engaging in dual use, which is associated with increased health risks (Krishna Rao et al. 2013).

Table 13.1 Landmark epidemiological research on addiction in South Asian countries and their major findings

Sl. No.	Country	Author, year	Methods	Results
1	Afghanistan	Afghanistan National Drug Use Survey (ANDUS) (Wankel et al. 2015)	A national urban and rural toxicological and self-report survey that covered 24 provinces, over 2000 households, and over 10,000 people including women and children	• 2.5–2.9 million people (11% of the population) use drugs • 1.9–2.3 million use opiates (7% of the population) and 0.9–1.1 million use cannabis • Drug use is present in 31% of all households, including 11% in urban centers and 39% in rural areas
		Afghanistan National Urban Drug Use Survey (ANUDUS) (Cottler et al. 2014)	Household sample survey of 19, 025 participants	• Opioids were the most prevalent drugs in biological samples • Prescription medications were the most commonly reported used substances in the past month • Opioids were the most common substance detected in women and children • Cannabinoids were the most common substance detected in males The individual prevalence of substance use was 7.2% in men and 3.1% in women • National prevalence was 5.1% and prevalence in Kabul was 5%

(continued)

Table 13.1 (continued)

Sl. No.	Country	Author, year	Methods	Results
2	Bangladesh	Mohit et al. (2018)	Review of 15 studies in Bangladesh on addiction from 2010 to 2018. Most of the studies were conducted in clinical settings in urban areas	• The mean age of the respondents was 28.10 years. The majority were males, unmarried, and from urban dwellings • About 67%, 44%, and 39% of respondents considered heroin, yaba, and cannabis as their drugs of choice, respectively
		Alam et al. (2020)	A two-stage national multicentric community-based cross-sectional study by the NIMH (2017–2018)	• The prevalence of substance use was 3.3% in adults with a prevalence of 4.8% in males and 0.6% in females The most frequent substances of abuse included Cannabis (42.7%), alcohol (27.5%), Yaba (15.2%), Opioids (5.3%), and sedatives (3.4%)
		Dewan and Chowdhury (2015)	Narrative review	Prevalence of alcohol consumption is 3.8%, heavy drinking is 20.2%, and dependence is 0.7%
3	Bhutan	Wangdi and Jamtsho (2019)	Data from the National Health Survey 2012 of Bhutan. A questionnaire was developed using the WHO STEPwise approach	The prevalence of lifetime drug use among teenagers and young adults was 3.2% (n = 672) • Prevalence of alcohol consumption is 30.9% • Male, single, 18–24 years, alcohol and cigarette smoking were some of the factors associated with ever drug use

(continued)

Table 13.1 (continued)

Sl. No.	Country	Author, year	Methods	Results
4	India	National Survey on Extent and Pattern of Substance Use in India (2019) (Ambekar et al. 2019)	Household sample survey of 10–75 years population—4,73,569 individuals from 186 districts were interviewed Respondent-driven sampling survey—72,642 from 135 districts for illicit drugs	• Alcohol is the most common substance used (14.6% or 16 crore people), with higher use in men (27.3%) compared to women (1.6%) • About 2% or 2.2 crore people use bhang (legal form of cannabis), and 1.2% or 1.3 crore people use illegal cannabis products • About 2.1% or 2.26 crore people use opioids, the most common of which is Heroin (1.14%) • 2.7% of the general population or 19% of current users of alcohol are dependent on alcohol. Another 2.5% of the general population consumes alcohol in a harmful pattern • 8.5 lakh individuals inject on drugs (IDU)—most of whom inject opioids • Only 1 in 38 people with alcohol dependence report getting help with alcohol problems • Only one in four individuals dependent on illicit drugs has ever received treatment

(continued)

Table 13.1 (continued)

Sl. No.	Country	Author, year	Methods	Results
		Nadkarni (2018)	A systematic review of 52 papers on alcohol use among adolescents in India	Prevalence of ever-use and lifetime use of alcohol ranged from 3.9 to 69.8%. Prevalence of alcohol consumption at least once in the past year ranged from 10.6 to 32.9%. The mean age of initiation was from 14 to 18 years. Factors associated with alcohol use included male, older age, parental use, abuse, and academic difficulties
		National Mental Health Survey, 2015–2016. (Gururaj et al. 2016)	Multi-stage, stratified, random cluster sampling, with random selection based on probability proportionate to size at each stage. ICD 10 diagnostic criteria for research was used	Prevalence of alcohol use disorders is 4.7%, tobacco use disorders is 20.9%, and other substances 0.6%. The treatment gap for alcohol use disorder is 86.3%, and for tobacco use disorder is about 92%. The median amount spent for care and treatment is 2250 rupees for alcohol use disorder
		Eashwar et al. (2020)	Epidemiological review of alcohol use in various parts of India	Prevalence of alcohol consumption: 16.8–65.8% Hazardous and harmful use of alcohol: 14–52.5% Dependent users: 2.6–14.7%

(continued)

Table 13.1 (continued)

Sl. No.	Country	Author, year	Methods	Results
5	Maldives	National Drug Use Survey Maldives 2011–2012 (UNODC 2013)	Household survey, multiplier survey, and qualitative analysis	• Number of drug users was 3,154 (2.02%) and 4342 (6.64%) in the Atolls and Malé, respectively, with majority of the users being males and between ages 15 and 19 • Alcohol, cannabis, and opioids were the most common substances used in the country • The number of injecting drug users were 200–300 • In the Atolls the highest number of problem drug users were among opioid users (66%)
		Fallati et al. (2020)	Wastewater-based epidemiology. Raw wastewater 12 h composite samples were collected from nine pumping stations serving the city area. Samples were analyzed by liquid chromatography coupled to mass spectrometry for estimating the profile of use of a large number of substances including illicit drugs, alcohol, caffeine, tobacco, and pharmaceuticals	The illicit drugs most used were cannabis (THC) and heroin (700 and 18 g/day), with lower consumption of cocaine and amphetamines (0.1–1.2 g/day). Consumption of alcohol, which is not allowed in Maldives, was found (1.3 L/day/ 1000 inhabitants)

(continued)

Table 13.1 (continued)

Sl. No.	Country	Author, year	Methods	Results
6	Nepal	Chapagain et al. (2020)	• A cross-sectional study from July 2018 to December 2018 • Self-administered structured questionnaire • 1125 higher secondary school students	• Prevalence of ever users of tobacco were 46.04% of which the current users were 20.46%, ever users of alcohol were 37.58% of which 15.20% were current users and ever users of drugs was 18.19% of which 18.13% were current users • More than half of the drug users (50.71%) used cannabis
		Poudel et al. (2016)	Cross-sectional descriptive study in drug rehabilitation centers in Kathmandu. Tool used was drug use screening inventory-revised	About 54% of respondents initiated substance use between ages 15 and 19 Approximately 75% of the respondents used alcohol, 56% cannabis, 47% opiates, 37% sedatives, and 10% stimulants Over 59% of participants used substances >3 times/day
		Nepal National Mental Health Survey, 2020 (Jha et al. 2020)	Survey from 2019 to 2020 with a sample size of over 15,000 from 7 provinces	Alcohol use disorders: 4.2% Other substance use disorders: 0.2%
7	Pakistan	Ghazal (2019)	• Cross-sectional survey • Semi-structured questionnaire • Rehabilitation settings • Sample size 102 • Only males	• A third of the participants initiated drug abuse in their teenage years • Heroin was the most abused substance (48%) followed by Cannabis (28%)

(continued)

Table 13.1 (continued)

Sl. No.	Country	Author, year	Methods	Results
		Drug Use Report, UNODC (2013)	• National survey • Age 15–64 • Four provinces • Sample: 4533 high-risk drug users, 58 drug treatment center representatives, 1,198 key informants; and 51,453 participants randomly selected from the general population	• Six percent of the population, i.e., 6.7 million had used any controlled drug in the past year • Over 4 million people were considered dependent on substances and require treatment • Cannabis was the most commonly used drug (4 million users) • Around 860,000 people used heroin regularly. The number of people who inject drugs was estimated to be 430,000 nationwide (0.4%) • 19,000 people reported they had used methamphetamine • 1.6 million people reported misuse of prescription opioids for non-medical use
		Jamal et al. (2022)	• Cross-sectional survey • 600 prisoners in Karachi • Instrument: WHO ASSIST version 3	• About 97% of prisoners had a lifetime history of substance abuse • For tobacco, 80.5% of prisoners were at moderate risk of use • For opioids, 13% were at high risk, 12.7, and 9.5% of prisoners were at high risk for using cannabis, and tobacco, respectively

(continued)

Table 13.1 (continued)

Sl. No.	Country	Author, year	Methods	Results
8	Sri Lanka	Jayamaha et al. (2022)	A descriptive cross-sectional study was conducted among 205 individual rehabilitation centers	Cannabis was the most commonly used illicit drug (89.3%) followed by heroin (83.9%), methamphetamine (73.2%), and cocaine (38%). The most (n = 152, 74.1%) problematic substance for life was heroin
		National Prevalence Survey on Drug Use, 2019 (National Dangerous Drugs Control Board 2019)	Sample surveys/domestic surveys (direct methods) and benchmark multiplier, capture re-capture methods (indirect methods)	2,406,581 cigarette/ tobacco products users, 3,035,143 alcohol users, 92,540 users of heroin, 301,898 users of cannabis, 24,211 users of prescription tablets Only 7% of the drug using population have been admitted for treatment or rehabilitation The most common illicit drug of abuse is cannabis followed by heroin

13.3 Research on Neurobiology of Addiction in South Asia

The research on neurobiology of addiction from South Asia has been conducted largely in India and limited to a few centers where facilities to conduct such research are available. In this section, we will review some of the important studies pertaining to genetics, epigenetics, neuroimaging, and electrophysiology of addiction from South Asia.

13.3.1 Genetics

A few Indian studies have used a candidate gene approach to investigate the genetic associations of alcohol, nicotine, and opioid-related phenotypes. The first study from India studied the association between Taq 1a polymorphism in the DRD2 gene and early onset of alcohol dependence, but found no difference in frequency of the polymorphism between cases and controls (Shaikh et al. 2001). A study among two culturally distinct tribal communities in South India found that the DAT1 VNTR was significantly associated with AD in the Badaga population but not in the Kota population (Bhaskar et al. 2012). The same group also found an association between three polymorphisms in the DRD2 gene and polymorphisms in the EPHX1 gene and AD in the Kota population (Bhaskar et al. 2010, 2013). A study from North India investigated the association between rs1229984 in ADH1B and rs671 in ALDH2 with alcohol dependence and found that rs1229984 in ADH1B was monomorphic (minor allele frequency = 0.0014), while, somewhat surprisingly, the minor allele frequency of rs671 in ALDH2 was 0.19. The study also found that the presence of two copies of the minor allele was associated with a later age at first alcohol use, age at dependence, and a shorter duration of dependence suggesting some protection from severe forms of alcohol dependence. The presence of the typical alcohol flush reaction in these individuals was not documented (Vaswani et al. 2009). A study from Central India on a tribal population also found that the minor allele frequency of rs671 in ALDH2 was 0.21, while rs1229984 in ADH1B was monomorphic, although there was no association found with alcohol dependence (Mansoori and Jain 2018). This is in contrast to the findings from an evaluation of haplotypes of the ALDH2 locus belonging to six ethnic populations, from four linguistic groups of India, which found that there was strong linkage disequilibrium across the region (Bhaskar et al. 2007). A more recent study from North India found that rs671 in ALDH2 was monomorphic and rs2066702 in ADH1B was extremely rare, suggesting that there was no role played by these polymorphisms in the Indian population (Malhotra et al. 2016). The same study also found homozygotes at the recessive allele of the rs4680 polymorphism in COMT were at increased risk for the development of AD, while homozygotes at the recessive allele of rs279871 in GABRA2 were at reduced risk of AD. Polymorphisms in genes for serotonin transporter and cholinergic receptors were not found to contribute to the genetics of AD (Malhotra et al. 2016). A study from South India found an association between SNP rs1806201 in *N*-Methyl-D-Aspartate receptor 2B Subunit (GRIN2B) and an earlier age of alcohol withdrawal in patients with AD, suggesting the importance of glutamatergic mechanisms in the pathophysiology of AD (Paul et al. 2017). A small study from North India found that individuals carrying the A1 allele of rs1800497 in the ANKK1 gene had higher self-reported alcohol and nicotine consumption. The Fagerström test for nicotine dependence (FTND) and heaviness of smoking index (HSI) scores were up to six and four times higher among A1 allele carriers (Quraishi et al. 2017). The same group also found that the odds of consuming alcohol and nicotine were four times higher among Met allele carriers of the COMT gene. The FTND and HSI scores were also up to four and eight times higher among Met allele carriers (Quraishi et al. 2021). An interesting study from Eastern India found an association of the G allele of the SNP rs1799971 in exon1 of the human OPRM1 gene (hOPRM1), with heroin and alcohol addiction. The functional significance of the G allele in A118G single-nucleotide polymorphisms was also evaluated by studying the regulation of protein kinase A (PKA), pCREB, and pERK1/2 by morphine in Neuro 2A cells, stably transfected with either wild-type or A118G mutant hOPRM1. It was seen that, unlike acute morphine treatment, both chronic morphine exposure and withdrawal precipitated by naloxone were differentially regulated by A118 and G118 receptor isoforms when both PKA and pERK1/2 activities were compared. This suggested that the association of A118G polymorphism to heroin and alcohol addiction may be because of the altered regulation of PKA and pERK1/2 during opioid and alcohol exposures (Deb et al. 2010).

Studies from Pakistan have also shown an association between the G allele of the SNP rs1799971 in exon1 of the human OPRM1 gene (hOPRM1) and heroin addiction (Ahmed et al. 2018). An enhancer variant, rs12364283, which increases DRD2mRNA expression was also found to be significantly associated with heroin addiction (Jabeen et al. 2019). There is also a significant association of ACHE 3′UTR SNP, related to a miRNA binding site with addiction vulnerability (Javed et al. 2019).

A study from Bangladesh has suggested the role of the Catechol-O-Methyltransferase (COMT) (Val158Met) polymorphism and the Dopamine receptor D4 gene (DRD4) (120 bp tandem duplication) in patients with addiction. There was also an association with a longer duration of drug use problems (Sonia et al. 2021). There was also found to be an association between variants rs16969968 and rs578776 in the CHRNA5-A3-B4 gene cluster and smoking status (Chaity et al. 2021).

There are currently no genome-wide association studies related to addiction from South Asia and this represents a major thrust area for future research and offers a possibility for multi-center collaborations across countries in the region.

13.3.2 Epigenetics

There is extremely limited research related to epigenetics of addiction from South Asia. An Indian study of male patients with severe alcohol use disorder found that epigenetic modifications were observed to persist over 3 months of treatment. The changes observed were at the genes specific to alcohol metabolism (ALDH2) and homeostasis (MTHFR) and at global levels. The higher methylation levels of specific genes ALDH2 and MTHFR may point towards a complex regulatory mechanism among individuals at the severe end of the AUD spectrum. While lower methylation at a global level may suggest cellular adaptation to manage alcohol metabolites (Soundararajan et al. 2021). Given that there are population-specific differences in the consequences of substance use, there is a need for more studies from South Asia that focus on the role of epigenetics and gene expression changes in addiction.

13.3.3 Neuroimaging and Electrophysiology

The neuroimaging and electrophysiological studies pertaining to addiction from South Asia can be broadly divided into those conducted in individuals at high risk for development of addiction and those in individuals with established addictions.

In substance-naïve children of persons with AUD, it was seen that there was altered cortical thickness in key areas critical for executive function, emotion regulation, and social cognition during adolescence. It was also seen that these alterations were associated with externalizing symptom scores (Holla et al. 2019). Similar alterations were also observed in functional brain networks which displayed reduced clustering, small-worldness, and local network efficiency and corresponded to brain regions subserving cognitive, affective, and sensorimotor processes (Holla et al. 2017). Lower P300 amplitudes were also seen over frontal brain areas with a strong association between this reduced brain activation and an excess of externalizing behaviors (Silva et al. 2007). The utility of auditory P300 event-related potentials and neurocognitive functions as an endophenotype of addiction has also been demonstrated (Singh et al. 2009).

Two studies have described the development and testing of visual cue-induced craving paradigms for alcohol (Holla et al. 2014) and heroin (Shukla et al. 2021). These are promising tools to be able to elicit cue-induced craving and understand its neural substrates. This paradigm was used in a study where greater activation of the bilateral dorsolateral pre-frontal cortex and right anterior cingulate cortex (ACC) was seen following baclofen treatment in comparison with the control group. This increased activation of ACC and deactivation of insular cortex (IC) was associated with longer time to first alcohol use only in the baclofen treatment group but not in the control group (Holla et al. 2018). The use of the P300 auditory oddball paradigm in the midline region and visual N400 semantic incongruity task in the centro-parietal region has also been shown to be useful as a biomarker for chronicity in patients with AUD (Mishra et al. 2020).

13.4 Research on Addiction Law and Policy in South Asia

There are three broad law and policy approaches undertaken to address substance use and addictions across the world namely, supply reduction, demand reduction and harm reduction. An overview of addiction laws and policies in South Asia is covered in Chap. 10. This section will review research related to implementation challenges and effectiveness of these strategies in the countries under study.

There are a number of viewpoint articles from authors in the region on challenges around addiction law and policy. A report from Maldives identified a preponderance of law enforcement approaches, underutilized rehabilitation services, gaps in prevention strategies, and difficulties in controlling drug supply. The key reasons identified for the ineffectiveness of the policy implementation include inappropriate strategy development, inadequate stakeholder participation, ineffective monitoring and evaluation, inappropriate budget allocation and management, and lack of integration between components and actions in isolation from problem and context (Mariyam Zaahiya 2008). Two reviews from Nepal and Sri Lanka also emphasize the predominance of punitive approaches and the need to orient services more towards evidence based approaches such as prevention, demand reduction, and harm reduction (Pant et al. 2023; Patabendige 2021).

There are also a few articles which have evaluated implementation and effectiveness of policy measures in South Asia. A study from Nepal on perceptions of key stakeholders on taxation on alcohol and tobacco demonstrates that both industry and government officials felt that higher taxation has limited potential to reduce consumption of alcohol and tobacco products and may lead to more illicit trade (Acharya et al. 2023). A study from Bhutan evaluated the compliance with alcohol service laws through outlet visits, staff education, development of a toolkit, and implementation checks. The study reported that after the intervention, compliance with laws improved from 20 to 34%. Outlets with younger staff, stand-alone bars, and indoor smoking areas were less likely to comply with Bhutan's alcohol service laws (Dorji et al. 2016). Similar findings were seen in another larger study, suggesting that alcohol control requires ongoing government enforcement, supplemented by public awareness and knowledge (Gyeltshen et al. 2021). In India, the Bihar Excise Amendment Act of 2016 imposed complete prohibition on alcohol within the state of Bihar. A recent study reported a 41.78% reduction in the proportion of men consuming alcohol in the state, a reduction of about one-third among those who reported daily alcohol use, and a reduction of 69.5% in the proportion of women who reported alcohol use (Balhara et al. 2023). However, there have been criticisms about the estimated loss of revenue, employment and for being stringent (Kumar and Prakash 2016; Samanta and Narayan 2017). The National Family Health Survey (NHFS) is a large-scale survey conducted in a representative sample of households in India which provides pertinent state and national-level information on substance use, among other data. Studies evaluating the NFHS data have shown that raising the minimum legal drinking age (MLDA) decreases the prevalence of alcohol consumption, tobacco smoking, and domestic violence (Luca et al. 2019). Alcohol prohibition policies in India have also demonstrated a 40% decrease in the quantity of alcohol consumed using household expenditure data (Rahman 2003). Research on pricing of alcohol has shown that when alcohol prices rise, households spend a larger portion of their budget on alcohol, which is contrary to the assumption that price policies improve welfare (Subramanian and Kumar 2017).

Among the South Asian countries under review, Bhutan and India have successfully enforced regulations around public smoking. Bhutan is the first country in the world to impose a complete ban on the sale and consumption of tobacco products (Griffith et al. 2008). Bangladesh and Pakistan have also banned smoking in public spaces, yet the enforcement remains incomplete ("List of Smoking Bans" 2024). In spite of comprehensive legislations for tobacco control in India, only half of the states have mechanisms for smoke-free rule enforcement, less than half of the states collected penalties for public smoking violations, only three states collected fines for the violation of the section on advertisements, promotion, and sponsorship, less than half of the states have district level tobacco cessation clinics and the enforcement of a ban on the sale of tobacco to minors and within hundred yards of educational institutions are incomplete (Kaur and Jain 2011). Studies have demonstrated that the barriers hindering the success of tobacco cessation interventions include lack of awareness, societal acceptance of tobacco use, and poor implementation of anti-smoking laws (Iqbal et al. 2022). A study on 19,643 individuals from Pakistan, India, Bangladesh, and Nepal showed that adolescent males who were not exposed to anti-tobacco media messages and were not taught about the harmful effects were more likely to be current smokers than those who were (Rao et al. 2014). A community-based cross-sectional study on 389 adult past and current tobacco users in Kaski, Nepal examined the perceived effectiveness of pictorial health warning labels of various tobacco products (Budha et al. 2019). According to this study, about 12% of users wanted to quit tobacco use after seeing the pictorial health warnings.

The South Asia region has a sizeable proportion of people who inject drugs. HIV prevalence is about 20% or higher in some regions of India and Opioid Substitution therapy (OST) is an important HIV prevention intervention in this region (Reid et al. 2014). Despite an incremental growth in the knowledge of OST, increasing availability of Buprenorphine and Methadone, and wider response to the HIV epidemic through intervention packages, capacity building remains critically important (Reid et al. 2014). Moreover, regular monitoring and evaluation of the effectiveness of OST programs for this region would inform policymakers and stakeholders on how to further improve the expansion of such services. Since 2003, several non-governmental organizations offer harm reduction services in Afghanistan including needle syringe exchange programs, wound care, and first aid. However, there are challenges in implementation such as lack of resources, staff, inconsistent governmental support, and a fractured polity (Todd et al. 2012). The Colombo Plan provides abstinence based treatment facilities in Afghanistan, however, differs in ideology from harm reduction practices and treatment of dependency (Todd et al. 2012). Moreover, there continue to be shortages of Methadone despite Methadone being listed as an Essential Drug by the World Health Organization.

In summary, supply reduction has been the primary approach employed by most countries in the region for addressing issues related to substance use and addictions. The laws enacted criminalize drug use and employ a punitive approach, although some also emphasize referral to treatment as an alternative. Research into the effectiveness of these approaches is limited. Demand reduction approaches, including prevention, early identification, and treatment have also been employed and will be reviewed in the subsequent sections. Harm reduction approaches have been under-utilized and this remains a matter of concern.

13.5 Research on Interventions for Addictions and Outcomes from South Asia

There have been a number of studies testing pharmacological and psychosocial interventions for the treatment of addictions in South Asia. These studies are largely from India, once again underlining the need for more support for such studies in other countries.

13.5.1 Pharmacological Interventions

There have been a number of studies that have evaluated the use of anti-craving agents such as Naltrexone, Acamprosate, and Baclofen in patients with AUD. These have been exclusively conducted in India with no data from other South Asian countries. The methodology for the majority of studies has been retrospective. Acamprosate was seen to be associated with higher rates of abstinence and better functioning at follow-up when compared to Naltrexone (Basu et al. 2005). A systematic review in 2018 studied the pharmacotherapeutic interventions from 18 studies from Indian settings demonstrated that Disufilram was the most common pharmacological agent studied before 2000, whereas the subsequent decade compared Disulfiram with Naltrexone and Acamprosate, and newer agents such as Baclofen and Topiramate (Bharadwaj et al. 2018). In this review, disulfiram was reported to have better affordability, social support, and abstinence rates, whereas newer agents were more effective for the control of craving in India. An open-label trial on 122 alcohol-dependent subjects in India reported that Baclofen had significant improvements in drinking outcomes compared with participants receiving benfotiamine (Gupta et al. 2017). A double-blind placebo-controlled randomized trial of Varenicline for smokeless tobacco users in India showed that patients on Varenicline had higher self-reported end of treatment abstinence versus placebo (Jain et al. 2014).

13.5.2 Biological Interventions

A prospective, single-blind sham controlled study on 45 patients with alcohol dependence syndrome included 30 patients who received 10 rTMS to the right dorsolateral prefrontal cortex with a 1 month follow-up. This study reported significant reductions in craving as measured with the Alcohol Craving Questionnaire (ACQ-NOW) (Raikwar et al. 2020). Another randomized double-blind sham controlled parallel arm study from India demonstrated the clinical utility of transcranial direct current stimulation (tDCS) in the treatment of alcohol use disorders with a 3 month follow-up. The prefrontal tDCS on resting-state functional magnetic resonance imaging (rsfMRI) revealed that verum tDCS significantly reduced the likelihood of relapses and led to reductions in impulsivity (Holla et al. 2020). A study examined the effect of continuous theta burst stimulation rTMS (CTBS-RTMS) over the right orbitofrontal cortex as an adjunct to Naltrexone for Opioid Use Disorder, however, both sham and active arms of the study showed a significant reduction in craving (Ankit et al. 2022).

13.5.3 *Psychosocial Interventions*

In a study in India, 90 male inpatients with alcohol dependence syndrome were randomly assigned to individual relapse prevention (IRP), dyadic relapse prevention (DRP) with a family member, and treatment as usual (TAU) for 3 weeks (Nattala et al. 2010). In the 6 month follow-up, DRP performed better in reducing the quantity of alcohol consumed, number of drinking days, and number of dysfunctional days compared to IRP and TAU. Motivation enhancement therapy (MET) is a client-centered intervention that aims to decrease ambivalence in clients with substance use disorders. One study in Varanasi, India, demonstrated that patients who received 10 sessions with MET along with TAU had higher values of self-efficacy (Kumar et al. 2021). Behavior change interventions for smokeless tobacco cessation have been studied in community, school, and hospital settings in Pakistan (Hussain et al. 2018; Rasool et al. 2023; Siddiqi et al. 2016). An ongoing randomized controlled trial in Pakistan is attempting to study the feasibility and acceptability of a culturally adapted manually assisted motivational interviewing with cognitive behavior therapy (CBT) and mindfulness-based relapse prevention for substance use disorders (Asif et al. 2023). Research from Kabul, Afghanistan, has shown that patients who attend Motivational Interviewing (MI) sessions were more likely to complete drug addiction treatment (Rasekh et al. 2018). Integrated CBT has been shown to be an effective strategy for post-traumatic stress symptoms and substance use in Afghanistan veterans (Capone et al. 2018). A study from Nepal demonstrated the need for healthcare worker training to improve skills in behavioral support for tobacco cessation in primary health care (Elsey et al. 2015). Community-based intervention trials including physician education, self-help materials, telephone counseling, and awareness campaigns have also led to reductions in smoking rates in Kerala and Tamil Nadu, India (Kumar et al. 2012; "Smoking Cessation Intervention in Rural Kerala, India" 2013). There is overall a dearth of good quality trials on clinical psychosocial interventions for substance use disorders from South Asian countries.

13.6 Research on the Prevention of Addictions in South Asia

There is limited research on the prevention of substance use or addiction in South Asia. A review of popular media and the gray literature indicates that almost all of the countries in the region conduct programs to raise awareness about the perils of substance use among school and college students, both at a local level and as part of larger government-supported initiatives. However, there is a conspicuous absence of peer-reviewed studies on any of these programs.

There are two studies from India that focus on school-based prevention. The first study was a UNODC and Ministry of Social Justice and Empowerment, Government of India supported, life skills-based, teacher-conducted, school drug awareness program titled "I Decide—I will not take drugs." It was implemented in the states of Delhi, Chandigarh, West Bengal, Maharashtra, Assam, Haryana, and the North Eastern States, across about 250 schools and 400,000 students. Two teachers from each school were selected and trained through a 3 day training workshop. Training included awareness of what substances are drugs, the effects of their use, vulnerabilities and protective factors related to youth, and a thorough knowledge of life skills. Drug use prevention activities were carried out through "I Decide" clubs set up at schools. This program observed a positive attitudinal shift in several aspects as an outcome (Pattojoshi and Tikka 2020). The second study was the Mobilizing Youth for Tobacco-Related Initiatives (MYTRI) project. It was a school-based intervention that included 14,063, 6th and 8th grade students across 32 schools in Delhi and Chennai. It was essentially a behavioral classroom curriculum-based program that also included parental involvement and peer-led activism components. The findings showed that over the next 2 years, the likelihood of exhibiting an increase in cigarette or bidi smoking and also the intention to smoke or chew tobacco was significantly less in the intervention group (Perry et al. 2009).

An interesting study from Afghanistan described the implementation of the Child Intervention for Living Drug-free (CHILD) intervention protocol for children with substance use and reported preliminary outcome data on its impact. The protocol included age-appropriate education, drug education, information on nutrition, hygiene, and personal safety, along with communication skills and trauma-coping skills. The intervention leads to improvements in well-being in both younger and older children over time (Momand et al. 2017). There were also seen to be differences in treatment entry based on gender, with girls entering treatment with higher past-three-month use of opioids and sedatives, and boys with higher past-3 month use of tobacco, cannabis, and alcohol (Momand et al. 2020).

A study from India presented the development of a skill-based intervention for college students based on a disease prevention and health promotion approach by addressing psychoactive substance use as a risk factor for several major illnesses and providing practical guidance on how to overcome use. It received positive feedback regarding its applicability and acceptance among college students (Doraiswamy et al. 2022).

Given the key role of preventive and promotive interventions, the need for robust research that provides support for these approaches in the South Asian context would be imperative.

13.7 Research on Treatment Systems for Addictions in South Asia

South Asia faces several challenges in the context of the provision of treatment for persons with addictions. These include poor allocation of funds for the treatment of SUD, a paucity of SUD treatment services and trained professionals with expertise

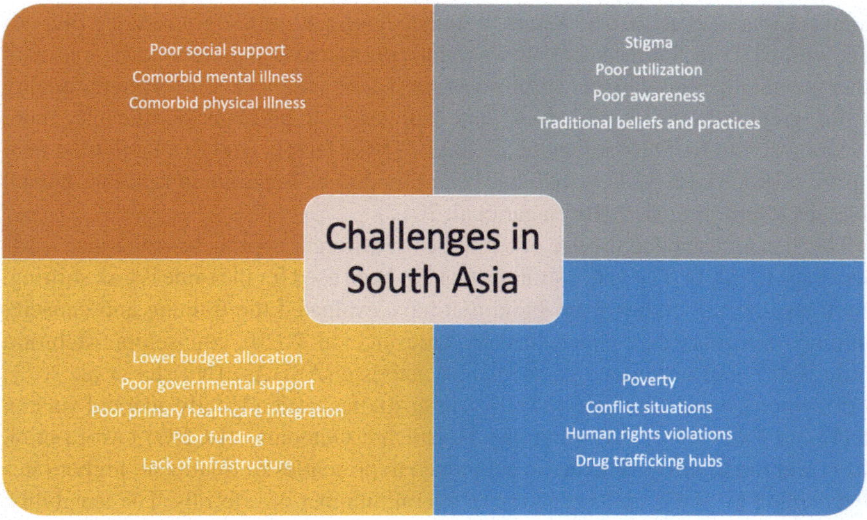

Fig. 13.1 Challenges in service delivery in South Asia

in the treatment of SUD, cultural beliefs and societal attitudes towards SUD, and stigma surrounding treatment (Fig. 13.1).

The countries in the region, except for Afghanistan allocate less than 1% of their total national health budget to mental health, leading to a scarcity of psychiatrists, clinical psychologists, and social workers (Trivedi et al. 2007). This shortage is evident since the median number of mental health providers has increased from 9 to 13 per 10,000 population globally, but declined from 4.8 to 2.8 from 2014 to 2020 in South Asia (Mental Health ATLAS 2020 n.d.). In terms of mental health professionals, all these countries are characterized by having very few trained psychiatrists and other mental health professionals. The World Health Organization Mental Health Atlas 2020 suggests that all SAARC countries except Maldives have less than one psychiatrist per 100,000 population. The situation is similar for psychiatric nurses, psychologists, and psychiatric social workers (Grover 2023). The exposure to psychiatry as a subject among undergraduate students in these countries is very poor (Trivedi and Dhyani 2007). In Afghanistan and Bangladesh, less than 1–2% (Tripathi and Kumar 2015) and 4% (Karim et al. 2006), respectively, of the medical training is devoted to mental health. It has also been seen that persons with mental illnesses including SUD often seek treatment from the unorganized sectors comprising faith healers, magico-religious practitioners, and underqualified professionals in remote regions of these countries (Mishra et al. 2011). Several magico-religious practices involve the use of local substances, which could potentially also be liable to abuse. There is a significant delay between the onset of drug use and first contact with care (Bhad et al. 2020). SU are often comorbid with various physical (Narasimha et al. 2019) and mental illnesses (Subodh et al. 2017), rendering such individuals exposed to financial crises, homelessness, unemployment, poor social support, and stigma (Kulesza et al. 2013). A review found significant self-stigma among individuals with SUD in South Asia that was more pronounced than among people with other mental illnesses. Greater stigma was consistently associated with poorer quality of life, greater disability, and inadequate help-seeking, and was significantly more for women with SUD (Manthey et al. 2022). These factors lead to a large treatment gap for persons with SUD, which has been found to be higher than for other mental illnesses (Gururaj et al. 2016; Sagar et al. 2017).

This has necessitated the use of a number of different approaches to reduce treatment gaps for SUD. The major strategy that has been used for the same is task shifting. There are several studies from India that have evaluated the training and capacity building of primary care physicians (Mahadevan et al. 2020), counselors (Mehrotra et al. 2018), and accredited social health activists (ASHAs) (Nirisha et al. 2023) to carry out the management of SUD. These studies used a locally adapted version of Project Extension for Community Healthcare Outcomes (ECHO) (Arora et al. 2014) and found improvements in adherence to principles of treatment, higher rates of screening of SUDs, and reduction in overall number of referrals. The feasibility, acceptability, and efficacy of training lay counselors using a manualized intervention called Counselling for Alcohol Problems consisting of problem identification, skill development, and relapse prevention techniques has also been demonstrated in Randomized Control Trial (RCT). A reduction was seen in AUDIT scores and mean alcohol consumed in the 14 days preceding the outcome assessment in the intervention group compared to the control group with received enhanced usual care (Nadkarni et al. 2019; Nadkarni et al. 2017a, b). It was seen that the end-of-treatment effects seen at 3 months were largely stable over time till 12 months after the intervention and were mediated by a readiness to change (Nadkarni et al. 2017a, b). The intervention was also found to be safe to deliver in individuals with AUD and comorbid depression although evidence of its efficacy in this population was not seen (Synowski et al. 2021).

The use of digital technology has been another strategy that has been employed to reduce the treatment gap. Studies have shown that the use of a mobile-based brief intervention for hazardous alcohol use leads to a reduction in percent days heavy drinking, and mean grams of ethanol consumed per week at follow-up (Nadkarni et al. 2022). The participants also reported a positive experience, with factors such as customized intervention delivery and personal motivation facilitating their engagement (Fernandes et al. 2023). A short text message-based mobile health program (the "mCessation" program) was also found to be effective to support tobacco users to quit, with a quit rate of 19% (Gopinathan et al. 2018). An app for relapse prevention, "Quest" was also found to be feasible and acceptable among users (Sharma et al. 2023).

A number of studies have evaluated SUD treatment and their outcomes in different countries across South Asia using a range of methodologies.

Afghanistan provides addiction treatment primarily through Drug Treatment Centers (DTCs). These are run both by the government through the Ministry of Public Health and Non-governmental Organizations, often supported by international agencies, including the US government. The treatment settings include residential, outpatient, and community and treatment is typically abstinence oriented. An independent evaluation conducted across 32 Afghan DTCs trained in Universal Treatment curriculum included data from 1022 individuals followed up for 1 year. There was a 30% decrease in the use of any substance between baseline and follow-up. A 39% decrease in opioid use, 36%–46% decrease in stimulant use, 43% decrease in sedatives and benzodiazepine use, 23% decrease in hashish use, and 67% decrease in alcohol use. There was also a 70 and 67% decrease in 30 day overdose and attempted suicide, as well as decreases in criminal behavior and arrest rates. There were no significant differences across residential, outpatient, and home based drug treatment (Shamblen et al. 2022). Another study from Afghanistan described the development of a village-based treatment program for SUD, which was adapted from the camp approach for community-based treatment of SUD pioneered by Ranganathan Clinical Research Foundation or TTK Hospital in India (Ranganathan 1994). It consisted of a pre-treatment phase of community engagement, a treatment phase where a 21 day camp-based treatment for drug users was implemented in a building identified by the local community, and a post-treatment follow-up phase. A total of 15 camps were conducted and 280 patients were treated with approximately 70% of them receiving aftercare support. There was no information available on substance use-related outcomes. The challenges faced included the security of the project staff, lack of access to medications for managing opioid use, and ill sustained engagement in some of the communities due to socio-cultural factors (How et al. 2014). The camp-based approach has been used in India and found to be a reasonable alternative to more formal treatment approaches in certain cases but has not been investigated in depth (Chavan and Priti 1999; Raj et al. 2005).

The treatment for SUD in Bangladesh broadly fall into; the medical hospital model and the ashram model of spiritual treatment. The public hospitals have dominated the treatment market under a state-run health care system; however, private for-profit as well as nonprofit drug treatment centers are also available (Hossain and Ahmed 1999). These centers predominantly use abstinence-oriented approaches. A study of 150 male and 110 female PWUDs admitted to the 3 month drug detoxification-rehabilitation treatment programs of three non-governmental organization-run drug treatment clinics in Dhaka, Bangladesh found high rates of relapse; 71.9% and 54.5% for females and males, respectively. The factors associated with relapse for both men and women included unstable housing. The presence of high risk sexual behaviors and selling sex were also associated with higher relapse rates (Maehira et al. 2013). A cross-sectional study from Bangladesh identified factors such as family unrest, peer pressure, alleviation of depression and craving for drugs as major factors for relapse following treatment (Nabi et al. 2022).

The treatment for SUD in Bhutan is carried out in four different settings, namely, through government agencies, Buddhist monasteries, civil society organizations and community outreach. A qualitative study from Bhutan described the use of a Buddhist approach, *Choeshed Layrim* in the prevention and treatment of SUD and reported its acceptability amongst treatment providers and youth in bringing about attitudinal changes related to substance use (Doma 2020).

There are a number of studies of community-based treatment for addictions from India. Community Drug Treatment Clinics at the National Drug Dependence Treatment Center, AIIMS provide opioid agonist treatment, treatment for alcohol use disorder, psychosocial interventions and liason. It was seen that these clinics were able to provide quality care at low cost with minimal personnel and infrastructure. This was associated with improved access and acceptability to treatment (Rao et al. 2021). Another study which tested the effectiveness of brief intervention for alcohol and tobacco integrated into primary healthcare settings found reduction in mean ASSIST scores for tobacco and alcohol in the intervention site and a reduction in heavy alcohol users. This emphasizes the role of timely, minimal intervention at community settings in reduction of alcohol and tobacco use (Sridhar et al. 2017). A nurse-delivered, on-campus screening and brief intervention (SBI) for hazardous alcohol use was also found to reduce AUDIT scores and lead to a reduction in WHO risk drinking levels among college students (Kamal et al. 2020).

In Nepal, there are currently 235 drug and alcohol treatment and rehabilitation centers, none of which are operated by the Government. However, due to the lack of regular surveillance and monitoring, the effectiveness of such centers in the treatment of addictive disorders is largely unknown. There are also reports that such centers are largely profitable businesses, with a lack of uniformity, human rights violations, lack of training among staff, lack of evidence-based practices and several restrictions within the center for both inpatients and their families. Nepal does not yet have a national treatment center dedicated to the treatment of substance use disorders. Barring a few district-level NGOs and self-help groups, community mental health services for substance use are virtually non-existent (Pant et al. 2023).

The treatment for SUD in Pakistan has largely been through the NGO sector, with 73 such centers in 2012. Following this, the Ministry of Narcotics Control and the Anti-Narcotics Force (ANF) aimed at setting up new treatment and rehabilitation centers and upgrading existing ones. However, these programs have not been implemented and no data is available on outcomes. The treatment approach in these centers is abstinence oriented (Uddin and Rahman 2021). An early study which followed up 100 patients with heroin dependence for 5 years after treatment. The treatment consisted of an extended inpatient detoxification for 30 days along with motivational interviewing and training in coping strategies, followed by community-based group therapy and self help. It was seen that 77% had relapsed but there was a reduction in associated harms (Mufti et al. 2004). A more recent study from Pakistan of 636 HIV-uninfected male PWIDs enrolled in a harm reduction program consisting of needle syringe exchange and risk reduction counselling found a retention rate of 74.5%. Younger age, poor education, a history of incarceration, and being homeless were associated with lower retention rates (Samo et al. 2016).

The treatment of SUD in Sri Lanka is carried out by several governmental and non-governmental organizations. The treatments include inpatient medical detoxification, outpatient medical detoxification, outpatient abstinence-oriented treatment, and long-term residential rehabilitation. A total of 3613 individuals were enrolled to the residential treatment island-wide and were treated in 2019 (Jayamaha et al. 2022). A retrospective chart review conducted across seven different rehabilitation centers reported significant improvement in the HRQoL of the participants during the residential treatment in comparison to the enrolment (Jayamaha et al. 2023). However, there was no comparison group and no description of post-discharge outcomes.

In summary, there are a wide number of stakeholders involved in treatment of SUD across both governmental and non-governmental organizations across the region. The treatment approaches tend to favour abstinence but the importance of harm reduction for injecting drug use is recognized, though wider implementation of these approaches remains limited. Further, treatment for SUD in community settings. There are also large gaps in our knowledge about short- and long-term outcomes of various treatments, due to the lack of methodologically rigorous studies.

13.8 Challenges in Addiction Research in South Asia

The inadequacy in mental health research and resources available for the research has been pointed out by the mental health research mapping project (Sharan n.d.). The research output related to mental health is poor and there are many factors responsible for this including limited opportunities for training, poor network for research, lack of knowledge on the publication process how to write a journal paper and poor funding for mental health services (Petersen et al. 2017). The policies and procedures followed in the region has limited evidence based background and poor implementation due to poor resource allocation. Mental health Budget in the region varies from 0.5 to 2.5% of total health budget (Kuruvilla and Jacob 2015). These factors also influence those who are highly trained in the research to emigrate from the South Asian region to developed western nations where they have higher resources to conduct research (Mullan 2005). Further, the limited training opportunities are also unevenly distributed, mostly concentrated in countries like India, Sri Lanka, and Pakistan (Sharma and Razzaque 2017). Financial and infrastructural support in academic institutions is inadequate, hindering research and training development. A lack of experienced mentors and a research-oriented culture within health sectors further impedes the growth of early-career researchers. Research institutes struggle to translate findings into policy due to minimal collaboration with policymakers and civil society. Additionally, intense competition for scarce research funding, especially for those in early or mid-career stages, presents another major challenge, as guidance for developing effective grant proposals is often lacking.

13.9 Conclusions

The landscape of addiction is inherently dynamic, with multifaceted intricacies—the complexities of which are compounded by the socio-cultural layers in South Asian countries. There is a considerable need for translational research, psychosocial interventions, long-term course and outcome studies, studies on implementation of policies, and the effectiveness of various preventive and management strategies in the field of addiction from the South Asian countries. In low-resource settings, there arises a compelling need for innovative interventions in substance use disorders, particularly in the realm of community health.

References

Acharya, Y., Karmacharya, V., Paudel, U., Joshi, S., Ghimire, R., & Adhikari, S. R. (2023). Perceptions of key stakeholders on taxes on tobacco and alcohol products in Nepal. *BMJ Global Health, 8*(Suppl 8), e012040. https://doi.org/10.1136/bmjgh-2023-012040

Ahmed, M., Ul Haq, I., Faisal, M., Waseem, D., & Taqi, M. M. (2018). Implication of OPRM1 A118G Polymorphism in Opioids Addicts in Pakistan: In vitro and In silico Analysis. *Journal of Molecular Neuroscience: MN, 65*(4), 472–479. https://doi.org/10.1007/s12031-018-1123-1

Alam, M., Sarkar, M., Alam, M., Ahmed, H., Bhowmik, A., & Roy, S. (2020). Prevalence of substance use in Bangladesh. *Bangladesh Journal of Psychiatry, 32*, 1–8. https://doi.org/10.3329/bjpsy.v32i1.53043

Ambekar, Atul, Chadda, Rakesh Kumar, Khandelwal, Sudhir Kumar, Rao, Ravindra, Mishra, Ashwani Kumar, & Agrawal, Ashok. (2019). *Magnitude of Substance Use In India*. Ministry of Scoial Justice and Empowerment, Government of India and NDDTC, AIIMS, New Delhi.

Ankit, A., Das, B., Dey, P., Kshitiz, K. K., & Khess, C. R. J. (2022). Efficacy of continuous theta burst stimulation—repetitive trancranial magnetic stimulation on the orbito frontal cortex as an adjunct to naltrexone in patients of opioid use disorder and its correlation with serum BDNF levels: A sham-controlled study. *Journal of Addictive Diseases, 40*(3), 373–381. https://doi.org/10.1080/10550887.2021.2007716

Arafat, S., & Kar, S. (2024). Epidemiology of psychiatric disorders and overview of access to mental health care in South Asia. In: S. M. Y. Arafat, S. K. Kar, *Access to mental health care in South Asia*. Springer Nature Singapore. https://doi.org/10.1007/978-981-99-9153-2_1

Arora, S., Thornton, K., Komaromy, M., Kalishman, S., Katzman, J., & Duhigg, D. (2014). Demonopolizing medical knowledge. *Acad Med, 89*(1), 30–32. https://doi.org/10.1097/acm.0000000000000051

Asif, M., Khoso, A. B., Husain, M. A., Shahzad, S., Van Hout, M.-C., Rafiq, N.-Z., Lane, S., Chaudhry, I. B., & Husain, N. (2023). Culturally adapted motivational interviewing with cognitive behavior therapy and mindfulness-based relapse prevention for substance use disorder in Pakistan (CAMAIB): Protocol for a feasibility factorial randomised controlled trial. *Pilot and Feasibility Studies, 9*(1), 67. https://doi.org/10.1186/s40814-023-01296-0

Balhara, Y. P. S., Sarkar, S., Singh, P. K., Chattopadhyay, A., & Singh, S. (2023). Impact of three years of prohibition on extent and pattern of alcohol use in Bihar: Observations and insights from the National Family Health Survey. *Asian Journal of Psychiatry, 82*, 103479. https://doi.org/10.1016/j.ajp.2023.103479

Basu, D., Jhirwal, O. P., & Mattoo, S. K. (2005). Clinical characterization of use of acamprosate and naltrexone: Data from an addiction center in India. *The American Journal on Addictions, 14*(4), 381–395. https://doi.org/10.1080/10550490591006933

Bertholet, N., Winter, M. R., Heeren, T., Walley, A. Y., & Saitz, R. (2023). Polysubstance Use Patterns Associated With HIV Disease Severity Among Those With Substance Use Disorders: A Latent Class Analysis. *Journal of Studies on Alcohol and Drugs, 84*(1), 79–88. https://doi.org/10.15288/jsad.21-00440

Bhad, R., Gupta, R., & Balhara, Y. P. S. (2020). A study of pathways to care among opioid dependent individuals seeking treatment at a community de-addiction clinic in India. *Journal of Ethnicity in Substance Abuse, 19*(3), 490–502. https://doi.org/10.1080/15332640.2018.1542528

Bharadwaj, B., Selvakumar, N., & Kuppili, P. P. (2018). Pharmacotherapy for relapse prevention of alcohol use disorder in the Indian setting: A systematic review. *Industrial Psychiatry Journal*, *27*(2), 163–171. https://doi.org/10.4103/ipj.ipj_79_17

Bhaskar, L. V. K. S., Thangaraj, K., Non, A. L., Singh, L., & Rao, V. R. (2010). Population-based case-control study of DRD2 gene polymorphisms and alcoholism. *Journal of Addictive Diseases*, *29*(4), 475–480. https://doi.org/10.1080/10550887.2010.509274

Bhaskar, L. V. K. S., Thangaraj, K., Osier, M., Reddy, A. G., Rao, A. P., Singh, L., & Rao, V. R. (2007). Single nucleotide polymorphisms of the ALDH2 gene in six Indian populations. *Annals of Human Biology*, *34*(6), 607–619. https://doi.org/10.1080/03014460701581419

Bhaskar, L. V. K. S., Thangaraj, K., Patel, M., Shah, A. M., Gopal, K., Saikrishna, L., Tamang, R., Singh, L., & Rao, V. R. (2013). EPHX1 Gene Polymorphisms in Alcohol Dependence and their Distribution among the Indian Populations. *The American Journal of Drug and Alcohol Abuse*, *39*(1), 16–22. https://doi.org/10.3109/00952990.2011.643991

Bhaskar, L. V. K. S., Thangaraj, K., Wasnik, S., Singh, L., & Raghavendra Rao, V. (2012). Dopamine transporter (DAT1) VNTR polymorphism and alcoholism in two culturally different populations of south India. *The American Journal on Addictions*, *21*(4), 343–347. https://doi.org/10.1111/j.1521-0391.2012.00244.x

Boileau-Falardeau, M., Contreras, G., Garipy, G., & Laprise, C. (2022). Patterns and motivations of polysubstance use: A rapid review of the qualitative evidence. *Health Promotion and Chronic Disease Prevention in Canada: Research, Policy and Practice*, *42*(2), 47–59. https://doi.org/10.24095/hpcdp.42.2.01

Budha, K. B., Adhikari, C., & Gahatraj, N. R. (2019). Perceived Effectiveness of Pictorial Health Warning Labels of Tobacco Products and Associated Factors among Smokers and Quitters in Kaski District, Nepal. *Journal of Health and Allied Sciences*, *9*(2), Article 2. https://doi.org/10.37107/jhas.126

Capone, C., Presseau, C., Saunders, E., Eaton, E., Hamblen, J., & McGovern, M. (2018). Is Integrated CBT Effective in Reducing PTSD Symptoms and Substance Use in Iraq and Afghanistan Veterans? Results from a Randomized Clinical Trial. *Cognitive Therapy and Research*, *42*(6), 735–746. https://doi.org/10.1007/s10608-018-9931-8

Chaity, N. I., Sultana, T. N., Hasan, Md. M., Shrabonee, I. I., Nahid, N. A., Islam, M. S., & Apu, M. N. H. (2021). Nicotinic acetylcholine gene cluster CHRNA5-A3-B4 variants influence smoking status in a Bangladeshi population. *Pharmacological Reports*, *73*(2), 574–582. https://doi.org/10.1007/s43440-021-00243-1

Chapagain, K., Rai, D., Koirala, B., & Rauniyar, G. P. (2020). Exploring the Prevalence and Correlates of Substance Abuse Amongst the Adolescents of Dharan, Eastern Nepal. *Journal of Nepal Health Research Council*, *18*(2), 263–267. https://doi.org/10.33314/jnhrc.v18i2.2484

Chavan, B. S., & Priti, A. (1999). Treatment of alcohol and drug abuse in cAMP setting. *Indian Journal of Psychiatry*, *41*(2), 140–144.

Cottler, L. B., Ajinkya, S., Goldberger, B. A., Ghani, M. A., Martin, D. M., Hu, H., & Gold, M. S. (2014). Prevalence of drug and alcohol use in urban Afghanistan: Epidemiological data from the Afghanistan National Urban Drug Use Study (ANUDUS). *The Lancet. Global Health*, *2*(10), e592–e600. https://doi.org/10.1016/S2214-109X(14)70290-6

Deb, I., Chakraborty, J., Gangopadhyay, P. K., Choudhury, S. R., & Das, S. (2010). Single-nucleotide polymorphism (A118G) in exon 1 of OPRM1 gene causes alteration in downstream signaling by mu-opioid receptor and may contribute to the genetic risk for addiction. *Journal of Neurochemistry*, *112*(2), 486–496. https://doi.org/10.1111/j.1471-4159.2009.06472.x

Dewan, G & Chowdhury, FR. (2015). *Alcohol Use and Alcohol Use Disorders in Bangladesh.*

Doma, D. (2020). Interventions for Substance Abuse by the Central Monastic Body (Gzhung Gra Tshang) in Bhutan. *Bhutan Journal of Research and Development*, *9*(1). http://103.133.216.36/index.php/bjrd/article/view/70

Doraiswamy, P., Nattala, P., & Murthy, P. (2022). Development and pilot-testing of a skill-based intervention to prevent psychoactive substance use among college students: A study from Bangalore, India. *Journal of Family Medicine and Primary Care, 11*(7), 3600–3606. https://doi.org/10.4103/jfmpc.jfmpc_2488_21

Dorji, G., DeJong, W., Bor, J., Bachman DeSilva, M., Sabin, L., Feeley, F. R., Udon, P., Wangchuk, N., Wangdi, U., Choden, T., Gurung, M. S., Chogyel, T., Wangchuk, D., & Kypri, K. (2016). Increasing compliance with alcohol service laws in a developing country: Intervention trial in the Kingdom of Bhutan. *Addiction (Abingdon, England), 111*(3), 467–474. https://doi.org/10.1111/add.13202

Eashwar, V. M. A., Umadevi, R., & Gopalakrishnan, S. (2020). Alcohol consumption in India—An epidemiological review. *Journal of Family Medicine and Primary Care, 9*(1), 49–55. https://doi.org/10.4103/jfmpc.jfmpc_873_19

Elsey, H., Khanal, S., Manandhar, S., Sah, D., Baral, S. C., Siddiqi, K., & Newell, J. N. (2015). Understanding implementation and feasibility of tobacco cessation in routine primary care in Nepal: A mixed methods study. *Implementation Science, 11*(1), 104. https://doi.org/10.1186/s13012-016-0466-7

Fallati, L., Castiglioni, S., Galli, P., Riva, F., Gracia-Lor, E., González-Mariño, I., Rousis, N. I., Shifah, M., Messa, M. C., Strepparava, M. G., Vai, M., & Zuccato, E. (2020). Use of legal and illegal substances in Malé (Republic of Maldives) assessed by wastewater analysis. *The Science of the Total Environment, 698*, 134207. https://doi.org/10.1016/j.scitotenv.2019.134207

Fernandes, D., D'Souza, E., Sambari, S., Pacheco, M., D'Souza, J., Velleman, R., Bhatia, U., & Nadkarni, A. (2023). Experiences of a mobile phone delivered brief intervention for hazardous drinking: A qualitative study nested in the AMBIT trial from Goa, India. *Cambridge Prisms: Global Mental Health, 10*, e58. https://doi.org/10.1017/gmh.2023.51

Ghazal, P. (2019). Rising trend of substance abuse in Pakistan: A study of sociodemographic profiles of patients admitted to rehabilitation centres. *Public Health, 167*, 34–37. https://doi.org/10.1016/j.puhe.2018.10.020

Gopinathan, P., Kaur, J., Joshi, S., Prasad, V. M., Pujari, S., Panda, P., & Murthy, P. (2018). Self-reported quit rates and quit attempts among subscribers of a mobile text messaging-based tobacco cessation programme in India. *BMJ Innovations, 4*(4). https://doi.org/10.1136/bmjinnov-2018-000285

Griffith, G., Welch, C., Cardone, A., Valdemoro, A., & Jo, C. (2008). The global momentum for smokefree public places: Best practice in current and forthcoming smokefree policies. *Salud Pública de México, 50 Suppl 3*, S299-308. https://doi.org/10.1590/S0036-36342008000900006

Grover, S. (2023). Status of mental health in South Asian countries. *Journal of SAARC Psychiatric Federation, 1*(1), 1. https://doi.org/10.4103/jspf.JSPF_15_23

Gupta, M., Verma, P., Rastogi, R., Arora, S., & Elwadhi, D. (2017). Randomized open-label trial of baclofen for relapse prevention in alcohol dependence. *The American Journal of Drug and Alcohol Abuse, 43*(3), 324–331. https://doi.org/10.1080/00952990.2016.1240797

Gururaj, G, Varghese, M, Rao, GN, Pathak K, Singh LK, Mehta, RY, Ram, D, Shibukumar, TM, Kokane, A, Lenin Singh, RK, Chavan, BS, Sharma P, Ramasubramaniam C, Dalal PK, Saha PK, Deuri SP, Giri AK, Kavishkar AB, Sinha VK, … Singh SK. (2016). *National Mental Health Survey of India 2015–16*. https://main.mohfw.gov.in/sites/default/files/National%20Mental%20Health%20Survey%2C%202015-16%20-%20Mental%20Health%20Systems_0.pdf

Gyeltshen, T., Penjor, T., Dorji, L., Tshering, L., Dorji, K., Subedi, B. N., Tshering, D., Xu, Y. Y., Dorji, G., & Gueye, G. N. (2021). Alcohol policy compliance among retailers in Bhutan: A multisite community intervention study. *BMC Public Health, 21*(1), 1893. https://doi.org/10.1186/s12889-021-11932-0

Holla, B., Bharath, R. D., Venkatasubramanian, G., & Benegal, V. (2019). Altered brain cortical maturation is found in adolescents with a family history of alcoholism. *Addiction Biology, 24*(4), 835–845. https://doi.org/10.1111/adb.12662

Holla, B., Biswal, J., Ramesh, V., Shivakumar, V., Bharath, R. D., Benegal, V., Venkatasubramanian, G., Chand, P. K., & Murthy, P. (2020). Effect of prefrontal tDCS on resting brain fMRI graph measures in Alcohol Use Disorders: A randomized, double-blind, sham-controlled study. *Progress in Neuro-Psychopharmacology & Biological Psychiatry, 102*, 109950. https://doi.org/10.1016/j.pnpbp.2020.109950

Holla, B., Karthik, S., Biswal, J., Viswanath, B., Jayarajan, D., Bharath, R. D., Venkatasubramanian, G., & Benegal, V. (2018). Brain Functional Magnetic Resonance Imaging Cue-reactivity Can Predict Baclofen Response in Alcohol Use Disorders. *Clinical Psychopharmacology and Neuroscience: The Official Scientific Journal of the Korean College of Neuropsychopharmacology, 16*(3), 290–301. https://doi.org/10.9758/cpn.2018.16.3.290

Holla, B., Panda, R., Venkatasubramanian, G., Biswal, B., Bharath, R. D., & Benegal, V. (2017). Disrupted resting brain graph measures in individuals at high risk for alcoholism. *Psychiatry Research. Neuroimaging, 265*, 54–64. https://doi.org/10.1016/j.pscychresns.2017.05.002

Holla, B., Viswanath, B., Agarwal, S. M., Kalmady, S. V., Maroky, A. S., Jayarajan, D., Bharath, R. D., Venkatasubramanian, G., & Benegal, V. (2014). Visual Image-Induced Craving for Ethanol (VICE): Development, Validation, and a Pilot fMRI Study. *Indian Journal of Psychological Medicine, 36*(2), 164–169. https://doi.org/10.4103/0253-7176.130984

Hossain, M., & Ahmed, S. K. (1999). A Natural Response to Drug Misuse Problems: A Review of Drug-User Treatment Services of Bangladesh. *Substance Use & Misuse, 34*(12), 1605–1617. https://doi.org/10.3109/10826089909039418

How, T. B., Morales, B., Thirumagal, V., & Ayub, M. (2014). Development of a Village Based Treatment Model for Afghanistan. *International Journal of Prevention and Treatment of Substance Use Disorders, 1*(2), 28. https://doi.org/10.4038/ijptsud.v1i2.7689

Hussain, A., Zaheer, S., & Shafique, K. (2018). School-based behavioral intervention to reduce the habit of smokeless tobacco and betel quid use in high-risk youth in Karachi: A randomized controlled trial. *PLOS ONE, 13*(11), e0206919. https://doi.org/10.1371/journal.pone.0206919

Iqbal, S., Barolia, R., Petrucka, P., Ladak, L., Rehmani, R., & Kabir, A. (2022). Smoking cessation interventions in South Asian Region: A systematic scoping review. *BMC Public Health, 22*(1), 1096. https://doi.org/10.1186/s12889-022-13443-y

Jabeen, S., Pinsonneault, J. K., Sadee, W., Lee, S.-H., Zafar, M. M., Raja, M. S., & Raja, G. K. (2019). Significant association of DRD2 enhancer variant rs12364283 with heroin addiction in a Pakistani population. *Annals of Human Genetics, 83*(5), 367–372. https://doi.org/10.1111/ahg.12322

Jain, R., Jhanjee, S., Jain, V., Gupta, T., Mittal, S., Goelz, P., Wileyto, E. P., & Schnoll, R. A. (2014). A Double-Blind Placebo-Controlled Randomized Trial of Varenicline for Smokeless Tobacco Dependence in India. *Nicotine & Tobacco Research, 16*(1), 50–57. https://doi.org/10.1093/ntr/ntt115

Jamal, M., Waheed, S., & Shakoor, A. (2022). The prevalence of substance abuse and associated factors among male prisoners in Karachi jails, Pakistan. *Journal of Taibah University Medical Sciences, 17*(6), 929–935. https://doi.org/10.1016/j.jtumed.2022.05.001

Javed, T., Habib, R., Ghafoor, S., Rumman, B., Awan, S., Ntepe, L. J. M., Batool, S., & Nurulain, S. M. (2019). Association of status of acetylcholinesterase and *ACHE* gene 3' UTR variants (rs17228602, rs17228616) with drug addiction vulnerability in pakistani population. *Chemico-Biological Interactions, 308*, 130–136. https://doi.org/10.1016/j.cbi.2019.05.036

Jayamaha, A. R., Dharmarathna, N. D., Herath, N. D., Ranadeva, N. D., Fernando, M. M., Samarasinghe, K. L., Amarabandu, P. N., Senanayake, B., Darshana, T., Renuka, N., Rajapakse, I. H., Gunasekara, C. P., Meegoda, L., & Fernando, N. (2022). The Pattern of Substance Use and Characteristics of the Individuals Enrolled in Residential Treatment at Selected Rehabilitation Centers in Sri Lanka: A Descriptive Cross-Sectional Study. *Substance Abuse: Research and Treatment, 16*, 11782218221100823. https://doi.org/10.1177/11782218221100823

Jayamaha, A. R., Herath, N. D. M., Dharmarathna, N. D., Sandakumari, H. S., Ranadeva, N. D. K., Fernando, M. M., Samarakoon, N. A. W., Amarabandu, P. N., Senanayake, B., Darshana, T., Renuka, N., Samarasinghe, K. L., & Fernando, N. (2023). Health-related quality of life in patients with substance use disorders enrolled to the residential treatment in Sri Lanka: A retrospective cross-sectional study. *Quality of Life Research: An International Journal of Quality of Life Aspects of Treatment, Care and Rehabilitation, 32*(2), 435–445. https://doi.org/10.1007/s11136-022-03270-4

Jha, A. K., Ojha, S. P., Adhikari, K., & Koirala, P. (2020). *Nepal National Mental Health Survey 2020.*

Kamal, K., Sunita, S., Karobi, D., & Abhishek, G. (2020). Nurse-Delivered Screening and Brief Intervention Among College Students with Hazardous Alcohol Use: A Double-Blind Randomized Clinical Trial from India. *Alcohol and Alcoholism (Oxford, Oxfordshire), 55*(3), 284–290. https://doi.org/10.1093/alcalc/agaa014

Karim, M. R., Shaheed, F., & Paul, S. (2006). Psychiatry in Bangladesh. *International Psychiatry, 3*(3), 16–18. https://doi.org/10.1192/S1749367600004835

Kaur, J., & Jain, D. C. (2011). Tobacco Control Policies in India: Implementation and Challenges. *Indian Journal of Public Health, 55*(3), 220. https://doi.org/10.4103/0019-557X.89941

Krishna Rao, S. V., Mejia, G., Roberts-Thomson, K., & Logan, R. (2013). Epidemiology of oral cancer in Asia in the past decade—An update (2000-2012). *Asian Pacific Journal of Cancer Prevention: APJCP, 14*(10), 5567–5577. https://doi.org/10.7314/apjcp.2013.14.10.5567

Kulesza, M., Larimer, M. E., & Rao, D. (2013). Substance Use Related Stigma: What we Know and the Way Forward. *Journal of Addictive Behaviors, Therapy & Rehabilitation, 2*(2), 782. https://doi.org/10.4172/2324-9005.1000106

Kumar, M. S., Sarma, P. S., & Thankappan, K. R. (2012). Community-based group intervention for tobacco cessation in rural Tamil Nadu, India: A cluster randomized trial. *Journal of Substance Abuse Treatment, 43*(1), 53–60. https://doi.org/10.1016/j.jsat.2011.10.026

Kumar, S., & Prakash, N. (2016). Bihar's Alcohol Ban: Good Intentions, Impractical Policy. *Economic and Political Weekly, 51*(1), 13–15.

Kumar, S., Srivastava, M., Srivastava, M., Yadav, J. S., & Prakash, S. (2021). Effect of Motivational Enhancement Therapy (MET) on the self efficacy of Individuals of Alcohol dependence. *Journal of Family Medicine and Primary Care, 10*(1), 367–372. https://doi.org/10.4103/jfmpc.jfmpc_1578_20

Kuruvilla, A., & Jacob, K. S. (2015). Mental Health Resources in South Asia. In J. K. Trivedi & A. Tripathi (Eds.), *Mental Health in South Asia: Ethics, Resources, Programs and Legislation* (pp. 191–219). Springer Netherlands. https://doi.org/10.1007/978-94-017-9017-8_11

Lemon, C. A., Svob, C., Bonomo, Y., Dhungana, S., Supanya, S., Sittanomai, N., Diatri, H., Haider, I. I., Javed, A., Chandra, P., Herrman, H., Hoven, C. W., & Sartorius, N. (2023). Priorities for research promoting mental health in the south and east of Asia. *The Lancet Regional Health—Southeast Asia, 0*(0). https://doi.org/10.1016/j.lansea.2023.100287

List of smoking bans. (2024). In *Wikipedia*. https://en.wikipedia.org/w/index.php?title=List_of_smoking_bans&oldid=1201211275

Luca, D. L., Owens, E., & Sharma, G. (2019). The effectiveness and effects of alcohol regulation: Evidence from India. *IZA Journal of Development and Migration, 9*(1), 4. https://doi.org/10.1186/s40176-018-0139-1

Maehira, Y., Chowdhury, E. I., Reza, M., Drahozal, R., Gayen, T. K., Masud, I., Afrin, S., Takamura, N., & Azim, T. (2013). Factors associated with relapse into drug use among male and female attendees of a three-month drug detoxification–rehabilitation programme in Dhaka, Bangladesh: A prospective cohort study. *Harm Reduction Journal, 10*(1), 14. https://doi.org/10.1186/1477-7517-10-14

Mahadevan, J., Shukla, L., Chand, P., Komaromy, M., Murthy, P., & Arora, S. (2020). Innovative virtual mentoring using the Extension for Community Healthcare Outcomes model for primary care providers for the management of alcohol use disorders. *Indian Journal of Medical Research, 151*, 609. https://doi.org/10.4103/ijmr.IJMR_1851_18

Malhotra, S., Basu, D., Khullar, M., Ghosh, A., & Chugh, N. (2016). Candidate genes for alcohol dependence: A genetic association study from India. *The Indian Journal of Medical Research, 144*(5), 689–696. https://doi.org/10.4103/ijmr.IJMR_1018_14

Mandal, P., Mittal, S., & Chadda, R. K. (2023). Polysubstance use in South Asia. *Current Opinion in Psychiatry, 36*(4), 269–276. https://doi.org/10.1097/YCO.0000000000000869

Mansoori, A. A., & Jain, S. K. (2018). ADH1B, ALDH2, GSTM1 and GSTT1 Gene Polymorphic Frequencies among Alcoholics and Controls in the Arcadian Population of Central India. *Asian Pacific Journal of Cancer Prevention: APJCP, 19*(3), 725–731. https://doi.org/10.22034/APJCP.2018.19.3.725

Manthey, J., Benegal, V., Kilian, C., Mahadevan, J., Mejía-Trujillo, J., Morojele, N., Murthy, P., Neufeld, M., Pérez-Gómez, A., & Rehm, J. (2022). International Perspectives on Stigma toward People with Substance Use Disorders. *The Stigma of Substance Use Disorders*, 107.

Mehrotra, K., Chand, P., Bandawar, M., Sagi, M. R., Kaur, S., Aurobind, G., Raj, A., Jain, S., Komaromy, M., & Murthy, P. (2018). Effectiveness of NIMHANS ECHO blended telementoring model on Integrated Mental Health and Addiction for counsellors in rural and underserved districts of Chhattisgarh, India. *Asian Journal of Psychiatry, 36*, 123–127.

Mental Health ATLAS 2020. (n.d.). Retrieved December 30, 2023, from https://www.who.int/publications-detail-redirect/9789240036703

Mishra, N., Nagpal, S. S., Chadda, R. K., & Sood, M. (2011). Help-seeking behavior of patients with mental health problems visiting a tertiary care center in north India. *Indian Journal of Psychiatry, 53*(3), 234–238. https://doi.org/10.4103/0019-5545.86814

Mishra, P., Nizamie, S.-H., Jahan, M., Garg, S., Tikka, S. K., Goyal, N., & Mishra, J. (2020). Predictors of chronicity in alcohol use disorder: An evoked response potential study. *Journal of Addictive Diseases, 38*(4), 411–419. https://doi.org/10.1080/10550887.2020.1780185

Mohit, M., Huq, N., Mali, B., Akter, H., & Arafat, S. M. Y. (2018). *Epidemiology of Substance Abuse in Bangladesh: A Narrative Review. 4*, 1000165. https://doi.org/10.4172/2471-271X.1000165

Momand, A. S., Mattfeld, E., Gerra, G., Morales, B., Browne, T., Haq, M. U., O'Grady, K. E., & Jones, H. E. (2020). Implementation and Evaluation of a Psychoactive Substance Use Intervention for Children in Afghanistan: Differences Between Girls and Boys at Treatment Entry and in Response to Treatment. *Global Journal of Pediatrics & Neonatal Care, 2*(1), 527. https://doi.org/10.33552/gjpnc.2020.02.000527

Momand, A. S., Mattfeld, E., Morales, B., Ul Haq, M., Browne, T., O'Grady, K. E., & Jones, H. E. (2017). Implementation and Evaluation of an Intervention for Children in Afghanistan at Risk for Substance Use or Actively Using Psychoactive Substances. *International Journal of Pediatrics, 2017*, 2382951. https://doi.org/10.1155/2017/2382951

Mufti, K. A., Said, S., Farooq, S., Haroon, A., Nazeer, A., Naeem, S., & Hussain, I. (2004). Five year follow up of 100 heroin addicts in Peshawar. *Journal of Ayub Medical College, Abbottabad: JAMC, 16*(3), 5–9.

Mullan, F. (2005). The Metrics of the Physician Brain Drain. *New England Journal of Medicine, 353*(17), 1810–1818. https://doi.org/10.1056/NEJMsa050004

Murthy, P. (2015). Culture and alcohol use in India. *World Cult Psychiatry Res Rev, 10*, 27–39.

Murthy, P., Manjunatha, N., Subodh, B. N., Chand, P. K., & Benegal, V. (2010). Substance use and addiction research in India. *Indian Journal of Psychiatry, 52*(Suppl1), S189. https://doi.org/10.4103/0019-5545.69232

Nabi, M. H., Masud, I., Humaira, T., Hussain, A., Naz, F., Chakraborty, P. A., & Hawlader, M. D. H. (2022). Reasons of relapse and pattern of drug use among the substance users in Bangladesh: A nationwide study. *Journal of Ethnicity in Substance Abuse, 21*(3), 876–885. https://doi.org/10.1080/15332640.2020.1801549

Nadkarni, A. (2018). Increasing access to psychosocial interventions for alcohol use disorders: Home based interventions. *Indian Journal of Psychiatry, 60*(Suppl 4), S564–S570. https://doi.org/10.4103/psychiatry.IndianJPsychiatry_25_18

Nadkarni, A., Fernandes, D., Bhatia, U., Velleman, R., D'souza, E., D'souza, J., Pacheco, G. M., & Sambari, S. (2022). Brief intervention for hazardous drinking delivered using text messaging: A pilot randomised controlled trial from Goa, India. *Public Health Nutrition, 25*(5), 1365–1374. https://doi.org/10.1017/S1368980022000313

Nadkarni, A., Weiss, H. A., Velleman, R., McCambridge, J., McDaid, D., Park, A.-L., Murthy, P., Weobong, B., Bhat, B., & Patel, V. (2019). Feasibility, acceptability and cost-effectiveness of a brief, lay counsellor-delivered psychological treatment for men with alcohol dependence in primary care: An exploratory randomized controlled trial. *Addiction (Abingdon, England), 114*(7), 1192–1203. https://doi.org/10.1111/add.14630

Nadkarni, A., Weiss, H. A., Weobong, B., McDaid, D., Singla, D. R., Park, A.-L., Bhat, B., Katti, B., McCambridge, J., Murthy, P., King, M., Wilson, G. T., Kirkwood, B., Fairburn, C. G., Velleman, R., & Patel, V. (2017a). Sustained effectiveness and cost-effectiveness of Counselling for Alcohol Problems, a brief psychological treatment for harmful drinking in men, delivered by lay counsellors in primary care: 12-month follow-up of a randomised controlled trial. *PLoS Medicine, 14*(9), e1002386. https://doi.org/10.1371/journal.pmed.1002386

Nadkarni, A., Weobong, B., Weiss, H. A., McCambridge, J., Bhat, B., Katti, B., Murthy, P., King, M., McDaid, D., Park, A.-L., Wilson, G. T., Kirkwood, B., Fairburn, C. G., Velleman, R., & Patel, V. (2017b). Counselling for Alcohol Problems (CAP), a lay counsellor-delivered brief psychological treatment for harmful drinking in men, in primary care in India: A randomised controlled trial. *The Lancet, 389*(10065), 186–195. https://doi.org/10.1016/S0140-6736(16)31590-2

Narasimha, V. L., Ganesh, S., Reddy, S., Shukla, L., Mukherjee, D., Kandasamy, A., Chand, P. K., Benegal, V., & Murthy, P. (2019). Pellagra and Alcohol Dependence Syndrome: Findings From a Tertiary Care Addiction Treatment Centre in India. *Alcohol and Alcoholism, 54*(2), 148–151. https://doi.org/10.1093/alcalc/agz004

National Dangerous Drugs Control Board. (2019). *National Prevalence Survey on Drug Use, 2019.* https://www.nddcb.gov.lk/Docs/research/National%20Prevalence%20Survey%20on%20Drugs%20Use%202019.pdf

Nattala, P., Leung, K. S., Nagarajaiah, null, & Murthy, P. (2010). Family member involvement in relapse prevention improves alcohol dependence outcomes: A prospective study at an addiction treatment facility in India. *Journal of Studies on Alcohol and Drugs, 71*(4), 581–587. https://doi.org/10.15288/jsad.2010.71.581

Naveed, S., Waqas, A., Chaudhary, A. M. D., Kumar, S., Abbas, N., Amin, R., Jamil, N., & Saleem, S. (2020). Prevalence of Common Mental Disorders in South Asia: A Systematic Review and Meta-Regression Analysis. *Frontiers in Psychiatry, 11*, 573150. https://doi.org/10.3389/fpsyt.2020.573150

Nirisha, P. L., Malathesh, B. C., Kulal, N., Harshithaa, N. R., Ibrahim, F. A., Suhas, S., Manjunatha, N., Kumar, C. N., Parthasarathy, R., Manjappa, A. A., Thirthalli, J., Chand, P. K., Arora, S., & Math, S. B. (2023). Impact of Technology Driven Mental Health Task-shifting for Accredited Social Health Activists (ASHAs): Results from a Randomised Controlled Trial of Two Methods of Training. *Community Mental Health Journal, 59*(1), 175–184. https://doi.org/10.1007/s10597-022-00996-w

Pant, S. B., Gurung, B., & Howard, J. (2023). Recovery and Rehabilitation from Alcohol, Substance Use and Related Disorders in Nepal: Call for Paradigm Shift. *Journal of Psychosocial Rehabilitation and Mental Health, 10*(2), 131–134. https://doi.org/10.1007/s40737-023-00337-4

Patabendige, C. L. C. M. (2021). *Legal implications on narcotics; a threat to national security.* Sri Lanka Military Academy Journal. https://www.defence.lk/upload/doc/LEGAL_IMPLICATIONS_ON_NARCOTICS_THREAT_NATIONAL_SECURITY.pdf

Pattojoshi, A., & Tikka, S. K. (2020). School-based substance use disorder prevention in India: A brief appraisal. *Indian Journal of Psychiatry, 62*(4), 427–430. https://doi.org/10.4103/psychiatry.IndianJPsychiatry_43_19

Paul, P., Dahale, A., Kishore, B., Chand, P., Benegal, V., Jain, S., Murthy, P., & Purushottam, M. (2017). Association of N-Methyl-D-Aspartate receptor 2B Subunit (GRIN2B) polymorphism with earlier age at onset of withdrawal symptoms in Indian alcohol dependent subjects. *Journal of Addictive Diseases, 36*(1), 48–52. https://doi.org/10.1080/10550887.2016.1140434

Perry, C. L., Stigler, M. H., Arora, M., & Reddy, K. S. (2009). Preventing Tobacco Use Among Young People in India: Project MYTRI. *American Journal of Public Health, 99*(5), 899–906. https://doi.org/10.2105/AJPH.2008.145433

Petersen, I., Marais, D., Abdulmalik, J., Ahuja, S., Alem, A., Chisholm, D., Egbe, C., Gureje, O., Hanlon, C., Lund, C., Shidhaye, R., Jordans, M., Kigozi, F., Mugisha, J., Upadhaya, N., & Thornicroft, G. (2017). Strengthening mental health system governance in six low- and middle-income countries in Africa and South Asia: Challenges, needs and potential strategies. *Health Policy and Planning, 32*(5), 699–709. https://doi.org/10.1093/heapol/czx014

Poudel, A., Sharma, C., Gautam, S., & Poudel, A. (2016). Psychosocial problems among individuals with substance use disorders in drug rehabilitation centers, Nepal. *Substance Abuse Treatment, Prevention, and Policy, 11*, 28. https://doi.org/10.1186/s13011-016-0072-3

Quraishi, R., Jain, R., Mishra, A. K., & Ambekar, A. (2017). Association of ankyrin repeats & kinase domain containing 1 (ANKK1) gene polymorphism with co-morbid alcohol & nicotine dependence: A pilot study from a tertiary care treatment centre in north India. *The Indian Journal of Medical Research, 145*(1), 33–38. https://doi.org/10.4103/ijmr.IJMR_458_14

Quraishi, R., Sharma, J., Jain, R., & Ambekar, A. (2021). Influence of catechol-O-methyltransferase enzyme gene polymorphism on alcohol and tobacco consumption in North Indian treatment seeking population. *Indian Journal of Psychiatry, 63*(3), 240–244. https://doi.org/10.4103/psychiatry.IndianJPsychiatry_465_20

Rahman, L. (n.d.). *Alcohol Prohibition and Addictive Consumption in India.*

Raikwar, S., Divinakumar, K. J., Prakash, J., Khan, S. A., GuruPrakash, K. V., & Batham, S. (2020). A sham-controlled trial of repetitive transcranial magnetic stimulation over left dorsolateral prefrontal cortex and its effects on craving in patients with alcohol dependence. *Industrial Psychiatry Journal, 29*(2), 245–250. https://doi.org/10.4103/ipj.ipj_53_19

Raj, L., Chavan, B. S., & Bala, C. (2005). Community 'de-addiction' camps: A follow-up study. *Indian Journal of Psychiatry, 47*(1), 44–47. https://doi.org/10.4103/0019-5545.46074

Ranganathan, S. (1994). The Manjakkudi experience: A camp approach towards treating alcoholics. *Addiction (Abingdon, England), 89*(9), 1071–1075. https://doi.org/10.1111/j.1360-0443.1994.tb02783.x

Rao, R., Dhawan, A., Parmar, A., Yadav, D., & Bhad, R. (2021). Improving Treatment of Substance Use Disorders through Community Drug Treatment Clinics: An Experiential Account. *Indian Journal of Community Medicine : Official Publication of Indian Association of Preventive & Social Medicine, 46*(3), 370–373. https://doi.org/10.4103/ijcm.IJCM_998_20

Rao, S., Aslam, S. K., Zaheer, S., & Shafique, K. (2014). Anti-smoking initiatives and current smoking among 19,643 adolescents in South Asia: Findings from the Global Youth Tobacco Survey. *Harm Reduction Journal, 11*, 8. https://doi.org/10.1186/1477-7517-11-8

Rasekh, B., Mon Saw, Y., Azimi, S., Kariya, T., Yamamoto, E., & Hamajima, N. (2018). Associations of treatment completion against drug addiction with motivational interviewing and related factors in Afghanistan. *Nagoya Journal of Medical Science, 80*(3), 329–340. https://doi.org/10.18999/nagjms.80.3.329

Rasool, S., Holliday, R., Khan, Z., Dobbie, F., & Bauld, L. (2023). Behavior Change Intervention for Smokeless Tobacco Cessation Delivered Through Dentists in Dental Settings: A Pragmatic Pilot Trial. *Nicotine & Tobacco Research*, ntad243. https://doi.org/10.1093/ntr/ntad243

Reid, G., Sharma, M., & Higgs, P. (2014). The long winding road of opioid substitution therapy implementation in South-East Asia: Challenges to scale up. *Journal of Public Health Research, 3*(1), 204. https://doi.org/10.4081/jphr.2014.204

Sagar, R., Pattanayak, R. D., Chandrasekaran, R., Chaudhury, P. K., Deswal, B. S., Lenin Singh, R. K., Malhotra, S., Nizamie, S. H., Panchal, B. N., Sudhakar, T. P., Trivedi, J. K., Varghese, M., Prasad, J., & Chatterji, S. (2017). Twelve-month prevalence and treatment gap for common mental disorders: Findings from a large-scale epidemiological survey in India. *Indian Journal of Psychiatry, 59*(1), 46–55. https://doi.org/10.4103/psychiatry.IndianJPsychiatry_333_16

Samanta, D., & Narayan, S. (2017). *Human Development in Bihar and impact of Liquor Prohibition Policy: An Analysis.*

Samo, R. N., Agha, A., Shah, S. A., Altaf, A., Memon, A., Blevins, M., Qian, H.-Z., & Vermund, S. H. (2016). Risk Factors for Loss to Follow-Up among People Who Inject Drugs in a Risk

Reduction Program at Karachi, Pakistan. A Case-Cohort Study. *PloS One, 11*(2), e0147912. https://doi.org/10.1371/journal.pone.0147912

Shaikh, K. J., Naveen, D., Sherrin, T., Murthy, A., Thennarasu, K., Anand, A., Benegal, V., & Jain, S. (2001). Polymorphisms at the DRD2 locus in early-onset alcohol dependence in the Indian population. *Addiction Biology, 6*(4), 331–335. https://doi.org/10.1080/13556210020077055

Shamblen, S. R., Courser, M., Young, L., Schweinhart, A., Shepherd, C., Morales, B., & Redpath, B. (2022). The Efficacy of Drug Treatment in Afghanistan: Overall Results and Implications From a New Evaluation. *International Journal of Mental Health and Addiction, 20*(1), 541–552. https://doi.org/10.1007/s11469-020-00382-1

Sharan, P. (n.d.). Research capacity for mental health in low- and middle-income countries: Results of a mapping project. Retrieved January 3, 2024, from https://cir.nii.ac.jp/crid/113000079581 3657856

Sharma, A. K., Shadakshari, D., Chand, P., & Murthy, P. (2023). Design, development and pilot testing of "Quest", a smartphone-based relapse prevention app for patients with alcohol dependence. *Asian Journal of Psychiatry, 83*, 103572. https://doi.org/10.1016/j.ajp.2023.103572

Sharma, M., & Razzaque, B. (2017). Research capacity strengthening in South Asia: Based on the experience of South Asian Hub for Advocacy, Research and Education on Mental Health (SHARE). *Global Mental Health, 4*, e9. https://doi.org/10.1017/gmh.2017.5

Shukla, S., Ghosh, A., Ahuja, C. K., Basu, D., & Holla, B. (2021). An instrument for visual cue associated craving of HEroin (IV-CACHE): A preliminary functional neuroimaging-based study of validity and reliability. *Indian Journal of Psychiatry, 63*(5), 448–455. https://doi.org/10.4103/indianjpsychiatry.indianjpsychiatry_1391_20

Siddiqi, K., Dogar, O., Rashid, R., Jackson, C., Kellar, I., O'Neill, N., Hassan, M., Ahmed, F., Irfan, M., Thomson, H., & Khan, J. (2016). Behaviour change intervention for smokeless tobacco cessation: Its development, feasibility and fidelity testing in Pakistan and in the UK. *BMC Public Health, 16*(1), 501. https://doi.org/10.1186/s12889-016-3177-8

Silva, M. C., Benegal, V., Devi, M., & Mukundan, C. R. (2007). Cognitive deficits in children of alcoholics: At risk before the first sip! *Indian Journal of Psychiatry, 49*(3), 182–188. https://doi.org/10.4103/0019-5545.37319

Singh, S. M., Basu, D., Kohli, A., & Prabhakar, S. (2009). Auditory P300 event-related potentials and neurocognitive functions in opioid dependent men and their brothers. *The American Journal on Addictions, 18*(3), 198–205. https://doi.org/10.1080/10550490902786975

Smith, D. E. (2015). *South Asian Politics and Religion*. Princeton University Press.

Smoking Cessation Intervention in Rural Kerala, India: Findings of a Randomised Controlled Trial. (2013). *Asian Pacific Journal of Cancer Prevention, 14*(11), 6797–6802.

Sonia, J. A., Kabir, T., Islam, M. M. T., & Kabir, Y. (2021). Catechol-O-methyltransferase and dopamine receptor D4 gene variants: Possible association with substance abuse in Bangladeshi male. *PLOS ONE, 16*(2), e0246462. https://doi.org/10.1371/journal.pone.0246462

Soundararajan, S., Agrawal, A., Purushottam, M., Anand, S. D., Shankarappa, B., Sharma, P., Jain, S., & Murthy, P. (2021). Changes in DNA methylation persist over time in males with severe alcohol use disorder-A longitudinal follow-up study. *American Journal of Medical Genetics. Part B, Neuropsychiatric Genetics: The Official Publication of the International Society of Psychiatric Genetics*. https://doi.org/10.1002/ajmg.b.32833

Sridhar, O. S., Murthy, P., & Kumar, K. K. (2017). Integrated brief tobacco and alcohol cessation intervention in a primary health-care setting in Karnataka. *Indian Journal of Public Health, 61*(5), 29.

Subodh, B. N., Hazari, N., Elwadhi, D., & Basu, D. (2017). Prevalence of dual diagnosis among clinic attending patients in a de-addiction centre of a tertiary care hospital. *Asian Journal of Psychiatry, 25*, 169–174. https://doi.org/10.1016/j.ajp.2016.10.020

Subramanian, A., & Kumar, P. (2017). The impact of price policy on demand for alcohol in rural India. *Social Science & Medicine, 191*, 176–185. https://doi.org/10.1016/j.socscimed.2017.08.024

Synowski, J., Weiss, H. A., Velleman, R., Patel, V., & Nadkarni, A. (2021). A lay-counsellor delivered brief psychological treatment for men with comorbid Alcohol Use Disorder and depression in primary care: Secondary analysis of data from a randomized controlled trial. *Drug and Alcohol Dependence, 227*, 108961. https://doi.org/10.1016/j.drugalcdep.2021.108961

Todd, C. S., Macdonald, D., Khoshnood, K., Mansoor, G. F., Eggerman, M., & Panter-Brick, C. (2012). Opiate use, treatment, and harm reduction in Afghanistan: Recent changes and future directions. *International Journal of Drug Policy, 23*(5), 341–345. https://doi.org/10.1016/j.drugpo.2012.05.004

Touw, M. (1981). The Religious and Medicinal Uses of *Cannabis* in China, India and Tibet. *Journal of Psychoactive Drugs, 13*(1), 23–34. https://doi.org/10.1080/02791072.1981.10471447

Tripathi, A., & Kumar, J. (2015). *Mental Health in South Asia: Ethics, Resources, Programs and Legislation* (Vol. 58). https://doi.org/10.1007/978-94-017-9017-8

Trivedi, J. K., & Dhyani, M. (2007). Undergraduate psychiatric education in South Asian countries. *Indian Journal of Psychiatry, 49*(3), 163–165. https://doi.org/10.4103/0019-5545.37314

Trivedi, J. K., Goel, D., Kallivayalil, R. A., Isaac, M., Shrestha, D. M., & Gambheera, H. C. (2007). Regional cooperation in South Asia in the field of mental health. *World Psychiatry, 6*(1), 57–59.

Uddin, S., & Rahman, S. (2021). *Pakistani Laws on Drug Use and Addiction: Need for Reform. 4*, 105. https://doi.org/10.1016/j.puhe.2018.10.020

United Nations Office on Drugs and Crime. (2022). *World Drug Report 2022*. United Nations.

UNODC. (2005). *South Asia Regional Profile.*

UNODC. (2013). *National Drug Use Survey Maldives 2011/2012*. https://www.unodc.org/documents/southasia/reports/National_Drug_Use_Survey_-_Report.pdf

Vaswani, M., Prasad, P., & Kapur, S. (2009). Association of ADH1B and ALDH2 gene polymorphisms with alcohol dependence: A pilot study from India. *Human Genomics, 3*(3), 213–220. https://doi.org/10.1186/1479-7364-3-3-213

Wadley, S. S. (2014). *South Asia in the World: An Introduction: An Introduction*. Routledge.

Wangdi, K., & Jamtsho, T. (2019). Drug use among Teenagers and Young Adults in Bhutan. *Indian Journal of Psychological Medicine, 41*(6), 535–540. https://doi.org/10.4103/IJPSYM.IJPSYM_348_19

Wankel, Harold D, Rothenbaum, Donal K, Ghani, Mohammad Asrar, Martin, David M., Gold, Mark S, Goldberger, Bruce A., Jones, Joseph, Morales, Brian, Chitturi, Pallavi, Brown, Thomas, Spirko, Lauren Nicole, & Weber-Roark, Julie. (2015). *Afghanistan National Drug Use Survey*. SGI Global.

Zaahiya, M. (2008). *An analysis of current policy and future directions on illicit drugs: A case study on the Maldives.*

Chapter 14
Substance Use Disorder Among Women and Children in South Asia

Amit Singh, Mohita Joshi, and Arpit Parmar

14.1 Introduction

South Asia is home to approximately a quarter of the world's population. However, being situated between the prolific opium cultivating and drug trafficking regions—the Golden Triangle and the Golden Crescent, this region finds itself at the crossroads of global drug trafficking routes (UNODC 2023). This location makes the countries of South Asia particularly vulnerable to the illicit flow of opiates and other addictive drugs. The drug use problem has continuously increased in this region over the past few decades. Besides, poverty, instability, and conflicts in this region have only helped to escalate the problem. The region harbors over a third of the world's opiate users (UNODC South Asia 2023) and high proportions of people using other substances.

Certain sections of the people who use drugs are particularly disposed to face compounded challenges. Women and children and among such vulnerable populations. Women, due to their socially disadvantaged position in many societies face much higher problems related to substance use than their male counterparts. They often face high levels of stigma, violence, and deprivation (Meyers et al. 2021). Similarly, children and adolescents, not only are at risk of initiating the use of substances and engaging in high-risk behaviors but also experiencing severe drug-related consequences (Poudel and Gautam 2017). Women constitute about half of the population in South Asia, whereas children and adolescents account for a third of the population (World Population Prospects 2022). Since the needs and challenges of these populations regarding the drug use problem are unique, there are significant implications for understanding and addressing substance use-related issues, particularly in the broader context of the region's distinct cultural and complex drug-related landscape.

A. Singh (✉) · M. Joshi
Department of Psychiatry, King George's Medical University, Lucknow, Uttar Pradesh, India
e-mail: amitsingh0612@gmail.com

A. Parmar
Department of Psychiatry, All India Institute of Medical Sciences, Bhubaneswar, Odisha, India

S. M. Y. Arafat and S. K. Kar (eds.), *Current Perspectives on Substance Use Disorders in South Asia*, https://doi.org/10.1007/978-981-97-6619-2_14

14.2 Substance Use Landscape and Challenges in Different South Asian Countries

14.2.1 Afghanistan

Afghanistan is among the leading producers of opium and other illicit drugs. The decades of conflict, instability, and change of regimes have put enormous stress on the general population, making them vulnerable to drug use. The easy availability of drugs and the presence of life stressors resulted in a high prevalence of drug use in all the population subgroups including women and children (SGI-GLOBAL 2015).

Though there are limited data available regarding the drug use scenario post-reoccupation of Afghanistan by the Taliban in 2021, the national drug use surveys conducted in 2005, 2009, 2015, and 2020 shed light on substance use and related problems in women and children. In a nationwide survey conducted in 2015, involving the analysis of hair, urine, and saliva samples from 3,723 women aged 15 and above, the prevalence of drug use was reported to be 9.5%. Notably, the prevalence was significantly higher in rural areas at 11.2% compared to urban areas, which stood at 4.3% (SGI-GLOBAL 2015). A survey conducted in 2009 found that the prevalence of injecting drug use among women was 0.07% (UNODC 2009). The prevalence of drug and alcohol use is detailed in Table 14.1. Women tend to predominantly ingest opium products orally, either by placing them under the tongue or swallowing, in contrast to men who prefer smoking opiates (SGI-GLOBAL 2015; UNODC 2009). The use of opioids among women is often driven by the desire for analgesia and relief from general discomfort. Also, the women may inadvertently test positive for alcohol due to its presence in alcohol-based cough syrups (SGI-GLOBAL 2015). Another population-based survey of 3,956 adults aged 18–69 found alcohol use in 0.2% of women and tobacco smoking in 2.6% (Ministry of Public Health and World Health Organization 2018). Women predominantly used drugs such as opium, opioid painkillers, and sedatives at home. However, they also used it in recreational gatherings and at abandoned places or buildings (UNODC 2009).

Table 14.1 Prevalence of drug use in Afghanistan (SGI-GLOBAL 2015)

	Alcohol	Cannabis	Opioids	Benzodiazepines	Amphetamine	Barbiturates
Women (15 years and above) (%)	0.3	1.5	6.7	1.4	0.1	0.1
Children and adolescents (less than 15 years) (%)	<0.1	0.2	0.6	<0.1	<0.1	<0.1

The 2015 national survey also revealed that among children (up to 14 years old), the prevalence of drug use was 0.8%, with rates slightly higher in rural areas (1%) compared to urban areas (0.2%) (SGI-GLOBAL 2015). Interestingly, a significantly greater number of children tested positive for opioids and cannabis in Afghan households than those who admitted to using them (approximately 9%). This phenomenon is attributed to second-hand and third-hand exposure to opiates, either through environmental contact or administration by adults. The primary potential source of second or third-hand environmental exposure to opioids is suggested to be men's drug use within households. This results in even infants testing positive for opiates. Additionally, adults have been reported to administer opioids to children for calming effects or analgesia, with instances of blowing opioid smoke in children's faces also documented in many households (SGI-GLOBAL 2015). Nearly half of the children who have used opioids reported that their parents introduced them to these substances (UNODC 2014). Regardless of the manner of exposure, childhood contact with opioids or cannabis has been linked to significant developmental challenges and later-life addiction.

In a 2018 study involving students aged 15–18, 15.6% admitted to using drugs, alcohol, or psychoactive medications for recreational purposes at some point in their lives. Over the past 12 months, 12% acknowledged such behavior, with 7.8% indicating usage within the last 30 days. The prevalence of past-year cannabis use was 5.6%, painkillers 4.5%, inhalants 4.1%, sedatives 3.5%, opium 2.0%, heroin 1.3%, morphine 1.1%, methamphetamine 1.3%, and amphetamine 0.9%. Additionally, 1.8% of adolescents reported using MDMA-containing tablets (UNODC 2021). The study also reported a lifetime prevalence of smoking among adolescents aged 13–18 at 19.7%, with past-year and past-month smoking rates at 12.0% and 7.4%, respectively. Another study reported tobacco use among students aged 13–15 at 8.3% for current use (boys, 10.1%; girls, 5.6%) and 26.2% for ever-use (World Health Organization 2017). Overall, repeated surveys have consistently highlighted the pervasive issue of substance use among adolescents.

14.2.2 Bangladesh

Bangladesh, situated in close proximity to the Golden Triangle, has become deeply entangled in the web of drug use. Over the years, it has transitioned from being merely a transit country for drug trafficking to one where drugs, opioids, amphetamines, cannabis, and pharmaceutical drug use have become increasingly prevalent. The significant volumes of drug seizures by Bangladesh's narcotics control agencies serve as a tangible indicator of the magnitude of the issue (Department of Narcotics Control 2023). Despite concerted efforts by law enforcement agencies, the influx of "Yaba" (containing methamphetamine), particularly, has witnessed a concerning surge. The pervasive problem of substance addiction has permeated every aspect of society, transcending geographical boundaries.

Multiple studies have highlighted substance use among women, especially those conducted in collaboration with agencies working with this population. These studies have documented the use of a variety of substances, including alcohol, cannabis, opioids (natural, semi-synthetic, and synthetic), methamphetamines, and prescription drugs (UNODC ROSA 2010). However, surveys consistently report a low prevalence of substance use among women. A nationwide multicentric community-based survey found a substance use prevalence of 0.6% among females, in contrast to 4.8% among males (Alam et al. 2020). Similarly, the national mental health survey of Bangladesh, 2018–2019 reported substance use in only 0.1% of females. The Global Burden of Diseases 2017 reported the estimates of substance use to be 1.4% (1.2–1.6%) with alcohol use in 1.0% (0.9–1.2%) females and drug use in 0.4% (0.3–0.5%) (WHO 2020a). Nevertheless, methodological constraints in these studies may have contributed to these low figures, given that substance-using females constitute a hidden population (UNODC ROSA 2010). There is no proper system in place to track information on women with drug addiction (Hasan 2024). However, there has been a manifold increase in women seeking treatment in government health facilities. As fewer women seek treatment for substance use, these trends provide a glimpse of the upcoming drug use problem (Khaled 2020).

The substance use is prevalent in children as well. The prevalence among the population aged 7–12 years and 13–17 years is around 0.2% and 1.5%, respectively (Alam et al. 2020). A survey of Bangladeshi high school students (n = 424) found "ever-use" rates of drugs, alcohol, and tobacco at 14.4% (males, 22.2% and females, 5.8%), 15.1% (males, 25.8% and females, 3.7%) and 21.2% (34.2%, males and 6.6%, females) participants, respectively. Current tobacco use was found in 10.4% of participants (20.1% males and 0.6% females) (Moonajilin et al. 2021).

14.2.3 Bhutan

Bhutan has traditionally been an agrarian economy. Now, with technology and modernization making their way into the lives of people, the public health challenges have also shifted to include substance use problems which has made inroads in the lives of youth. Despite efforts, Bhutan remains vulnerable to drug trafficking from Nepal and proximal Indian states such as West Bengal and Assam.

In women, the Bhutan STEPS survey 2019 reported a prevalence of "past year" alcohol use at 34.9% and heavy episodic drinking at 7.9%. Tobacco use was present in 11.8% of women (smokeless, 8.3%; and smoke, 3.7%) (Ministry of Health 2020). A community-based assessment survey for drug use conducted in 2009 revealed that "ever use of alcohol" was higher in the respondents living in areas bordering India (92%) compared to the participants from the capital city (77%). 88% of females who use drugs (FWUDs) had reported "ever use" of alcohol (Bhutan Narcotics Control Agency and UNODC 2009). "Every day" use of alcohol in the past month was present in 29%. The drug use patterns of female and male drug users were similar, except for the absence of "Yaba" or heroin use within the last month among females.

Global Youth Tobacco Survey (GYTS) reported tobacco use among students aged between 13 and 15 to be 22.2% for current use (boys, 31.2%; girls, 13.5%) and 38.4% for "ever use" (boys, 51.7%; girls, 25.4%) (World Health Organization 2019). A survey among students aged 13–17 years found past month alcohol use in 24.2% of students (male, 33.4% and females, 16.1%) and lifetime cannabis use in 16.0% of students (male, 28.3% and female, 5.3%) (World Health Organization 2016). A survey conducted in 2008 in Phuentsholing town in Bhutan to rapidly assess the drug use situation, found alcohol use once in a quarter of the male students and one-fifth of the female students, and inhalant use once in 11% of males and 4% of females. One percent of the female students reported single-time use of cannabis or pharmaceutical drugs, the rates were 5% and 4%, respectively, for cannabis and pharmaceutical drugs among male students. Injecting drug use ever was reported by an equal proportion of male and female students (0.01%) (Panda et al. 2009). Occasional alcohol use was reported by 8% of males and 3% of females. Occasional solvent use was present in 8% of male participants but only 1% of the female participants in the school-based assessment (Panda et al. 2009). As opposed to males, everyday use of alcohol, cannabis, pharmaceutical drugs, or solvent use was absent in females. The study found that the mean age at onset for males was 16 years for alcohol use and 17 years for drugs like inhalants, pharmaceutical medicines, and heroin. The mean age at onset for females was 19 years for alcohol use and 18 years for drugs. According to the survey, various substances, including cannabis, glue sniffing, codeine-containing cough syrups, dextropropoxyphene, benzodiazepine or nitrazepam tablets, and antihistaminic tablets, were used by PWUDs (Panda et al. 2009).

School-based assessment carried out in 60 schools in 2009 revealed daily tobacco use in 5% (in classes 7–8) and 8% (in classes 9–10) in male students. In female students, tobacco use was found to be less than 1%. However, a higher prevalence of use was reported from classes 9–12 (13% and 1% in males and females, respectively). Daily solvent use (sniffing) was reported only by 1% of male students from classes 9–10 (Bhutan Narcotics Control Agency and UNODC 2009).

14.2.4 India

In India, the women currently constitute 48.3% of the population. However, gender disparities persist as India has been traditionally a patriarchal society. The intersection of gender repression and substance use makes women in India particularly vulnerable.

The prevalence and patterns of substance use among women and children vary significantly across different states, mirroring the diversity observed among men. For instance, data from the National Family Health Survey-5 revealed alcohol use rates among women aged 15 years and above ranging from 0.3% in states like Gujarat and Rajasthan to as high as 14.9% in Arunachal Pradesh, compared to the national average of 1.3% (International Institute for Population Sciences 2021). Similarly, findings from the second round of the Global Adult Tobacco Survey conducted

Table 14.2 Substance use prevalence in women and children in India (Ambekar et al. 2019)

	Alcohol	Cannabis	Opioids	Cocaine	Inhalants
Women (10–75 years) (%)	1.6	0.6	0.2	0.01	0.07
Children and adolescents (10–17 years) (%)	1.3	0.9	1.8	0.06	1.17

during 2016–2017 indicated tobacco use prevalence rates of 40% and above in states such as Mizoram, Tripura, and Manipur, while in Punjab, the prevalence was as low as 0.5% (Tata Institute of Social Sciences and Ministry of Health and Family Welfare 2018). The national level prevalence of tobacco use in women was 14.2% (Tata Institute of Social Sciences and Ministry of Health and Family Welfare 2018). The National Mental Health Survey reported the prevalence of alcohol use disorder in women to be 0.5% (Gururaj et al. 2016). The north-east Indian states of Manipur and Nagaland, consistently report high prevalence of injecting drug use in women as well as high HIV seroprevalence. Moreover, over 80% of female sex workers (FSUs) in India report not receiving formal treatment for substance use (Kumar et al. 2015).

The Global Youth Tobacco Survey—fourth round reported the prevalence of tobacco use among school-going children aged 13–15 at 8.5% (Tata Institute of Social Sciences and Ministry of Health and Family Welfare 2019). A large epidemiological survey comprising 82,875 adolescents (aged 10–19 years) reported the prevalence of alcohol and drugs in this population (Table 14.2) (Ambekar et al. 2019). The prevalence of substance use among street children is much higher, falling in the range of 40–70% (Sharma and Joshi 2013). A national-level survey conducted by the National Commission for the Protection of Child Rights in 2013 in 4024 children below the age of 18 years found that the most common substances used were tobacco and alcohol. Cannabis, inhalants, pharmaceutical opioids, heroin, and sedatives were also used by them (Tikoo et al. 2013). Recent reports indicate a substantial increase in substance use prevalence among young children, emphasizing the urgent need for age-appropriate sensitization about the dangers of drug use, the necessity to report drug use, and the importance of developing resistance to peer and social pressures in India (Dhawan et al. 2020). Protecting children from the widespread prevalence of substance use stands as one of the most significant policy challenges facing the country.

14.2.5 Maldives

The Republic of Maldives has faced significant challenges related to substance use, particularly among its youth. Its proximity to the Golden Crescent and Golden Triangle makes it susceptible to illegal shipments of precursor chemicals and large quantities of drugs. With the influx of tourists, especially from Europe, South East Asia, and South Asia, the Maldives faces a critical drug problem, particularly among its youth, who constitute over 45% of the population. Over the past three decades, the availability of various drugs in the Maldives has increased, with cannabis products, alcohol, and heroin being the most commonly used substances (UNODC 2013b).

According to the STEPS survey conducted in 2011 to assess chronic disease risk factors, the prevalence of current tobacco use among women was 3.4%, with tobacco smoking reported by 2.2% of women. Alcohol consumption among women was relatively low, with only 0.2% reporting alcohol use in the past month. It is noteworthy that none of the women reported engaging in heavy episodic drinking. Notably, none of the women reported engaging in heavy episodic drinking (WHO 2011). A subsequent survey aimed at evaluating the drug use situation in the Maldives found that females were implicated in 6% of substance-related offenses. While females constituted 12.2% of illegal substance importers, they accounted for only 4.5% of total drug users (Suzana and Ismail 2023). Additionally, significantly more female participants (45.8%) admitted to trading sex for drugs, a striking difference compared to the 1.06% reported among males.

In a survey involving 2,984 students aged 13–15 years, the prevalence of current tobacco users was 45.7% (boys, 48.0% and girls, 43.2%) with smokeless tobacco use (46.1%) being significantly more common than smoked forms (8.3%) (WHO 2020b). The Global School-Based Student Health Survey in 2014, which covered 3,493 students aged 13–17 years, revealed that 4.4% (boys, 6.7%, and girls, 1.7%) had ever used cannabis (WHO 2014).

Underage offenders (<18 years old) accounted for 3–13% of overall instances across the Maldives' Atolls. Over the decade spanning 2010–2020, there was a consistent rise in cases received by the Juvenile Justice Unit (JJU), with the highest number involving 15-, 16-, and 17 year-olds (17%, 25%, and 43%, respectively). Notably, more than half of underage offenders were not attending school (51.6%). A remarkable proportion were detained for substance use (24.8%) and possession of drugs (38.2%). A decade ago, juvenile offenses primarily involved substance use (40%), possession of drugs (20%), alcohol use (20%), and substance use and possession of drugs (10%). However, in 2020, juveniles were predominantly involved in possession of drugs (20%), drug use (18.7%), drug trafficking (10.7%), production of alcohol (5.3%), possession of liquor (1.3%), and substance use and possession of drugs (44%) (Suzana and Ismail 2023).

14.2.6 Nepal

The drug use situation in Nepal has evolved. While cannabis traditionally played a significant role in Nepalese culture, recent years have seen a troubling shift towards synthetic opioids and other drugs, presenting new challenges.

A national survey conducted by the Ministry of Home Affairs, with technical assistance from the Central Bureau of Statistics (CBS) in 2020, sheds light on the severity of the situation (Table 14.3). The findings revealed that out of 130,424 PWUDs identified, 6.7% were female (Government of Nepal 2020). A population-based household survey of 5593 adults aged 15–69 years found that past-year use of tobacco and alcohol was present in 11.6% and 10.8% of women, respectively (Nepal Health Research Council 2019). The Nepal Drug Users Survey, 2076 found that the majority of FWUDs consumed drugs at home (47.5%), while 35.4% reported using them in isolated locations. A higher proportion of female drug users were unemployed (71.7%) compared to males (38.0%) (Government of Nepal 2020). The age group of 20–24 comprised the largest proportion (51.5%) of current female drug users, followed by the 25–29 age group (29.3%). All FWUDs were under the age of 40, with approximately 90% having completed education up to the 10th grade or less. Of the users, 29.3% were married, and 71.7% of the females were unemployed, compared to 38.0% of males. Nearly one-third started drugs before the age of 15, with almost half initiating use between the ages of 15 and 19. A significant majority of FWUDs, approximately 93.9%, began smoking before reaching the age of 20. Similarly, around 91.3% initiated alcohol consumption before reaching the same age threshold. Among FWUDs, the majority commenced their drug journey with cannabis (77.8%), followed by opiates (10.1%) and diazepam (9.1%). The prevalence estimates of "ever use" of drugs are shown in Table 14.3. The other drugs used include pregabalin, gabapentin, and tramadol. Despite a greater proportion of females seeking treatment compared to males (27.3% vs. 10.2%), none made more than two visits to treatment centers. Also, a larger percentage of FWUDs (54.5%) faced arrest for drug use or associated offenses, compared to their male counterparts (45.2%). Approximately one-third of these arrested females were subsequently referred to treatment centers by law enforcement. Notably, a significantly higher proportion of women reported experiencing mental violence during treatment compared to men (81% vs. 4.3%) (Government of Nepal 2020). Only 8.1% of female drug users received assistance or treatment from government agencies in the past year. Among their expressed needs, the majority sought employment opportunities (57.6%), followed by skills training (36.4%), and access to free treatment (31.3%) (Government of Nepal 2020).

About substance use among adolescents, findings from a school-based survey involving 6,529 students aged 13–17 revealed notable rates of alcohol and tobacco consumption within the past month. Specifically, 5.2% of respondents reported alcohol use (with 6.7% among males and 3.65% among females), while 8.1% reported

Table 14.3 Percentage of drug users who had ever used drug by background characteristics, Nepal, 2019 (Government of Nepal 2020)

	Tobacco	Alcohol	Cannabis	Opiates	Sedatives	Stimulants	Inhalants	Others
Women	98.0	69.7	81.8	48.5	83.8	3.0	3.0	33.3
Children and adolescents								
• Less than 15 years	38.4	17	66.7	0.0	33.3	0.0	33.3	33.3
• Age 15–19 years	55.6	71.4	88.9	41.7	56.3	0.7	18.1	45.8

Table 14.4 Annual prevalence of drug use in Pakistan in 2012 (UNODC 2013a)

	Cannabis	Opioids	Sedatives	Solvents	Amphetamine-type stimulants
Women (15–64 years) (%)	0.2	1.5	1.6	0.001	0.1

tobacco use (11.0% among males and 5.0% among females). Additionally, the survey indicated that 3.8% of participants had ever used cannabis, with 5.0% being males and 2.5% being females (WHO 2015a).

14.2.7 Pakistan

Pakistan is ensnared in a complex web of drug-related problems. Being situated along one of the busiest drug trafficking corridors, primarily fueled by opium cultivation in neighboring Afghanistan and precarious socioeconomic factors amplifies its vulnerability to drug-related issues. Substance use in women and children is also common.

A 2010 study conducted by UNODC across 13 cities in Pakistan estimated that there were approximately 4,632 female drug users, indicating a significant presence of FWUDs (UNODC 2010). However, women were less likely to have received treatment for drug dependence compared to men. A subsequent report in 2013 revealed an annual prevalence of illicit drug use among women at approximately 2.9% (n = 1.6 million), with injecting drug use recorded in about 0.01% of women (approximately 7000 females), though it suggested that actual prevalence might be higher than reported (UNODC 2013a). The annual prevalence of drug use among women is represented in Table 14.4. Additionally, tobacco use among females aged 15 years and above was reported at 5.8%, with smokeless tobacco being more prevalent (3.7%) than smoking (2.1%) (PHRC 2016). The prevalence of alcohol use disorder among females was found to be 0.1% (WHO 2019).

Among adolescents aged 15–19, the overall prevalence of drugs was around 2.6%, with cannabis being the most commonly used drug, followed by prescription opioids (UNODC 2013a). In students aged 13–15, the prevalence of tobacco use stood at 7.2%, with higher rates among males (9.2%) compared to females (4.1%) (PMRC 2015).

14.2.8 Sri Lanka

Sri Lanka is a nation with a high human development index of 0.782 (United Nations Development Programme 2021). However, the prevalence of drug use is a significant concern across various demographics. The National Prevalence Survey on Drug

Use—2019 was conducted to estimate the drug use pattern and profile of users in the country. The drug use rates were low in women. The survey found that, in the female population above 14 years, cannabis was the most widely used drug with a prevalence of 0.02%. It was followed by heroin (0.018%) and prescription drugs (0.004%). Stimulants and other drugs such as cocaine, amphetamine, ecstasy, and areca nut preparations were used by 0.054% of females. 0.3% of females above age 14 were reported to smoke tobacco and 0.26% consumed alcohol (National Dangerous Drugs Control Board 2019). However, in the STEPS survey of noncommunicable diseases, the current tobacco use rates were 5.3% (for all forms of tobacco) and current alcohol use rates were 0.5% among women aged 18–69 (WHO 2015b). The number of females who inject drugs has also been reported to be minuscule (Herath and Ambekar 2019).

Among adolescents aged 13–15 years, the prevalence of tobacco use is 3.7% (boys, 6.7 and girls, 0.7%) (WHO 2016b). The Global School-Based Student Health Survey reported tobacco use in the past month in 9.2% (male, 15.6%, and female 3.0%) adolescents aged 13–17 years (WHO 2016a). The prevalence of alcohol use was 3.2% (boys, 5.5% and girls 1.0%) and cannabis use was 2.8% (boys, 4.6% and girls, 0.8%) (WHO 2016a).

Sri Lanka's militarized approach to drug control, entailing the involvement of security forces in treatment and prevention, sparks human rights concerns. The stigmatization of PWUDs, coupled with arbitrary detention and compulsory rehabilitation, stands in contradiction to international standards. The absence of harm reduction services and reliance on abstinence-based models in rehabilitation programs, both public and private, reflects a critical gap in addressing the complex issue (Satkunanathan 2021).

14.3 Factors Influencing Substance Use Vulnerability

For children and adolescents, the susceptibility to substance use is often intertwined with various developmental and environmental elements. While genetics plays a major role, peer influence, family dynamics, socioeconomic status, and exposure to trauma can significantly impact the initiation and progression of substance use during these formative years. Additionally, the developing brain in children and adolescents may render them more susceptible to the addictive properties of substances, further complicating the picture.

In women, the initiation and progression of substance addiction are found to be shaped heavily by environmental factors (UNODC 2004). Societal pressures, changing roles, increasing stress, and lifestyle changes are rendering South Asian women vulnerable to new problems. The intersectionality of these factors further magnifies the vulnerability of women to newer challenges in the realm of substance use (UNODC 2004).

Women and children in South Asia face numerous factors that make them vulnerable to substance use, classified as individual-related, familial, and societal factors. Poverty is widespread in South Asian countries (United Nations Development Programme 2022), leading to limited access to education, healthcare, and opportunities for children and women, especially those from rural or marginalized communities, which can increase feelings of hopelessness and despair, driving them towards substance use as a coping mechanism (Lal et al. 2015; Nawi et al. 2021; Tikoo et al. 2013). Insufficient education and awareness programs about addiction risks contribute to the underestimation of substance dangers among children (Nawi et al. 2021). Even when women recognize their addiction, accessing treatment can be challenging due to cultural norms, financial constraints, and lack of female-friendly facilities (Lal et al. 2015).

Moreover, the easy availability and affordability of substances like tobacco, alcohol, and prescription drugs contribute to experimentation and addiction among children. Peer pressure is also significant, especially in South Asian societies where community ties are strong, pushing children towards substance use to fit in or gain acceptance (Tikoo et al. 2013; Zafar et al. 2021). Family dynamics, including hierarchical structures and traditional gender roles, can lead to stress and anxiety among children, while family dysfunction like domestic violence or substance use further increases vulnerability to addiction.

Traumatic events such as conflicts and natural disasters expose children to mental health issues like depression and PTSD, increasing susceptibility to substance use as a coping mechanism. Similarly, women in South Asia may experience trauma from domestic violence or forced marriage, leading to mental health disorders and substance misuse (Ray et al. 2004). Involvement in the drug production industry and transitioning cultures also contribute to the complex landscape of substance use vulnerability in South Asia (Department for International Development and British Embassy Kabul 2011; Dolkar 2016).

Addressing the unique vulnerabilities of women in South Asia requires a comprehensive approach that addresses social, cultural, and economic factors. This includes promoting gender equality, raising awareness about the impact of addiction on women, providing accessible and gender-sensitive treatment services, and challenging cultural norms that perpetuate stigma and shame around women's substance use.

The challenges confronting children who use drugs are complex and extend across developmental, academic, familial, and health domains. Early substance use onset is associated with higher comorbidity, chronic courses, and poorer outcomes, impacting not only immediate well-being but also long-term trajectories (Poudel and Gautam 2017). It hinders the development of crucial cognitive skills including memory and judgment (Hamidullah et al. 2020). The academic repercussions include impairments in declining grades, frequent absenteeism, truancy, confrontations with teachers, and the grim outcomes of suspension, expulsion, and early dropouts. Drug-using students are more prone to committing crimes, exhibiting violent behavior, and being involved in bullying; posing additional challenges for both the educational and societal systems (Pichel et al. 2022). The vicious cycle of mental and cognitive issues and substance use disorders (SUDs) in youth adds layers of complexity to their challenges; making them even more vulnerable (Hingson et al. 2009).

14.4 Needs of Women and Children with Substance Use

Women and children impacted by substance use require comprehensive support tailored to their unique needs including healthcare needs and social support.

14.4.1 Healthcare Needs

The population using substances may have substance use behavior falling at different places on a severity spectrum. There may be hazardous use, harmful use, or dependence on the substance. Appropriate services matching the problem are required to address the issue. For instance, those with harmful use may need screening and brief interventions only while others injecting opioids may need opioid maintenance treatment (Murthy 2012).

The SUDs rarely occur in isolation. It is often associated with a host of other health issues related to physical health and mental health. The health problems may be a direct complication of the substance used such as overdose due to opioids or bronchitis due to tobacco smoking or indirectly related to the substance use behavior such as contracting tuberculosis while using drugs in unhygienic spaces (Kumar et al. 2015). In FWUDs, their male partners often play a significant role, as they are frequently the ones who introduce them to drug use (Murthy 2002). This dynamic not only underscores the social and relational aspects of substance use but also amplifies the health risks associated with it. There is a risk to sexual health of contracting infections such as syphilis, herpes, fungal infections, and reproductive health in the form of unintended pregnancies and abortions (Murthy 2012). Unplanned pregnancies not only add to the physical strain on a woman's body but also carry substantial mental health implications. The stress and uncertainty surrounding unplanned pregnancies can exacerbate existing mental health issues and further compound the challenges faced by individuals grappling with SUDs. Also, the risk of blood-borne infections such as HCV, HIV, and HBV is much higher in people who inject drugs. These infections not only pose immediate health threats but also contribute to the overall burden of health complications faced by drug users. The shared use of needles or engaging in risky sexual behaviors within the context of substance use can significantly increase the likelihood of transmission. Thus, the programs and facilities intended for managing substance use problems should be able to address these diverse sexual health, reproductive health, and other healthcare needs (Sharma et al. 2017).

Substance use often co-occurs with mental health disorders. Access to mental health services, including counseling and therapy, is essential for addressing underlying issues contributing to substance use. Many women and children with SUDs who have experienced trauma, such as physical violence, emotional abuse, or sexual abuse may need mental healthcare and support.

14.4.2 Others Needs

- Prenatal and Maternal Care—Pregnant women with SUDs require specialized prenatal care to ensure the health and well-being of both the mother and the baby. Children born to mothers with SUDs may require specialized pediatric care to address neonatal abstinence syndrome, potential developmental delays, and growth issues (Murthy 2012).
- Education and Skills Training—Empowering women with education and vocational skills can improve their economic prospects and reduce the risk of relapse by providing alternative sources of fulfillment and income (Murthy 2012).
- Legal Assistance and Advocacy—Women with SUDs may face legal challenges, such as child custody issues or involvement in the criminal justice system. Access to legal assistance and advocacy services can help protect their rights and navigate legal complexities.
- Basic entitlements—Providing FWUDs with basic entitlements such as a ration card, voter identity card , and a bank account is essential for ensuring their access to government welfare schemes and services. These documents not only enable them to access essential commodities and exercise their right to vote but also facilitate their participation in financial transactions and formal employment opportunities.
- Travel concessions for treatment—Accessing treatment for SUDs often requires travel, whether it is to attend counseling sessions, medical appointments, or rehabilitation programs. Providing women with travel concessions, such as subsidized or free transportation options, can help alleviate the financial burden associated with seeking and accessing treatment.
- Direct financial help—FWUDs may face financial instability due to various factors, including unemployment, low-income levels, or economic dependence on partners involved in substance use. Direct financial assistance, in the form of cash transfers or emergency grants, can provide them with the means to meet their immediate needs and address financial crises without resorting to risky behaviors or further entrenching themselves in poverty.
- Housing schemes—Stable and secure housing is fundamental to the well-being of FWUDs. Housing schemes that offer affordable and safe accommodation options, including shelters, halfway houses, or subsidized housing programs, can provide them with a supportive environment conducive to recovery and reintegration into society.
- Livelihood support—Empowering FWUDs to secure sustainable livelihoods is essential for promoting their economic independence and social inclusion. This can involve providing them with vocational training, job placement assistance, or entrepreneurship programs tailored to their skills and interests, thereby enhancing their prospects for long-term financial stability and self-sufficiency.
- Insurance—Access to health insurance coverage is critical for ensuring that FWUDs can afford essential healthcare services, including treatment for SUDs, preventive care, and management of co-occurring health conditions. Providing them with access to affordable health insurance plans or subsidizing their

healthcare costs can help mitigate the financial barriers to accessing quality healthcare.

- Pension schemes—Many FWUDs may face challenges in building a secure financial future, particularly if their substance use has affected their ability to work or save for retirement. Pension schemes tailored to their needs, such as social security benefits or pension plans for marginalized populations, can provide them with a safety net in their later years and alleviate concerns about financial insecurity.
- Nutrition support—Ensuring adequate nutrition for both FWUDs and their children is crucial for promoting their physical health and well-being. Nutrition assistance programs, such as food vouchers, subsidized meals, or nutritional counseling, can help address food insecurity and dietary deficiencies, thereby improving their overall health outcomes.
- Legal aid—FWUDs may encounter legal challenges or face discrimination due to their substance use, ranging from involvement in criminal activities to child custody disputes. Access to legal aid services, including legal advice, representation, and advocacy, can help them navigate the legal system, protect their rights, and access justice without fear of stigma or discrimination (Murthy 2012).

14.5 Barriers to Healthcare

Barriers to accessing treatment for SUDs can be categorized into structural, social, and individual-level barriers. Structural barriers encompass policies and practices in services/programs that hinder women's access to substance use treatment, extending beyond substance use services to other health services as well (UNODC 2004). Social barriers refer to the conditions under which people are born, develop, live, study, work, and age, which can have an adverse impact on an individual's access to treatment (CDC 2019). The individual-level barriers refer to sociodemographic factors like age, education, and occupation, as well as psychosocial and behavioral aspects including attitudes, beliefs, and information about the condition that impede access to healthcare.

The structural barriers to substance addiction treatment encompass various challenges, from the distant or indiscreet locations of treatment facilities to the high costs associated with treatment and transportation. Additionally, long waiting times and the lack of immediate response further impede access to care, compounded by the absence of quality and comprehensive services. Facilities often lack appropriate treatment protocols and may favor forced detoxification over other evidence-based treatments. Female-centered services are scarce, with facilities predominantly designed for men. Lack of ancillary psychosocial services such as childcare and support for pregnant women hinder women from seeking treatment and healthcare (UNODC 2004). Integration between different services remains poor, and facilities are often ill-equipped to manage co-occurring psychiatric disorders and other health issues. Women are often shuttled between facilities without addressing their holistic needs. Referral processes are hindered by inadequate knowledge and coordination, while treatment costs and efficacy remain significant barriers. Service facilities frequently lack safety and discretion, discouraging women from seeking assistance. Under-resourced staff and limited public treatment facilities contribute to substandard care and overcrowding, while rigid schedules and bureaucratic hurdles further impede access (Motyka et al. 2022). The attitude of service providers can be poor, characterized by judgmental behavior and stigma, while confidentiality concerns persist, particularly regarding personal information disclosure outside of clinic settings. Inadequate training and high caseloads among staff, along with rigid program schedules, deter women with family and household responsibilities from seeking treatment, while challenges with therapeutic teams, including a lack of empathy and poor relationships between care providers and patients, hinder progress. The absence of support networks exacerbates the situation, with limited family and community backing hindering long-term healthcare adherence. Punitive policies and state violence further compound the challenges, exposing individuals to harassment and violence from law enforcement officers. Gender-based violence, including intimate partner violence and exploitation of female sex workers, further undermines women's autonomy and access to healthcare services (The Global Coalition on Women and AIDS 2011; UNODC 2004).

Moreover, legal constraints, such as the absence of a legal framework governing organizational relationships in settings like prisons and medical facilities, pose significant obstacles. Exclusionary attitudes, policies, and programs perpetuate barriers, while the continued criminalization of drug use and individuals who use drugs exacerbates the situation (Malinowska and Rychkova 2015). Policy barriers also stem from the failure to address social determinants of health and contextual factors. Ultimately, the complex interplay of these structural and policy barriers severely limits access to substance addiction treatment for women, highlighting the urgent need for comprehensive reform and support.

In South Asia's predominantly male-dominated society, women encounter obstacles in asserting their rights and often grapple with disadvantaged life circumstances, including poverty, limited access to healthcare and education, low literacy rates, financial dependence, and domestic violence. Besides they encounter substantial barriers to treatment due to entrenched social and cultural norms dictating gender roles and behavior and the stigma towards women with substance use issues. Cultural norms force them to engage in childcare and household responsibilities and do not permit them to leave their communities for treatment. Women seeking treatment get exposed to scorn, discrimination, and opposition from their families (Yousafzai 2020). Juggling familial responsibilities and financial burdens, they often prioritize their family's needs over their treatment, perpetuating a cycle of neglect. The societal stigma surrounding substance use amplifies feelings of shame and guilt among women, hindering their ability to seek help. Particularly vulnerable groups, such as women in sex work or those unable to care for their children, may feel further alienated due to societal norms. The stigma associated with drug use in children also compounds their challenges, creating a barrier to open discussion and access to much-needed treatment (Mukolo et al. 2010). In the context of South Asia, where violence against women is high, FWUDs or victims of HIV/AIDS face additional layers of complexity (Kumar et al. 2015; Murthy 2012; UNODC 2010). The stigma associated with drug use and HIV/AIDS further silences and hides this group, hindering their access to treatment, and support. Fear of losing custody of their children further deters pregnant or parenting women from disclosing substance use issues and seeking treatment. Additionally, many women find themselves reliant on their families or male partners for any form of medical assistance concerning their substance use issues, and lack of support from family, particularly partners, can discourage women from seeking help, especially if their partners also use substances. Fear of partner abandonment and intimate partner violence further compound these challenges (Kumar et al. 2015; Murthy 2012; UNODC 2010).

Additionally, difficulties in establishing non-drug-using social networks, as well as breaking ties with existing drug-using circles, create barriers to recovery. In some cases, women may view substance use as a coping mechanism for emotional distress or as a solution to overwhelming circumstances (Irfan et al. 2021). Some women lack confidence in the effectiveness of treatment and hesitate to seek help independently. Some believe that treatment is unnecessary and prefer to withdraw from substance use alone without assistance. Psychological barriers such as low self-esteem, poor motivation, low self-confidence, privacy concerns, and feelings of loneliness further hinder engagement with treatment. Additionally, co-occurring mental illnesses can complicate the treatment process and decrease the likelihood of seeking help for SUDs. Safety concerns, especially prevalent among women who have endured abuse or are in vulnerable situations like sex work, can hinder their access and retention in treatment programs (Irfan et al. 2021).

14.6 Healthcare Initiatives for Women and Children

In South Asian countries, public healthcare initiatives for addressing substance use problems specifically among women and children are lacking. The government programs and funds are focused on managing substance use in males which forms the largest chunk of the substance-using population. However, there is a need for comprehensive and tailored to address the specific needs and vulnerabilities of these populations. In the region, substance use in women and children is also being managed along the lines of adult males. Various Non Governmental Organizations (NGOs), however, are involved in providing dedicated services to this population. Since social, economic, and cultural factors play a big role in drug addiction in women the related issues need to be effectively managed. Also, women should be empowered to deal with the stereotyped gender responsibilities to seek help for substance use and maintain in the recovery process. Also, the stigma they are facing for being into addiction needs to be effectively dealt with. However, as people avoid even discussing substance use in women this issue is largely getting ignored. The ser Here are some potential initiatives.

14.6.1 *Awareness and Prevention Programs*

Public awareness campaigns targeting women and children aim to educate them about the risks of drug use and available resources for treatment and support. Various channels like schools, community centers, healthcare facilities, and media platforms are used to reach policymakers, clinicians, parents, young people, and teachers. Educating these key stakeholders about the consequences of prescription drug misuse can lead to more informed decision-making and proactive interventions (Wiedermann et al. 2023). Tailored prevention programs in schools, communities, and healthcare settings are crucial, alongside support for women facing disadvantaged circumstances. Overcoming the barriers to treatment-seeking is essential. Structural barriers such as the lack of services for pregnant women and childcare options must be dismantled to create a more inclusive and accessible treatment environment. Additionally, social and cultural barriers like stigma, shame, and guilt should be actively countered through awareness campaigns and community education (Lal et al. 2015).

School-based prevention programs should emphasize life skills education, equipping students with tools to handle stress and peer pressure. Creating awareness of the potential harm associated with substance use should be an integral part of these programs, ensuring a universal intervention that resonates with diverse student populations. Prevention programs must be meticulously designed to target multiple settings, including schools, communities, and streets (Kirchhoff and Keller 2021). Special attention should be given to vulnerable children, such as working children and out-of-school children. By addressing multiple risk factors, these programs can proactively deter substance initiation among children. Rehabilitation efforts should extend beyond cessation programs. NGOs should take the lead in providing skill-building and vocational training, empowering individuals recovering from substance use to reintegrate into society with enhanced capabilities.

14.6.2 *Screening and Early Intervention*

Screening, brief intervention, and referral to treatment (SBIRT) is a well-recognized early intervention strategy that is used in various combinations and settings in developed nations. In various South Asian nations, early intervention programs in schools, healthcare settings, and communities are implemented to screen women and children for SUDs, provide counseling and other appropriate interventions, and referrals to treatment services (National Health Mission 2014). However, the implementation of this strategy is not uniform across the demography. Many difficult-to-reach geographies and socio-economically deprived populations are not getting covered under this public health initiative.

14.6.3 Gender-Sensitive Treatment Services

While states acknowledge the importance of tailoring treatment programs to meet the unique needs of women and children, including considerations of gender roles, child-care responsibilities, and cultural sensitivities, implementation at the ground level remains inadequate. Public healthcare systems continue to fall short in providing easily accessible, affordable, and quality care in a supportive and non-judgmental environment. General practitioners and pediatricians are key in identifying and addressing substance use issues but often lack appropriate training in this area. Future efforts should prioritize sensitizing these healthcare professionals to effectively deal with the complexities of substance use, ensuring timely intervention and support. NGOs can play a crucial role in leading rehabilitation efforts specifically tailored for women, focusing not only on cessation programs but also on skill-building, vocational training, and empowerment to foster independence and resilience among women in recovery. Understanding the impact of pregnancy, motherhood, and societal expectations on women's engagement with treatment is paramount for designing effective interventions (Polak et al. 2015).

14.6.4 Integration of Health Services

Integration of health services to meet the diverse needs of patients remains deficient in many areas, despite ongoing efforts to improve coordination (WHO 2022). Resource constraints, inadequate infrastructure, and a lack of coordination mechanisms pose significant barriers to achieving seamless integration (NACO 2023). Pregnant women with SUDs require specialized care that considers both maternal and fetal well-being. Treatment programs must offer comprehensive support, necessitating collaboration between addiction specialists and maternal health professionals. Similarly, effectively addressing substance use among children requires coordinated efforts across different ministries. Collaborative approaches should adopt a holistic stance to tackle the multifaceted challenges faced by vulnerable children. Inter-ministerial coordination is essential for developing targeted strategies and interventions that address the root causes of substance use among children effectively (Dhawan et al. 2017).

14.6.5 Community-Based Support Groups

Established community-based support groups and peer-led interventions for women and children affected by drug use are providing them with a safe space to share their experiences, receive peer support, and access information about available resources and coping strategies.

14.6.6 Service Provision in Juvenile Homes and Correctional Settings

Providing services for the management of substance addiction in correctional settings is essential to address the complex needs of incarcerated women struggling with addiction. Access to evidence-based interventions such as medication-assisted treatment and counseling should be prioritized to support recovery and reduce the risk of relapse. Additionally, harm reduction measures such as needle exchange programs and overdose prevention education should be implemented to promote the health and safety of incarcerated individuals. Juvenile homes and children's homes under the Ministry of Women and Child Welfare should include specialized service provisions for substance-using children. Tailored rehabilitation and support programs within these facilities can significantly contribute to the holistic well-being and recovery of young individuals (Sharma 2023). Collaboration between correctional facilities, healthcare providers, and community-based organizations is crucial to ensure continuity of care and support successful reintegration into the community post-release. Rehabilitation programs addressing substance addiction should be integrated into broader efforts to address recidivism and promote rehabilitation within correctional settings.

14.6.7 Capacity Building for Healthcare Providers

Healthcare providers, social workers, educators, and other frontline workers should be provided training for identifying and addressing drug use problems in women and children (WHO 2020a). Skills needed to screen, assess, counsel, treat and refer these special populations can be enhanced through regularly conducted capacity building programs for healthare providers.

14.6.8 Policy and Legal Reforms

Advocating for policy and legal reforms is crucial to address the underlying social determinants of drug use among women and children, including poverty, gender inequality, and limited access to education and healthcare. These efforts may encompass initiatives aimed at improving socioeconomic opportunities, strengthening laws related to substance use prevention and treatment, and enhancing access to justice and support services for victims of gender-based violence.

14.6.9 Research and Data Collection

Through collaboration with governments and civil society organizations, UNODC engages in diverse activities such as research, evidence generation, quality assurance, advocacy, and policy advice. However, research and data collection efforts should be increased to better understand the prevalence, patterns, and determinants of drug use among women and children in South Asia. This is important as many nations do not have updated gender and age-wise data on substance use problems to guide the response measures in the form of policies and programs to address the unique needs of these populations.

By implementing these public healthcare initiatives, policymakers, healthcare providers, and community stakeholders can work together to prevent and address drug use problems among women and children in South Asia, promoting health, well-being, and resilience in these vulnerable populations.

14.7 Conclusion

Addressing the complex challenges faced by women and children in South Asia regarding substance use requires a multifaceted approach that acknowledges their unique vulnerabilities and needs within the broader cultural and societal context of the region. Women and children, particularly those from marginalized communities, encounter compounded obstacles such as stigma, violence, and limited access to resources, exacerbating their susceptibility to substance use. The challenge posed by drugs demands a comprehensive and evidence-based strategy rooted in global cooperation. Structural, social, and individual-level barriers hinder their access to healthcare and support services, necessitating comprehensive healthcare initiatives tailored to their specific circumstances. These initiatives should encompass awareness and prevention programs, screening and early intervention strategies, gender-sensitive treatment services, integration of health services, community-based support groups, capacity building for healthcare providers, policy and legal reforms, research and data collection, and service provision in juvenile homes and correctional settings. By implementing these initiatives collaboratively, policymakers, healthcare providers, and community stakeholders can effectively address substance use problems among women and children in South Asia, promoting their health, well-being, and resilience.

References

Alam, M. F., Sarkar, M., Alam, M. T., Ahmed, H. U., Bhowmik, A. D., & Roy, S. (2020). Prevalence of substance use in Bangladesh. *Bangladesh Journal of Psychiatry*, *32*(1), 1–8. https://doi.org/10.3329/bjpsy.v32i1.53043

Ambekar, A., Agrawal, A., Rao, R., Mishra, A., Khandelwal, S., & Chadda, R. (2019). *Magnitude of Substance Use in India*. Ministry of Social Justice and Empowerment.

Bhutan Narcotics Control Agency, & UNODC. (2009). *National Baseline Assessment of Drugs and Controlled Substance Use in Bhutan—2009*. UNODC. https://www.unodc.org/documents/southasia/reports/National_Baseline_Assessment_of_Drugs_and_Controlled_Substance_use_in_Bhutan_2009.pdf

CDC. (2019, September 4). *Disability and Health Disability Barriers | CDC*. Centers for Disease Control and Prevention. https://www.cdc.gov/ncbddd/disabilityandhealth/disability-barriers.html

Department for International Development, & British Embassy Kabul. (2011). *Growing poppies instead of opium in Afghanistan*. GOV.UK. https://www.gov.uk/government/case-studies/growing-poppies-instead-of-opium-in-afghanistan

Department of Narcotics Control. (2023). *Annual Drug Report Bangladesh, 2022*. Ministry of Home Affairs, Bangladesh. https://dnc.gov.bd/sites/default/files/files/dnc.portal.gov.bd/annual_reports/37a9ace4_624d_4650_80ad_9f4041db6b2b/2023-05-10-07-21-ca4e1390829fc7f031c5df30419878f6.pdf

Dhawan, A., Mishra, A. K., Ambekar, A., Chatterjee, B., Agrawal, A., & Bhargava, R. (2020). Estimating the size of substance using street children in Delhi using Respondent-Driven Sampling (RDS). *Asian Journal of Psychiatry, 48*, 101890. https://doi.org/10.1016/j.ajp.2019.101890

Dhawan, A., Pattanayak, R., Chopra, A., Tikoo, V., & Kumar, R. (2017). Pattern and profile of children using substances in India: Insights and recommendations. *The National Medical Journal of India, 30*(4), 224. https://doi.org/10.4103/0970-258X.218679

Dolkar, T. (2016). Prevention of Illegal Substance Use and Abuse in Bhutan. In J. L. Romano & M. Israelashvili (Eds.), *The Cambridge Handbook of International Prevention Science* (pp. 597–605). Cambridge University Press. https://doi.org/10.1017/9781316104453.026

Government of Nepal. (2020). *Nepal Drug Users Survey: 2076*. Government of Nepal, Ministry of Home Affairs.

Gururaj, G., Varghese, M., Benegal, V., Rao, G. N., Pathak, K., Singh, L., Mehta, R., Ram, D., Shibukumar, T., & Kokane, A. (2016). National mental health survey of India, 2015–16. *Bengaluru, India: NIMHANS*.

Hamidullah, S., Thorpe, H. H. A., Frie, J. A., Mccurdy, R. D., & Khokhar, J. Y. (2020). Adolescent Substance Use and the Brain: Behavioral, Cognitive and Neuroimaging Correlates. *Frontiers in Human Neuroscience, 14*, 298. https://doi.org/10.3389/fnhum.2020.00298

Hasan, K. (2024). *Female drug abusers most vulnerable among addicted population*. Dhaka Tribune. https://www.dhakatribune.com/bangladesh/bangladesh-others/142203/female-drug-abusers-most-vulnerable-among-addicted

Herath, S., & Ambekar, A. (2019). *Rapid Assessment of Drug Use Patterns (RADUP) among People Who Use and/or Inject Drugs (PWUD/PWID) in Sri Lanka*. National STD/AIDS Control Program, (NSACP) & Sri Lanka National Dangerous Drugs Control Board, NDDCB, Sri Lanka.

Hingson, R. W., Edwards, E. M., Heeren, T., & Rosenbloom, D. (2009). Age of Drinking Onset and Injuries, Motor Vehicle Crashes, and Physical Fights After Drinking and When Not Drinking. *Alcoholism, Clinical and Experimental Research, 33*(5), 783–790. https://doi.org/10.1111/j.1530-0277.2009.00896.x

International Institute for Population Sciences. (2021). *National Family Health Survey—5, 2019–21*. Ministry of Health and Family Welfare. http://rchiips.org/nfhs/NFHS-5_FCTS/Final%20Compendium%20of%20fact%20sheets_India%20and%2014%20States_UTs%20(Phase-II).pdf#toolbar=0&navpanes=0

Irfan, S. D., Khan, M. N. M., & Khan, S. I. (2021). Tales of gender-based oppression and violence: Risks and vulnerabilities of women who inject drugs (WWID) in Dhaka, Bangladesh. *International Journal of Drug Policy, 92*, 103144. https://doi.org/10.1016/j.drugpo.2021.103144

Khaled, S. (2020). Alarming rise in drug abuse. *The Financial Express*. https://thefinancialexpress.com.bd/views/opinions/alarming-rise-in-drug-abuse-1578932293

Kirchhoff, E., & Keller, R. (2021). Age-Specific Life Skills Education in School: A Systematic Review. *Frontiers in Education, 6*. https://doi.org/10.3389/feduc.2021.660878

Kumar, S., Oinam, A., Mukherjee, D., Mittal, A., & Kishore, K. (2015). *Women Who Use Drugs in Northeast India*. UNODC, Regional Office for South Asia. https://www.unodc.org/documents/southasia/publications/research-studies/FINAL_REPORT.pdf

Lal, R., Deb, K. S., & Kedia, S. (2015a). Substance use in women: Current status and future directions. *Indian Journal of Psychiatry, 57*(Suppl 2), S275–S285. https://doi.org/10.4103/0019-5545.161491

Malinowska, K., & Rychkova, O. (2015). *The Impact of Drug Policy on Women*. Open Society Foundations. https://www.opensocietyfoundations.org/publications/impact-drug-policy-women

Meyers, S. A., Earnshaw, V. A., D'Ambrosio, B., Courchesne, N., Werb, D., & Smith, L. R. (2021). The intersection of gender and drug use-related stigma: A mixed methods systematic review and synthesis of the literature. *Drug and Alcohol Dependence, 223*, 108706. https://doi.org/10.1016/j.drugalcdep.2021.108706

Ministry of Health. (2020). *Non-communicable disease Risk Factors: Bhutan STEPS Survey 2019*. Department of Public Health. https://www.who.int/publications/m/item/2019-steps-country-report-bhutan

Ministry of Public Health, & World Health Organization. (2018). *Afghanistan STEPS Noncommunicable Disease Risk Factors Survey 2018*. World Health Organization (WHO). https://cdn.who.int/media/docs/default-source/ncds/afghanistan_2013_steps_survey_article_ba6e2792-c004-4774-afe8-954ff8dd0bfd.pdf?sfvrsn=9d28454e_8&download=true

Moonajilin, Mst. S., Kamal, M. K. I., Mamun, F. al, Safiq, M. B., Hosen, I., Manzar, Md. D., & Mamun, M. A. (2021). Substance use behavior and its lifestyle-related risk factors in Bangladeshi high school-going adolescents: An exploratory study. *PLoS ONE, 16*(7), e0254926. https://doi.org/10.1371/journal.pone.0254926

Motyka, M. A., Al-Imam, A., Haligowska, A., & Michalak, M. (2022). Helping Women Suffering from Drug Addiction: Needs, Barriers, and Challenges. *International Journal of Environmental Research and Public Health, 19*(21), 14039. https://doi.org/10.3390/ijerph192114039

Mukolo, A., Heflinger, C. A., & Wallston, K. A. (2010). The stigma of childhood mental disorders: A conceptual framework. *Journal of the American Academy of Child and Adolescent Psychiatry, 49*(2), 92–103; quiz 198. https://doi.org/10.1097/00004583-201002000-00003

Murthy, P. (2002). Women and drug abuse: The problem in India. *New Delhi: Ministry of Social Justice and Empowerment and United Nations International Drug Control Programme, Regional Office for South Asia.*

Murthy, P. (2012). *Female injecting drug users and female sex partners of men who inject drugs: Assessing care needs and developing responsive services*. UNODC & NACO. https://eha-health.org/downloads/category/45-documents-materials?download=85:fidus

NACO. (2023). *Guidance Document: Integrated Package of Services for People Who Use Drugs*. Prevention Division, National AIDS Control Organisation, Government of India.

National Dangerous Drugs Control Board. (2019). *National Prevalence Survey on Drugs Use 2019*. Research Division, National Dangerous Drugs Control Board. https://www.nddcb.gov.lk/Docs/research/National%20Prevalence%20Survey%20on%20Drugs%20Use%202019.pdf

National Health Mission. (2014). *Rashtriya Kishor Swasthya Karyakram Operational Framework: Translating Strategy into Programmes*. National Health Mission. https://nhm.gov.in/images/pdf/programmes/RKSK/RKSK_Operational_Framework.pdf

Nawi, A. M., Ismail, R., Ibrahim, F., Hassan, M. R., Manaf, M. R. A., Amit, N., Ibrahim, N., & Shafurdin, N. S. (2021). Risk and protective factors of drug abuse among adolescents: A systematic review. *BMC Public Health, 21*(1), 2088. https://doi.org/10.1186/s12889-021-11906-2

Nepal Health Research Council. (2019). *Nepal—STEPS 2019*. World Health Organization. https://extranet.who.int/ncdsmicrodata/index.php/catalog/771/related-materials

Panda, S., Chowdhury, L., Dendup, T., & Pahari, S. (2009). *Drug use situation and responses in schools and communities—A Rapid Assessment in Phuentsholing, Bhutan*. UNODC.

PHRC. (2016). *Pakistan—Global Adult Tobacco Survey 2014*. Pakistan Health Research Council. https://extranet.who.int/ncdsmicrodata/index.php/catalog/257/related-materials

Pichel, R., Feijóo, S., Isorna, M., Varela, J., & Rial, A. (2022). Analysis of the relationship between school bullying, cyberbullying, and substance use. *Children and Youth Services Review, 134*, 106369. https://doi.org/10.1016/j.childyouth.2022.106369

PMRC. (2015). *Pakistan—Global Youth Tobacco Survey 2013*. Pakistan Medical Research Council. https://extranet.who.int/ncdsmicrodata/index.php/catalog/334/related-materials

Polak, K., Haug, N. A., Drachenberg, H. E., & Svikis, D. S. (2015). Gender Considerations in Addiction: Implications for Treatment. *Current Treatment Options in Psychiatry, 2*(3), 326–338.

Poudel, A., & Gautam, S. (2017). Age of onset of substance use and psychosocial problems among individuals with substance use disorders. *BMC Psychiatry, 17*, 10. https://doi.org/10.1186/s12888-016-1191-0

Ray, R., Mondal, A., Gupta, K., Chatterjee, A., & Bajaj, P. (2004). *The Extent, Pattern and Trends of Drug Abuse in India: National Survey*. United Nations Office on Drugs and Crime, Regional Office for South Asia and Ministry of Social Justice and Empowerment, Government of India.

Satkunanathan, A. (2021). *A Broken System: Drug Control, Detention and Treatment of People Who Use Drugs in Sri Lanka*. Harm Reduction International.

SGI-GLOBAL. (2015). *Afghanistan National Drug Use Survey 2015*. https://colombo-plan.org/wp-content/uploads/2020/03/Afghanistan-National-Drug-Use-Survey-2015-compressed.pdf

Sharma, G. (2023). *Special Home Under "Juvenile Justice (Care and Protection of Children) Act, 2015": Analysing the Practical Implementation of Section 47(1)*. https://legalvidhiya.com/special-home-under-juvenile-justice-care-and-protection-of-children-act-2015-analysing-the-practical-implementation-of-section-471/

Sharma, N., & Joshi, S. (2013). Preventing-substance abuse among street children in India: A literature review. *Health Science Journal, 7*(2), 137.

Sharma, V., Sarna, A., Tun, W., Saraswati, L. R., Thior, I., Madan, I., & Luchters, S. (2017). Women and substance use: A qualitative study on sexual and reproductive health of women who use drugs in Delhi, India. *BMJ Open, 7*(11), e018530. https://doi.org/10.1136/bmjopen-2017-018530

Suzana, D., & Ismail, S. (2023). *Situational Analysis of Drugs in the Maldives 2021*.

Tata Institute of Social Sciences, & Ministry of Health and Family Welfare. (2018). *Global Adult Tobacco Survey GATS 2 India 2016–17*. Ministry of Health and Family Welfare, Government of India. https://ntcp.mohfw.gov.in/assets/document/surveys-reports-publications/Global-Adult-Tobacco-Survey-Second-Round-India-2016-2017.pdf

Tata Institute of Social Sciences, & Ministry of Health and Family Welfare. (2019). *Global Youth Tobacco Survey GYTS 4 India*. Ministry of Health and Family Welfare, Government of India. https://ntcp.mohfw.gov.in/assets/document/National_Fact_Sheet_of_fourth_round_of_Global_Youth_Tobacco_Survey_GYTS-4.pdf

The Global Coalition on Women and AIDS. (2011). *Women who use drugs, harm reduction and HIV*. The Global Coalition on Women and AIDS, Geneva. https://www.aidsdatahub.org/sites/default/files/resource/women-who-use-drugs-harm-reduction-hiv.pdf

Tikoo, V., Dhawan, A., Pattanayak, R., & Chopra, A. (2013). Assessment of pattern and profile of substance use among children in India. *National Commission for Protection of Child Rights (NCPCR) by National Drug Dependence Treatment Centre [NDDTC], All India Institute of Medical Sciences [AIIMS], New Delhi.*

United Nations Development Programme. (2021). Unsettled Lives: Shaping our Future in a Transforming World. *Human Development Report, 2022*.

United Nations Development Programme. (2022). *Unpacking Deprivation Bundles to Reduce Multidimensional Poverty: Global Multidimensional Poverty Index 2022*. United Nations. https://doi.org/10.18356/9789210028035

UNODC. (2004). *Substance abuse treatment and care for women: Case studies and lessons learned*. United Nations Publication, Geneva. https://www.unodc.org/pdf/report_2004-08-30_1.pdf

UNODC. (2009). *Drug Use in Afghanistan: 2009 Survey*. https://www.unodc.org/documents/data-and-analysis/statistics/Drugs/Drug%20use/Drug_use_in_Afghanistan_2009_survey.pdf

UNODC. (2010). *Female Drug Use in Pakistan—Mapping Estimates, Ethnographic Results & Behavioural Assessment*. United Nations Office on Drugs and Crime (UNODC) Country Office Pakistan. https://www.unodc.org/documents/pakistan/female_drugs_use.pdf

UNODC. (2013a). *Drug use in Pakistan 2013*. United Nations Office on Drugs and Crime. https://www.unodc.org/documents/pakistan/Survey_Report_Final_2013.pdf

UNODC. (2013b). *National Drug Use Survey Maldives—2011/2012*. UNODC.

UNODC. (2014). *Impacts of drug use on users and their families in Afghanistan*. https://doi.org/10.1163/2210-7975_HRD-9924-2014008

UNODC. (2021). *Study on Substance Use and Health among Youth in Afghanistan 2018*. United Nations Office on Drugs and Crime (UNODC). https://www.unodc.org/documents/data-and-analysis/statistics/Drugs/Drug%20use/Study_on_substance_use_and_health_among_youth_in_Afghanistan_2018.pdf

UNODC. (2023). *World Drug Report 2023*. United Nations.

UNODC ROSA. (2010). *Female Drug Users and Female Regular Sex Partners of Male Drug Users in Bangladesh—A Report*. United Nations Office on Drugs and Crime, Regional Office for South Asia. https://www.unodc.org/documents/southasia//reports/BGD-_FIDU_printed_report.pdf

UNODC South Asia. (2023). *South Asia: Understanding and Addressing the Threat of Opiate Trafficking*. https://www.unodc.org/southasia//frontpage/2023/May/south-asia_-understanding-and-addressing-the-threat-of-opiate-trafficking.html

WHO. (2011). *Maldives—STEPS 2011, Male*. World Health Organization. https://extranet.who.int/ncdsmicrodata/index.php/catalog/661

WHO. (2014). *Maldives—Global School-Based Student Health Survey 2014*. World Health Organization. https://extranet.who.int/ncdsmicrodata/index.php/catalog/546/related-materials

WHO. (2015a). *Nepal—Global School-Based Student Health Survey 2015*. World Health Organization. https://extranet.who.int/ncdsmicrodata/index.php/catalog/655

WHO. (2015b). *Sri Lanka—STEPS 2014*. World Health Organization. https://extranet.who.int/ncdsmicrodata/index.php/catalog/614/related-materials

WHO. (2016a). *Sri Lanka—Global School-Based Student Health Survey 2016*. World Health Organization. https://extranet.who.int/ncdsmicrodata/index.php/catalog/648

WHO. (2016b). *Sri Lanka—Global Youth Tobacco Survey 2015*. World Health Organization. https://extranet.who.int/ncdsmicrodata/index.php/catalog/226/related-materials

WHO. (2019). *Global status report on alcohol and health 2018*. World Health Organization. https://www.who.int/publications-detail-redirect/9789241565639

WHO. (2020a). *Bangladesh WHO Special Initiative for Mental Health Situational Assessment*. World Health Organization. https://www.who.int/docs/default-source/mental-health/special-initiative/who-special-initiative-country-report---bangladesh---2020.pdf?sfvrsn=c2122a0e_2

WHO. (2020b). *Maldives—Global Youth Tobacco Survey 2019*. World Health Organization. https://extranet.who.int/ncdsmicrodata/index.php/catalog/928

WHO. (2022). *WHO Special Initiative for Mental Health—Nepal*. World Health Organization. https://cdn.who.int/media/docs/default-source/mental-health/special-initiative/who-special-initiative-country-report---nepal---2022.pdf?sfvrsn=714028db_3&download=true

Wiedermann, C. J., Barbieri, V., Plagg, B., Marino, P., Piccoliori, G., & Engl, A. (2023). Fortifying the Foundations: A Comprehensive Approach to Enhancing Mental Health Support in Educational Policies Amidst Crises. *Healthcare, 11*(10), 1423. https://doi.org/10.3390/healthcare11101423

World Health Organization. (2016). *Global School-based Student Health Survey 2016: Fact Sheet Bhutan*. World Health Organization. https://www.who.int/publications/m/item/2016-gshs-fact-sheet-bhutan

World Health Organization. (2017). *Global Youth Tobacco Survey Afghanistan (Kabul)*. World Health Organization (WHO). https://cdn.who.int/media/docs/default-source/ncds/ncd-surveillance/data-reporting/afghanistan/afghanistan-(kabul)-gyts-2017-factsheet-(ages-13-15)_508tagged.pdf?sfvrsn=5553af79_1&download=true

World Health Organization. (2019). *Global Youth Tobacco Survey: Fact sheet Bhutan 2019*. World Health Organization (WHO). https://www.who.int/publications/m/item/2019-gyts-fact-sheet-bhutan

World Population Prospects. (2022). *World Population Prospects—Population Division—United Nations*. https://population.un.org/wpp/

Yousafzai, A. R. (2020, April 2). *Pakistan government urged to do more for female drug addicts*. Arab News. https://arab.news/rsstz

Zafar, A., Raha, S. A., Rana, S., & Fariha, M. Z. (2021). *Exploring Older Adolescents' (Age 15–19) Perceptions About Substance Abuse in Urban Slums: Policy Brief*. BRAC University.

SPRINGER NATURE

GPSR Compliance

The European Union's (EU) General Product Safety Regulation (GPSR) is a set of rules that requires consumer products to be safe and our obligations to ensure this.

If you have any concerns about our products, you can contact us on ProductSafety@springernature.com

In case Publisher is established outside the EU, the EU authorized representative is:

Springer Nature Customer Service Center GmbH
Europaplatz 3
69115 Heidelberg, Germany

The manufacturer's authorised representative in the EU is Springer Nature Customer Service Centre GmbH, Europaplatz 3, 69115 Heidelberg, Germany. If you have any concerns regarding our products, please contact ProductSafety@springernature.com

Printed and bound by CPI Group (UK) Ltd, Croydon, CR0 4YY
01/10/2026
02225858-0011